London Literature, 1300–1380

English literary culture in the fourteenth century was vibrant and expanding. Its focus, however, was still strongly local, not national. This study examines in detail the literary production from the capital before, during, and after the time of the Black Death. In this major contribution to the field, Ralph Hanna charts the development and the generic and linguistic features particular to London writing. He uncovers the interactions between texts and authors across a range of languages and genres: not just Middle English, but also Anglo-Norman and Latin; not just romance, but also law, history, and biblical commentary. Hanna emphasises the uneasy boundaries legal thought and discourse shared with historical and 'romance' thinking, and shows how the technique of romance, Latin writing associated with administrative culture, and biblical interests underwrote the great pre-Chaucerian London poem, William Langland's *Piers Plowman*.

RALPH HANNA is Professor of Palaeography at the University of Oxford and Tutorial Fellow in English at Keble College, Oxford.

CAMBRIDGE STUDIES IN MEDIEVAL LITERATURE

General editor
Alastair Minnis, *Ohio State University*

This series of critical books seeks to cover the whole area of literature written in the major medieval languages – the main European vernaculars, and medieval Latin and Greek – during the period *c.* 1100–1500. Its chief aim is to publish and stimulate fresh scholarship and criticism on medieval literature, special emphasis being placed on understanding major works of poetry, prose, and drama in relation to the contemporary culture and learning which fostered them.

Recent titles in the series

A complete list of titles in the series can be found at the end of the volume.

London Literature,
1300–1380

RALPH HANNA

CAMBRIDGE
UNIVERSITY PRESS

CAMBRIDGE UNIVERSITY PRESS
Cambridge, New York, Melbourne, Madrid, Cape Town, Singapore, São Paulo

Cambridge University Press
The Edinburgh Building, Cambridge CB2 2RU, UK

www.cambridge.org
Information on this title: www.cambridge.org/9780521848350

First published 2005

Printed in the United Kingdom at the University Press, Cambridge

A catalogue record for this book is available from the British Library

ISBN-13   978-0-521-84835-0 hardback
ISBN-10   0-521-84835-0 hardback

For the old people
Rosa Hirshfeld-Fries
and
R. N. Hanau

Contents

Abbreviations

Age:	*Age of Chivalry: Art in Plantagenet England 1200–1400*, ed. Jonathan Alexander and Paul Binski. London: Royal Academy, 1987.
Apoc:	*An English Fourteenth Century Apocalypse Version*, ed. Elis Fridner, Lund Studies in English 29. Lund: Gleerup, 1961.
Beves:	*The Romance of Sir Beues of Hamtoun*, ed. Eugen Kölbing, EETS es 46, 48, 65 (1885–94).
BRUO:	Emden, A. B. *A Biographical Register of the University of Oxford*, 3 vols. Oxford: Clarendon Press, 1957–9.
Cavanaugh:	Cavanaugh, Susan H. 'A Study of Books Privately Owned in England: 1300–1450', 2 vols. Unpub. University of Pennsylvania Ph.D. diss., 1980.
Comp:	*The Middle English Complaint of Our Lady and Gospel of Nicodemus*, ed. C. William Marx and Jeanne F. Drennan, Middle English Texts 19. Heidelberg: Winter, 1987.
Digby 86:	*Facsimile of Oxford, Bodleian Library, MS Digby 86*, ed. Judith Tschann and M. B. Parkes, EETS ss 16 (1996).
GEC:	C[ockayne], G[eorge] E., rev. Vicary Gibbs. *The Complete Peerage*, 12 vols. in 13. London: St Catherine's, 1910–59.
Glanvill:	*The treatise on the laws and customs of the realm of England commonly called Glanvill*, ed. G. D. G. Hall. London: Nelson, 1965.
Guy:	*The Romance of Guy of Warwick*, ed. Julius Zupitza, EETS es 42, 49, 59 (1883–91).

IMEV: Brown, Carleton, and Rossell H. Robbins (eds.). *The Index of Middle English Verse*. New York: Columbia University Press, 1943. With Robbins and John L. Cutler (eds.). *Supplement to IMEV*. Lexington KY: University of Kentucky Press, 1965.

IPMEP: Lewis, R. E., N. F. Blake, and A. S. G. Edwards (eds.). *Index of Printed Middle English Prose*. New York: Garland, 1985.

Ker, MLGB: Ker, N. R. *Medieval Libraries of Great Britain: A List of Surviving Books*, RHS Guides and Handbooks 3, 2nd edn. London: Royal Historical Society, 1964. With Andrew G. Watson. *MLGB: Supplement to the Second Edition*, RHS Guides and Handbooks 15. London: Royal Historical Society, 1987.

Ker, MMBL: — (volume 4 with A. J. Piper; volume 5, indexes, by I. C. Cunningham and A. G. Watson). *Medieval Manuscripts in British Libraries*, 5 vols. Oxford: Clarendon Press, 1969–2002.

LALME: Angus McIntosh, M. L. Samuels, *et al. A Linguistic Atlas of Late Mediaeval English*, 4 vols. Aberdeen: Aberdeen University Press, 1986.

Letter-books: *Calendar of Letter-Books . . . of the City of London*, ed. Reginald R. Sharpe, 11 vols. London: Guildhall, 1899–1912.

Milemete: *The Treatise of Walter de Milemete De nobilitatibus sapienciis et prudencijs regum*, ed. M. R. James, Roxburghe Club. Oxford: Horace Hart, 1913.

Minot: *The Poems of Laurence Minot*, ed. Joseph Hall. Oxford: Clarendon Press, 1887, 1897, 1914.

Mirror: the Middle English translation of Robert of Gretham's *Mirur*, Cambridge, Magdalene College, MS Pepys 2498, pp. 45^a–212^b, partly ed., *The Middle English* Mirror*: Sermons from Advent to Sexagesima . . .* , ed. Thomas G. Duncan and Margaret Connolly, Middle English Texts 34. Heidelberg: Winter, 2003.

PAL: Schmitt, Charles B., and Dilwyn Knox. *Pseudo-Aristoteles Latinus: A Guide to Latin Works Falsely*

                      Attributed to Aristotle before 1500, Warburg Institute Surveys and Texts. London: Warburg Institute, 1985.

Paues Version: *A Fourteenth Century English Biblical Version,* ed. Anna C. Paues. Cambridge: Cambridge University Press, 1904.

Richard: *Der Mittelenglische Versroman über Richard Löwenherz,* ed. Karl Brunner. Vienna: Braunmüller, 1913.

STC: A. W. Pollard and G. R. Redgrave, rev. Katherine F. Panzer, *A Short-Title Catalogue of Books Printed 1475– 1640,* 2nd edn, 3 vols. London: Bibliographical Society, 1976–91.

In Thrall

Stories are all the human race has got. You just got to find the one you like and stay with it.

Belmont Pugh to Dave Robicheaux, as reported by James Lee Burke

The team, the buckboard, went on in the thick dust of the spent summer. Now he could see the village proper – the store, the blacksmith shop, the metal roof of the gin with a thin rapid shimmer of exhaust above the stack. It was now the third week in September; the dry, dust-laden air vibrated steadily to the rapid beat of the engine, though so close were the steam and the air in temperature that no exhaust was visible but merely a thin feverish shimmer of mirage. The very hot, vivid air, which seemed to be filled with the slow laborious plaint of laden wagons, smelled of lint; wisps of it clung among the dust-stiffened roadside weeds and small gouts of cotton lay imprinted by hoof- and wheel-marks into the trodden dust. He could see the wagons too, the long motionless line of them behind the patient, droop-headed mules, waiting to advance a wagon-length at a time, onto the scales and then beneath the suction pipe.

William Faulkner, *The Hamlet*, in *Novels 1936–1940*
(New York: The Library of America, 1990), p. 878

Faulkner smells the lint, but he misses out another smell, the detail I remember about ginning, always associated with late August drives up old US highway 79 into East Texas. These, necessarily, went straight through Thrall, with its gin beside the highway. The same heat, the same brightness suffused with dust from the unpaved gravel that led to the highway, seen through squinted eyes. But I remember most the smell of the gin, a second heat in the day. Perhaps they did not in Mississippi *c.* 1900 have an idea what to do with gin waste, the seed and stubs the machinery removes to leave the fibre you can spin.

In my day, like provident ants, ginners profited even from the waste; they used it for cattle feed. To do that, they cooked it. By the gin was a huge open-walled circular oast, its floor glowing red with smouldering cotton seed, and from it emanating the smell I always think of – more heat, and something strangely disgusting and inviting, all at once. The oil burns out of the cotton stubs, at once acrid and sweet, and, when they gin, it permeates everything. Whole towns, in the heat of summer's end, smell of it for weeks. What the oast leaves behind, once the odour has at last dissipated, stamped into large pellets, cottonseed-cake, can be tossed into the lots to keep the cattle going through the winter when the grass is gone.

I am telling you this because it is an experience you (or most of you) will not share. It will be alien because it is a product of being of a time and, most importantly, of a place. It was eight hundred miles up that same road through East Texas to the nearest professional baseball team then; we'd only had a teevee for three years, and usually still got our news off the radio. But we weren't conscious of cultural blight; we shared those unspoken commonalities, the things that construct culture – among them, that sometime the last two weeks of August, the man would start ginning, and they would fire up the oast, and we would be suffused with that smell, at once bitter and saccharine. Indeed, our very alienation, that we were who we were because of where we were, made of us a community, in Thrall and places like it – Kyle and Blanco and Manshack.

The voice in what I have just written is of course, that of unvarnished nostalgia. But one must be aware that not all local knowledges are responsible, or recuperable through the dusty haze of the late August in which they were first experienced. However enthralling the cotton gin may be in memory, one knew that it was only the visible (and smellable) manifestation of something larger – and if not then guilt-inducing, at least embarrassing.

The trucks that drove to the gin were steered by white hands. They had earlier been filled, first by the stoop labour, and the scarred hands (cotton isn't docile, and the stiff leafy edges of the bolls rip and tear), of black men and women, then by the hard work of black people emptying the sacks into truck beds. The bossman (or his white foreman) drove the truck, and he took the money for the usable fibre; the black labour that produced his profit got paid at piecework wages. Memory holds voices (both the following citations excerpted from the *dicta* of southern belles who ended up with college degrees) that are equally part of the experience of ginning:

> Daddy always says to hire n–rs because the Mexicans will rob you blind
>
> *
>
> Of course when you hire n–rs you know you are getting the culls; all the ones with any gumption got up and left here

Faulkner comments at the end of his introductory description of Frenchman's Bend, 'There was not one negro landowner in the entire section. Strange negroes would absolutely refuse to pass through it after dark' (733).

Experiences are complex and fractured, and include resistances, as well as joys. It is possible to sentimentalise ginning, just like you can railroad whistles at grade crossings or sitting under the live oaks in the back at Scholtz's (the opening scene in the best literary evocation of the site, Billy Lee Brammer's *The Gay Place*). You can possibly – a la Nashville – have a nostalgia for rednecks and bubbas ('Hank Williams, you wrote my life'). But it takes a voluntary act of forgetting to do so, or do so without some deep qualifications. Ultimately, just as I will argue in chapter 1 of so small a detail as fourteenth-century London English, being in Thrall resists any totalising narrative.

I emphasise this resistance because postmodern medievalism, for example that enunciated in both David Wallace's *Chaucerian Polity* and Richard F. Green's *A Crisis of Truth*, often seems to me so keen to submerge it. Both writers pursue master-narratives and an emphasis upon the longue durée. Yet in so doing, they often fail to respond to, to render comprehensible and narratable, a history I would take as responsive to something like lived experience and practice. This would actually occur somewhere, in a fragmented locality. (Contrast with their treatments the local knowledge of Steven Justice's agrarian communities, presented in *Writing and Rebellion* as unified by the threat of dearth.)

Since law will flicker in and out of my argument, I restrict detailed comments to Green's work (although *mutatis mutandis*, much the same critique would address Wallace's return to Burckhardt). *Crisis of Truth* works through Green's postulating an oral *Volksrecht* beginning deep in the pre-Conquest past. In his argument, this reflects a local community immune to writing and dependent on face-to-face personal integrity, a community of interest lost before a royal incursion associated with the advent of written law. But this centralisation might be perceived as having occurred long before Green's postulated fourteenth-century moment of disaster:

> After many nations received the faith of Christ and the religion spread, many synods gathered throughout the world . . . and in these gatherings, they established compensation for many misdeeds, and they wrote them, whatever their source (or content?), as chapters in many synod-books. Then I, X the king, gathered them together and commanded that they be written down . . .
>
> Postquam contigit quod plures nationes Christi fidem susceperunt, religione crescente, plures synodus circumqueque conuenerunt. . . . Et in multis synodis suis multorum forisfactorum emendationes aptauerunt et ex multis synodalibus libris undecumque capitula conscripserunt. Ego tunc X rex hec collegi simul et scribi precepi . . .

One might think this a statement about canon law, and a regal gesture, perhaps precocious, of the Central Middle Ages. But, of course, it is not – and indeed might be perceived as a beneficent royal gesture designed to protect the populace in dispersed localities from predations of local lords. Both my Latin and my 'X' perhaps unfairly anonymise the passage; the latter should be replaced by 'Ælfredus', Alfred the Great (reigned 871–900); the former, a twelfth-century translation into Latin, by a surviving Anglo-Saxon version. The king continues:

> Then I, King Alfred, gathered together many of those judgements my ancestors had made and commanded that they be written down, at least those that pleased me . . . . But I gathered here those that appeared most just to me and that I found from the days of my kinsman Ine, or of King Offa of Mercia, or of Ethelbert, first to be baptised among the English, and I put the remainder aside.
>
> Ego tunc Ælfredus rex hec collegi simul et scribi precepi, multa eorum que predecessores nostri tenuerunt et mihi placuerunt . . . . [Q]ue repperi de diebus Inae regis, cognoti mei, uel Offa Mircenorum regis uel Æþelbrihtes, qui primus in Anglorum gente baptizatus est, que michi iustiora uisa sunt hic collegi, ceteraque dimisi (*Gesetze* I, 45, 47, the Anglo-Saxon on the facing pages).

From Alfred at least, one must see Law as a written pronouncement centrally imposed and, in localities, deriving its sense of procedure and penalty from such promulgations. Impressive recent study (Patrick Wormald 1999) shows clearly the extent to which Green's local community was centrally directed and restrained from its own factionalism through received, textually inscribed behaviours subject to learned editing and emendation and to a royal power of promulgation. Late fourteenth-century audiences know that of Alfred as well, and both John Trevisa and at least one Lollard author take his vernacular assays seriously, as model textual promulgations – Alfred 'turnede þe best lawes into his moder tunge and þe Sawter also' ('A Lollard tract' 149–50, cf. Trevisa's 'Dialogue' 135–8).

Moreover, Wormald's masterful demonstration – the projective force of 'ancient' Anglo-Saxon law, its flowing into the twelfth-century 'birth of Common Law' – is only half the story. For Alfred's preface to the *Laws* scarcely shows itself as an originary document. The king could accession, and (as he says) preserve where it suited him ('ancient custom' is always already malleable), what must be the originary *written* English code, that of Æthelbeorht of Kent, the first baptised English monarch (s. vii in.).

But more to the point, Alfred's very conception of what creates and sanctifies law, what gives it its power to bind, is nothing less than writing itself. The *Laws* are not oral, and Alfred does not begin by reproducing those of Æthelbeorht. His very lengthy prologue focuses law as a royal imitation of God-given written practice: it is mainly (*Gesetze* 1, 26–45) quotation – of Exodus 20–3 and Acts 15:23–9. While one may be immensely sympathetic to Green's sense that something dire occurred in the later fourteenth century, the loss of organic local community (something that must have happened long since, that Law had been created to adjudicate) neither discovers what preceded that date nor defines the nature of the subsequent disaster.

The book that follows will be primarily concerned with what gets repressed, as literary history, in accounts like these of a longue duree. For implicitly, critics like Green and Wallace are writing about centralising procedures, canonical authors, and in the voice of traditional 'English Literary History'. This, as everyone knows, sanctions an origin – 'Chaucer the Father of English Poetry'. Silenced behind it, and the repressed that somehow must have contributed to and enabled it, is 'locality', the local literary culture of discrete places. With a certain irony, I choose here to offer London as an exhibit of the distinctive productive character of a locale. In conventional accounts (cf. Wallace's 'Absent City', *Chaucerian Polity* 156–81), London functions as 'dys-topic', not a place at all. Master narratives of national culture require that London reflect a universal metropolitanism, the very opposite of a resistant and fragmented locality. Absorptive, it simply overwhelms everything else, eradicating difference, its success its ability to submerge any perception of different procedures, whether biographically/personally or culturally.

This volume seeks a fragmentary restoration. I here return to a local (and thus pre-canonical) site in an effort to render intelligible what, in accounts like those I describe, now is only, to cite one prominent example, the trace of Auchinleck romances subsumed in the parody of 'Sir Thopas'. Most especially the book returns to the great repressed voice, which Chaucer found so strong he could only ignore (and parody), that of William Langland, a visible, and far from unique, connective between diverse versions of local community. So this will be a topical study. The word 'topic', after all, means primarily a place and a commonplace – the representation (which is not the same as the existence) of a 'commune'.

I am particularly indebted to the models for such an inquiry provided by my colleagues and interlocutors, Thorlac Turville-Petre and Richard Beadle. Their writings have suggested ways of using localisable manuscript records to construct a polyvocal and topical cultural surround. Here I adopt methods they have developed to a different (and in many respects, less promising) locale. In addition to their scholarly tutelage, I remain grateful to both for many kindnesses (including meals and shelter) and stimulating conversations over the years.

Following such expert guidance, my argument will return to the manuscripts, the local instantiations of textual culture, forgotten behind the printed editions of canonical authors like Chaucer. I would insist, at the outset, what attentive readers of my past work will recognise, that these documents contain their own resistances to any fetishisation or nostalgia. Most typically, as I have often argued, it is their vicissitudes and misrepresentations that identify a locale in which one can begin some form of historical inquiry. One of my major indebtednesses remains to the present custodians of my central exhibits, most especially to Aude Fitzsimons at the Pepys Library and to the long-time facilitators of my work in Duke Humfrey's Library, William Hodges, Russell Edwards, Jean-Pierre Maillon, and Alan Carter.

To balance what may appear a heavy dose of manuscript bibliography, I have tried to keep reference so light as possible. In general, I note my indebtednesses parenthetically within the text, and simply group all my authorities in a list of references at the end. Readers will probably recognise a number of studies not here cited, although ostensibly relevant. Quite simply, I attempt to maintain bonhomie by not feeling compelled to cite, much less offer a critique of, works I have found generally unhelpful. All translations are my own, with the exception of biblical citations (from the Douay-Rheims version). I follow one convention throughout: unmarked references to *Piers Plowman* are always to the B Version, A and C only being explicitly marked.

Finally, I remain acutely aware of the partiality of my account. At various points, I have wished that I might provide a thicker description of my chosen locale, fourteenth-century London. I am conscious of having scanted a great deal I know I should have discussed, in particular further specific Anglo-Norman texts and manuscripts, as well as a deeper historical surround predicated on documents like the London Letter-Books and London Chronicles. But, although it goes against the grain to cite Chaucer here, 'The remenant of the tale is long ynough', and I hope not to 'letten eek noon of this route', scholar-pilgrims who may well have access to stronger plough-teams than I.

This book has a long gestation and has been through a large number of fits and changes since I first conceived it. If it has an only begetter, it was my late colleague Robert P. apRoberts, who in autumn 1981 invited me to read a Chaucer paper at the Philological Association of the Pacific Coast. In a rash moment, I discussed Chaucer's method as translator in his *Boece*. This resulted in a very long bout (and eventually a 350-page draft) on the status of formal prose translation in Middle English culture.

This study, some bits of which get recycled in chapter 4, depended upon the largesse of a patron, the John Simon Guggenheim Memorial Foundation. I am particularly indebted, not only to the Foundation for its support, but to those who helped draw its attention to that transmogrification of my project: Steve Barney, Larry Benson, John Burrow, Tony Edwards, Del Kolve, and Traugott Lawler. Tony read one whole draft of that iteration, with his usual trenchant scepticism. Traugott and I have collaborated on four projects; he has been a ceaseless inspiration, both for his Latinity and his humanity.

The Guggenheim fragment never actually reached its projected subject, 'Ricardian-Lancastrian prose translation'. In writing it, I became more fascinated by the cultural centrality of *Ancrene Riwle*, a fascination that forced me into the middle of Pepys 2498. A major turning point in the development of the project occurred in March 1998, when my friend Sally Mapstone commanded me come to a conference she had organised in Scotland; at that point, library tourism introduced me to the Hunter MS of the London sermon cycle called *The Mirror*, and I began to have an inkling how a dormant project might receive new purchase.

As will be obvious, like all those who deal with Middle English manuscripts, I owe immense debts to A. I. Doyle and Malcolm Parkes. As he does for all who approach him, Ian has constantly offered advice and information. I hope that he will accept my gratitude, although my hope is qualified by our very different responses to medieval Christianity. Malcolm, as he has done for many, has bailed me out of all sorts of tight spots, queried or verified what I thought of a number of scribal hands, and, through his engaging raconteurism, suggested to me a great many avenues of inquiry I should never otherwise have thought to take up.

Three people offered intense encouragement and support at various points of gestation. Rita Copeland and David Lawton read full drafts of what stood in 1991. Lynn Staley has been constantly and thoroughly supportive, and has read large blocks of the current draft. I am also grateful for advice on specific chapters to Helen Cooper and Helen Barr. While he forebore reading anything, most of what I know about medieval English religious writing has been shaped by long (and beery) communions with the field's greatest expert, Vincent Gillespie, whose influence has always impinged on my writing.

I am particularly grateful to my current employers, Keble College and Oxford University. Their combined generosity enabled a year's sabbatical in 2001–2; during this time, I managed to research and draft about 40 per cent of what ensues. My Warden, Averil Cameron, and the Keble Governing Body were especially generous in allowing me an unusual extra term without duties. I'm also conscious of the friendship of Tony Phelan and how much I have learned from my Keble colleagues, Michael Hawcroft and, a fount of London lore, Ian Archer, as well as from the monitory example of Daniel Butt.

Various pieces of the volume have been read in public fora, and a few bits published. All these occasions have placed me in the debt of those who thought I must have something to say (and of the sceptical audiences they assembled to hear me): John Alford, Kate Bennett, Linda Brownrigg, John Burrow (once again), Larry Clopper, Andrew Cole, Andy Galloway, David Ganz, Jill Havens (cf. Hanna 2003, portions reproduced in the conclusion), Nigel Palmer, Derek Pearsall (cf. Hanna 2000, some pieces recycled in chapter 3), Ad Putter, Pamela Robinson, Vance Smith, Jane Tolmie, and Thorlac Turville-Petre (again).

I owe particular gratitude to Cambridge University Press and its series Studies in Medieval Literature for the care and attention they have bestowed on my work. Alastair Minnis, the series editor, must deserve an award for long-suffering perseverance, finally cajoling a manuscript from me fifteen years after first asking. My two readers, Andy Galloway and John Burrow, were full of suggestions about the submitted version, from which it has invariably profited. At the press, Linda Bree has been a magnificently supportive editor, and my script has been ably seen through the production process by Maartje Scheltens and my copy-editor, Ann Lewis.

The dedication honours the two people who first and most strongly, from my childhood, inspired me. They, a woman of valour and a self-defrocked rebbe, are quite peculiarly my locality. Were I not compelled to remember them (and it), this volume would have to be for the two Annes, Middleton and Hudson. The first, my friend for more years than either of us will care to remember, has offered more than constant encouragement, something more like sheer inspiration, as I attempted to raise my scholarly game to a level of which she might approve. The second, a friend of a later, if still antique, vintage, convinced me (as she has everyone else) of the centrality of Wycliffism and has long been my model of scholarly industry and acumen. With both, I have enjoyed the exchange of drafts; both have read substantial chunks of the book in one shape or another and offered their customarily bracing commentary. Particularly, as I tried to respond to my readers, Anne M. has been a font of productive suggestions, many silently incorporated here. Like all those named above, they should be considered immune from critique for the errors of what follows, all of my own propagation.

Kait and McGee are simply immune from critique.

CAMBRIDGE STUDIES IN MEDIEVAL LITERATURE

English vernacular culture in London before 1380: the evidence

In 1978, Ian Doyle and Malcolm Parkes inaugurated a new era of manuscript study. In their discussion of an early *Confessio Amantis* manuscript, Cambridge, Trinity College, MS R.3.2, they identified five important scribes sharing out the production, in London just after 1400. In the course of the study, Doyle and Parkes located the inception of a London book-trade that specialises in works of Chaucer and Gower and that is vitally important to understanding the development of English Literature as we know it. Their work has stimulated numerous daughter studies and squarely fixed critical attention on the development, in London, of a canon of English Authors.

Another comment by one of these scholars, now a few years later, fills in a further aspect of these seminal findings. Doyle, discussing 'English books in and out of court' (1983, 164–5), points out how few of them can be associated with the metropolis before 1400. And he comments upon the likelihood that before that date, the vernacular book-trade was in the main 'provincial' in nature. Although he notices the existence (and Chaucer's possible use) of 'The Auchinleck MS' (Edinburgh, National Library of Scotland, MS Advocates' 19.2.1), it appears in his account as a fairly isolated accident of London work.

But this was simply a moment of inattention on Doyle's part. He certainly knew, in his 1953 dissertation, more than anyone before or since about pre-1400 London books (and what will follow is pervasively indebted to his work). Moreover, both Doyle and Parkes obviously knew that records of book-trade organisation, in this case evidence that a guild including 'scriptores scribentes curiam ac textum' (both court and text hand, see further pp. 44–5) existed by 1357 (Pollard 3–9; documents at Riley 295, 372–3). This professional group was presumably prepared to answer vernacular – English – as well as Latinate and French, demands. Equally, Doyle and Parkes knew these 1357 regulations scarcely represented the origins of the local trade; a 'venditor librorum', Michael of Ludgate Hill, is recorded as early as 1223 (Pollard 5), and a substantial number of surviving deluxe books was produced in the capital, probably Westminster, rather than the City, from at least 1270 (cf. Rosser 1989, 207). However, in directing attention towards the fifteenth century – and to the foundations of Modern Literary Culture – these great palaeographers replicated the act which always accompanies the construction of national identity, forgetting the past.

This amnesia surely inheres in Doyle's bland reference to 'provincial' book-production. During the period he is addressing, such work should be perceived as something other than the randomly dispersed and fitful book-activities his adjective might imply. At least two English regions, to both of which my argument will return, were established centres of English literary activity and promulgation well before the initiatory London gesture Doyle and Parkes identify: the ancient diocese of Worcester (in this case, carrying on Anglo-Saxon traditions continuously) and, from the later thirteenth century, a number of West and North Yorkshire locales. Further evidence suggests that another centre, perhaps neither so distinguished nor so protracted in its output, existed in the neighbourhood of King's Lynn from an early date; work from this area, initially signalled by Angus McIntosh (1976), is placed within its long-term context in Richard Beadle's seminal study of this county literary community (1991, esp. 102–3). Similarly, Thorlac Turville-Petre has, on several occasions, pointed to the rich remains of early fourteenth-century literary production, at times concentrating upon early Lincolnshire communities (as well as much later Nottingham and Derbyshire ones). Rather than the 'provincial' identifying the backwater, ample evidence implies that the developed London booktrade Doyle and Parkes discuss had been preceded by a discontinuous series of robust indigenous literary cultures.

So where does this leave London, The Metropolitan Centre? If fourteenth-century evidence would indicate the literary vitality of 'provincial' book-activities, continuous and proliferated, what should one make of the apparent silence of The Metropolis? Perhaps one needs to reverse Doyle's telescope; before Chaucer, London may truly have been 'provincial', among England's vernacular literary backwaters, just another locality. This will be a discovery perhaps surprising in the light of the City's general cultural hegemony, both developing and achieved.

'Developing', however, may be the operative term here, for at the opening of the fourteenth century, London might be perceived as culturally deprived, the chief amenities and ornaments of high literary activity originated and disseminated mostly outside its walls. The universities were elsewhere, unlike Paris; and unlike the centres provided by great religious foundations in Worcester and the North, the local religious houses were not urban, but formed an arc around the periphery, outside the walls that define 'The City' (Brooke 38; Barron 1989, 47).[1] Indeed, the cultural developments I intend to outline here might be seen as most easily aligned with the City's growth in commercial centrality, associated with the decline of the provincial wool-trade after about 1270 (cf. Nightingale's revisionary arguments, 1996, 90, 93–5). Moreover, although eventually government followed commerce, in the usual formulation, the process of centralising administrative offices in London only became fixed and complete with the inception of Edward III's French adventure in the 1340s. No one would wish to dispute the relative size and power of the later book-trade described by Doyle–Parkes, perhaps a reflection of new products now available to purvey.[2]

But before the century's end, this place may not have been an English literary centre of any great distinction whatever. Indeed, it resembles a locale a good deal more like the customary meaning of 'provincial' than what Doyle takes the term to describe. London, in the earlier fourteenth century, is notable chiefly as an absence from the continuum constructed by scholars as 'The History of English Literature'.

The paradox I am posing invites the revival of the repressed and consideration of a generally ignored medieval literary history. Customarily, scholars examine 'The History of English Literature'; at least one inference to draw from my opening would be that no such beast existed in the fourteenth century. The literary history that this book seeks to uncover remains largely peripheral, because customary critical practice often (Beadle and Turville-Petre being notable exceptions) neglects to notice the polyvocal and individuated voices of discrete local/regional literary cultures.

3

Necessarily, I will attend to but a small portion of this array, the range of options that characterised literature in England before a legibly single 'The History of English Literature' existed. I describe but one local variation overwhelmed in some measure (my final chapter will problematise this easy narrative) by the Lancastrian project of prioritising a national identity. I address the literary culture of what I call 'Edwardian London', an adjective I invoke to imply a broad cultural continuum covering the reigns of three Edwards and about a century, 1270–1370. Although most of my local exhibits come from *c.* 1310–80, the lower date does not signal abrupt cessation of earlier textual practices, which certainly overlap Doyle–Parkes's originary moment chronologically. For example, the London production of the city's most important Edwardian author, William Langland, occurred *c.* 1377–95 but is largely known, inferentially, from later copies (here certainly contemporary with, and some in fact produced by, members of the Doyle–Parkes team).

As will be evident from Doyle's prioritisation of the 'provincial', one can only begin such a study by identifying what the master himself had momentarily forgotten, some corpus of fourteenth-century London writing. Here only dialect and provenance studies can offer the tools for constructing a group of books (and subsequently works) on which to operate. The most useful, although not entirely compelling and potentially very fraught, work has come from the studies of M. L. Samuels, subsequently included in LALME. Whatever the difficulties with Samuels's formulation of his procedures (to which I return in section III below), his work serves to isolate a sequence of medieval English books written in roughly comparable languages, and languages associable with the London area.

I Defining the corpus of London texts

Developing findings he first announced in 1963 (87–8 and 87 n. 7), Samuels singles out (1972, 166) nine sources for London English of the period *c.* 1330–75.[3] Two of these scribes appear in the same volume (Auchinleck), and one copyist is alone responsible for three separate books. Further, as Thomas G. Duncan pointed out, one can add a tenth writer to this group. And following one of Doyle's myriad generous suggestions, I will add an eleventh.

4

Significantly, like Doyle and Parkes, Samuels adduces this sequence of books in the course of mapping what he argues constituted a cataclysmic change. For him, London language shifted dramatically around 1380. Before that date, he argues, the language of these eleven writers, an Essex-tinged dialect, was reflective of local usage, his 'Type II London'. But around 1380, in his account, local usage changed abruptly, to a dialect influenced by a 'central Midland standard', his 'Type III London'. This latter language first appears in local documents, most notably Thomas Usk's 'Appeal' (1386) and the vernacular reports of London guild regulations in 1388–9 (Chambers–Daunt 18–60, Barron–Wright). Type III will subsequently become the language in which Chaucer's poetry is transmitted.

Samuels's materials must testify to a London vernacular book-trade. As is well known, no sample of London English (and thus, no product of, or evidence for, such an institution) survives between two brief texts of Henry III's reign and those eleven writers identified by Samuels. Further, before 1258, evidence for vernacular literary production in the capital is negligible. Margaret Laing lists only two items remotely likely to represent London transmission, much less authorship, 'the Trinity homilies' (Cambridge, Trinity College, MS B.14.52 [335], s. xii²; 1993, 37–8), an identification which she has subsequently retracted (see Laing–McIntosh); and 'A Prisoner's Prayer' (IMEV 322; London, Corporation of London Records Office, 'Liber de antiquis legibus', fols. 160ᵛ–61ᵛ, s. xiii²ᐟ⁴; 1993, 108). Further, leaving aside a number of early vernacular legal documents, only two other books show even a ghostly sign of having been copied in London at a time before those items Samuels assembles.[4] The evidence, in short, would suggest that this was a locale with virtually no English literary culture at all before about 1300.

At this point, I turn to consider the composition and contents of the books written in Samuels's 'Type II' London English. There are, in all, ten relevant manuscripts. All these volumes are written on vellum, and they are datable, in the main on a palaeographical basis, at various points in the fourteenth century:

(1) Cambridge, University Library, MS Gg.iv. 32, s. xiv in., perhaps, given the inclusion in part II of local ecclesiastical documents dated 1312 and 1315, before 1320: a Latin priest's book, with diagrammes,

English and Anglo-Norman snippets, mainly verse (IMEV 2703, 1064, 3201, 476, 3248, 1282, 1062 + 1024). The scribe of the English also copied extensive materials for Andrew Horn in the 1320s (see further p. 69). David Rollenhagen, author of a Cornell Ph.D. dissertation concerning part II, generously tells me that this portion of the book, mostly London ecclesiastical records of the late 1310s, certainly belonged to John Skip, rector of St Martin in the Vintry (*c.* 1300–18), or to his successor, William of Norwich.

(2) The two most widely dispersed hands of 'The Auchinleck MS', those designated scribe 1 (the director of the entire operation) and scribe 3, conventionally dated *c.* 1330–40, and probably, because of the affiliations of its decorators (see pp. 79–81), earlier in that period, rather than later.[5]

(3) Glasgow University Library, MS Hunter U.4.8 (250): s. xiv$^{2/4}$, probably *c.* 1340 or a little later: *The Mirror*.

(4) British Library, MS Additional 17376, part I, fols. 1–149 (the front nine leaves, all Latin, now preserved separately as Bodleian Library, MS Lat. th. e. 32; see Hunt), palaeographically s. xiv med. (*c.* 1330–70): the prose Psalter (IPMEP 114). The style of one colophon (fol. 198^{rv} in part II, not in London language but the same hand), outlining indulgences which 'are granted by Archbishop Simon' ('a domino Symone Archiepiscopo Cantuarie conceduntur'), may permit a narrower placement, *c.* 1330–48.[6] A copy of the text appears to have been circulating in London by the later date (see the discussion of Robert de Felstede's will, p. 11). Doyle (1953, 1, 106) could read under ultraviolet light an inscription I can no longer see: 'William Pelka civis London'.

(5) Cambridge, St John's College, MS S.30 (256), pp. 233–70, s. xiv med. (*c.* 1340–70): basic instructional materials, an unpublished English Office of the Dead, 'Speculum Gy de Warwyke' (IMEV 1101), added to a copy of Lorens of Orleans, *Somme le roi*, produced in London in the 1320s.

(6–8) The three books in a single hand, late s. xiv$^{3/4}$ (1365–75; see Hanna 2003, 142–4):

(6) Cambridge, Magdalene College, MS Pepys 2498: *The Mirror, Ancrene Riwle*, prose Psalter, Apocalypse, and other prose texts; belonged to Stephen Batman (*d.* 1584; see Parkes 1997, 139–41).

(7) Bodleian Library, MS Laud misc. 622: *Kyng Alisaunder, Titus and Vespasian*, excerpts from *The South English Legendary*, etc.

(8) British Library, MS Harley 874: the prose Apocalypse, with an excerpt from a *South English Legendary* item (IMEV Sup. 1907.5, from IMEV 3458).

(9–10) The two remaining volumes may be dated towards the end of the century and very likely after the appearance of Samuels's Type III London English:

(9) Cambridge, Corpus Christi College, MS 282, s. xiv$^{4/4}$ (Christopher de Hamel suggests to me 1380s, on the basis of decoration): *The Mirror.*

(10) British Library, MS Harley 5085, s. xiv/xv: *The Mirror*, including additional sermons.[7]

In addition to these manuscripts, external evidence, historical and codicological, will place *Piers Plowman* B within the context of books such as these. Work on any version of the poem, if Lady Meed, central to the opening vision, represents Alice Perrers, cannot predate 1365, the first record implying her liaison with Edward III. The last clear historical references of the B Version allude to events of 1376–7. Thus, Langland composed his poem contemporary with the production of manuscripts 6–8 above. Further, the early visible manuscript tradition of *Piers Plowman* B is London centred, although associated with Type III scribes (see Samuels 1985, 240–1). Like most propositions about the poem, these are contentious and require protracted demonstration. This I defer until chapter 6, where I examine Langland as the inheritor of early London traditions visible in the ten books listed above.

These manuscripts do not simply share, as Samuels argues, a distinctive local language, but an extensive group of texts as well. Particularly central in this regard is Pepys 2498, devoted entirely to a lengthy sequence of prose texts. In addition to their prose form, unusual at this date, these share a variety of other features: all provide reasonably direct access to biblical texts, all encourage a relatively learned textual consumption through their inclusion of explanatory commentaries, and all have been translated from Anglo-Norman sources.

In the manuscripts I have singled out for discussion, the most widely dispersed of these items is the largely unpublished *Mirror*. This extensive sermon-cycle is composed of fifty-nine homilies, with an appended sixtieth text, not properly a sermon; the later copies include further, often extensive, additions. The first fifty-three sermons offer fairly direct translations into English prose of the comparable portions of an Anglo-Norman poetic cycle, Robert of Gretham's *Mirur* (s. xiii$^{2/4}$ or med.), also largely unpublished (see Aitken, Duncan 1983, 1998; Sinclair).

The following six sermons differ from the preceding in not presenting and expounding, as Gretham's *Mirur* is subtitled, 'Les ewangelies des domnees' (line 423), the standard Sunday gospel readings. As Charlton Laird showed long ago, five of these six have been derived from an expanded Anglo-Norman version, where they are assigned to feastdays and the commons of saints. The sixtieth text differs further still, since it treats an epistle (1 Cor. 13), rather than a gospel, and is brief and hortatory, rather than a translation of a biblical text with attached homiletic commentary. In one form or another, this extensive text would appear utterly central to London preoccupations; in spite of its very great length (in the in-progress edition, something like 350 close-spaced printed pages), it occurs in four of the books, in three as the sole text.

Pepys 2498 shares two further texts with others of the ten manuscripts, and there is more attenuated evidence for the persistent London provenance of two additional items. This manuscript also includes a translated and commented version of the Apocalypse. The text appears to have been a modest demand item, for it is the only one the scribe copied more than once. It forms the only substantial contents item of another of his volumes, Harley 874.

'The Early English Prose Psalter' in Pepys 2498 recurs among the early London books. This is a lightly glossed translation, derived from a French version not known to survive in any manuscript produced in England (see St-Jacques). It also is found in Additional 17376, part I, where it follows Latin materials suitable for use by a parish priest.

Pepys includes two further works with more attenuated, but equally certain, London traditions of transmission. Among the most interesting of its texts is a heavily revised and interpolated copy of the early thirteenth-century West Midland spiritual classic, *Ancrene Riwle*. The interpolation, as will become clear shortly, certainly represents London work, at least inspired by the *Mirror*. And although later copies do not reflect these revisions, fifteenth-century circulation of the *Riwle* appears strongly London-centred.[8]

Finally, among shorter texts in the Pepys MS, once more derived from Anglo-Norman (in this case, an example occurs in a London book of *c.* 1340), is a narrative combining the Virgin's complaint and the pseudo-biblical *Gospel of Nicodemus*. Not widely attested, the text recurs *c.* 1500, in a London miscellany, Huntington Library, MS HM 144 (also including Chaucer's *Melibee* and a variety of excerpts from Caxton's print of Trevisa's *Polychronicon*). There existed in London a community of readers, served by both translators and, initially, by a scribal community writing Type II English.

If translated biblical prose provides one centre of the early London book-trade, it certainly does not form a unique emphasis. Although earlier and very different in its general tenor, a substantial grouping of romances, the Auchinleck MS may be connected with other books I have singled out. It includes both the historical romance *Kyng Alisaun-der*, shared with Laud misc. 622 (the Auchinleck copy now mostly cut away), and the 'Speculum Gy de Warwick' (IMEV 1101), shared with the St John's MS. Moreover, numerous Auchinleck (and Laud 622) texts remained alive in London well into the sixteenth century and the age of print, works like *Of Arthour and of Merlin*, *Beves of Hamtoun*, *Guy of Warwick*, *The Seven Sages of Rome*, and the loosely related *Lybeaus Desconus* (cf. chapter 3, n. 3).

The translated biblical commentaries that form one centre of early London work clearly appeal to considerable religious sophistication. Their readers were precocious in their desire for Scripture in English, and they not only wanted access to the biblical letter but to commentaries, academically based aids to reading. However, manuscripts written in Type II English show London religious materials extending to encompass the opposite end of the intellectual spectrum; some texts accommodate the parishioner utterly naïve. In the fourteenth century, the need to provide the most fundamental guides to salvation was perceived as considerably more important (and was more widespread) than biblical reading. This address to the quasi- and non-literate, in accord with the injunctions of the fourth Lateran council (1215) and those of echoing local councils, was to become a major emphasis of vernacular religious writings later in the century (Hanna 1997, xvii–xxii).

Such work is modestly represented in the volumes here assembled. At the least august, one could point to the scraps of CUL Gg.iv.32; the verse-form here imposed on instructional lists may identify this doggerel as mnemonic devices to outline basic points for a not very sophisticated congregation. Similar are the translations of basic prayers and of the extensive Office of the Dead, together with lists of basic beliefs, in St John's 256. Both manuscripts also include lyrics indicating a shared interest in Marian devotion. Even tiny and unpromising bits here are capable of surprising. The Anglo-Norman versified Pater Noster of CUL Gg.iv.32, for example, is accompanied by Latin glosses which convert it into a full-scale septenary mnemonic. These align the petitions of the prayer, the seven deadly sins, and the gifts of the Holy Spirit (ed. Meyer 342). This treatment renders the text comparable to the elaborate painted instructional diagrammes that appear elsewhere in the book (see Sandler 1999, Maurice Hussey), although it is still simpler than these.

In short, one can argue that the ten manuscripts provide a fairly coherent, if diverse, centre of earlier fourteenth-century London reading, its concerns extended (as I will argue in chapter 6) in *Piers Plowman*. Yet simultaneously, to concentrate uniquely on this group of texts would substantially misrepresent contemporary literary culture. This was, of course, overwhelmingly polylingual, a point that will persistently recur in my argument (cf. Turville-Petre 1996, 182–5, on the trilingual culture underlying Harley 2253). Early London readers were not engaged in an 'English or . . .' situation but one that likely moved between the ten central books – portions of which are in clerical Latin and continental French, after all – and other volumes.

Moreover, such behaviours would persist, as two legacies in the 1392 will of Isabella, duchess of York, will indicate:

> Also, I leave to my beloved son Edward, count of Rutland, my two books, Machaut and Launcelot . . . . Also, to Sir Lewis Clifford, my book of vices and virtues.[9]

Strikingly, both legatees, although recipients of French materials, actively participated in English literary culture, Edward as translator of Gaston Phebus's *Livre de chasse* (*The Master of Game*, 1406 × 1413), Clifford not only as member of 'the Chaucer circle' and intermediary between Chaucer and Deschamps, but as owner of Lollard and other English materials, one such item bequeathed in his English will of 1404.[10]

External evidence implies that materials like those in Pepys 2498, especially, in Auchinleck, and in the other eight volumes I have isolated provided the greater part of Londoners' English reading. The use of testamentary evidence in book-history has, ever since Margaret Deanesly (1920b) introduced the subject, been fraught with difficulties, and certainly testamentary information, as the example in my last paragraph may indicate, is never anything other than provocative. So far as it goes, however, the very few references to English books in contemporary London documents speak to the prevalence in local culture of texts like these.

Doyle was the first to point out London testamentary evidence for two probable lost copies of the texts I am considering (1953, 1, 105–6, 233–4; 2, 65–6, 304). In 1349, Robert de Felstede, a London vintner, willed a copy of 'a psalter written in Latin and English' to the clerk of another prominent vintner, Henry la 'Vanneve' (cf. Cavanaugh 335–6, citing Reginald Sharpe 1, 636).[11] The will might be seen, in conjunction with the Additional MS, as giving a *terminus ad quem* for the active circulation of this text; this book was being used by men presumably associates of the child Geoffrey Chaucer's vintner father.

Yet another copy of the prose Psalter may appear in an early inventory. The goods of Thomas of Woodstock, earl of Gloucester, whose seat was at Pleshey (Essex), just at the edge of Type II London language, were inventoried after his attainder (and not quite judicial murder) in 1397; among them was 'j. veil' sauter glosez d'engleis pris xx. *d*' (Dillon–Hope 299). One cannot be altogether certain just what this volume was, just as one must express uncertainty about 'un livre d'engleis de les evangelies coverez de quyr' rouge pris xj. *s* viij. *d*' (300), perhaps another copy of the prose *Mirror*. The difficulty here is that Thomas lived within the ambit of Lollard translation. His surviving two-volume Wycliffite Bible, now British Library, MSS Egerton 617–18 also appears in the inventory (300). Indeed, Thomas appears something of a fanatic for Lollard materials, having organised a debate between a Lollard and a friar (recorded in Dublin, Trinity College, MS 244); certainly, his 'novel livre de les evangelies glosez en engleis x. *s*' (301) is more apt to have been the Lollard glossed gospels than an earlier London text.

Again, John Clifford, a London mason, wrote his will, only probated 1417, in 1411. He bequeathed to his parish church, St Olave's, Southwark, along with his best (probably Latin) psalter, a 'lib[er] de Evangelijs dominicalibus in Anglicis verbis transposit[is]', a designation that very likely refers to the *Mirror* translation.[12] In addition, he willed a copy of another Pepys 2498 text to the 'monialibus iuxta Towrhill', 'the Minories', a convent of Franciscan nuns. Called in the will a 'lib[er] ... vocatus ... "Recti diligunt te"', this was a copy of *Ancrene Riwle*, identified by its incipit and its language not specified. The second bequest also included a book of saints' lives, its language again unspecified (cf. Cavanaugh 1980, 196–7, citing PRO, MS Prob. 11/2b, fol. 301).

There is also early London evidence, beyond the surviving copies, for *Piers Plowman*. The work appears in a bequest of 1400, nearly two decades before the first London will that mentions a Chaucer text. William Palmer, rector of St Alphege, Cripplegate, left Agnes Eggesfeld 'librum meum vocatum Peres Plowman' (Wood).

At least sporadic evidence suggestive of early London reading of texts like those in Auchinleck also occurs. In 1348, the prominent fishmonger Henry Graspays bequeathed 'To Henry his son divers chattels and household goods, including his wardrobe, his books of "Romanse", and others' (Cavanaugh 1980, 381, citing Reginald Sharpe 1, 627). While the form of reference is notoriously imprecise – Graspays may simply have meant his French/Anglo-Norman books, or even if 'romances', not English ones – the will potentially indicates that he was reading something like Auchinleck contents. Similarly, the post mortem inventory of property belonging to John Sandele, bishop of Winchester, and at his Southwark townhouse, Winchester Palace, includes, among twenty-six volumes, one of 'Romanc' (here probably French) (Carlin 50–1). Or again, Thrupp cites (162) two bankruptcy inventories for London grocers. One of these, that of Roger Chalket, a pepperer, in 1361, includes three quires of paper (since described as 'spendable', perhaps only for wrapping, not sale) and 'iiij. libri de romaunc' prec. xj. *s* iiij. *d*' (Cavanaugh 1980, 175, citing PRO, MS C 131/12/24).[13]

Another of Thrupp's bankruptcy inventories, that of the grocer William Cost in 1392, implies somewhat different interests, yet ones familiar from materials in the ten manuscripts. Along with a great deal of paper and parchment, which may imply Cost was (or was supplying) a practising scribe or stationer, the inventory includes:

ij. libros de Englyssh prec' viij. *d*
j. tabulam cum calendar[i]o prec' viiij. *d*
unum librum vocatum prymer' prec' xvj. *d*
j. tabulam vocatur Penybrede prec' ij. *d*
j. librum vocatur prymer prec' iiij. *d*
j. tabulam longam prec' iiij. *d.*

(Cavanaugh 1980, 210, citing PRO, MS C 131/42/2)

'Penybrede' might speak to Cost's commercial interests; although the title implies that this item, perhaps unusually, was in English, it was probably some version of the legal text, 'The Assise of Bread [and Ale]', which governed the pricing of staples according to the cost of grain (*Statutes* I, 199–200). But the remainder of Cost's holdings falls squarely in that area of modest devotions attested in CUL Gg.iv.32 and St John's 256. The 'tables', and especially the one with attached calendar, important for scheduling daily devotions, should recall the 'Turris sapientie' illustrations to CUL Gg.iv.32, graphic outlines of basic Christian responsibilities. The two primers address similar needs; the term refers to the basic private prayerbook (in modern terminology a 'book of hours'), customarily also equipped with a calendar. Quite routinely among its contents, in the main successions of Psalms (whose comprehension would have been aided by the translation in Pepys and Additional), appears the Office of the Dead and accompanying Commendation of All Souls, the basic prayer of penitential memorial. This text appears in (unpublished) Middle English in the St John's MS. Liturgical books of this stripe seem to have been ubiquitous in fourteenth-century London households; the great majority of books bequeathed in contemporary wills are primers, more extensive breviaries (the usual referent for 'porthors' or 'portiforium'), or books of liturgical readings ('legenda', some explicitly saints' lives).[14]

One English example of this last genre is also known from the legal record and will, like *Ancrene Riwle*, broach an issue to which I will return shortly, 'imported' English texts in London. In 1376, following his impeachment by the Good Parliament, an inventory was prepared of the goods of Richard Lyons, vintner (see Thrupp 354). In his counting house, the government agents found 'j. livre appellé legende sanctorum en engleis, pris 10 *s*', pretty certain to have been a copy of *The South English Legendary* (Myers 327). Trace elements from works associated with this western text of the later thirteenth century appear in Auchinleck, Laud misc. 622, and Harley 874.

Inventories of possessions made in the course of various legal actions augment the testamentary evidence. One pair of references resists identification and/or points towards interests of a sort unrecorded in the ten central volumes. After his 1386 attainder by the Lords Appellant, an inventory was made of the goods of Simon Burley, Richard II's tutor (see further pp. 232–3 and n. 18 there). Among the rash of French books one expects at this date, there was a single English item, the 18th: 'j. liure de englys del forster et del sengler'. This was probably, as Scattergood says (1968), *Fachliteratur*, a manual for a huntsman.

More problematically, in 1376, the goods of John Sharnebrok, chandler, were inventoried in yet another action for debt. Sharnebrok's possessions included a single book, 'unum Clensyng syne, prec. viij. *d*' (Cavanaugh 781, citing PRO, MS C 131/24/20). The only surviving text with a similar title, 'Þe clensyng of mannes soule', remains unpublished (Jolliffe E.14, Everett; neither his nor Catherine Regan's 1963 Harvard dissertation has appeared in print). This prose exhortation is about 'cleansing sin', a work in three sections of seven chapters each, each section devoted to one of the traditional three 'parts' of the sacrament. It provides, in the vernacular, teaching (based on the metaphor of Ps. 50:9 and 4 Reg. 5:10) analogous to Latin discussions John Skip or William of Norwich copied into CUL Gg.iv.32. It has additional connections to Latin instructional literature communicated in a polylingual early London context; part of the text is derived from Robert Grosseteste's popular diagrammatic manual *Templum Dei* (Everett 273–6). This work will be reminiscent of other 'tabulae' already mentioned, both the 'Turris sapientie' of CUL Gg.iv.32 and those in William Cost's inventory; moreover, a (now fragmentary) copy of Grosseteste's text appears in Bodleian Library, MS lat. th. e.32, originally integral with Additional 17376.

There is independent corroboration for 'Þe clensyng of mannes soule' as an 'early London' text. MS Bodley 923, the oldest of the four copies, is written in anglicana formata of about 1400. Fol. 153ᵛ has the inscription 'Iste liber constat Sibille de Felton' Abbatisse de Barkyng' and, in a different hand, but one that could be contemporary, 'anno domini 1401'.

However one interprets this addition, Felton's style means that she could have owned the book at any time 1393 × 1419, the dates of her tenure as abbess of the important east London/Essex nunnery (see further Doyle 1958, esp. 239–41).

There are, however, difficulties about the identification of the text with Sharnebrok's book.[15] At least in part (some forms of address are much more general), the abbess's book sounds as if written for a community of women like Felton's; this group owned other books, both French and English, including the text called *The Chastising of God's Children* (Bodley 923, fol. 145ᵛ). But *The Chastising*, whose sources are datable so late as the early 1370s, may postdate 1382, and yet must predate 'Þe clensyng' (see *Chastising* 35–7). Whether or not the community addressed is Felton's Barking, *The Chastising* may also be a London work from just at the end of the period (and it was to be extensively propagated in the capital in the later fifteenth century).[16] Nonetheless, both 'Þe clensyng' and *Chastising* resemble much more closely instructional materials typical of the period *c.* 1380–1410, and stand somewhat apart from the biblical emphases of most religious texts in the other central books. One might compare with Sybil Felton's penitential interests, for example, the most widely transmitted single sermon in Middle English; this was delivered at St Paul's Cross by Thomas Wimbledon in 1388 (IPMEP 560).

In sum, with the exception of Doyle–Parkes's early Chaucer and Gower manuscripts (see further Parkes 1995), all pre-Henry V evidence of London English reading points to texts found in, or analogous to those found in, the ten manuscripts. They might be perceived as forming, for the period under discussion, a set local canon, analogous to, yet more modern and literarily less distinguished than, those of 'provincial' centres like Worcester, York, or King's Lynn. However, unlike these locales, London was a place of persistent resort from throughout the kingdom. Thus, the extant manuscript record requires careful interrogation from two directions – as an exporting and an importing literary community.

II London as import–export centre for texts

Certainly by 1400, and probably earlier, London had begun to function as a community not simply engaged in local literary production but export. Rather than the preserve of local scribes, London texts found in the ten manuscripts began to be carried back to outlying locales by interested readers. There they will have become involved in divergent local textual traditions, collocations foreign to the locale in which they began. The clarity that one might hope for – London works appearing only in the metropolitan context – does not exist; indeed, the absence of that clarity testifies to the perceived success of London work at meeting general, and not just local, expectations.

The earliest visible behaviour of this kind involves dissemination of the romances gathered in the Auchinleck MS. Here I restrict myself to mentioning a particularly clear-cut example, London, Lincoln's Inn, MS Hale 150, copied shortly after 1400 in south-west Shropshire (LALME LP 4037). This book, with one exception, is composed of well-known London-circulating texts – the large Auchinleck romances *Of Arthour and of Merlin* and *Kyng Alisaunder*, the more ephemeral *Lybeaus Desconus* (not in the extant Auchinleck, but associated with its contents by Chaucer), and a copy of *Piers Plowman* A. The exemplars underlying Hale 150 presumably ended up where they did as the result of forays in and out of the capital by a servant of prominent local lords as he went about the business of his masters, the Fitzalan earls of Arundel, in their guise as barons of Clun and Oswestry. (For a distinguished argument that such behaviour represents the normal state of affairs, see Salter 1983, 52–85.)

Such dispersed transmission clearly appears with the texts of Pepys 2498 subject to repeated London copyings. The *Mirror* survives in six manuscripts total, and appears solidly in its transmission an early London text. Four of the manuscripts mentioned above (Corpus, Pepys, Hunter, and Harley 5085) contain it, in all instances except Pepys as the book's single text. The remaining two copies are temporally belated. Bodleian Library, MS Holkham misc. 40 (s. xv in.), however, appears mainly in Type III London language and thus should be perceived as a descendent of a local London scribal and textual tradition. The remaining copy of the *Mirror*, John Rylands University Library, MS Eng. 109 (formerly MS Lat. 179), was copied in 1432 and shows every sign of being a non-metropolitan production. It was preserved at Welbeck (Notts.), where it belonged to the Premonstratensian abbey.[17] Indeed, LALME places one of the manuscript's two scribal languages (LP 169) in the Welbeck area, and the main language of *The Mirror* in a proximate area of extreme south Yorkshire (LP 70).

The Pepys/Harley 874 prose Apocalypse (there are several versions) shows a similar, but more extensive, pattern of dispersal. The text is known from twelve manuscripts. These two, in a single hand, much the oldest of the survivors, and from a common archetypal source, are London work, but the remainder, all probably copied after 1400, reflect a range of locales. Aspects of this later transmission will figure prominently in my conclusion.

The case of the Pepys prose Psalter provides an especially interesting example of dispersed transmission. Heretofore, I have discussed two of the four extant copies. However, the two dispersed examples, like Hale 150, even if not in London language, imply an unusually concerted access to London texts. Excepting its last four leaves, Dublin, Trinity College, MS 69 (fols. 1–64, 73–83 only) presents in order: 'The Early English Prose Psalter', the prose Apocalypse, and what it entitles 'a tale of charite', in fact the sixtieth sermon of the *Mirror* (present in Corpus, Hunter, and Harley 5085). The remainder of the book, besides two brief fillers, is given over to an early copy of a widespread instructional text involving biblical exposition, the 'standard tract on the Decalogue' (IPMEP 48). The second scribe of this volume, who copies *The Prick of Conscience* (IMEV 3428) may be localised in south central Sussex, near Brighton (LALME LP 9300). My rather cursory survey of the first scribe's spelling forms suggests that he should be from the same general area, although a bit further west, near Arundel; he shares many forms with the scribe of Bodleian Library, MS Rawlinson poet. 157 (LALME LP 5690).

Trinity MS 69 quite obviously belongs with the others I have described. Its scribe, although 'provincial' in language, and thus probably in training, draws almost totally upon those texts available to the London book-producers whose work I have outlined above. The majority of the manuscript's contents, in fact, replicates MS Pepys 2498, pages 45–370, in reverse order (although the two books have certainly been derived from different exemplars). The Dublin scribe is no passive receptor, either; he here recontextualises his brief excerpt from the *Mirror*. Fols. 78–82^v present an instructional collocation later to become conventional on the basis of gospel precept, analysis of the two biblical statements of The Law, the New (sermon 60 has for its text 1 Cor. 13 and Matt. 22:37–40) and the Old (the Decalogue of Exod. 20).

Indeed, the scribe may have derived all his English texts from London. Some contents in another early copy (1392 × 1409) of the 'standard Decalogue', Oxford, University College, MS 97, imply that this text, although not appearing in any of the ten central manuscripts, may be another early London work of parochial instruction. In University 97, a composite volume, the scribe, perhaps William Contour, vicar of Pirton (Worcs.), writing for his patron, the former London-based courtier and sometime Chancellor of the royal household, William Beauchamp, lord Abergavenny, includes notes on the affairs of St Paul's, all of them referring to events before 1382 (fols. 175–76).[18] Yet the book is squarely West Midland in some emphases; a series of Latin documents (fols. 171–74^v) records events of 1392 × 1400 but mainly ones in Worcestershire and adjacent counties. Further, either the book or its exemplars were available in the Lichfield area to the producers of British Library, MS Additional 22283 (see further Doyle 1981).

Moreover, the fourth copy of 'The Early English Prose Psalter' can scarcely be ignored either. For as Malcolm Parkes has pointed out to me, the same Sussex scribe who copied Trinity College MS 69 is responsible for this book, Princeton, Scheide Library, MS M.143, as well. It contains only the Psalter.[19] In this context, it is difficult to be certain that the Trinity/Scheide scribe was not a London workman, like those others whose books I have described. His Sussex language may simply represent the early training of a person then immigrant to London, *c*. 1400 (after Samuels's posited transition between Types II and III); as a 'home counties' dialect, this may not have appeared particularly outlandish in that rich linguistic mixture that I will show in a moment characteristic of the capital. Against such a hypothesis, one must weigh the work shared (recto and verso of the same leaf) with the second Sussex copyist of the Trinity MS (although they could have come to the City as a team). The early medieval ownership of the Trinity MS by a John Hyde does not elucidate the problem; the name may imply a London provenance for the book (cf. Thrupp 349), although equally, Hyde might be a Winchester surname.[20]

Simultaneously, this example, either of the export of early London texts or of migration into the City, implies a further qualification.

Although the Dublin/Scheide scribe may show an early London culture transmitted to rural locales, other 'Type II' London manuscripts show quite the reverse movement. Transmission was, from an early period, two-way, not simply a process of dispersal from London, but also, especially strongly given the greater riches of other local cultures, into it from elsewhere. In chapter 3 (pp. 104, 125–8), I will examine some of the most extensive examples of such importation procedures, in the Auchinleck MS. Here I need only draw attention to the number of items in these volumes associated with *The South English Legendary*, a widely dispersed work, yet one whose primary circulation occurred in the south-west Midlands, especially northern Gloucestershire; in addition to Richard Lyons's recorded copy, it has left its traces in Laud misc. 622 and Harley 874 (see Görlach *passim*, esp. 95–7, 127–8).

However, imported materials provide the securest method of dating the onset of London literary activities. Although the manuscript record allows one to register circulation, it does not speak particularly strongly to the age (or the precise extent) of that circulation. But the reappearance in London books of items placeable within some relative chronology in more continuously recorded literary communities would imply that the imported literary texts still available for our scrutiny are unlikely to have been circulating in London before late in the reign of Edward I.

Leaving aside the Pepys 2498 version of *Ancrene Riwle* (reflecting a similarly Western community), the oldest textual remains in the London books are, like *The South English Legendary*, products of the south-west Midlands and from the last third or so of the thirteenth century. Perhaps the oldest, although subjected to 'the newe gise' in an Auchinleck revision, is the fourth item in the extant headless manuscript, a lengthy 'Life of St Margaret' (IMEV 203, fols. 16rb–21ra). This poem recasts a considerably older one, the version presented in Cambridge, Trinity College, MS B.14.39 (323) (IMEV 2672; cf. Reichl's extensive discussion and edition 119–40, 163–288). The Trinity manuscript, a communal book of preaching materials, is a particularly hand-to-mouth production (nowhere more evidently so than in the copying of this poem) and probably dates from the 1260s; there is at least some likelihood that it reflects activities at the Worcester Franciscan convent.

Similarly, the 'Anonymous Short Chronicle' (Auchinleck item 40, fols. 304ra–17rb) is derived from materials from the West of England and survives in a fragment from that area of *c.* 1270. Auchinleck also relies, particularly for booklet-ending filler materials, but for more extensive texts as well, upon items circulating in south-western Worcestershire in the 1280s, where they were copied into the household manuscript, Bodleian Library, MS Digby 86 (Hanna 2000, 99–101; for Digby, see the extensive introduction to the Tschann–Parkes facsimile). Given normal patterns of manuscript circulation, it is hard to imagine these texts appearing in the capital much before the turn of the century.

The Auchinleck romances themselves have resisted dating. Their exemplaristic themes and absence of anything like contemporary allusion have left their editors typically settling for the rather weaselly assessment '*c.* 1300'. However, in contrast to the customary belatedness usually ascribed them (e.g. by Colledge, who thought some of them Lollard, or Duncan 1998), there is some evidence for dating the prose texts relatively early. They appear to have emerged well within the first quarter of the fourteenth century, and then probably to have been the result of fairly intense, yet not particularly protracted, endeavour.

A minor palaeographical feature allows some chronological specificity. Although niggling, it is a detail of the kind which renders but a single example of its occurrence definitive, and points to composition of *Mirror*, Apocalypse, and Psalter before 1320. Although the Pepys MS itself probably dates to *c.* 1365–75, the texts it communicates are far older, indeed probably contemporary with an indeterminate number of the Auchinleck romances. Consider the following two passages:

> Her gorge is an open biriel; hij deden trecherouusliche wiþ her tunges; venim of aspides, id est nedders, is vnder her lippes. Of whiche þe mouþe ys ful of *paryynge* and bitternysse; her fete ben swift to shade blode (Additional 17376, fol. 9ᵛ; 'The Early English Prose Psalter', the translation of Ps. 13:5–6; cf. edn 13).

*

> We ben dombe of alle goodnesse whan we speke noȝt of God in bysechynge oþer in techinge and amenden *oþer* defautes, ȝif we mowen ne conseyl nouȝt usseluen forto knowen our synnes and to schewe hem to þe prest. (Holkham misc. 40, fol. 33ᵛ; early in *Mirror* sermon 16, for the third Sunday in Lent)

In the first passage, the translator's rendition of the Vulgate's 'maledictione et amaritudine plenum est' is not, as written, Middle English. But the anomalous 'þaryynge' must represent the appropriate 'waryynge' CURSING. Similarly, in the second example, as the later 'usseluen' shows, the scribe should have written 'ower' or 'owre' OUR, not 'oþer'. Both errors depend upon analogous failures to 'translate' the scribes' exemplars, to replace the archaic letter *wynn* appropriately with *w*, as all scribes of the texts did fairly automatically in most instances.[21] Although neither of these examples involves the Pepys scribe, the point should nonetheless stand, that even in the early fifteenth century, when the Holkham MS was copied, exemplars for these texts were circulating that included *wynn*'s.

The demise of this grapheme is a roughly datable feature. In some contexts, this old runic form was becoming passé by the 1270s, and I should not put the latest example I have noticed, in a book copied near King's Lynn, after 1320.[22] In the metropolitan context (*wynn* does not occur in the clerical hand of the London 'Proclamation of 1258'), the letter may have passed out of use even earlier. But the exemplars must postdate composition of the texts, and hence, both Prose Psalter and *Mirror* must have been composed, at the latest, early in the fourteenth century.

Another pair of passages allows some further specifications:

> And þerfore God ordeyned þre ordres of holy chirche, of wynners and of defendours and of assailours. God haþ sette þe wynners for to feden alle wiþ her trauaile and þat ben þe commune poeple. þe defendoures – þat ben þe kniȝttes þat schull defenden hem and al þe londe fram yuel. And assailours – þat ben men of holy chirche þat schulde techen boþe þat on and þat oþer wiþ far speche and wiþ reddure. ȝif þat hij duden any synne and trespasseden aȝeins God, hij it schulden adressen and turnen hem to Godward, ac as þe werlde schapeþ now, hij ben þe moste deel rauysschours and rauisshen þe poeple from Godward, boþe wiþ her ensample ȝiuynge and wiþ her werk. (*The Mirror*, early in the second prologue, Pepys 2498, p. 46[b]; edn. 9/10–9).[23]

> *
>
> For þis londe is departed in þre, in wynners and defendours and in assaillours. þe wynners, þo ben þe commune poeple, and hij han ben chastised wiþ hunger. þe defendoures, þat ben þise grete lordes þat schulden defende þe commune poeple; hij ben chastised wiþ hongeynge and draweynge – here is proue of ynouȝ; alle men it witen wel. þe assailours, þat is þe clergie þat schulde teche boþe þat on and

þat oþer þe lawȝe of god and chastise hem ȝif þat hij duden amysse. And as by siȝth in þe werlde hij þat schulden ben chastisoures ben meyntenoures of synne and hij ben vnchastised ȝutt. (*The English Text . . . Magdalene* 90/36–91/3).

The first passage, partly a translator's elaboration, contains distinctive English terms substituted for those in the parallel discussion in Gretham's Anglo-Norman. Most notably, the term 'assailer' ONE WHO CORRECTS OR CHASTISES, beyond being exceptionally unusual in Middle English, does not correspond to Gretham's language, 'lettrez ço sunt conseillurs' and 'les ordenez' (258, 262).[24] The two passages share an elsewhere unparalleled vocabulary to reproduce a commonplace and clearly are connected. Moreover, both here are engaged in at least similar anti-clerical interpolations. While the reviser of the Pepys *Ancrene Riwle* may simply have intruded bits from a reading of the *Mirror*, it is at least possible that the two texts are products of the same hand.

Yet simultaneously, the Pepys *Riwle* here interpolates into an interpolation. While all the *Mirror* MSS I have checked include the subsequent interpolation/expansion, none of them glosses the three estates as the *Riwle* does here. Moreover, one should recognise that this glossing is historically allusive. While complaints about clerical performance are regrettably eternal (and led Colledge mistakenly to identify the Pepys MS with Lollardy), those about the other two estates are not. They probably refer to events late in the reign of Edward II. Although subpar harvests and famine may have been endemic in England through much of the fourteenth century (Frank 1990), the most notorious example was the first, savage onslaught, the European pandemic of 1315–17 (Jordan). Similarly, even jaded contemporaries were shocked by one aspect of the conclusion of Edward's reign, the number of magnates who went to deliberatedly grisly ends on the scaffold – a carnage not to be repeated until near the end of the century.

Indeed, this indictment of the current failure of all estates sounds very much like the opening summary view of society in a poem always associated with Edward II's disruptive career, *The Simonie*, the final text in the Auchinleck MS:

> Whij werre and wrake in londe and manslauht is icome,
> Whij hungger and derþe on eorþe þe pore haþ vndernome,

Whij bestes ben þus storue, whij corn haþ ben so dere,
ȝe þat wolen abide, listneþ and ȝe muwen here
   þe skile.
I nelle liȝen for no man, herkne whoso wile.

           *

God greteþ wel þe clergie and seiþ þeih don amis
And doþ hem to vnderstonde þat litel treuþe þer is.
(1–8)

The poem develops through amplification of these complaints: clerical malfeasances in the opening section (to line 210 of the Auchinleck
version), agrarian disaster at lines 373–420, the opening stages of 'the
tyranny of Edward II' at lines 421–56 (see further Salter 1988, 158–69).
Yet one of these evils is in certain respects timebound, with a sell-by date.
At least, magnatial fratricide did reach its own end; Roger Mortimer,
earl of March and usurper of crown perquisites through his relation with
the Queen Mother Isabella, was probably the last such victim, in 1330.
It is thus hard to see the complaint voiced by both Pepys reviser and
poet of *The Simonie* as at all timely much after the later 1330s and the
new king's galvanising the realm to participate in his French adventure.
That should provide a *terminus ad quem* for the activities which have
produced at least this portion of the Pepys revisions.

But, if the *Mirror* has contributed to the invective of the Pepys *Riwle*,
it is scarcely the unique source of such concerns about estates (and especially clerical) performance. Although I would not dismiss out of hand
the possibility that the Pepys *Riwle* was revised by the translator/adaptor
of Gretham's *Mirror*, both in some measure depend, often in linguistic specifics, upon the Anglo-Norman prose Apocalypse, in its Middle
English translation. The dependency is especially overt in part 8 of the
Pepys *Riwle*, where Apoc. 21–2 with its commentary is allowed to replace
much of 'the outer rule' (*English Text . . . Magdalene* 177/30–182/29). As a
consequence, this English translation must predate both the other texts.

The English prose Apocalypse is parasitic on earlier Latin and Anglo-
Norman fashions, a topic to which I will return in chapter 4. Books of
this type begin to appear in profusion from the 1250s, and, from about
1270 are well attested as London productions, often with Westminster
court associations (Morgan 2, 103). But initially, the texts and commentaries provided for these books were composed in Latin. The Middle

English version depends upon a further development, the replacement of earlier textual content with comparable materials in Anglo-Norman. This shift, in content as well as in linguistic presentation, is datable, and has occurred in books produced just around 1300 (see *Lambeth Apocalypse* 93, 271–4). Thus, the Middle English prose Apocalypse is likely to have been translated contemporaneously with the earliest certainly London-authored text, Adam Davy's dreams. In this escalating sequence of prophetic visions, Davy imagines, at the head of the new reign (*c.* 1308), Edward II's eventual fusion of sustaining communal roles, both crusading papal emperor and Becket-like cardinal priest (see Scattergood 1970, Phillips).[25]

The other texts then can be disposed over the next three decades. The kinds of complaints voiced in *The Simonie* and in the Pepys *Riwle* intrusions into *Mirror* materials belong in the period around 1322 (see edn 22–3), thus marginally later than that date marked as palaeographically most probable for the *Mirror* and Psalter translations. The latest literary work in the manuscripts here discussed, contemporary with interpolations into the Pepys *Riwle*, would be those additions that update 'An Anonymous Short Chronicle' to at least the accession of Edward III, probably into the 1330s (see n. 5 above). These are much of a piece with other adjustments to Auchinleck texts, tailoring to modernise, unify, and provide a consistent local patina to diverse materials.

III London language and London texts: chronologies and geographies

Thus, books in 'Type II' London English recycled the same texts for something like eighty years. Moreover, scribal output securely localisable to mid-century, *c.* 1340–65, appears to have been minimal (perhaps only the two hands adding English texts in St John's 256). Fourteenth-century London book-history is doughnut shaped, with a big hole in the middle. And in fact, relatively minimal book-trade evidence in any language exists for a substantial mid-century period, roughly 1340s to early 1370s.

One can proliferate examples of this absence. Any reader of Sandler's history of English illumination will note this substantial gap, extending roughly from the Neville of Hornby Hours (British Library, MS Egerton 2781) to John Palmer's *Omne bonum* (British Library, MSS Royal

6 E.vi–vii). The most recent art-historical discussions, particularly those of Lynda Dennison (e.g. 1999), have concerned possible migrations of atéliers once apparently metropolitan to dispersed centres. At this writing, Cambridge is the current favourite.

Similarly, London chronicle writing shows a significant mid-century gap until 1377 and later. The continuations to the Anglo-Norman *Brut* end with Halidon Hill in 1333 (although see some qualifications below, pp. 127–8), and the end-of-century Middle English translation uses a continuation to Ranulf Higden's *Polychronicon* to update the text through to Edward III. The *Annales Paulini* end in 1341, and the Westminster continuations to the *Flores historiarum*, while chronologically continuous, were updated from alien sources in 1345 and then carried forward only in spurts of 1366–9 (John of Reading) and post 1377. The Anglo-Norman *Croniques de London* break off in 1344. (Cf. Taylor *passim* and, for the French text, Cox.)

It is, of course, likely that we have lost a great deal. For example, Chaucer considered the romance *Lybeaus Desconus*, recorded in neither Auchinleck nor Laud 622, of a piece with the similar texts extant there (cf. 'Sir Thopas' 900). However, such possibilities aside, there is negligible sign of metropolitan literary production between the Pepys *Riwle* or local additions to the Auchinleck MS and William Langland in the 1370s. While I am reluctant to insist upon some form of economic determinism, books do represent luxury expenditures; in light of this fact, it does not seem entirely accidental that London economic development was not smooth and may have undergone a substantial decline that began just before the Great Famine, recovery only occurring in the 1350s or 1360s (cf. Nightingale 1996, 98–102). Clearly, demand fell in the face of demographic failure, first of famine, then significantly aggravated by the Plague in 1348. Not only books but the non-royal construction industry seems to have been affected (Carlin 46; Rosser 1989, 65–74).

This hiatus makes it clear that, insofar as Langland considered himself a London writer, 'siþ þe pestilence tyme' may well stand as an aesthetic statement about the poem. The poet's perceived sense of local antecedence gazes back across some divide. He draws his local inspiration and thematic from materials in many cases contemporary with his birth, if not before – 'Edwardian literature', most particularly writings associable with late Edward I and Edward II (cf. n. 36 below). One might further note that the dating I suggest for texts in Pepys 2498 implies that, like Langland, these writers may have been stimulated into literary production by a perception of social emergency or discord.

This gap in the London textual record should underwrite a re-evaluation of Samuels's views on the evolution of London English. The Type II/Type III conjunction may only appear sudden in a faulted historical retrospect. It is possible that silence cloaks something like a measured transition, with elaborate mixtures of forms typical of Types II/III in combination. Or it might reflect what Dennison's hypothesised exodus of limners would suggest, a thorough break in scribal tradition, with later scribes assembling Type III, after an interim, as a different combination of formal features out of Type II and other forms in competition.

Samuels states his views succinctly:

> The London dialect changed suddenly and radically in the fourteenth century. The theory that two distinct dialects coexisted in fourteenth-century London, even if it were acceptable, is not really relevant here, since all material of Type II is from before 1370 and all that of Type III from after that date. (1963, 88)

He then invokes Eilert Ekwall to draw attention to shifts in London migration patterns over the fourteenth century. Essex and East Anglia provided many early London migrants and are reflected in Type II; in the course of the fourteenth century, although Norfolk migration continued, prominent was an influx from Bedfordshire and Northants. Samuels continues:

> This immigration from the Central Midlands in the fourteenth century amply explains the great differences between our Types II and III; there seems no reason to doubt that the same trend must then have continued, as it will explain the further changes from Type III to Type IV ('Chancery Standard').

But leaving aside methodological complaints that might be lodged against a migration model of change (cf. McClure), the linguistic evidence for it is scarcely compelling. The Central Midland writers whom Samuels associates with this shift are practitioners of a third linguistic form, Type I, 'central Midland standard', certainly used in London from the late fourteenth century. But the features Samuels himself cites as most distinctly constitutive of Type I – sich, mych, ony, silf, stide, 30uun, wijf – are absolutely foreign to the greater run of both Type II and Type III scribes; indeed, all of them frequently agree in the same non-Type I form (the major exception being substantial minority evidence for 'stide' in Type III).

One major problem with Samuels's arguments about this issue – and a great many similar topics in Middle English dialectology – is his totalising impulse: he frequently overlooks inconvenient local evidence, often (as one would expect in an urban environment) pluralistic and polyvocal in nature. A telling example illustrates this tendency and its consequences. One early Type II scribe, that of MS Hunter 250, uniquely among the writers at issue, relies upon a Type I form (excepting 'stide'); he writes 'lijf' LIFE. But the scribe neither has this as his consistent form for the item (although it is massively preponderant), nor does he have 'ij' in any of the analogous forms where it is normal in Type I, but writes 'wife/wyfe' and 'wise'.

While one reason for Samuels's problematic formulation is his confla-tion of two distinct linguistic categories, 'attested graphemic system' and 'linguistic standard', his dismissive rejection of two coexisting dialects adumbrates other problems in his temporal schematisation of change. Quite simply, as Samuels is occasionally aware in his acknowledgements that a number of Type II books seem to have been copied in what should be his exclusively Type III period, London books were being copied si-multaneously in both Types II and III over something like a century and one half. Two examples from either end of the relevant time-period illustrate the problem: Type III language occurs much earlier than this division proposes, while Type II persists well past 1380.

CUL Gg.iv.32, mostly Latin, includes exiguous bits of Anglo-Norman and Middle English. Much of the Middle English (fols. 21ra–22ra), al-though brief, is in archaic Samuels Type II English and may resemble more closely still 'The Proclamation of 1258'. But such is not the case with the most extensive English text of the manuscript, the Marian lyric at fols. 23vb–24va (Brown 1924, 230–3): if anything, its language resembles a Type III text. Similarly, one might adduce those London guild returns copied in English in 1388/9 (see Barron–Wright). These documents are taken as nearly originary examples of Type III, but they are of course, copies of older London texts, in one case of the 1330s;

were one to believe them literatim copies, a point which is very far from established, they would testify to similar early prevalence of Type III.

At the other chronological extreme, Type II London English persists for a considerable time, a fact inconsequentially noted in Samuels's study and thoroughly masked in LALME. In one manifestation, Type II forms appear residually in late copies, otherwise mainly in Type III, of texts first evidenced in Type II books. As an example, one might cite Bodleian Library, MS Holkham misc. 40, a copy of the *Mirror*, perhaps produced as late as 1410. But there is considerably more extensive evidence for the persistence of Type II in London. As Samuels argues (and LALME thoroughly demonstrates), Type II is an Essex-tinged dialect. Hence, LALME simply places several prominent Type II scribes (perhaps the majority of the evidence for the type) in Essex – the persons responsible for Pepys 2498 and two other books (LP 6260); for the London portions of Additional 17376 (LP 6280); and St John's MS 256 (LP 6340).

These texts are geographically displayed in this way because the Atlas editors refuse to present a London blow-up map indicative of the linguistic diversity in the metropolis or to provide 'three-dimensional mapping' (1, 12). Profiles like these presumably represent the languages identified by the statement, 'the earlier texts are placed east and northeast of the city centre, the later manuscripts centrally or north and north-west of the centre'. The latter statement probably signals such placements in Middlesex as those assigned to Corpus Christi MS 282 (LP 6490); MS Harley 5085 (LP 6520); or the main hand of Auchinleck (LP 6510). But there are substantial problems with this formulation, signalled by Samuels's willingness, at one point in his researches, to place the language of Pepys 2498 precisely in suburban Essex (at Waltham Abbey [OSA], see *English Text . . . Magdalene* xvii–xviii). And indeed, LALME maps without comment, as examples of Essex language to be localised adjacent to the three scribes I have mentioned, a number of certainly London books copied in the metropolis after 1400. The geographical, as well as temporal, neatness of this statement is thus open to some revision.

Here I simply return to an old friend, one in fact from rather far afield, LALME's LP 6030, placed far out along the Thames estuary, in the Rayleigh area near Southend. This scribe, active *c.* 1415–25, is presented on the basis of his two copies of Chaucer's *Troilus*, Huntington Library, MS HM 114 and British Library, MS Harley 3943. The editors of LALME did not know his third English book, Lambeth Palace Library, MS 491 (I). The scribe's version of *Piers Plowman*, also in HM 114, shares for portions of its conflated text an examplar elsewhere visible only in a certainly London book (see pp. 243–4), and Lambeth 491 has an extensive London provenance history ably discussed by Boffey–Meale (161–2).

Lest that evidence of his London connections seem a little too attenuated to place the scribe in the metropolitan book-trade, his Latin copying should certainly do so. In addition to his literary English work, this individual is responsible for a series of entries in City of London Record Office, Letter-Book I (for 1421) and for several quite substantial stints in the same repository's MS Cust. 12, the *c.* 1420 collection of City records called 'The Liber Albus'. Plainly, he was a professional engaged in various City writing tasks and continued to write, if he came from Essex at all, an English Samuels presents as markedly Essex.

This would seem a sufficient demonstration that Essex English (whether it's Type II or Child of Type II) is a perfectly acceptable mode of professional London writing in the fifteenth century, indeed well into the century. Nor is this scribe an isolated example; were one to take this scribal placement as indicating the limits of a(n acceptable) London language, ample evidence would identify much of LALME's (south)-west Essex English with the City instead. A substantial number of books provides, on the basis of contents, provenance, or scribal associations, compelling examples extending into the 1470s.[26]

In short, overwhelming evidence indicates that Essex language of a sort resembling Type II remained persistently acceptable within London book-production for a very long time. It must reflect acceptable London linguistic practice, in short a dialect in use. In fact, Essex speech, in some form, was alive and well in London as late as the eighteenth century, when it provided a variety of Standard English forms, including a universal phonetic feature, the collapse of the two Middle English mid-front long vowels into one (see Jeremy Smith 1996, 105–11).

Thus, evidence for temporally distinguishing Samuels's Types II and III frays at both ends. His construction of the evidence is nowhere near so hermetically sealed as he presents it. As one expects in any urban locale, the language of London is not easily subjected to clear typing, and the evidence would support a more robustly variant set of alternatives than Samuels allows.[27] A more plausible reading of fourteenth-century London evidence would show that Type II already is a great deal more like Type III than Samuels is willing to credit and that early fourteenth-century language allowed considerably greater variation than he states. Samuels's own practice elsewhere provides excellent support for such a claim. Particularly in his discussion of 'Langland's Dialect' (1985), Samuels silently yet properly invokes the concept of 'scribal competence', that forms within the scribe's ken, whether or not majority or consistent, represent forms of the dialect he is writing.

Yet a look at a broader conspectus of Type II and III usage than Samuels uses argumentatively is revealing. For this purpose, I simply assembled Samuels's own data, provided by LALME, from the relevant books for about fifty-five dialect features, nearly fifty items from the original LALME questionnaires of the mid-/late sixties and seven items Samuels himself adduced as typically Type II Essexisms in 1963. These show, first, a substantial amount of disagreement among forms between different books designated variously Type II or Type III; a considerable amount of special pleading is required to believe these provide coherent single groups of forms. Further, if the books differ, the individual scribes themselves offer quite substantial variation within their individual stints.

If one examines the evidence retrospectively, Type III has certainly deselected a rich variety of forms available in Type II. For example, Chaucer and Hoccleve show a substantial reduction of the range of words allowing possible representation of OE *y* as *u* or *e*. Yet even this evidence needs qualification, for early London English wills, even after 1400, retain such forms as 'church', 'mende' MEMORIAL, 'kechyn' KITCHEN, and 'fulfelle'. Viewed prospectively, and relying primarily on the two prominent Auchinleck scribes and that of Pepys 2498 etc., the evidence shows the utter persistence of forms across these Types, with a frequency that Samuels's more schematic claims occlude. More than forty of the items are usually identical in representation somewhere in the sample. For instance, for an item capable of wide variation, routine 'swich, swiche' occurs universally in both types (and both unanimously reject Type I 'sich'). Moreover, even Type II forms Samuels insists upon because they are unusual have clear reflections in Type III.[28]

From evidence like this, it is difficult to see how a model of rupture, frequently predicated upon a minority of or conflict between usages, performs a descriptive service. The evidence suggests considerable flux and contestation among forms, already substantially advanced in Type II. Some very prominent Type II forms do disappear, but in most cases, these are not testimony to dying dialect 'types' but to developments whose influence Samuels unaccountably deprecates, a general isoglossic movement of northerly forms southward, e.g. Type II 'hij' replaced by Type III 'they'. But 'they' is, in any case, known to all and the majority form of many Type II scribes, the main hand of Auchinleck, for example. And some Type II forms persist within Type III, even rather surprising ones, for example the scribe of Cambridge, Trinity College MS B.15.17 retaining 'þeiȝ' (AL) THOUGH in close to 20 percent of his uses (ignored in LALME, it also appears, rarely, in the Hengwrt *Canterbury Tales*). The evidence, it seems to me, is best explained quite simply, as a sequence of individual decisions to prioritise slightly differing sets of variants out of a robustly mixed but reasonably continuous sample (cf. Horobin's recent argument that Type III might represent a carefully crafted 'sociolect').

To conclude, I return to the end-of-century Type II books (Harley 5085 and Corpus Christi 282), in both cases, copies of *The Mirror*. This text includes literal translations of the gospels, as well as heady support for a lay ministry. Only in 1409 did Thomas Arundel prohibit any vernacular Bible produced since the time of John Wycliffe. But in the context of a go-getter local bishop like Robert Braybrooke, any time after 1382, and particularly after 1386, production of something like this text may have appeared dangerous in London. It is possible that the scribes were copying from archetypes prepared a good deal earlier in the century. Moreover, they may have been deliberately creating their own particular 'sociolect' in their acceptance of archaising forms from their exemplars, for they may have had good reason to do so. Given that Arundel in 1409 was protecting some imagined pre-Wycliffite scripture and that he seems unlikely to have manufactured his clause excluding some books from prohibition out of whole cloth, it is possible to imagine later Type II scribes in fact ensuring that what they wrote had the look of something incontrovertibly old.

One learns a good many things by being consciously of a locality, a distinct place with its own customs, as cities proudly were in the Middle

Ages. One local custom (and a source of pride) is linguistic habit (and I'm conscious of being locally marked in this way in three different languages). But it is the precise knowledge of living and experiencing these customs in their full variousness as products of time (historical circumstance), place, and social interaction that creates devolved selves, citizens of the locality. That seems to me precisely the consciousness that Samuels is unable to bring to this project. Indeed, his effort of detached totalisation undoes everything that defines a local urban culture.

IV Some cultural environments of London texts

To this point, I have discussed the received literary record. But equally, ample evidence speaks to a largely unrecorded London cultural surround with some claim to literary attention. Often ephemeral, in some instances it impinges upon the literary texts I will discuss. Such materials, because they frequently involve quasi-dramatic presentations (masquing, costume, disguise), have received increasing attention from theatre historians (see the full listings of sources, Lancashire 31–65). With equal frequency, they have appealed as potential expressions of civic or national *communitas* (Barron 2000, 407–9, but contrast Lindenbaum's provocative analyses).

Bill-posting, the most evanescent of these behaviours, is the only one of these forms purely verbal. In the fourteenth century primarily a function of social disorder, the broadsheet affixed in a prominent locale, particularly St Paul's, performed as an un- or counter-official statement. These documents almost parody governmental promulgation, the way in which Statutes, for example, were customarily published (see pp. 52–3 and Scase 1998, with later examples). Bills were certainly intended to drum up popular support for causes that might be controversial or embarrassing to a more official or sanctioned culture.

The earliest recorded example is the least typical, because involving a permanent placard and a statement at least grudgingly official. Around 1311, duke Thomas of Lancaster had some form of memorial, probably a copy, of the Ordinances that he and his magnate coalition had extracted from Edward II affixed to a pillar in St Paul's. (These had been locally promulgated in the churchyard.) In Paul's, the document would publicly indicate to suspicious Londoners the constraints under which a capricious monarchy was committed to operate. The matter seems to have rested there – the Ordinances benign or to be ignored – until after Thomas's armed revolt and execution in 1322. At that point, when Thomas was widely perceived as saintly martyr to Edward's tyranny and when his grace was alleged to have been manifested at the site through miracles, the king ordered the posted text removed. Although political fortune led to the restoration of this countercultural shrine, it was gone by the fifteenth century.[29] Unusual in its persistence, Thomas's placard was not different in nature from Queen Isabella's second letter soliciting the City's aid in 1326 – the first had been ignored by timorous officialdom – said by chroniclers to have been posted everywhere almost immediately (*Annales Paulini* 315, *Croniques* 51, *Great Chronicle* 29–30).

More typically, however, bills appear to have been documents libellous in tone, testimonies to that propensity towards slanderous confrontationalism perceived as a besetting urban sin. Expressions of social division, they challenged behaviour deemed abusive in similarly abusive language. Considerably more typical than Thomas's placard would have been the defamatory bills against the Dominican convent posted in 1314 by runaways from the order (*Flores* 161–7, with text; Riley 111–13). Another surviving fourteenth-century example, this in the vernacular and associated with the impeachment and execution of a royal crony in 1388, was nailed up in the chapter houses of both Westminster and St Paul's. It seeks to split king from counsellor by lampooning the archbishop of York, Alexander Neville, as 'Kyng Alisaundre Nero', a surrogate predator in his region (Illingworth, Saul 184–5, and cf. 219). Certainly, the invective of 'The twelve conclusions of the Lollards' (posted 1395?) does not seem especially indecorous in such a rhetorical context. Although exceptional occurrences, bills testify, not to associative community, but to potentially deep fractures and conflictual interests in the locale. After all, the most basic definition of urban status remains dissimilation of economic function (cf. Keene 1989, 99) and, from that, follow other dissimilations as well.

Libelling has particular importance in London. In a situation at its highest level mercantile, much depends upon 'credit', not simply of the economic stripe but what Londoners persistently call 'good fame'. And in a packed urban environment, the potential for quarrel, beginning at the verbal level (but clearly more pressing as business misunderstanding), was so expected that virtually every guild, but perhaps most especially those of voluntary association, built into its regulations compulsory arbitration of private disputes, not necessarily economic ones (cf. Hanawalt 1998, 29–31, 35–52, and see further pp. 200–1, 271 below).

Such insistence on being credible, trustworthy, replays itself in basic policing procedures and the ludic aspects of the pillory and tumbrel. Libel, or more usually slander, is one subset of most basic civic crime, misrepresentation – particularly of wares and especially of the foodstuffs on which communal wellbeing depends. Punishment is pantomimic; in the routine penalty for spoiled food, the criminal publicly displayed to abuse in the presence of his or her foul wares.[30] And similar, if less frequent, crimes of verbal misrepresentation have their pantomimes as well, for instance, scriveners who forge false property deeds placed in the pillory with the offending documents (e.g., Riley 333–5, 1367). For verbal crimes like slander or perjured charges, attacks on the 'good fame' of another, the convicted appear in the Pillory with a token of their sin, a whetstone inscribed 'A false liar', suspended from their neck. They must enact the sharpening of the tongue's knife, the fomenting of discord (cf. Ps. 56:5, 58:8; Prov. 12:18, 25:18). Ludic demonstrations of 'credit' like these might be seen to interface with a particularly prominent discursive strand in *Piers Plowman*, the ambivalence about satire, 'lakking'.[31]

Other local activities may have been considerably less fraught. Like people in most locales, Londoners participated in ceremonials associated with the ritual year, many with ludic components. Stow, the assiduous chronicler of vanishing and vanished civic custom, twice mentions organised Mayings, although called 'plays' probably only Maypole festivities (1, 98–9, 350; cf. Hutton 27–34 and *passim*). All of these had their seasonal proprieties.

Organised civic Christmas mummings may have occurred with some regularity in the fourteenth century; at least there are such festivities in 1334 and 1352 (Lancashire 41). In the most elaborate recorded example, one clearly unusual, at Candlemas 1377, masked citizens rode to Kennington to fete prince Richard. They processed outward into Surrey on a ceremonial track that reversed the customary path of royal entries (see further below). The elaborate costumes – emperor, pope, cardinals, potentially hostile aliens – bear more than a passing resemblance to those in another reported pageant associated with Richard's father and his retinue, *Winner and Waster* 50–8, 137–96.[32] But the purport of the whole show, an example of the strong desire of civic government to retain royal favour (in this instance, at a time when relations with the powerful royal uncle John of Gaunt were not in good odour), was to honour the prince with wishes of good fortune. The celebrants diced with him, his allowed victory a hopeful presage of the future; the civic stakes on the occasion – golden ball, cup, and ring – alluded to the regalia, as well as the gifts the Magi had presented a king whom one might hope the child would imitate (Stow 1, 96–7, probably from *Anonimalle Chronicle* 102–3).

Stow also refers twice to 'pageants showed at midsummer in the Watch' in West Cheap (1, 159–60, 257–8). He will have had in mind a later, highly formalised version, first recorded in 1378 and to become a central civic show. But at this date, the Watch was clearly ritualising, as a civic display of legal power, policing activities imposed on a precedent Midsummer Night festivity – and probably disorder.[33] The ceremonial grew out of routine local peacekeeping regulations (e.g. the 1282 promulgation, Riley 21). City nights were generally regarded as lawless. Persons out after curfew were, ipso facto, taken to be suspicious, probably criminous; many guild statutes forbade evening work, whether as disturbing, conducive to bad workmanship, or simply allowing disorder; and the evening market in Langland's Cornhill seems to have been perceived as a perpetual magnet for criminal activity.[34] As Lindenbaum (1994) argues, appeal to tradition and civic solidarity here likely is susceptible to conflicting readings.

Also near midsummer, parishes celebrated Corpus Christi with processions. London had more than one hundred parish churches, a set of microdivisions typical of larger English towns (Brooke 35). Expressions of an extremely local devotion and solidarity in a metaphoric union explicitly corporate, one imagines these celebrations might represent true bonding and associationalism. But such seems unlikely to have been the universal case, as a bizarre eruption of 1389 illustrates. On this occasion, the parishioners of St Nicholas Acon were prevented from following the long-accustomed route of their Corpus Christi procession; it required passage through a private house, whose residents prevented and threatened the marchers and were consequently imprisoned (Riley 509–10). But other examples were clearly a great deal more opulent and decorous, for example the elaborate procession of the Skinners, whose passing Stow laments (1, 230–1). (See further Rubin, 1987, 247–71, with due attention to non-associative and disruptive features.)

The Skinners' processional exemplifies one aspect of guild practices, which I will argue in chapter 4 are integral to an understanding of early London devotional prose. Such organisations were utterly ubiquitous and ranged from the 'great companies', craft guilds with independent power in civic affairs, all the way down to exiguous parish fraternities, capable of little beyond a candle on an altar and a hired priest to say requiem masses for deceased members. But like the Skinners Stow describes, all agreed in having statutes, supervisory wardens, a special livery, and a festival capped off by a meal (cf. Rosser 1994). At their most expansive, like the Skinners, they were capable of considerable display. Certainly, the outstanding example would be the totemic procession of the powerful Fishmongers, with their images of four golden sturgeons, three silver salmon, and forty-six knights mounted on horses dressed as luces. The ceremonial is recorded only twice, on the first occasion in honour of Edward I's victory at Falkirk in 1298, representing the first clearly mimic London pageant of which record survives.[35]

One guild organisation, the London Puy, was specifically committed to written (and sung) literary activity (Sutton, Butterfield 88–9). This group, perhaps ten men, nearly all Mercers, met, like all guilds, for an annual mass and banquet. In this organisation, however, conviviality was supplemented by song; beyond pious bonding, the banquet chose the best example of an essay in a fixed French verse-form, a *chansoun reale*, submitted by a member. While there may have been later court analogues, this particular posh gentlemen's club seems to have been active for only about a decade around 1300. Its prominence has been assured, however, by the decision of Andrew Horn, Chamberlain of the City, to write into his massive collection of City documents, the 'Liber custumarum' (*Munimenta* 216–28, 579–94) one set of the organisation's statutes. In doing so, he may only have sought, as he did on other occasions, to indicate the nobility of his City, that it had fostered institutions that might rival those of its continental trading partners, here perhaps especially Arras. But the existence of such an organisation functions as a reminder of the rich linguistic surround, nurtured by the urban locale, in which literature in English is only a small part.

In chapter 3 I will look sympathetically at evidence concurring with Caroline Barron's view (2000, 410–12) that London citizens lacked a participatory interest in chivalry.[36] But that does not mean they were not avid and interested tournament spectators, having often equipped the show in the first place (Lysons, Staniland 1978). Generally speaking, modern knowledge of tournament culture in the period – it peaked in the 1340s, when these events are recorded virtually every year – depends almost entirely upon London chronicle accounts of local and suburban (e.g., Smithfield, Stepney, Windsor) aristocratic *hastiludia*. And such notices, already profuse in the early record, were not stillborn but passed on into the local vernacular chronicle tradition of the fifteenth century. It is difficult to understand the record, were tournaments not perceived as important entertainments, although it is informative that one typically discovers more (still not a great deal) about costuming and by-play than the results, identification of the best jouster. Given the emphases of Auchinleck romances on supplementing prowess with other virtues, notably guile, such a discovery should not perhaps surprise.[37]

Costuming, the ludic element of the show, is particularly intriguing. In one of the earliest recorded London examples, a Round Table of Edward I purportedly held in 1299, perhaps a dozen knights impersonated their Camelot avatars and were assigned quests by an elaborately guised Loathly Damsel.[38] More pointedly, in the 1359 Smithfield joust to celebrate John of Gaunt's marriage to Blanche of Lancaster, Edward III, his sons and associated courtiers to the requisite number of twenty-four, appeared as London's aldermen, a bit of camp cross-dressing that probably combines both compliment and satire.

Langland does not seem to have been immune to an interest in these occasions. We can never know how much detail of passus 5 may be indebted to the costuming in the 1362 jousts in which some combatants were disguised as the Seven Deadly Sins (John of Reading 131). In the Smithfield tournament of 1375, Alice Perrers led the processional in a costume identifying her as the Lady of the Sun, a turn of royal concubinage into courtly splendour that Clopper (2000a, 130–1) argues underlies the initial presentation of Lady Meed. (See further Stow 1, 268; 2, 29–31; and Juliet Vale's voluminous illustration and analysis, 59–75.)

The one kind of civic display London surprisingly lacked was a municipal play cycle. Although there are spotty references to biblical plays and players from the end of the fourteenth century, taking these as references to cycle drama seems mistaken and the 'performances', the earliest in 1384, explicable on other grounds (Clopper 2000b, cf. 2001, 15–16, 160–6, 278–84, 302).[39] Instead, the City involved itself in elaborate processional pageantry, typically to herald the onset of a new reign. The earliest full example, for the coronation of Richard II, has appeared constantly in discussions of the prologue to *Piers Plowman* B, and I will take it up again (see Clopper 2000a, 127–30 and pp. 248–9).[40]

But best described of all these events is not a coronation, but the enforced ceremony of reconciliation that followed Richard II's 'quarrel with the City' in 1392. In Gordon Kipling's description (1–21), the pageant enacted a biblical scene, the City implicitly the descending New Jerusalem seen by John in Apoc. 21.[41] The pageants involved a series of castles, typically inhabited by citizens in the guise of angels; in gestures reminiscent of the 1377 mumming to the child-prince or of his coronation, these actors imitated the Epiphany visit of the Magi and their presentation of symbolic gifts (118).

Yet equally, one might see the ceremonial echoing or interfacing with aspects of local literate culture. Kipling finds (36–7) the 'jasper green' castles, an allusion to Rev. 21:11, a repeated local dramatic scene. But, as I will suggest in chapter 3 (p. 122), they may be otherwise locally allusive; green castles appear with radically other implications in earlier royal culture. Of course, the pageant presentation will also be reminiscent of Langland's 'tour on a toft', the 'tabernaculum' of Ps. 14:1, probably a more proximate source than the often-cited *Castle of Perseverance*. Moreover, behind such imagery of apocalyptic reconciliation there stretches a vast amount of thinking about the immediate Christian implications of Apocalypse, carried through a bulky sequence of Pepys 2498 texts, the subject of chapter 4 below.

Before passing on to a consideration of the texts I have mentioned, I turn to a more general question. If London was, until some time in the early fourteenth century, a community negligible in English literary terms, what changed? Why, in the decades after 1300, did it, apparently suddenly, develop a voluminous and sophisticated local literary culture? In the next chapter, I will examine the most extensive and absorbing developments in local book-production in the immediately preceding period and assess their literary implications. Developing governmental function, perhaps especially in its interface with civic interests, and always emphatically as written function, is central to the growth of local London culture.

NOTES

1. Friars, of course recent arrivals, were literally *penetrans domos* and set up inside; see Röhrkasten. The best preserved of the peripheral religious houses, although a late foundation, is the Charterhouse; see Schofield 1994, 71–3 (no. 48). The adjacent St Bartholomew's the Great represents remains of the twelfth-century chapel of a house of Augustinian canons.

2. Christianson's figures for named London book-artisans (14) reveal the exponential growth after the period I study here. During the years 1300–79, known persons associated with the trade average about three per decade, with a range of one to six. From 1380–89, there are sixteen known book-trade persons, from 1390–99, thirty-four; and for the fifteenth century generally, the average is 42.5 per decade, with a range of thirty-four to fifty.

3. Samuels was much more forthright in his earlier publication about suggesting an early dating (pre-1370) for these books.

4. For the legal documents, a writ for the 'ridingknights' of Portsoken Ward 1042/4, three writs for St Paul's, and thirty-four of Edward the Confessor for Westminster, see Laing 1993, 119. The faintly possible literary manuscripts, both with copies of the extremely popular 'Poema morale' (IMEV 1272), include:

   (a) Bodleian Library, MS Digby 4 (s. xiii in.) (Laing 1993, 127), described by Samuels to Betty Hill (1977, 110) as Kentish with a London admixture but 'perhaps a homogeneous dialect of NW Kent or NE Surrey'. This is a monastic book, from Canterbury Cathedral, where it was no. 954 in the early fourteenth-century catalogue (Ker, MLGB 38, 242).

   (b) Cambridge, Fitzwilliam Museum, MS McClean 123 (s. xiii/xiv) (Laing 1993, 27), described by Samuels to Hill as 'Essex with a western admixture' (*ibid.*). In the fourteenth century, the book belonged to the Benedictine nuns of Nuneaton (Warws.) (Ker, MLGB 140).

   See further Laing 1992.

5. But, as Helen Cooper points out to me, some portions can have been produced no earlier than 19 October 1330; she notices that, at the added lines A 1075–82, this manuscript's version of 'An Anonymous Short Metrical Chronicle' uniquely offers a description of the cellars of Nottingham Castle, integral to Edward III's putsch against Mortimer and Isabella of that date. In the 'Chronicle', Lancelot seeks his Queen, a bizarrely ironic, although, as I will show in chapters. 2 and 3, far from unparalleled, troping of the King in search of Queen Mother and *her* lover as romance hero.

6. The colophon indicates that William of Shoreham, the author of instructional poetry forming part II of the book, for whom prayers are to be offered, died during the archiepiscopate of Simon Meopham (1327–33; no register survives to indicate when William was replaced as vicar of Chart iuxta Leeds, Kent). At least the exemplar from which this colophon itself is derived probably predates 1349, when it should have been necessary to designate Meopham by his surname, Simon Islip having been appointed to the see.

7. Modern descriptions and facsimiles include:
    (1) Hardwick-Luard 2, 177–82; Montague R. James, a handwritten revision of the preceding, kept in the Department of Manuscripts; Meyer 341–3 (not surveyed in LALME).
    (2) A full facsimile, as well as a colour digitisation at 'www.nls.uk/auchinleck/contents.hmtl'. As M. B. Parkes pointed out to Pamela Robinson (1972, 128–31), the editors' scribe 6 is simply scribe 1, in a different duct and ruling system than elsewhere, this quire perhaps originally intended for some other use. See further Kölbing 178–91, Bliss, Robinson 120–38, Cunningham, Cunningham–Mordkoff, Mordkoff, Shonk. Scribes 1 and 3 described as LALME LPs 6510 and 6500, respectively; subsidiary hands are LPs 6940, 6350 and 7820 ('scribe 6').
    (3) Young–Aitken 201, *Middle English Mirror* xii–xiv, with a facsimile of fol. 4ᵛ (not surveyed in LALME).
    (5) James 1913, 291–3; Sandler 1986, 2, 68–9, and plates 148–9 (neither showing portions of the manuscript in English), LALME LP 6340.
    (6) *English Text . . . Magdalene* ix–xvi, McKitterick–Beadle 86–8 (by Beadle), *Middle English Mirror* xv–xvi, LALME LP 6260. Page 40 is reproduced as the frontispiece to EETS 157, page 371 as that to EETS 274.
    (7) G. V. Smithers, *Kyng Alisaunder* 2, 1–3; fol. 49 reproduced as the frontispiece to vol. 1.
    (8) Fridner, *Apoc* vii–ix, with reproduction of fol. 26ᵛ as the frontispiece.
    (9) James 1909–12, 2:48; *Middle English Mirror* xiv–xv, LALME LP 6490.
    (10) *Middle English Mirror* xix, LALME LP 6520.
8. The fifteenth-century contents table to British Library, MS Royal 8 C.i ascribes this redaction to William Lichfield, a known London rector and preacher who died in 1447; and Wynkyn de Worde in 1493 printed a version translated from an excerpted and redacted French version as his *Tretys of Love* (IPMEP 751), a companion volume to his edition of another local classic, *The Chastising of God's Children* (see p. 15). Further, the French version of British Library, MS Cotton Vitellius F.vii was given by a long-time pious widow, Joan Holland, relict of Thomas, earl of Kent, to Eleanor Cobham, the ill-fated wife of Humfrey, duke of Gloucester, c. 1433–41.
9. Item ie deuise a mon tres amé fils Edward counte de Ruttellond mes deux liures, Machaut et Launcelot. . . . Item a mon Seigneur Lewys Clyfford, mon liure de vices et vertuz (Cavanaugh 460–1, from Kew, PRO, MS Prob. 11/1, fols. 48ᵛ–49).
10. In describing the legacies as 'courtly', I assume Clifford received a copy of Lorens's *Somme le roi* (the original text of St John's 256), a devotional book for Philip the Fair. For the overwhelming persistence of French courtly materials in booklists associated with the Court, see, e.g., Cavanaugh 1988 or Scattergood 1983, 32–6, and Malcolm Vale's discussion of cross-Channel culture 21–47. Scattergood also draws attention (35) to the 1391 will of Margaret Courtenay, countess of Devon, also in French (Cavanaugh 1980, 213, from Kew, PRO, MS Prob. 11/1, fol. 15ʳᵛ). For Clifford, see McFarlane, esp. 207–18.
11. In spite of the vagueness of the description, I would take the identification of Felstede's Psalter with the text of Pepys 2498 as fairly axiomatic. This is far too early to be finding a copy of Rolle's prose Psalter in the south, and the only other early candidate, the so-called 'Surtees Psalter' (IMEV 3103), circulated only in a small area of extreme West Yorkshire. I assume that 'Vanneve' is in fact Henry Vanner, vintner; a 1349 description of his house survives (Myers 306). His son, also Henry and a vintner, was an alderman

and, in a standard act of mercantile diversification into real estate, held rural estates in suburban Poplar and Hackney (Thrupp 371; McDonnell 30, 157, 159).

12. Although New Testaments and full sets of Gospels abound in the tradition of the Wycliffite Bible, a liturgical presentation, like that of the *Mirror*, is rare, since it would detract from Lollard insistence on access to the full biblical text.

13. A 'Romance of King Alexander in verse' was valued by two stationers at £10 in 1382. Pledged as security for a loan by the Bruges merchant John Salman to the former mayor William Walworth, it was surely a continental book (*Calendar of Select Pleas* 3, 11).

14. Explanatory notes to *Piers Plowman* C 5.45–8 typically are a trove of information about such 'lomes' of prayer; see, more extensively, Donaldson 208–11, 221. For a view that such books are specifically women's reading, see Clanchy 1993, 189–96.

15. The identification of the text strikes me as plausible but not absolute; Ian Doyle points out to me that the work might have been an import, the Lincolnshire canon Robert Manning's *Handlyng Synne*.

16. E.g. Bodleian Library, MSS Bodley 505 and Rawlinson C.57 (and another manuscript was taken from London to the Hull Charterhouse at the century's end). See Ker, MLGB 122, 278; 178, 305, respectively.

17. Ker, MLGB 194. For a description, see Ker, MMBL 3, 418–20; a heavily damaged fragmentary book, eight leaves are now in Norwich, Cathedral Library, MS 5.

18. About the time Beauchamp appears to have retired from court; see Given-Wilson 162. The text on St Paul's in University 97, in the form of a bill or placard (see further pp. 32–3 below), was, at least in the fifteenth century, affixed to a pillar in the Cathedral; see *Chronicle* 174–87.

19. A full description of the Trinity MS must await John Scattergood's catalogue of the library's English books; until then, see Lewis–McIntosh 134–5. For the Scheide MS, see Sotheby's, London, 21 November 1972, lot 547 (catalogue 50–2, with a facsimile).

20. In his 1402 will, PRO, MS Prob. 11/2a, fols. 12^v–13, 17, Thrupp's William Hyde, grocer and alderman, includes no bequests to a John. The 1403 will of a John Hyde, clerk of Petherton (Somt.) – an identification that just might indicate a royal appointee, since this was a forest, also administered at one point by Chaucer – appears at MS Prob. 11/2a, fol. 30^{rv}.

21. Although 'oþer' earlier in the sentence is apt to have facilitated the error in the second passage, the error itself is not very likely in the absence of the archaic form. At least two manuscripts of the Mirror, Hunter 250 and Holkham, enshrine confusions over other earlier (yet not clearly datable) forms, e.g. fusing 'hij' THEY (or a similar form) with singular 'he', with persistent switches between singular and plural.

22. Both confusion of *wynn* and *thorn* and the alternation/replacement of *wynn* and/by *w* have been a persistent theme in discussions of the manuscript versions of *The Owl and the Nightingale*, probably from the 1270s; see most recently *Owl* ix, xli–xlii, xlviii–l. For my latest examples, see the frontispiece to *Middle English Genesis*, from Cambridge, Corpus Christi College, MS 444 (note line 2 'wisseð þel', the scribe's single use of *w* on the page, a slip while accommodating himself to copying English, rather than Latin or French); cf. McIntosh 1976, 41, 45; and Laing 1993, 25. Andrew Horn wrote three notes into his books to explain the use of *wynn* (but also the far from archaic *thorn*); see Cambridge, Corpus Christi College, MS 70, fol. 2; London, Corporation Records Office, 'Liber custumarum', fols. 205^v, 362.

23. For the format of my citations from this mostly unedited text, see chapter 4, n. 44.

24. MED, s.v. assailour n. does not know the unpublished *Mirror*, provides only six citations, and gives the usage in my second citation as unique (sense c).

25. Similar prophecies, ascribed to Merlin, appear elsewhere in London texts, e.g., *Annales Londonienses* 151, *Brut* 242–7. The *Annales* record the birth of Andrew Horn's son in 1305 (137) and thus apparently are his composition.
26. Viz. Bodleian Library, MS Douce 322 (LP 6240, hand, illumination, contents) (see Doyle 1958); Cambridge, Corpus Christi College, MSS 80 (LP 6360, contents, provenance) and 387 (LP 6370, provenance); scribe 5 of the Auchinleck MS (LP 6350); formerly Maldon, Beeleigh Abbey, Christina Foyle (sold Christie's, 11 July 2000, lot 72) (LP 6250, provenance; again, see Doyle 1958, and perhaps only a representative example, since a great many copies of Nicholas Love's *Mirror*, the text here, in Sargent's account [Love lxxvii–xxxiv], are in similar Essex languages, e.g. Glasgow University Library, MS Hunter 77, copied by Stephen Dodesham, Carthusian of Sheen, in 1475, for whom see Doyle 1997); Alnwick, the Duke of Northumberland, MS 455 (LP 6040, only the tip of the iceberg, since the scribe and his associates were City professionals engaged in 'mass-production'; see Mooney–Matheson, Matheson 73, 215–28). In addition, note Cambridge University Library, MS Ff.vi.31 (II), hand 2, in LALME as an 'associated' Essex book (1, 196; provenance, see Scase 1992); similarly, called by LALME 'possibly language of SE Cambs' (1, 178), Bodleian Library, MS Bodley 423B (provenance – and again, copied by Dodesham).
27. Merely to allege a small passing example, Bodleian Library, MS Laud misc. 581, a copy of *Piers Plowman* B certainly produced in London and perhaps directly from Langland's fair-copy, is in a version of Type III comparable to Cambridge, Trinity College MS B.15.17. But it also has regular Essex 'cherche' CHURCH and regular northerly 'eyghen' EYES (as well as sporadic 'hiegh' and 'niegh' once).
28. To take one example not included among my forty-odd agreements, the majority of Type II scribes, early and late, reproduce for WHILE the archaic 'þe/þere-while-þat', taken by Samuels as typifying the dialect. Equally, many know the reduced form 'while(s) þat', without -s prominent in Chaucer manuscripts. Yet neither Auchinleck scribe nor that of Pepys 2498 participates in this Type II majority; they customarily write 'while' or 'whiles', the first, of course, the Type III form.
29. *Croniques* 46 and 54. Assertions of Thomas's sanctity provided one focus for City anti-royal cultural expression. See further such images as Thomas and George in Bodleian Library, MS Douce 231 (Sandler 1986, 2, 95; no. 87); the wallpainting of the martyrdoms of the London saints Becket and Thomas at South Newington (Oxon.), c. 1340 (Tristram 70–3, 226–9, plate 18); a Thomas of Lancaster pilgrimage badge (the shrine was at his tomb in Pontefract), found in Billingsgate, *Age* no. 80 (223); or the 'hanap of mazer with an impression of St Thomas of Lancaster thereon, and with a covercle' among goods sold to a London woman in 1338 by Walter Adrian, pepperer (Riley 203–4). See further p. 6.
30. The tumbrel and pillory, in Langland's Cornhill, were used for various commercial crimes (cf. Stow 1, 190); Stow also describes a 1383 charivari to shame whores, in which citizens take on themselves the prerogative of ecclesiastical court.
31. For this punishment, see, e.g., Riley 315–16, 352–3, 423 (events of 1364, 1371, and 1378, respectively). On 'lakking', see Martin 66–70, Simpson 1990; and cf. the portrayal of Envy, 'a knyf by his side', 'Ech a word þat he warp was of a neddres tonge' (5.79, 86).
32. These may be traditional Christmas mumming costumes, since, more nearly contemporary with *Winner*, 1352 Christmas sports featured Edward's courtiers dressed as Dominicans and merchants (Juliet Vale 73–5).
33. Although cf. Arnold Thedmar, describing a holiday with closed shops and the populace 'dancing jublilantly through the City's streets, singing for joy, just as happens each year

at the feast of St John the Baptist' ('per vicos civitatis tripudium ducentes et cantilenas facientes pre gaudio, sicut solet fieri annuatim in festo Sancti Iohannis Baptiste', 87).

34. For the civic effort at ridding the streets of brawlers, etc. in 1311 (those involved were perceived as so terrible that only slang English, 'rorers', would define them), see Riley 80, 86–9; *Letter-Books* 4, 262–7. The guild regulations, for example, those of the Spurriers (Riley 226–8; cf. 243, 246), are convincingly presented as background to the brief alliterative treatment of 'The Blacksmiths' at Salter 1988, 199–214. On the Cornhill market, prohibited in 1369 – and again in 1393 – see Riley 75, 339, 532–3; *Letter-Books* 7, 248. Both actions merely repeat a 1321 effort at civic suppression (Veale 1969, 136–7; *Letter-Books* 5, vii–viii, 156–9; *Munimenta* 426–7).

35. See Stow 1, 95–6, 213–14, and for his source, Withington 621. Withington remains the best survey of thirteenth-century civic pageantry, but surely overminimises the reference to 'various marvelous contrivances and strange conceits' ('quibusdam prodigiosis ingeniis et portentis') in Eleanor of Provence's 1236 entry (617–18). For the second Fishmongers' processional (1313), see Riley 105–7, *Annales Londonienses* 221, *Croniques* 37. Clearly, whatever the paucity of record, the guild did not dispose of, and must regularly have used, its rich emblems.

36. Thus, Langland's claim that 'sopares and here sones for suluer han be knyhtes' (C 5.72), if construed literally, addresses an abuse entirely imaginary. (*sopar*, also the name of a prominent mercantile Lane running out of Cheap, is a form of the noun *shoppere* 'shopkeeper'.) The only knighted London merchants in the century after 1334 were the local heroes who stood down Wat Tyler at Smithfield in 1381, the mayor William Walworth and his colleagues. But the next line, 'And lordes sones here laboreres and leyde here rentes to wedde', may imply a slightly different inflection. If the passage refers to encroachments produced by mercantile foreclosures on loans, Langland here imagines a non-abusive age that preceded his birth. See pp. 128–9, and cf. Nightingale 1995, 189 n. 4, for a pregnant example involving John Pyel.

37. Examples only: the *Annales Londonienses* describe Giles Argentein's costume as 'rex de Vertbois', presumably a woodwose/Green Knight, at Stepney in 1309 (157, repeated *Annales Paulini* 267). This latter chronicle includes additional references, e.g. 264, 352–5, 361. See further the Westminster monk John of Reading 129–32, 151, 152, 156; *Great Chronicle* 35, 37, 40, 46; and early Edward I examples in the first Westminster continuation of *Flores* 30–1, 53, 59, 62, 131–2.

38. This occasion, described Roger Loomis 118–21, is known only through a Flemish chronicle and may be entirely fictitious. Juliet Vale reformulates Loomis's Edward I evidence (15–21); she insists on the wealth of chivalric imagery in John of Howden's *Rossignos*, dedicated to Edward's mother, Eleanor of Provence (21).

39. On William FitzStephen's references to dramatic productions in the late twelfth century, see Scattergood 1995, 24–5, an analysis preferable to Lancashire 31–2.

40. On the processional, including a useful map and discussion of the route, see Manley 216–45. Schofield (1994a, 6–7) shows that this follows the great central axis of the City since Roman times (cf. also his illustration at 150). Generally missed out in the literature has been the 1371 welcome for the Black Prince on his return from Gascony; the surviving accounts include a huge £16 13s for minstrels, probably hired on to meet and to progress with the Prince (Riley 350–2).

41. Kipling merely replicates medieval perceptions considerably older than 1392, e.g. 'Then London appeared like the New Jerusalem adorned with gems' ('tunc visa est Londonia quasi nova Jerusalem monilibus ornata', *Annales Londonienses* 152, of the 1307 entry of Edward II and Isabella).

The 'Old' Law

Once, in an age more philologically concerned, 'The Proclamation of 1258' had a venerated, because originary, status. The text, a little inaccurately identified as the oldest surviving piece of London Middle English, remains of philological importance, and this the only guise under which it is published. But, whether originary or no, the proclamation repays scrutiny because of its characteristics as an early London document.

First of all, it is a legal document, not a literary text. In it, 'Henri, þurȝ godes fultume king on Englene loande', reassures a community of its rights, and in two languages, only one truly a vernacular, English and Anglo-Norman; Henry III promulgated this text, under duress, to hold off his rebellious barons (the 'rædesmen' whose power to legislate, exclusive of regal veto, the text acknowledges) after the Parliament of Oxford. As will appear, this is an important legal nexus. Two copies of the text survive: that normally printed, entered on the Patent Roll in the Public Record Office, in the form of an address to the sheriff of Huntingdonshire; and one surviving promulgated writ (English only), that sent to the sheriff of Oxford and to be preserved in the county muniments – as the document commands 'to halden amanges ȝew ine hord' (lines 20–2, 34–5).[1]

Secondly, befitting a legal text, the proclamation, in both renditions, is written in legal script. This is a hand associated with the production of documents, rather than that customary for copying books in the thirteenth century, the formal *littera gothica textualis*. The Exchequer clerk Robert of Fulham, responsible for composing the texts and preparing all the copies to be distributed to the county sheriffs, wrote in *anglicana*, an informal cursive script in the main reserved for legal and business purposes. On the Patent Roll, he distinguishes the two languages by script; that for the Anglo-Norman is marginally more careful and formal than that for the English.[2]

The uniqueness of this document of course testifies to the normal use of anglicana for Latinate or Anglo-Norman scribal record. But equally, with foresight, one can see here a distinction between formal learnedness and pragmatic record. In the thirteenth century, the use of textura is associated with the Bible and its commentaries, as well as the work of university scholars; anglicana has other, lesser uses. Such a distinction may be paralleled some seventy years earlier when 'Glanvill' explains his book to Latinate canon/civil lawyers put off by the vernacular (probably Anglo-Norman) argot of the Common Law: '[I am] adopting intentionally a commonplace style and the words used in court in order to provide knowledge of them for those who are not versed in this kind of inelegant language'.[3] And the distinction was enshrined in early regulation of London book-production, where writers of 'texthand' and scriveners, those adept at legal hands, formed separate guilds (Pollard).

The 1258 proclamation emerges from the insistence of the committee of twenty-four assembled at Oxford (twelve royal and twelve baronial appointments) that the king heed their reformist counsel. In its full development, this demand, hammered through at least three subsequent drafts and eventually, if somewhat grudgingly, adopted as royal policy in January 1263, modernises and restates the great guarantee of the Common Law, Magna Carta. An interest in such guarantees, the effort to collect binding precedents to protect one's own or one's client's interests, forms the basis of legal copying. Particularly in the wake of Edward I's great spate of legislation (Plucknett 1949), such textual dissemination proliferated in the last third of the thirteenth century. This vast increase in the copying of legal record forms the precondition of a comparable proliferation of private writing, and thence of English literary production at the opening of the following century.

In their classic discussion of 'the early Statutes', Richardson and Sayles identify (540, thence Skemer 1995, 202 n. 20) the seven texts central to any early collection of statute law. In order of antiquity, these are:

Magna Carta (usually not the charter granted at Runnymede in 1215, but either, the usual case, its 1225 reconfirmation, or one of the numerous later versions),

the Charter of the Forest (1217),

the Provisions of Merton, often with expansions (1236),

the Statute of Marlborough (1267),

the Statute of Westminster I (1275),

that of Gloucester (1278, frequently with its 'explanationes', since Edward I and his justices had later to gloss the text for actual enforcement; see 568),

and the Statute of Westminster II (1285).[4]

The occasion of the early London record is prescient, for this core Statute collection grew out of events surrounding the 1258 Proclamation. Richardson and Sayles argue (567) that the fully developed Provisions of Oxford were, like Magna Carta, a revolutionary exaction; they performed both as a treaty, a guarantee of respective rights between Henry III and his magnates, and as legislation. The Provisions themselves never appear in Statute MSS because they were subsumed in the 1259 Provisions of Westminster; these (as emended through to December 1264) were subsequently included, nearly verbatim, in chapters 9–29 of the Statute of Marlborough, after the collapse of the Barons' cause at Evesham (see, in detail, Brand 1974, 2–3, 11–43, 349–70). The last four of these core Statutes indicate the accelerating intensity of legal pronouncement, for all come from the narrow period 1267–85.

Moreover, also accelerating in this collection is a new language of promulgation. Westminster I is the first statute in Anglo-Norman, and Gloucester was issued in both Anglo-Norman and Latin (Brand 2000, 72). Although Anglo-Norman had been used in pleadings for a good while, possibly a full century, before 1275, its enduring presence in English culture, as a language learned and clerical, competitive with Latin for purposes broadly 'administrative', was ensured by promulgations like these, as well as by continuing oral use in the courtroom and in legal teaching and commentary. And the language remained alive in other quasi-legal, clerical areas – wills, accounts, business records, deeds, correspondence. Indeed, it proved so hardy as to survive in pleading, quite in defiance of statute, the supposed revolution of 36 Edward III, c. 1.15 (*Statutes* 1, 375–6), until abolished in 1731.[5]

Particularly important, the language displays a heavily and increasingly south-eastern tilt or bias. Its use is widely attested in the 'Cinque Portes' facing France across the Channel (note the language of the sobriquet) and commonplace over a large stretch of eastern England. This is strikingly an area almost coterminous with that identified by Derek Keene (2000, 101–3) as the limit of prevalent London-directed 'urban potential'. Anglo-Norman's influence in the capital is pervasive and overpowering, a topic to which I will return in discussing the texts of Pepys 2498 in chapter 4.[6]

The seven core statutes listed above became formalised as the centre of a common manuscript production of the late thirteenth and early fourteenth centuries, known in shorthand as *Statuta Anglie* (Richardson–Sayles 567, cf. 202). Books such as these are commonplace survivors from at least the mid- to later 1280s, although these 'early' versions, for example Huntington Library, MS HM 25782, almost instantaneous in following on Westminster II and (the final text of the book) the Statute of Exeter (1286) (Galbraith), simply fulfil a pattern that had emerged through the lengthy period of developing legislative pronouncement.

For example, Brand mentions (2000, 74–5) an unidentified book of *c.* 1240 with Magna Carta and the Charter of the Forest accompanying 'Glanvill' and writs. Similarly, Robinson describes (1969) Bodleian Library, MSS Douce 132 + 137 of the 1260s, with the Charter, Merton, and a few minor statutes, as well as 'Glanvill' and the 'Laws of William I'. British Library, MS Harley 746 (copied 1275 × 1278) is utterly up-to-date in including the second to sixth of the core set. Other similarly truncated volumes from the late 1270s include British Library, MSS Lansdowne 564 and Additional 38821, the latter fully demonstrating competition between learned legal languages, its statutes all rendered into French.[7]

A couple of further early copies deserve at least passing mention. Richardson and Sayles centre their discussion around a Chancery volume they call 'X', now Kew, PRO, MS E 164/9, which can be dated to 1291 (see further Ker's description, MMBL 1, 285–90). An inventory of the books confiscated in 1294 from Matthew Cheker, perhaps author of the legal treatise *Fleta* (Denholm-Young 1943, 1944), includes three *Statuta*-type volumes, one apparently quite opulent, with silver clasps. The most interesting of these contained both the original Magna Carta and one of its reconfirmations, the Charter of the Forest, the (two?)

Statute(s) of Westminster, and a manual of legal practice, 'Hengham' (Whitwell 399–400). The manual is so called from its putative author, Ralph Hengham, one of Edward I's chief justices and responsible for drafting some of his legislation (see amusingly, Plucknett 1949, 73, 133–4, 158).[8]

Manuscripts of this genre were copied out in profusion. Skemer counts (1999, 113; cf. 1995, 201 n. 16) more than four hundred surviving copies. Of these, in excess of half contain one form or another of the *Statuta vetera* or *Statuta antiqua*, the laws of Edward I and II; in the majority of examples, these books will have been produced by 1327 and virtually all of them before 1340, at which time they would have been obsolete in this form. This is an immense survival, especially given forces militating towards their disposal – the books were very early obsolete in not reflecting current legislative pronouncement; the text was very early published (first the *Nova statuta*, i.e. from 1327, by William de Machlinia *c.* 1485, STC 9264). As matters stand, if one assumes, as a rule of thumb, a 2 per cent survival and an English population of about three million, the country would have been utterly suffused with Statute collections, about one copy for every three hundred people. The Statutes will likely have been, *c.* 1330, the most ubiquitous book in England except for the Bible and liturgical volumes. And they will have been fundamental in acquainting people with the procedures of making and consulting books.

I offer one fairly typical example of such a collection, early (probably just around 1297) yet already fully developed, Oxford, Christ Church, MS 103.[9] (For some other early examples, see Adelaide Bennett, Camille 1993, Skemer 1997.) The Christ Church MS begins, as such volumes quite customarily do, with front-matter (fols. 1ᵛ–4); here, as very frequently (cf. Skemer 1999, 122–3), in a separate quire, the compiler of the volume provides an index of the 'capitula' for the seven seminal statutes, the only part of this corpus subjected to formal organisation at an early date. This core set of texts follows (fols. 5–51ᵛ), filled out by the so-called 'statuta sine anno', a somewhat random but here unusually full accumulation of twenty-eight items (fols. 51ᵛ–73ᵛ).

This completes the presentation of Statutes proper, but the volume is extensive, and the same scribe copied two further fascicles or booklets. These are bibliographically separate in execution, and each of roughly the same extent as the Statutes themselves. They provide practitioner material, instructions in the application of the central texts in actual legal/forensic situations. They constitute what a modern lawyer would learn as 'the rules of civil procedure'.

First appears a sequence of 'tracts' (fols. 77–155). More than 60 per cent of this portion is devoted to the old standbys, widely reproduced in books of this genre – the two 'summas' attributed to justice Hengham, George E. Woodbine's *Four Thirteenth Century Law Tracts*, and 'Cadit assisa', an abridged excerpt from the great early authority on the Common Law, Bracton.[10] Recent students (e.g., Beckerman, Brand 1992, 61–8, and 1999, esp. 69–70 and 79–81; Philbin) have insisted upon such writings as teaching texts for incipient pleaders. In this account, they likely represent *reportationes* of some formal classroom proceedings, and in their various Latin or Anglo-Norman forms originated in the metropolis, either in London or close to the Common Pleas in the Great Hall of Westminster Palace. But whatever their origins, they had a considerably wider audience than that initially intended.

In the Christ Church MS, the tracts are succeeded (fols. 156–237) by a *Registrum brevium*, a register of writs. Bracton states the necessity of the knowledge here assembled, 'From of old the rule has been that no one can bring an action in the King's courts of common law without the King's writ' (cited Haas xi).[11] Pursuing a legal case required pleading the proper action; the tracts explain the necessary procedures (and procedural defences), whilst the 'register' provides model forms to be filled in by Chancery clerks with the relevant information and submitted in court to initiate one's case. Such 'registers' were relatively precocious in their appearance; one was prepared in 1210 'to assist in the implementation of English law in Ireland' (Turner 101), and the oldest surviving example, printed by Haas and Hall, is an Irish register of 1227.

Writs are so vital that their appearance in the Christ Church MS is not limited to the scribe's formal text. The volume continued to be supplemented with additions, the majority from the 1340s, on blank and binding leaves, a feature which testifies to continued use as a privately tailored practitioner's collection (cf. Richardson–Sayles 544 on the ubiquity of this feature). For ultimately in English law, what matters is not high legal theory but the courtroom practice that will vindicate one's right; consequently, Christ Church 103, like many other *Statuta*, forms as complete a manual as its compiler could muster. The wealth of sophisticated materials on which the compiler could draw, at an early date and, as will appear, in a non-metropolitan setting, testifies to rapid and extensive propagation (see further Plucknett 1958, 31–3, 80–97; Maitland 2, 110–73; Davies).

The Christ Church MS, like most other *Statuta Anglie*, is written in full-fledged, relatively neat anglicana. Leaving aside its headings, decidedly in the style of the decorative top-lines of legal instruments (cf. Camille 1993, plate 1), it is a formalised and restrained version of the hand already visible in the Huntington MS (see Galbraith's plate of fol. 85^v opposite 182). There, one sees the standard late thirteenth-century split ascenders, including 'doubled' tops on *s* and *f*; and the uneven inking with thick dark vertical strokes and a broad dark cross-stroke on looped anglicana *d*. Legal scribes, unlike those who write textura book-hands, copy for speed with a flat-cut pen-nib, and as they write, they represent these strokes with the nib square to the writing surface, while they leave lighter impressions with the nib's edge as they write transversely the cursive connections between individual letters (cf. the hand of 1291 illustrated Parkes 1969, plate 4 (i), somewhat more formal, and his discussion xiii–xv).

Statutes regularly appear in anglicana – however inelegant it may be, and some palaeographers (Ker, for example) have discussed it with derision – because it is the appropriate professional script, that originally marked as 'of the law'. But the ubiquity of legal manuscripts, their dissemination of legal hand as one regularly observed in books, familiarises it and creates the conditions under which it appears a script style suitable for all formal writing purposes. Thus, anglicana, in less exaggerated forms, will come to typify not just the world of Edward I's laws, but the Edwardian literary world of fourteenth-century England. The script seems first to have escaped a strictly legal environment to appear recording literary texts (in all three of England's languages) in a book I have already mentioned (p. 20), Bodleian Library, MS Digby 86. This is the informal product, s. xiii ex. (conceivably, but unlikely, as early as 1272), of a household scribe plainly more used to copying accounts than texts. He was writing in an 'uplondish' area but one of continuous English literary composition, south-western Worcester (see the Tschann–Parkes facsimile, dating discussed xxxvi–xxxviii).[12]

Christ Church 103 is certainly accumulative in its method of textual selection, and in the process, its compiler may be aided by a certain haziness about the conception of a 'Statute'. Like most other Statute MSS, the book is a private collection; although its first section reproduces 'official documents', these are not necessarily drawn from any official source (as frequent textual variations among manuscripts show; see Richardson–Sayles 542–5, Reynolds 1989). Moreover, the book is self-tailored in contents (as are most medieval books); here the compiler sought to meet a practical objective, what would be useful when going to law. The amorphous sequence of miscellaneous statutes, as Richardson–Sayles suggest (566), represents texts the compiler, as potential litigant, knew judges would accept as binding principles. Insofar as *Statuta* might provide models for other kinds of manuscript, one might well keep such pragmatic rules of inclusion in mind; notions of 'the free space of the literary' may be utterly foreign to medieval book-production, and some more prosaic end may well have been in view.

Two features of the Christ Church MS may not, however, be taken as thoroughly typical, its size and its provenance. Like the earlier Huntington MS, this is, bibliographically, a small quarto; it measures about 240 mm × 160 mm, a bit larger than Huntington. While a great number of Statute manuscripts in this format certainly survive, there is a substantial group of distinctly undersized examples, many under 100 mm/4″ high – and often very thick – representatives of the genre.[13] The only common books of comparable size, generally dating from a much later date, the fifteenth century, are here instructive. The great majority constitutes either miniature books of private devotion (Hours of the Virgin, prayerbooks, etc.) or a similar style of practitioner volume, books of medical recipes.

'Junior' Statute MSS should be viewed in such a context. They are deliberately personal and private books. Further, they are also books for ready practice, designed to be carried easily on the person (in a sleeve, hung from a belt, in a purse), at hand for ready consultation (cf. Skemer 1995, 194–5 for discussion of their likely background, the private Statute roll, some produced commercially; and 198, 205 n. 43).

A further, perhaps atypical, feature of Christ Church 103 is its non-metropolitan provenance, to which I have alluded already. The ready assumption about *Statuta*, given that the materials emanated from

Westminster, has been one of London production; and such is certainly the case with a number of mass-produced, but very swank, copies of the late fifteenth century (Griffiths ch. 2 and Appendix; Scott 2, 319, 329, 345). But ample evidence indicates that the Christ Church MS was produced for (or by?) an individual in Cobham (Surrey). Two dated texts in the scribal hand (mentioned in n. 9) refer to Surrey affairs: a writ of Edward I to the sheriff concerning perambulations of the Forest[14] and a royal writ judging a transaction between Henry Gerard of Guildford and Henry Helegh, prior of Merton (OSA, Surrey). A later hand, datable *c.* 1345, adds writs on blank leaves in all three sections of the manuscript, two of these referring to Cobham and to nearby Weston. Yet a further hand, contemporary with the last mentioned but undated, copies on fol. 153 the Doomsday Book entry for Cobham. (Cf. another early non-metropolitan copy, Princeton University Library, MS Garrett 146, from Lincoln, 1297 × 1299, described Skemer 1997.)

One thus again needs to consider transmission, not origin. These books certainly 'are from' London/Westminster; they may have been teaching tools there, but central Statute texts are, increasingly, parliamentary acts. Parliament usually met in Westminster, increasingly so after Edward II, and the central government would have recorded its *acta* there. Eventually, in Edward III's reign, they would have been entered on the Great Roll of the Statutes kept by Chancery, a locale to which I will return in the next chapter (see Richardson–Sayles's discussion of the genesis of the Great Roll 209–12).

But, as I have signalled in my citation of the Proclamation of 1258, government pronouncements were routinely promulgated and archived in the shires. Perhaps, as with the proclamation and the brief 'Statutes sine anno', they were communicated as loose sheets. And, as Henry III's direction 'to halden ine hord' indicates, they should have remained available there for consultation and copying.

Unusually, the writ to the sheriffs accompanying such pronouncements survives from a London copy of Westminster I used in the printed *Statutes* (1, 39, cited Richardson–Sayles 545). The local legist Andrew Horn provides an excerpt: 'We order that these provisions be read and made public in your open Hustings and elsewhere, as it seems to you appropriate, within your jurisdiction' ('precipimus quod provisiones illas in pleno Hustengo vestro et alibi infra ballivam vestram ubi expedire videritis legi et publicari faciatur'). The enrolled writ sent with the copy to Cheshire (1, lxxxvi), a model from which Horn probably abbreviates, additionally commands 'that they be copied in various places within your jurisdiction, as it seems to you appropriate, and that copies be distributed to your loyal subjects in those places without delay' ('ea in singulis locis infra ballivam vestram ubi expedire videritis distincte et aperte conscribi et ea fidelibus nostris locorum illorum sic scripta sine dilacione liberari'). It further stipulates that copies are to be retained for the county community by two or four 'fidelioribus et discretioribus' knights (in later parallels, the local justices). These instructions indicate clearly that archiving and written availability, in addition to public proclamation (presumably in English, since the law was to reach all men), were expected on provincial receipt.

Thus, books like the Christ Church volume could be assembled from copies circulated by the sheriff. They did not even require that one visit a central record repository. A century earlier, in the time of Henry II, legal literacy among a dispersed knightly class was considered a necessity (Turner 110–11), and this group's increasing responsibility for local administration, for example, service as justices of the peace, would only have intensified the provincial traffic in legal literature. The capital was essentially involved in an act of cultural exportation; to make the common will known, its texts had to be available, in widely dispersed localities (for even wider traffic from Westminster, see Brand 1995).

But equally, whatever their promulgations, Statutes eventually returned to London. In the direst of instances, one's local matter may have ended before the Common Pleas or King's Bench. For the general proliferation of legal materials testifies (as my brief narrative of Statute origins 1258–67 implies) not to respect for law, but to a situation quite the opposite. People only need the law in situations where social unrest requires just dealing to be imposed by litigation.[15] Strikingly, the years 1294–8, the date of many early *Statuta* I have mentioned, are usually considered a debilitating stage of Edward I's reign, a crisis of regal lawlessness and undue expropriation (see, e.g., Prestwich 1980b; 1988, 401–35). Indeed, Matthew Cheker's booklist, which I have mentioned, only survives because he was a victim of a judicial purge associated with the crisis. And, of course, this state of affairs was to be cyclically repeated through to Edward III's war with Archbishop Stratford and his allies in

1340–1 (for this crisis, see *Croniques* 82–7; Ormrod 1990, 81–6, as well as the references at Ormrod 1989, 852 n. 16).

Thus, legal book culture may be perceived as central to the peaceful governance of England, and of the capital. In fact, London might be seen as unduly and specifically over-imbricated in legalism. This is true not simply of the (Westminster) site from which royal/parliamentary promulgation and legal instruction emanate but of the City as well. For this is a place thoroughly legally inscribed, like a royal forest defined by its own peculiar written institutions. In the remainder of the chapter, I investigate some distinctive features of this legal culture and their direct impact upon a contemporary culture more conventionally literary.

II

London as a community was committed to production of large legal books for local use (cf. Harding, esp. 48–51). These were especially prominent just after the period when the Statute book was developed, particularly in the activities, *c.* 1310–25, of Andrew Horn, Chamberlain of the City. Horn's work, which follows on models predating him by a century and more, can be integrally connected with the greatest contemporary London English literary book, the Auchinleck MS, in a variety of ways.

In his books, Horn draws upon a complex tradition of legal writing. This, on the one hand, at once embodies in an historical sweep a single developing tradition of royal law. Yet the books exist also to situate and to query the Edwardian perception of unique legal pronouncement. Within such a global legal history, Horn's book-work attends to the particular as well. Royal law, especially in its most recent avatar, the Statute, must both be seen as innovative, a single point in a long historical continuum, and accommodated to include the place of London. This distinctive local culture possesses unique forms of life that must be preserved – in this case, as an allegedly petrified history, one of inarguable and immutable 'ancient customs and liberties'.

Such compiling and compositional interests are deeply embedded in the peculiarities and the vicissitudes of London history itself. Although within a strongly centralised kingdom, the City, as a disparate particularity, a 'free borough', had developed its own unique legal custom to deal with specifically local problems, especially its commercial precociousness:

> Towns and cities are a product of a division of labour by which they provide goods and services in return for a proportion of the produce and income of the countryside. Rulers and other elite groups have a similar relationship with the basic rural resource . . . but almost invariably they will look to towns . . . for a location to express their standing, and for the supply of luxuries which were a necessary accompaniment of it. (Keene 1989, 99)[16]

Production of luxuries relies upon further divisions and, ideally, acts of mutual support, involving import trade, artisanal handiwork, mercantile entrepreneurship (and a working relation with 'rulers and other elite groups'). The supply of luxuries, of course, includes a further asset kings desired, one only the by-product and goal of luxury production – cash, and cash urban groups might provide monarchs in excess of what might be deemed strictly appropriate. London custom developed to balance these potentially divisive demands. These customs, most especially in the face of growing royal regulation by Statute, the City then felt required to defend against a monarchy intent on treating it like any other rich piece of royal demesne.

The London commune extorted its originary charter, partly verifying its 'ancient liberties', from the regent prince John, in 1191, a politically fraught moment of royal weakness. These guarantees were written into Magna Carta ('The City of London should possess its ancient liberties and free customs in both its lands and waters'; 'Civitas London' habeat antiquas libertates et liberas consuetudines suas tam per terras quam per aquas', *Statutes* I, 10, 23). At this moment of political crisis, London civic authority, as it was to do for more than a century, made (temporary) common cause with magnatial discontent to enforce its demands upon royalty.

But such efforts at the affirmation of 'ancient liberties' well predated Magna Carta. Like all Englishmen until the fourteenth century, the citizens considered the reign of The Confessor as a golden age of rights. And the Conqueror was prepared, as is general in Anglo-Norman culture, to adopt the view that his coming would ensure continuity, not cataclysm.[17] Thus, London received from William confirmation of its pre-Conquest institutions, 'that you deserve all those laws that you had in the days of Edward the Confessor' ('quod uos sitis omni lege illa digni, quod fuistis Edwardi diebus regis', *Gesetze* 1, 486).

Typically, rights depend upon written documentary evidences. As a scarcely surprising result, the Conqueror's original writ is still preserved in the Guildhall, and Andrew Horn copied its text three times, once in Anglo-Saxon, twice in Middle English (one example dated as the English of 1314) (*Munimenta* 25, 247, 504). Similarly, copies of the *Leges Henrici Primi* produced in London present within this text (although pretty certainly as interpolations dating from John's reign) London materials. The most flagrant example occurs at the very opening of the text; after citing Henry I's coronation charter, these London copies intrude Henry's charter for the City (1131 × 1133; *Gesetze* 1, 524–6; cf. *Leges* 3, 48, 80–1). A lesson civic officials learned from monastic cartularies, the fictive, forgery, may be the truest form of historical remembering and preserve the liberty that should have been textually instantiated, even if it hadn't actually been. (See Rumble 45–7; Gwyn Williams provides the best survey of the whole period to 1327.)

I will keep returning to a manuscript including one of these interpolated copies of the *Leges Henrici Primi* throughout this chapter and digress for a moment to introduce it here. The book, British Library, MS Additional 14252, is only the second half of a Guildhall volume now dispersed, begun in the reign of John (originally 1204 × 1215), in script of a decidedly late twelfth-century mien.[18] Most of this book is devoted to an extensive legal text, including the interpolated *Leges* and usually called 'the London collection'. At its end, the original scribe copied, *inter alia*, the earliest surviving and fragmentary London legal texts (fols. 98–100[v]).

Henry's charter states the most basic rights of London citizens. And the London legal texts, copied into Additional, assert these same freedoms. The charter understands the City to be self-governing, with its own unique institutions. These include an assembly, the folkmoot, with three annual meetings; it is implicitly recognised in Henry's clauses 8–9, and a note outlining its meeting place, dates of set meetings, and the requirement of attendance appears at Additional, fol. 100[v] (Bateson 502).

Yet even this first underpinning to urban rights is worth a pause. The Charter addresses the rights of 'citizens' or those 'admitted to the freedom of the City'; this category is not equivalent to London population or inhabitants, but, at any time in the later Middle Ages, only 5–10 per cent of that total. Inherent in the conception of City 'freedom' is the notion that it is not a widely shared privilege. This 'freedom' creates the potential for social friction, for example, between unenfranchised artisanal figures who may provide much of the City's skilled labour and entrepreneurial ones who may manage retail affairs and share both civic rights and excess profit.[19]

The folkmoot might perhaps sound a more communal and sustaining institution. In fact, the communal site was to have a fractious later history. Edward I allowed St Paul's Cathedral to enclose it, to convert public space to the uses of a quasi-private ecclesiastical corporation. And, although it might express its chagrin, the City ultimately was impotent, unable to regain what had been its own. In City perceptions, the Cathedral was something other than a benign public-service organisation, devoted to spiritual instruction and intercession, and the canons equally considered they had a use for the space that overrode pressing and longstanding needs of those whom they were, in some sense, committed to serve.[20] These examples will indicate that London always presents a fractured landscape, a locality irreconcilably plural, whatever the apparent glories of its legal status or the aggressiveness of its claims against outsiders.

To return to those rights granted in Henry's charter, the foundations of civic particularity: this document also treats the City as judicially independent. London has the equivalent of a shrieval county court, the Hustings (granted in clause 1, cf. clauses 8–9); the appended London records at Additional, fols. 98–99^v, include Anglo-Norman explanations of procedures for pleading property cases there (Bateson 492–5). The jurisdiction of the Hustings forms yet another zealously protected right, e.g. the City's refusal in 1311 to surrender to Edward II for punishment Welshmen arrested in London for felonies (Riley 89–90).[21]

Not treated in Henry's charter are matters of internal organisation over which he here waives control. These include a government predicated on a system of wards (eventually twenty-six of them), each of which elects one member of a supposedly representative aldermanic council.

The 'watch' of each ward, as I have indicated (p. 35), is responsible for peacekeeping and defence, including keeping the walls that originally define The City of London.

Further, Henry grants citizens (that relatively small upper class) valuable rights. They cannot be forced to plead outside the walls (clause 2), and they are freed from many customary exactions the king may impose elsewhere, most particularly tolls and military service (clauses 5 and 12, 2.1–2, respectively). These financial freedoms are bolstered by the king's grant to the City (actually to its elected sheriffs) of 'the farm', the right to collect royal taxes, the annual return to the king set at a bargain fixed price, £300 (clause 1).

As part of its grant of self-government, the City can create its own regulations, in practice ones which build upon preferential trading rights. Following clauses 5 and 12, Londoners have a freedom to engage in retail throughout the kingdom denied others. But for their part, they impose severe restrictions on alien trade in the City (a protectionism destroyed by Edward I in 1303).

The local texts in the Additional MS (fols. 99^v–101) offer an early version (*c.* 1130?, again in Anglo-Norman) of such thinking. The importance of regulation appears at the opening, with an extraordinary list of luxury items brought to the City's wharves for sale by Flemish and Rhineland shippers:

> Vessels of gold or silver or oriental work or precious stones or silks from Constantinople or Rennes or fine linen or whalebone from Mainz.[22]

These, however, are not freely available goods, but described so as to explain rules governing access to them. These reserve first right of purchase to royal officials, who are followed by London merchants, before any others can bargain (merchants of Oxford and Winchester then receive preference, in that order). Although the overseas visitors can sell their rich wares, they can neither own their own inns nor stay more than forty days in their (necessarily rented) lodgings (Bateson 499–502).

Henry also grants (clause 15), perhaps grotesquely to our eyes, extensive extramural hunting rights to the citizens. They extend to Middlesex, Surrey, the Chilterns, perhaps parts of Essex and Kent. Yet these were clearly valued. William FitzStephen (*c.* 1171) includes them in his account of the commodities of the City (110); and the City regularly opposed efforts at enclosure that would restrict its rights of the chase, e.g. at Stepney in 1294 or Greenford in 1307, in the latter case going up against a royal official to protect its own (McDonnell 64; *Letter-Book* 3, xx, 152). One of the Mayor's four esquires was 'communis venator' from at least 1379, and the City both solicited venison from lords and kept its own hunt of hounds (Masters 99–101). (As late as 1599, Thomas Dekker could still depict this 'common right' enthusiastically; cf. *The Shoemaker's Holiday*, scenes 5–6.)

The possibility of engagement in blood-sport speaks to the pretensions of at least some citizens. The ruling class, into the fourteenth century, considered themselves 'Barons' (and are so designated in Henry's clause 6, as well as by the civic historian Arnald Thedmar). Similarly, aldermen received burial with full baronial honours (O'Connor 1994b, 30, citing Thrupp 249–50). People of this class and pretension feel they are to be considered like other magnates of the realm, an opinion offering a logic for emulating, as well as making common cause with, fractious rural aristocrats, but also the potential for disgruntled factionalism and feelings of being disestablished by others who share space with them within the City walls.[23]

Henry's charter thus defines a distinctive local culture in terms of certain ancient rights. City history often appears a constantly renewed perception of threat to these legal arrangements, particularly from without. In this view, civic history is the preservation of ancient custom, and it depends upon a process fundamentally historical – legal memory. In part, such memory may be achieved by the preservation of evidences, which implies not just the Guildhall's locked chests that protect documents but equally their reproduction in writing as a guard against loss.

For example, Andrew Horn describes at length (*Munimenta* 169–79) an emergency which arose in 1314, when royal justices rejected a procedural concession the City thought it had gained thirty-three years earlier. Edward I had issued a writ, modifying for the City, it was alleged, provisions of the problematic Statute of Gloucester, chapter 12 (*Statutes* 1, 49, 52). But the justices remained sceptical, and faced with the loss of privilege, a two-year search ensued: where was the document which demonstrated the precedent on which the City based its interpretation? Once found and the City's understanding vindicated, the proper right was carefully re-entered, in both the rolls of Chancery and of the

Common Bench so that it could never again be questioned. Equally, Horn had it written into his book, where it might remain part of civic record and, with the accompanying account of the research that led to its recovery, civic history.[24]

As this narrative indicates, whatever the antiquity of right, local 'barons' might perceive it as hard won and in need of vigilant preservation. In the period leading up to, and continuing through, the formative period of Statute law, London persisted in having difficulties with and in resisting various forms of perceived monarchic incursion. Thedmar's history of the City, broken off at his death in 1274, describes ten occasions 1239–57 on which Henry III, petulantly 'motus in ir(acundi)am', suspended free City government for brief periods. Several of these involved intrusions into local elections, largely in the hope of finding officials complaisant about granting extra aids to royalty; that of 1249, significantly, City resistance to royal plans to improve the commercial prospects of the king's beloved Westminster through his instituting a fair there.[25]

Problems only intensified in the period of baronial 'reform', as I have shown, responsible for the development of Statute law. The City was the site of the baronial councils after the Oxford parliament of 1258, erupted in full revolt in 1263, was temporarily a Montfortian capital barred the king, and sent a contingent to Lewes in 1264 (it performed ignominiously – citizens might hunt but generally are not soldiers).[26] Following the reversal of baronial fortunes at Evesham, the king and Prince Edward suspended City government altogether for three years and imposed an enormous (20,000 *m*) fine, although they typically had difficulty extracting it (Gwyn Williams 205–9).

Nor did matters improve in early Edwardian England. To ignore a variety of minor altercations, Edward I governed the City through a royal warden and officials for thirteen years; he only returned the franchise in 1298, under coercion after several years of constitutional crisis. In this particularly disruptive period, the City oligarchy dissolved before rising guild control of industry and trade, restrictions on the activities of foreign merchants vanished with promulgation of the 'Carta mercatoria' in 1303, and the site of the folkmoot was lost.[27]

During the wardenship (1295), a minor emergency erupted (*Munimenta* 72–7, Riley 31–3) over a threatened French invasion of the

South Coast, another telling instance in which an escalating sense of lost 'ancient custom' came to the fore. On this occasion, the king, in the midst of his constitutional difficulties, sought military aid through rhetorical overkill, his infamous claim that Philip IV was seeking to destroy the English language itself (Prestwich 1988, 383 and n. 21). The problem for citizens was again a potential violation of right: were they being forced by a financially strapped king to offer military service (from which they were exempt)? or was this licit defence of the realm (to which they were obligated to contribute)? (They eventually decided the latter, and cooperated.)

Under Edward II, there were renewed emergencies; as Nightingale says (1995, 124), 'London politics seethed in a turmoil not equalled until the 1370s'. The situation was so fraught that rumour could prove as powerful as actual incursion, for example, in a civic riot of September 1312 over an unconfirmed possibility that City officials had been imprisoned in the Tower (*Annales Londonienses* 216–18, *Annales Paulini* 272). In a replay of the 1260s efforts to constrain royal power, the City supported the Ordainers, who abrogated the 'Carta mercatoria' that had destroyed the civic monopoly excluding alien merchants. In the wake of Thomas of Lancaster's fall at Boroughbridge in 1322, the legislation was restored, and oscillating promulgations and cancellations, a major source of mercantile disquiet and hostility, continued throughout the century.[28] As a result of his support (one will recall the bill with the Ordinances prominently displayed in St Paul's), the City staunchly endorsed Thomas's canonisation; Robert of Reading, in his continuation to the *Flores historiarum*, views his execution as a Christ-like martyrdom, with citation of Matt. 12:19, the result of persecution by a Herodian tyrant (see 176, 178–9, 183–5, 206–7, 213–14, 216 and Gransden 1974a). Local chronicles continued recording Thomas's miracles as late as 1358 (John of Reading 133–4, repeated at *Great Chronicle* 40).[29]

Most gallingly, in 1321 London was subjected to a crippling (and long-running, almost six months) general eyre, designed to root out its ruling class. This provides a major narrative centre in Horn's 'Liber custumarum' (*Munimenta* 285–432, 'Custumarum', fols. 224–63). Although the discussion absorbs nearly half the London records in this portion of his volume, Horn only records the corporate City as a defendant, not the large number of 'private' cases brought, in many cases for alleged (and sometimes appallingly real) abuse of civic office (see esp. *Eyre of London* 1, xi–xxii, xxxii–xxxiv; *Letter-Book* 5, v–xi).

On this occasion, the City was subjected, from the jump, to a sequence of deliberately outrageous demands. For example, Londoners were told they might not charge the king's justices for their lodging, a calculated violation of Henry I's charter, clause 4, which denied the royal *familia* any right to forced hospitality in the City (*Munimenta* 296). In a further provocation, the City was threatened with loss of its franchise on the first day of hearings (289); during much of the affair, the mayor's authority was suspended in favour of yet another warden, Sir Robert de Kendale, in fact appointed on the 41st day (late February, p. 378) and in office until 19 May.[30] Although the City nominally received back its franchise, the mayors until 1327 remained royal nominees, fundamentally still 'wardens' for the king (*Letter-Book* 4, x, 214).

It is probably no wonder that in 1326, after some initial dithering, London revolted on the news of Isabella and Mortimer's landing in Suffolk. The *Annales Paulini* is driven to the English phrase 'riffling time' to describe an uprising that included the assassination of the Treasurer bishop Stapledon of Exeter (315–22). Peace only came in the years after 1327, when the City's status was secured by an important royal charter.

Horn officiated at this watershed event of civic history, when on 9 March 1327, he read aloud in English this new statement of civic liberties. In it, Isabella and Mortimer restored unvarnished, pre-Edwardian 'ancient custom' (Gwyn Williams 299, 307; the event narrated and text fully cited *Annales Paulini* 322–32, summarised *Great Chronicle* 31–2). Perhaps most importantly (331), the document included a promise that the City would not have a warden imposed at caprice, for personal transgressions of citizens, but only for treason or rebellion of the corporate body. This not-so-ancient right was preserved inviolate until the 1391 royal 'quarrel'.

Yet even then, there were further throes. Until his downfall, anti-royalism became expressed as anti-Mortimerism, and another Lancaster, Henry of Grosmont, was considered the hero of the hour (cf. p. 229; see again succinctly, Gwyn Williams 301–4). Antipathy to centralising royal tendencies that would override what were perceived as venerable local customs is integral to early London history.

This is not quite the story that emerges, however, from an early Guildhall volume, Thedmar's 'Liber de antiquis legibus' (described Ker MMBL 1, 22–7). This volume provides a model for conceiving London civic right within a narrative history, although Thedmar remains unusual in any variety of ways. The grandson of German immigrants to London (cf. his hagiographic account, 238–9), he was alderman of the German merchant community; as a citizen, he was able to purchase for it the site of its great entrepot, the Steelyard, and was apparently instrumental in gaining Hanseatic merchants unparalleled trading terms (on these, see Nightingale 1995, 86–7).

As a 'naturalised alien', aloof from the typically protectionist policies which characterise London commercial culture, Thedmar was quite unusually a royalist, apparently patronised by Henry III's brother, Richard of Cornwall, king of the Romans. His book is unique in its sometimes heavily personalised royalism; for Thedmar, the 1258 Oxford meeting was an 'insane Parlamentum' (38), and the enormous royal fine of 1265 absorbs more than half Thedmar's 'biographical account', a self-defence against other citizens' retributive effort to force him, a loyalist and not a rebel, to pay a greater share than he considered just (239–42).[31]

Thedmar's book puts royal and local history in parallel. A sequence of professional scribes, writing textura, copied for him a core of historical notes, in the main material extracted from William of Malmesbury's *Gesta regum*, with further notes on royal activities to 1199, accompanied by briefish annals of London 1188–1257 (this last discussion at fols. 63ᵛ–71ᵛ). These materials Thedmar extended, in a rough anglicana, presumably the document hand he had learned as a businessman; he continued the royal annals, probably to 1272 (the portion to 1224 at fols. 36ᵛ–40, its continuation now lost), and he composed an enormously detailed extension of the London annals to cover events of 1258–74 (fols. 71ᵛ–144ᵛ, edn 1–173; for a facsimile, see Robinson 2003, plate 27).

Thedmar's book contains minimal Statute materials. Only one, that of Marlborough, actually appears (fols. 147–53); the book once also included an order about the Assise of Bread in the City, an important legal consideration, since controlling victualling trades and ensuring cheap food was a constant public concern (see Gwyn Williams 31, 78, etc.). But considerably more typical of Thedmar's work is the opening of a list of the charters kept in the 'scrineum civium' in 1270 (fol. 159). Thedmar was custodian of this chest, which held the City's invaluable documentary proofs of its rights and privileges, and he used these, and other documents, as mnemonic stimuli. A large number of fully cited texts provides a framework into which Thedmar places his personal experience and constructs a local history.[32] Thinking about being a Londoner, participant in great and troubling events, requires access to documentary record and the unvarnished provision of that record to other interested citizens. Thedmar's discovery provides a rule universal in London chronicling, followed by all his early fourteenth-century successors, not least Andrew Horn, in his considerably more extensive activities.

Thedmar's notion of the function chronicles serve is scarcely a surprising one (cf. Bede's letter to Ceolwulf). In his most overt statement, he applauds the memorial aid writing gives to an exemplaristic assessment of praiseworthy and ignoble action:

> The deeds and works of good men are committed to writing so that these might be brought to memory for their perpetual praise and glory. Likewise, the cruelty, malice, treachery, and criminality of evil men should be put in writing so that these may be noticed by the whole world in times to come for their disgrace, censure, and ill repute.[33]

One should be struck by the disparity between the two members of this sentence. Virtue is imagined matter of factly, while its opposite is subjected to a rhetoric both expansive and excessive. This excess appears both in the imagination of iniquity and the vehemence of condemnation the chronicle will allow 'the whole world in times to come' to draw from it.

The Chronicle also provides explicit statement about what 'gesta bonorum' might consist of:

> All those of the City, poor as well as rich, should be like a single body and a single man, to preserve faithfully the King's peace and the City's through their fidelity.[34]

All ranks are drawn together, in this statement, through a commonplace corporate metaphor. The City should act as one, an organic union of all its diverse constituent parts, imagined as 'peace', a normative quietness, and 'fidelity', a bond of cohesive loyalty. Generally without parallel elsewhere in pre-1327 London writings, Thedmar imagines this cohesiveness as that of a royal City, one extending to the locality's relationship with the realm at large.

Regrettably for someone capable of so high-minded a statement, Thedmar was forced to live through times where this ideal proved non-functional. The personal references that dot his chronicle suggest that he was required to cope with fractured and controversial moments of emergency.[35] These reveal nothing other than the failure of civic integrity, as Thedmar might have wished it.

Equally, under stress, the peculiarity of Thedmar's conception of corporate union emerges. For example, during the ascendancy of the Barons, Mayor Thomas FitzThomas and the populace

> made through their own acts new statutes and provisions (they can better be called perversions). They did this for their benefit alone, and with an intolerable loss to all merchants coming to London and English fairs, as well as to the greatest loss to the entire kingdom. And then nothing was done or treated that concerned the common profit of the City or the growth of its freedoms.[36]

In this account, faction seeks its own end, not communal good. That good is conceived in terms of old liberty, not 'new provisions better called perversions'. By definition, such a good is universal, not particular. Equally, efforts to improve the old are to be viewed, not as 'new' or innovatory, but only extensions or 'augmentations' of what has already existed. Thedmar's history, indeed London history generally, presents public good as a steady stream, always inherent in a long past, even when, as in the 1327 royal surrender of the right to impose a warden, a particular right can be assigned to or embedded in a specific narrative moment. Newness, innovation is thus always controversial (it is just as apt to be civic discord as royal incursion), and improving the City's lot must be seen as recovery of a franchise always implicit. Although events are situational and time-bound, they are also strangely timeless, imposed into a single past, and not developmental or progressive.

Just as his historical sense, Thedmar's definition of the communal good comes a bit unstuck here. While still appealing to a notion of the City as ideally integral, both within itself and to the realm at large, Thedmar manages to suggest an end in view that is particular, rather than generally shared commodity. 'Merchants *coming* to markets' implicitly refers to someone other than natives. Indeed, the passage allows public good to be defined as narrow interest, that of rich entrepreneurs, urban oligarchs, with the cash to trade with visiting foreign merchants. The antipathies in the passage reflect Thedmar's fear of government through local groups committed to versions of communal unity different from his own.

Thedmar's text, in spite of its pretences to unity, thus always is on the edge of fracture. Perhaps nowhere is this more true than the two villainous situations where he describes at length distracting lower classes erupting with their demagogic leaders – FitzThomas in 1262 and 1265, Walter Harvey in 1271–2 (traditionally seen by local historians as progressive movements). On these occasions, Thedmar laments the silencing of the City's 'discreti', frequently explicitly 'Aldermanni', that urban elite in a position to profit from long-haul trade. In this account, these persons are ceaselessly opposed by 'stulti et maliciosi' (77, 1265), 'fatui de wlgo' (86, 1265), 'vulgus Civitatis . . . magnum tumultum facientes', also called 'tantum multitudinem illius innumerabilis populi' (148, 1271).

Just as in that passage where Thedmar tries to theorise his chronicle, the common body fractures. Chronicle language no longer expresses the corporate, but violent difference and an invective-laden disrespect for others, indulged so as to match that disrespect to which Thedmar feels subjected. The note of social contempt is struck in one early instance, in which those operating 'without any semblance of reason' are described as 'from the populace, children of different mothers, many born outside the City, and many of a servile condition'.[37]

On one particularly stressful occasion, the 1262 'communa civium', one such mob claimed to be peacekeepers. In Thedmar's formulation, however, they were in fact 'pacis perturbatores' (55, 1262). This contention over who represents the peaceful communal City might return one to Thedmar's idealised definition of the single body/man in peace. An occasion like this permits a rereading of the metaphor: basically, one might see it as sustained, were these people actually quiescent, artisans and other menials going about their various labours. Invisible and peace-loving, they would elude narrative notice, and there would be none of the problems that so vex Thedmar. In such a situation, the unspoken but obvious implications of the corporate metaphor would also function – and offer comfort to those comprising the body's/man's proper head, people like Thedmar himself. Narrative might be restricted to his 'predecessores, Cives bone memorie', worthy of this designation for the 'privilegium libertatum ... perquisitum' (35–6) – or at least, attained for some.

Thedmar's book has always been seen as most relevant to English studies for its binding materials (fols. 160–62), reused from a servicebook, probably thirty-odd years older than the remainder. These leaves contain, among other things, an English poem, 'A Prisoner's Prayer'.[38] The poem represents a typical early London trilingual text, of a sort I will examine at much greater length in chapter 4. Its notation comes from learned Latin tradition, the 'Planctus ante nescia' of Godefroy of St Victor; but the actual Latin has been silenced, the poem itself in Anglo-Norman directly derived from the Latin, and the English a translation of the Anglo-Norman.

'A Prisoner's Prayer' gains whatever poignancy it has precisely from its recycling in this context. Only by its inclusion here does it refer to Thedmar's troubles after 1265 (as the book is now bound, his personal narrative begins on the next leaf), but it is impressive testimony to the fear of factionalism which underlies the entire historical collection. Specific about the guiltlessness of its speaker and the attacks he suffers from wicked men, 'Prayer' addresses the very conditions which render legal safeguards a necessity. Most noteworthy would seem the lines (27–34) on the transitoriness of worldly control, which generalise the argument and might be connected with the paintings of the London Lisle Psalter sixty years later; these feature images of Fortune and of the chilling confrontation with mortality, the meeting of the Three Living and Three Dead (including English captions) (Sandler 1999, 44–5).

In his activities, Thedmar presages the City's great writer of history and law, both chronicle (the *Annales Londonienses*) and legal research to construct the history of civic liberty, Andrew Horn, Chamberlain of the City 1320–8. Horn's will expresses his devotion to the City, and to its legal culture. In it, he leaves to the Guildhall in perpetuity five books, three of them still surviving (see Cavanaugh 1980, 440–2). The fifth, described as '"De statutis Anglie", with many liberties and other matters touching the City' is the Guildhall's surviving 'Liber Horn', dated 1311, but with expansions through to 1318 and its decoration continued into the 1320s.[39] This is presumably the book Horn described in a note at the foot of a leaf in another of his donations, Cambridge, Corpus Christi College, MS 70, p. 191, beneath an introduction and table of headings for the laws of Edward I:

> Neither these statutes (their rubrics are given above) nor the register of documents shall be written in this book, because *I have them elsewhere* and because I intend to compile, with God's grace, *from that book and others* a great codex of those things I think useful to portray to posterity the circumstances of our days. (my emphases)[40]

In this plan, Horn may have been very much a product of his age. At least two prominent occasions of City record dissemination he very likely witnessed stimulated him (and will certainly have aided him) in his London document gathering. In his own *Annales Londonienses*, Horn reports that Richer de Reffham (Mayor in 1310, see Breslow)

> had the ancient customs and liberties in the rolls and books of the Guildhall searched carefully and, having gathered, along with the aldermen, the wiser and more powerful, had these read and published in their presence.[41]

Reffham had those found read publicly, as Statutes were, and accepted by City and King (whose writ was also read). These activities were associated with a perambulation and restoration of civic properties 'ad pristinam dignitatem et indempnem'. In 1312, the Aldermen went further in ordering that, to instruct youthful citizens, all civic legislation should be registered, read aloud at least annually, and copies distributed to those who wished them (*Letter-Book* 5, 13; Gwyn Williams 274). In addition, Horn certainly had access to the papers of Hugh de Waltham, Common Clerk of the City (before 1311 × 1335); Waltham prepared, for private use in fulfilling his civic office, rolls of City precedents by consulting, as Horn was later to do, royal records in the Tower (see *London Eyre of 1244* xii–xvi, xxi, esp. xiii, xv; *London Eyre of 1276* xi–xii, xxv–xxvii; *Eyre of London* xv).

But Horn clearly found his task larger than envisioned, and the 'magn[us] cod[ex]' of his note ultimately spawned two, his greatest contribution to London civic life. These, 'Liber custumarum' and 'Liber legum antiquorum regum', he constructed from volumes already at the Guildhall, his private books, and from books of other legally engaged persons like Waltham. The 'Liber Horn' itself is marked with instructions for a copyist, 'non scribe' and 'hic incipe', followed exactly in constructing the huge customaries (see MMBL 1, 28). These two companion books, vastly larger than even the substantial volumes Horn left in his will, were not intended to be personal possessions but the expressions for posterity Horn's note mentions, tailor-made for the City as its communal records of memory.

Their current state is particularly vexatious. Lord Protector Somerset 'borrowed' the Guildhall Library in 1549, and the volumes were then split. They were returned, but only in part, in 1607/8 through the efforts of the antiquarian and lawyer of the Middle Temple Francis Tate (who signed as his own one still dispersed portion, Oxford, Oriel College, MS 46, fol. 65rb). Subsequently, the returned Horn books were rebound into a single volume, 'Liber custumarum' (Stow 1, 274–5; *Munimenta* xvii–xxiii, Glanvill lxiii).

These two books, produced in the period 1321 × 1325, have been reconstructed by Neil Ker (1985, 134–42). Pieces of each, in a confusing pattern, now survive as parts of the Corporation of London Library, 'Liber custumarum'; of British Library, MS Cotton Claudius D.ii; and of Oxford, Oriel College, MS 46. These are very large indeed, not just in their opulent page formats but in the sheer amount of material copied, well over 600 folios.[42]

Moreover, Horn took no chances about his record. Not only did he bequeath the Guildhall his own books, partial sources (and he knew that the Guildhall had other copies), but he also ensured substantial doubling of contents in his two volumes. Each book includes the same general sequence of materials:

(a) a Latin collection of pre-Statute law, extending from Ine of Wessex to Richard I (the logic for entitling one of the volumes 'Liber legum antiquorum regum');

(b) an extensive collection of *Statuta Anglie*, the latest items from *c.* 1321;

(c) another extensive collection, in this case of London legal materials (the 'custume').[43]

In historically arranging documents, both royal and civic, Horn's compositional gesture clearly reproduces Thedmar's presentation. But, designedly more thorough and expansive in its historical sweep, its expan-
siveness carefully contextualises Edwardian promulgation by placing it
as only the latest in a sequence of royal pronouncements beginning in
the deep Anglo-Saxon past.

These massive legal volumes reproduce and develop extensively a
book Horn found in the Guildhall, one that well predated Thedmar.
This, once again, survives in large dispersed fragments, as Manchester,
John Rylands Library, MS Lat. 155; and the previously mentioned Additional 14252. This conjoint volume, called 'the London collection',
has as its core the historical text I have identified above as Horn's (a),
the presentation of the pre-Statute laws of the English kings. Begun
at least a century before Rylands + Additional was copied, this text,
Quadripartitus, stands at an important juncture of English legal literature. Its author gives a summary of the law of the Anglo-Saxons, in
Latin translation, with a 'second book' continuation, the *Leges Henrici
Primi*, mentioned above.[44] This continuation is customarily seen as the
head of the twelfth-century Angevin legal revolution (e.g., Plucknett
1958 begins his discussion with it, 24–30).

Quadripartitus itself is a conscious historical gesture, and a considerable act of historico-legal research. Its author managed to assemble a
substantial chunk, the majority, of what is still known of Anglo-Saxon
legal codes. His second book may be a conscious forgery, predicated
on the reader accepting the presumptions of legislating kings underlying the first one. Rather than actual law promulgated by Henry I,
this represents an example of 'visionary legislation', a gesture recurrent
in English legal literature and law itself (for the phrase, see Middleton
1997, 216 *et seq.*) – an account of what the king should have promulgated (but didn't). As I have indicated, the ruse worked; the compiler of
'The London collection' intruded actual Henrican documents relating
to London into the text.

'The London collection' of John Rylands + Additional is noteworthy
for massive editorial work on the original *Quadripartitus*. The compiler
of this volume, or his source, quite conscientiously historicised the text
he received. Working from an early and incomplete version, he imposed a chronological order upon his materials, added various narrative

links, and constructed for it a sort of prologue, an explanation of Anglo-Saxon legal terms and a 'description of England' (taken from the Anglo-Saxon text called the 'Burghal Hidage'; see Rumble). Through these gestures, the compiler created a specifically London text that presented law as an organised continuum, an historical order (if not progression or development), and one susceptible to something like nascent literary presentation. Indeed, the compiler's work was so successful that his legal research could become the stuff of independently conceived historical narrative; Roger of Howden's *Chronica*, completed by 1201, cites a considerable chunk of the text (2, 215–52; see Plucknett 1958, 30; and cf. Patrick Wormald 1999, 142, 430). The legal and the historical approach become coterminous, as they also do in Andrew Horn's elaboration of this model in his two massive books for the Guildhall.

Moreover, again a model for Horn, the London compiler viewed what he had received as already dated (as it was), and he undertook further research to extend the text to the present day. Rylands lat. 155, fols. 124–26^v move past the limits of *Quadripartitus*, the laws of Henry I, and provide the coronation charter of Henry II and his letter to the City of London. The materials continuing from this point, now in the Additional MS, carry the legal narrative yet further, with the legal tract 'Glanvill' (fols. 1–87) and a Richard I narrative. The former text thus functions, not as instructional materials for practitioners, but as the historical survey its initial rubric implicitly promises, a summary 'de legibus et consuetudinibus regni Anglie tempore Regis Henrici Secundi' (1). This completes the set of materials that Horn commandeered to comprise his 'Leges regum', section (a) above.

Moreover, the last work of the original scribe in the Additional MS (fols. 92–104^v/1) provided a model to which Horn was clearly quite attentive. In an imitation of the revised opening to *Quadripartitus*, the scribe composed a prologue, to be discussed more fully below, to introduce the brief bits of specifically London legislation (some of them already described at pp. 56–8). This mirrors the presentation, earlier in the book, of the Anglo-Saxon 'Burghal Hidage' as a prologue; a text about Alfredian national defence gets recontextualised as if a 'Descriptio Anglie'. In making this decision, echoed through other legal books, the compiler of 'The London Collection' identifies the following contents, The Law, as tied to a landscape and a jurisdiction. The Law is associable with a locality, and a locality in the various stages of historical succession.

The two books Horn prepared for the Guildhall reflect different traditions of *Quadripartitus*. Thus, Claudius ('Leges regum') has been derived directly from Guildhall materials, the John Rylands MS, but for Oriel ('Liber custumarum' proper), Horn provided the scribe his own private copy. This is one of his surviving legacies to the Guildhall, Cambridge, Corpus Christi College, MS 70; its use in 'Liber custumarum' parallels the similar supply to the scribe of the still private 'Liber Horn' for Edwardian documents. This exemplar for copying relies on Horn's earlier private consultations and had been constructed independently of the Guildhall's Rylands MS.[45] One would surmise that this disparity of source materials reflects the simultaneous copying of the 'Leges regum' and 'Custumarum', and the consequent need for multiple exemplars.

Amid such a volume of material, I restrict myself to commentary on only two aspects of Horn's compilation, first his own appearances in his book. Like Thedmar, Horn can not resist presenting himself as a participant, and he is a kind of legalist hero in the history he constructed. In some sense, again like Thedmar, he 'enshrines' himself for that work with rolls out of civic document chests necessary to construct the volumes. At least part of this labour had an instrumentally civic function only accidentally enabling the surviving volumes; Horn himself researched the precedents necessary to prepare City officials for facing the King's judges in the Eyre of 1321 (*Eyre of London* xv), and his most prominent self-inscriptions in the narrative are as civic hero presenting the City's brief on this occasion (*Munimenta* 394, 399, 401, 403, 406, 408).

Yet civic heroism and commitment intertwine with modernised versions of Thedmar's divided City. On one occasion, Horn appears in his text as trade-protectionist, pleading for his own very prominent company of Fishmongers against poorer men trying to sell retail on the wharf (394). And civic record reveals that in 1307 (an experience perhaps repeated eight years later), he judicially revealed himself as profiteer in the sale of basic foodstuffs. On this occasion, Horn was serving as scrutiniser of fish panniers (their volume was regulated because used in wholesaling); he was found, presumably by his fellow scrutinisers, using an undersized example, forced to forfeit the contents and to have the container burned in Cheapside, the statutory penalty (*Letter-Book* 3, 157–8; cf. 5, 46).

These examples reveal the world of guild contentiousness, a major unpleasantness in Horn's customary. Having overturned the government of Thedmar's mercantile oligarchy, London trade unionism quickly forgot what may have been its egalitarian roots in parish fraternities (cf. Veale 1991) and promptly fissioned. The books Horn prepared for the Guildhall are replete with efforts at trade regulation. Some of this material records acts of communal protectionism one could perhaps applaud, e.g. efforts to ensure that wheelwrights from the Weald of Kent not import short-length spokes to the City, or the continuous efforts at enforcing adequate mesh in 'kidels' (*Munimenta* 85–6, 116–17, respectively).

But much of Horn's material records efforts by wealthier retailing trade associations to impose on the artisanal handicrafts who supplied constituent materials for fine goods. Disputes within the cloth trade, a typically dispersed medieval industry in which various menial steps eventually produced expensive finished product, occupy a substantial part of the record (for example, relations of the burellers, weavers, and fullers, *Munimenta* 121–32, 416–24). Again, the saddlers, who sold direct, very often to the court, appear to have been overbearing in their relations with their related artisanal crafts, the lorimers and the painters (78–81; on the last, see Staniland 1986). Whatever its pretensions to civic unity and ancient custom, the rule of law often exists as only a hierarchic enforcement procedure.

The contentious particularism of guild interests, the specialised group seeking power over others, may appear a far stretch from 'the common good'. Yet whatever factionalism enters Horn's account of civic history, his volumes proved constructive in ways perhaps far removed from his goal of recording the City. The main scribe of Horn's 'Liber legum', for example, is known elsewhere as a single practitioner, producing (whether before or after work for Horn) trilingual portions of CUL Gg.iv.32 for a London priest (Dennison 1990, 132 n. 62). But since Horn's volumes required cooperative work among an extensive group of book-artisans, these productions may have stimulated other particularisms and constituted a foundational experience, of use when these men and their associates turned to other tasks.

III

Horn's books can be seen as important models for London book-making in a variety of ways. They involve, as I have suggested, various compilational processes; rather than presenting set texts, like many contemporary liturgical volumes (e.g. Psalters), producing them required choices among potentially miscellaneous contents (and subsequent flexibility in using exemplars). Horn's work also will repay comparison with the Auchinleck MS for its repeated return to a nexus that joins legal precedent, the historicist insistence upon temporally descending antique right, with a fictive mode of thought that has often proved troubling to more legally inclined scholars.

Physically as well, the sheer size and the page format of Horn's custumals seem to have affected current practice. Book-production is, after all, learned human labour and, as such, it responds to and follows models, basically the totality of book-experiences shared by the production team. These can be conceived as doubly focussed; producers look both to similar current books (of say, the last twenty years or so), and they look to signals they find in whatever they are copying from. This happens because it is far easier to accept a received format, in which the text has already been processed for readers' consumption, than to invent one anew. Simply the thickness of Horn's books is reflected in large collected volumes like Auchinleck, Pepys 2498, and Laud 622 (only a fragment of what must have been, from the format, at least a rival to Pepys). Further, although Auchinleck now survives in severely cut-down form, on a relatively small and rather squarish page (the largest leaf now 264 mm × 203 mm), both Pepys and the Scheide Psalter are of sizes comparable to Horn's books for the Guildhall, Laud significantly larger.

More strikingly, the actual *mise-en-page*, in 'Liber custumarum' double columns of forty-two lines, the 'Leges regum' of thirty-nine, seems to have been equally generative, if not always in such a monumental script. The main scribe of Auchinleck normally has double columns of forty-four lines, a format usually emulated by other hands, and although Pepys and Laud are more packed, a comparable format recurs in smaller Type II books, Corpus Christi 282 in double columns of forty-two or forty-four lines, Hunter in forty-one, Scheide in forty-three. Indeed, such a sense of appropriate page content survived well into the fifteenth century in copies of Gower's *Confessio Amantis* (although frequently with a return to a larger display script and more expansive format).

Certainly, Horn's work implies that 'big book' production (although not in English) was scarcely foreign to the London book-trade. There are several ways in which this legal background can suggest that Auchinleck is not quite such an outré or overwhelming proceeding as has often been assumed. There is a consensus that this manuscript was not produced as a piece, but in twelve definable booklets or fascicles, independent units, many of them substantial and the work of five or six scribes (Bliss; *Auchinleck Manuscript* xii–xiii and ix; Robinson 1972, 120–38). Thus, there is no necessary connection between the bound order of the book we have – this was imposed on the booklets at the end of the procedure – and the various stages of its production.

Study of Auchinleck has generally sought to accommodate the book to some kind of production pattern familiar from other specifically literary work. Laura H. Loomis (whose extensive discussions of the manuscript have often been read as if they were *The Sun* – for the flashy bits and page 3) saw clearly the cooperative nature of the enterprise. For her, this could only mean that the book emerged from a laicised operation modelled on a monastic scriptorium (esp. 150–87, a view followed by Mordkoff). On the other hand, Pearsall, in the facsimile (viii–ix), and implicitly Robinson look to later models, forms of fifteenth-century book-production in which shared scribal work enables production economies. Dividing copy among a group of individuals allows the relatively prompt production of an extensive volume.

I think the evidence of the manuscript resistant to either view. First, it is difficult to see Auchinleck as anything other than a book prepared by the individual usually designated as its scribe 1. He copied something in the order of four times as much as the other four scribes with whom he shares work combined, and, as Timothy Shonk, in the finest single study of the manuscript, insists, he provided every catchword at a booklet boundary, as well as every surviving text title but one and all the numeration assigned to texts. Further, quite unusually for a book so large, where texts allowed it, every other scribe set out to imitate his ruling system and his double column format, as I have already suggested a feature closely resembling Horn's books.

Moreover, the scribal stints are conducive to viewing Auchinleck in this way. With the exception of the very interesting scribe 3, who originally copied the complete booklet 3, forty-three folios (three at the end left blank, eight now lost), the subsidiary scribes copied only full single texts in isolated sections of the manuscript. Particularly when the extent of scribe 1's copying is taken into account, the volume looks very much like a normal English book, if a very large one, a single practitioner volume with ad lib piecework. Like Ringo, scribe 1 called in his friends when the going got tough. The booklets then are probably not, as in fifteenth-century work, simultaneous in origin, a production economy, but largely the sequential efforts of a single individual.

Moreover, booklet structure supports such a view. Auchinleck is a great collection of romances, long narrative poems. Not altogether predictably, however, the booklet division reflects these separate big-ticket items. They most usually stand at the head of the runs of quires constituting individual booklets. (Booklet 1 is miscellaneous but also survives only from at best, its mid second quire on; in scribe 3's Booklet 3, the larger items are buried.) And concomitantly, the booklets conclude with fairly blatant filler, short texts written in to fill blank leaves at the ends of sections and create a sense of continuity. This tailoring, most of it by scribe 1 again, does not succeed in producing a thoroughly continuous manuscript.[46]

Such features invite speculation about the situation of production. At this date, the book must have been 'bespoke', a client's special order. The separable production may suggest that this was an order that, in some sense, got out of hand, that scribe 1 was provided with a succession of requested items ('Give me a *Beves*', 'This week I was thinking about *Richard Coer de Lion*') from someone perhaps imperious but certainly wealthy and enthusiastic. Hence the prevalence of top-heavy booklets: scribe 1 got started on the major texts his client requested.

But the central Auchinleck copyist may have differed in one important respect from Andrew Horn, who will have been able to provide his scribes continuous access to personal volumes and Guildhall materials. He may have had to fulfil a limited number of his client's orders simultaneously and as exemplars for copying came available, and in those situations he may simply have had to rely upon piecework contributions from colleagues. For (hypothetical) example, he might have acquired on short-term loan an exemplar for *Beves of Hamtoun* (copied by scribe 5 into the first third of what would, with scribe 1's additions and finishing, eventually become Booklet 5) at a moment when his client was clamouring for a look at *Kyng Alisaunder*, now the very fragmentary Booklet 8 but in any event at least a forty-folio stint (? two weeks' work) in its own right. As this narrative implies, I would not preclude the possibility that, perhaps even on multiple occasions at various stages of production, portions of the book may have passed from scribe 1, not just to the illuminator (which we would expect), but to the client for his or her use – and some disturbances in the system of numbering texts may imply that the scribe performed this task at a time when portions of the volume were unavailable to him.

There are certainly analogies for this kind of behaviour in early legal manuscripts. Huntington HM 25782, the early copy of the Statutes described by Galbraith, forms a legitimately 'loose-leaf' collection of contents. The volume looks as if quite possibly undertaken without a clear sense of what the assembly would eventually include, and with ample room left for additions. It has six booklets, with a separate one for the chapter table of the Statutes (the boundaries most easily discernible by conjoining Galbraith's discussion 180 and Dutschke's description 640–2).

This structure could be taken to forecast production behaviours something like those visible in Auchinleck. Significant large items, in HM 25782 often marked with marginal finding tabs (Galbraith 177), appear at the openings of booklets, and the miscellanea then completely fill in the blank leaves left at their ends. Quire 1 of the Huntington MS provides an apt example, its main contents a single item, the Runnymede charter, followed by two additions of a single leaf each, 'exposiciones verborum', a lexicon of Anglo-Saxon legal terms with Anglo-Norman equivalents, and the 'Assise of weights and measures'.

One of Andrew Horn's books, again a contemporary legal manuscript, offers equally suggestive analogues for the production procedures visible in Auchinleck. This is Corpus Christi College, MS 70, 'de veteribus legibus Anglie' (described James 1909–12, 1, 148–9). Horn here was having produced, not a one-off, free choice collection of recent romances, but *Quadripartitus* book 1, a fixed sequence of legal codes which had had some textual integrity for over a century. As I have implied above, this book may come from an early stage in Horn's book experiences; it was a private copy, made for his own consultation (and thus appears in his will). Moreover, he seems to have undertaken the production in a private fashion, not working from the formal full Guildhall text of Rylands + Additional 14252, but by gathering the constituent segments of the text from separate sources. Horn will certainly have had a clear enough sense of the general overall content (provided either by a list of kings or of existing royal codes). But the scribe who was producing his book, analogous to Auchinleck scribe 1, was clearly amassing the codex on a piecework basis.

The book, 98 folios, is in the main, the work of this single scribe. Certainly Horn's close acquaintance/regular employee, he is responsible for a second Horn book, the unique Anglo-Norman *Mirror of Justices* at Cambridge, Corpus Christi College MS 258, fols. 1–52 (the identification of the hands first made Catto 372–3). Originally, this was the second portion of a single volume with MS 70; Horn's will mentions these as a single book. But within two quires of Corpus 70 (the fifth and sixth), pages 75–105, this writer gave over *most* (not the last two pages or so) of a single text, 'Glanvill', to another scribe. The exchange, like those in Auchinleck, is textbound, not geared to a production unit; scribe 2 writes only within the two quires, and scribe 1's texts run continuously across quire boundaries before and after his companion's stint. While scribe 2 was engaged in this task, scribe 1 obviously was up to something else, one would presume copying his other text, the *Mirror*, as a separate book for later inclusion in the composite volume.

Moreover, Corpus 70, like Auchinleck, was certainly being stitched together in process. The quire where scribe 2 begins copying contains twelve leaves, as do all those in the remainder (the final quire is a three-leaf add-on), but this is preceded by four units, none of twelve leaves, indeed all unique in the number of leaves each contains, and divided among at least two booklets. This particularly raggedy production may have been driven by a feature absent from Auchinleck, in regular quires of eight – the pressure of chronology and the need to present codes in historical order. Setting quire length to correspond roughly with available copy would have ensured that the scribe might easily work currently absent pieces of the text into proper chronological sequence without having to resort to emergency measures (inserted leaves, for example).

Moreover, decisions about contents and presentation were being made *ad hoc*, during the production of Corpus Christi 70. Typically, the codes of individual monarchs, written in long lines, are preceded, within the text sequence, by double column tables of contents. However, that for William the Bastard's confirmation of the laws of the Confessor was added later on the still blank, booklet-ending page 52, analogous to scribe 1's provision of quire-ending fillers. Further, at the time of the addition, as a note on page 52 indicates, the subsequent quire to which the table referred was not to hand.

One more similar example (of several): at the end of the book, as I have already indicated, scribe 1 copied a table of contents for the voluminous legislation of Edward I. But Horn himself added a note in essence cancelling the text, saying that it is in another book, i.e. the current 'Liber Horn', fols. 36ff., and that he intends to have it copied into the 'magnum codicem' discussed above. Certainly, by the time Horn got round to having 'Liber custumarum' produced, he was vastly more aware of the difficulties involved in collecting and organising his materials, and he had access to Guildhall books where some of the work had already been done for him. In contrast, Auchinleck, unique in its extent and variousness among all medieval romance manuscripts, monumentalises such a fits and starts mode of production. Horn's note implies that his book ultimately was a fortuitous conjunction of materials originally intended for dispersed use, and one might suggest that this argument be extended to the romance codex as well.

If the mode of producing Auchinleck recalls and resembles the behaviours of legal book-producers, there are yet closer connections to be drawn between this manuscript and Horn's books. For Auchinleck includes more than the border-work that often adorns the opening leaves of vernacular books. The manuscript passed through the hands of a full-fledged illuminator – whose efforts have been generally ignored and unduly trashed. First of all, it's striking that the book has any illumination at all (Chaucer and Langland manuscripts don't, as a rule); second, how much there was of it – five miniatures survive, thirteen more have been cut out (leaving holes in the leaves, now patched), and eighteen leaves with text openings, places where one might have expected a painting, have been excised (Cunningham, in the facsimile xv).

The Auchinleck illuminator may be placed among 'the largest group of stylistically related English manuscripts of the early 14th century' (Sandler 1986, 2, 65). These limning hands are also responsible for the decoration of Horn's 'Liber custumarum'. They appear in something approaching twenty-five manuscripts total, all inferentially London products of the period *c.* 1310–35 and customarily known, after one of their grandest productions, British Library, MS Royal 2 B.vii, as 'the Queen Mary Psalter Group'.[47]

However, placement of the Auchinleck illuminator within this congeries remains somewhat problematic. Lynda Dennison has argued, for example, that the 'group' in fact represents the work of two separate teams, their contributions sometimes overlapping. In her account (1990), the Auchinleck painter is closely related to a probably peripatetic atélier, in origin East Anglian but resident in London for a substantial part of the 1320s. Some of the same hands, she argues, provided decoration both in Auchinleck and in Horn's 'Liber custumarum'. While the East Anglian chaps were engaged in work for Horn, *c.* 1321–25, Dennison believes (1986, esp. 304–5), the hands responsible for 'The Queen Mary Psalter' were illuminating what would eventually be extended into another early London English book, the *Somme le roi* originally the sole text in Cambridge, St John's College, MS 256.

However, this is not the only possible identification of the Auchinleck illuminator that has been advanced. Jonathan Alexander thought the artist identical with the hand of Paris, Bibliothèque nationale, MS fr. 13342 (Sandler 1986, 2, no. 58). He knew the book, a small devotional volume, nearly all the contents basic Anglo-Norman instructional materials, from Francis Wormald's profusely illustrated study.[48] Alexander was perhaps drawn to the identification because of similar compositional techniques in the two books, a tendency towards rows of figures within often strip-like rectilinear frames. While he has never published this opinion, Alexander passed it on to Pamela Robinson in conversation (see 1972, 135). Confusingly, Dennison (1986, 305) takes the hand of the Paris MS as representative of her central 'Queen Mary Group', not the dispersed one she would identify with Auchinleck; she dates the work to the mid-1320s.

These contradictory citings imply, I would think, that the conception 'Queen Mary Group' may require an interrogation that it has not
heretofore received. Specifically, difficulties of assignment seem to derive from a notion that one might consider the hands representative of
some 'atélier' system, a fixed group of artists working in concert. But
the expansive and shifting connections apparent in discussions might
better be explained by considering the books as dispersed piecework
among whatever hands happened to be available and capable of specific
tasks. One way forward could involve the very careful teasing out of
hands against production units of the various books, including very
small units like bifolia, similar to that analysis James provides (xxi–xxiv)
in discussing the contemporary Walter de Milemete illuminators (see
further pp. 122–4). But in any event, such an hypothesis would indicate
that contemporary London painters were engaged in production procedures like those I have argued are instantiated, not simply in Horn's
books, but in Auchinleck itself.[49]

In any case, however 'the Queen Mary Group' is conceived, the
Auchinleck team and Andrew Horn share access to the same cadre of
artists. Further, the content and provenance information one can glean
from materials the group produced implies their versatility at handling
a wide range of texts for a variety of purposes and audiences. Although
service books of one sort or another predominate (twelve of them), there
are equally seven devotional books (all but one in French, three of these
examples of the popular illustrated Apocalypse I will discuss at greater
length in chapter 4), and two lawbooks, in addition to those decorated
for Horn. At the learned end of the spectrum, the group also illustrated
an imported Latin Aristotle and a French translation of Giles of Rome's
handbook for princes.

The Queen Mary combine also appealed to a wide-ranging cast of
top-end patrons. One very small Psalter (Sandler 1986, 2, no. 74) was
executed for Edward III and queen Philippa c. 1328, and the French
Giles, as the next chapter will imply, might reflect a similarly courtly
context. Most Queen Mary items with discernible original patrons, five
in all, represent commissions for a range of dispersed religious houses, in
the main near southern or south-eastern (but one book, Sandler 1986, 2,
no. 69, so far away as Bangor Cathedral in North Wales); the Aristotle
is apt also to have been executed for a cleric, someone like a St Paul's

canon, for example.⁵⁰ (The ability to track these may only testify to clerical fastidiousness in marking their libraries.) Certainly, the two law books, like 'Liber custumarum', probably went to wealthy lawyers, men with careers and interests like Andrew Horn's, and the French devotional works to similarly prosperous lay people. They need not have been City dwellers, since three Psalters with illumination by the group show early signs of ownership by East Anglian gentry. But a list of patrons like these will imply the kind of range in which one might seek the person responsible for commissioning the Auchinleck MS.

Here again, one should stress the specifically legal, and perhaps specifically Horn/City context. The decorative programmes of Auchinleck and 'Liber custumarum' share features not the property of the greater run of 'Queen Mary' products, e.g. Psalters or Apocalypses. Painting in Horn's books appears most prominently in illustrations of kings in attitudes of authority or judgement, affixed to the heads of their legal acta. This is a presentation exactly analogous, so far as one can tell, to that of Auchinleck, where painting occurs at the heads of individual romances, depictions of the heroes in action (e.g., Reinbrun at fol. 167rb or the historiated initial with Beves at fol. 167ra; cf. also chapter 3, n. 21). At least in this kind of programme, models developed for the presentation of legal books (also evident in illustrated Statute MSS) have been transferred into a different context, that of romance.

Yet the ease of this transfer had already been facilitated by a prominent 'romance' strain already existing in Horn's, and other, legal work. One of the Chamberlain's sources will provide an initial example of this tendency. Just as he later accessioned Guildhall copies of Statutes to verify and correct his texts, Horn checked Corpus Christi 70 against yet another, non-Guildhall copy of *Quadripartitus*. This book, now British Library, MS Cotton Titus A.xxvii, contemporary with the Rylands + Additional volume at the Guildhall, was probably produced at St Augustine's abbey, Canterbury; it was certainly in its library in the late fifteenth century (James 1921, 1, 269–70; Ker 1985, 134 and MLGB 43; Catto 380; Patrick Wormald 1994, 121). Horn's marginalia in the Corpus MS, reminders for him to check the volume, refer to it as 'Liber Alex', a provocative signal of its mainly non-legal contents (Crick 156–8):

Geoffrey of Monmouth, *Historia regum*, with an excerpt from 'Nennius', *Historia Brittonum*, ed. Dumville 102–3; *Quadripartitus* (fols. 89–174^v; its differing order of contents indicated, Wormald 1999, 240–1 as T); Marbod of Rheims, *De lapidibus*; 'Prester John's letter (composed *c.* 1165; see Hamilton); a second excerpt from 'Nennius', ed. Dumville 103–5; Julius Valerius, *Res gestæ Alexandri magni*, with the letter of Alexander to Aristotle ('the Wonders of the East') and epitaphs of Alexander (see Hill 1975).

Horn's mode of referring to this volume suggests that it may in the fourteenth century have been bound in an order different from that one finds in the Canterbury catalogue of s. xv ex.[51]

Patrick Wormald (1999, 238) rather contemptuously dismisses the Titus MS's contextualisation of the legal materials as 'pseudo-historical marvels' (cf. Dumville 101 'various other romantic, pseudo-historical material'). While this categorisation of the works accompanying *Quadripartitus* here may be correct, the rejection strikes me as over-hasty. In fact, as I have tried to demonstrate at length, legal copying represents the construction of an historical record, and it should not be surprising, in the light of Thedmar's 'Liber de antiquis legibus', to find the two genres together.

Further, Wormald and Dumville's conception of 'true history', while it answers modern professional categories, certainly is non-responsive to medieval concerns. After all, among the soberer texts of Cotton Titus A.xxvii are an Alexander and a copy of Geoffrey of Monmouth. The former is one retelling of a narrative also appearing in a justly praised romance in Auchinleck, the version there derived from a different but equally historical authority, the *Historia de preliis* (see further pp. 105, 116–18). Geoffrey, whatever one may think of him as propagator of Brutus, the pre-Roman founder of Britain, is certainly most noteworthy for inspiring the late twelfth-century effusion of vernacular Arthurian romance. The boundaries of usable history in the early fourteenth century were certainly capacious enough to contain 'the romantic', just as in Auchinleck, romance appears with chronicle and complaint over contemporary legal abuse.

Examples of such juxtapositions occur a great deal more frequently than one might initially suspect; I limit myself to sketching out three instances. I have earlier (p. 47) mentioned Matthew Cheker and the three *Statuta* he owned in 1294. Of his remaining books, most were legal (including, in 26 loose quires, the Anglo-Norman 'Breton', *De legibus Anglie*, a Bracton derivative also transmitted in Horn's Corpus Christi 258). But Cheker also had 'quedam Summa de Alconomia et eciam vnum volumen in quo continentur duo libri qui vocantur Tobye et Poytrie' and 'Vnum Romaunz' (Whitwell 399–400). Whatever the last might have been, Cheker's interests extended to the literary, since the penultimate volume must include two works of Matthew of Vendôme, *Tobias* and *Ars versificatoria*, versified Bible and a rhetorical handbook, respectively (and both texts later used by Langland).

A booklet manuscript Robinson describes (1969), Bodleian Library, MSS Douce 132 + 137, shows a similar tendency. The three booklets that now form the latter shelfmark are completely composed of legal materials (see p. 47), but the portion now Douce 132 has eighty-two folios containing the romance *Horn* and three further Anglo-Norman imaginative texts: Robert Grosseteste's popular instructional poem *Le Château d'amour*, Marie de France's *Fables*, and Guillaume le Clerc's *Bestiary* (Dean nos. 151, 622, 179, and 702, respectively). Moreover, the two portions were indexed together by the owner *c.* 1270 (Robinson 1969, 61–2, with plate 7, a facsimile of the index leaf). Such mixed use of the volume continued; a late fourteenth-century owner reminded himself, in a list on a flyleaf, of books he had loaned others, a further melange of legal and imaginative texts, including three extensive romances (see Robinson 1969, 66).

Finally, one can adduce an example provided by Clanchy (1979, 112–13). He describes a roll (once owned by Joseph Mayer of Liverpool), a form in England with strong legal associations. On one side, it bears a history of England, in this form typically presented as a model of legal, genealogical succession, that property in the kingdom enforced by primogeniture. On the dorse is a copy of the romance 'Amadas and Ydoine' (see Dean no. 161).

Lest one think these random gestures or chance collocations, I return to the prologues that, as I have mentioned, appear attached to various forms of 'the London collection'. When Andrew Horn went looking at the concluding work of the original scribe in Additional 14252, he found materials that he sought to emulate in his own 'Liber custumarum'. Sandwiched around the London documents I have already discussed (fols. 98–100ᵛ) are two additional texts, the first of these (fols. 92–97ᵛ) Prester John's letter, that same text that appears in the Canterbury *Quadripartitus* Horn consulted.⁵² In the context of Cotton Titus A.xxvii, one could just about read this as a piece of 'orientalia', since the wonders of John's kingdom have in fact been derived from the surrounding texts, the Alexander materials and Marbod's lapidary. Moreover, all three texts are generically similar; John's epistle, an oriental potentate's inquiry allegedly sent to a Byzantine emperor, absorbs the marvels of Alexander's letter sent to the learned Aristotle, and Marbod 'authenticates' his lapidary as a text the learned Evax, king of Arabia, sent to Nero (cf. Nowell 435–6).

But surely, the recurrence of Prester John with legal materials in Additional 14252 implies that, in the thirteenth century, one could also read the Titus MS retrospectively. In so doing, one could put the epistle into the context of the legal text earlier in the book. A reading like this allows John to be perceived as a prologue analogous to that provided in *Quadripartitus* by 'The Burghal Hidage', as another piece of 'visionary legalism'. While John's letter surely appeals as a description of opulence and wonder, a Utopic neverneverland of the East, the text is pre-eminently a *descriptio terre*, an outline account of an extensive jurisdiction characterised by plenitude (including a richness with distinctly mercantile appeal) and that goal of all law, harmonious peace.⁵³

John's tone oscillates between a rhetoric almost Herodian in its arrogance ('dominus sum dominantium' par. 9, 910) and pious content. Perhaps nowhere is this more striking than in the statement of his priestly title: 'For this reason, Our Sublimity may not allow itself to be called anything more noble than a name befitting priesthood'.⁵⁴ Indeed, John's power depends upon his status as priestly potentate, ceaselessly served by pontiffs. The sources of his jurisdiction, embodied in his two palaces (pars 56–96, 917–22), draw attention to a double succession and basis for law, apostolic and patrilinear, St Thomas of India and John's father Quasideus (!). Moreover, Marbod's lapidary is scarcely appropriated here innocently, but underscores flagrant allusions to John's palaces as the New Jerusalem (nine stones from Apoc. 21 get a reprise). These gems are closely associated with the stairs ascending to one vehicle of John's wise lordship, his magic mirror (par. 71), an emblem of the monarch's prudential foresight and, not so obviously, humble self-analysis.

The most recent discussions (Hamilton, not to mention Umberto Eco's *Baudolino*) place John's letter as a visionary intervention in a long-running legal and jurisdictional dispute, between pope and emperor. But it might equally be perceived as visionary troping upon particularly local, English/London issues. John, an imperial king amidst Saracen lands, promises his participation in a Crusade (par. 11, 910); he thus might remind one of England's heroic Richard I. Again, in his piously visionary activities, he might be perceived as incarnation of the saintly Confessor, source of the Good Old Law. And, although with a royalist inflection, his priestlyness and the loyal priestly service he receives might suggest relationships compensating for failures in recent English history, the confrontation between Becket and Henry II. Beyond these more precise national allusions, the descriptive language of the epistle will resonate with persistent efforts to associate London with the heavenly City of the Apocalypse.

The second text juxtaposed with London regulations in Additional 14252 (fols. 101–4^v) is scarcely so exotic. It is composed of excerpts from Henry of Huntingdon in Anglo-Norman translation; at the conclusion, these are presented as if a prologue to a more extensive collection of London materials, 'Now we wish to show you part of the laws and freedoms of the City of London'.[55] Clerical, universalist Latin of the epistle is superseded by localism, a Latin text accommodated to the language of the surrounding legal texts.

Henry of Huntingdon certainly represents an updated version of the *Quadripartitus* prologue, 'The Burghal Hidage'. Avowedly foundational, this brief treatise 'de situ et habitu Britannie' (1.9, 24) quotes, with a little fleshing out from 'Nennius', nearly the entire first chapter of the authoritative statement of English identity and right, Bede's *Historia*. But it intrudes its own significant localising materials, an account of the heptarchy accompanied by a simultaneous listing of the shires and bishoprics of England, royal and ecclesiastical jurisdictions identified in parallel, within the history that founds them (1.4–5, 17–19). Equally, Henry's description vacillates between the fantastic and historical appropriation of the soberly legal: folkloristic enumerations of 'the five plagues' and 'four marvels' of Britain (1.4, 7; 14, 22) on the one hand, but the four 'royal roads' of England a citation of *Quadripartitus* codes (see 24 n. 35).

Horn's 'Liber custumarum', at the head of his London materials ('Custumarum', fols. ii, 1–11), repeats and modernises these gestures towards identifying jurisdictional foundation and succession. Horn here presents in order the Anglo-Norman selection from Henry of Huntingdon; William FitzStephen's 'Descriptio nobilissimæ civitatis Londoniæ', still viewed as foundational by Stow, who provides the text as an appendix to his *Survey* (2, 219–29); and an excerpt, typically described as an idealised description of communal government, from Brunetto Latini's French *Trésor* (the latter two selections *Munimenta* 1–25).[56]

One should interpret this material as, again, indulgence in the imaginary landscape that defines succession and jurisdiction. As Scattergood (1995) ably demonstrates, FitzStephen provides, not an historical document, but a Latin school exercise, a rhetorical 'descriptio urbis'. (One could, in this context, recall Matthew Cheker as reader of learned poetry, including a rhetorical handbook.) FitzStephen wrote the passage in his office as courtly rhetorician, as 'dictator episcopi'. But it is more important to see how, contextually, his effort situates the locality, the jurisdiction of London, within England, Henry of Huntingdon's subject. For Horn might be seen as using FitzStephen precisely because of the latter's office and the context in which he produced this text, and using him in ways that resituate Prester John materials. FitzStephen did not write his encomium in a vacuum but as a praise prologue attached to the life of a local hero, 'Thomas of London' – the *episcopus* he had served, Becket.

Although Erkenwald may occupy the local shrine site (as the Confessor does that of the church of St Peter in Westminster), Becket, born in Cheapside, is the London saint. His image, along with Paul's, appears on the thirteenth-century seals of the City, with their own forms of local 'descriptio', geographical panoramas. These, of course, are legal implements, used to identify documents approved by the City, but the earliest example (?1219) also bears the intercessory legend, 'Thomas, do not cease protecting me who gave thee birth' (*Age* nos. 193–95, 273–4). If 'Prester John' imagines bishops as humble servitors to sacral royalty, FitzStephen might be seen as an inscription of sanctified resistance and local independence.

The Brunetto materials are rhetorically very much of a piece with FitzStephen.[57] The description, actually that of an Italian podestà, instructively the external man of dignity brought in to govern a squabbling commune, forms the climax of Brunetto's encyclopaedic instruction. But he imagines his trained governor as a man constructed by rhetorical/dictaminal culture, precisely the sort of training FitzStephen, Becket, and Cheker represent. Precept here is heavily textualised by classical citation (Seneca, Cicero, and always implicitly, Aristotelian moderation). Strikingly in Horn's account, various features of the Italian city-state carry over pretty much intact; government proceeds according to the City constitutions alone (two references 21), without recourse to external authority, and 'le meire ou le governour', although expected to be moderate, governs without visible restraint, as if a king (cf. the unpacking of Thedmar's metaphor, that the Mayor should be 'the healthy head of the citizens', 'seyne teste [des cyteyns]', or the juxtaposition of governour and king in chapters 7 and 8).

London legal prologues thus imply that, while specific regulation may be important, imaginative citation/situation of legal thought is equally so. The Titus A.xxvii contextualisation of *Quadripartitus* and the provision of Prester John as an originary legal description further imply that legal imagining is not considered limited by the plausible or the veridically historical. Indeed, gestures of this sort are not restricted to documents that seek to situate law, but occur quite constantly in tiny details of the regulatory record itself. For example, the London interpolations into the early twelfth-century confection 'Leges Edwardi Confessoris' (see Patrick Wormald 1999, 409–11) attribute one regulation to King Arthur (32 A 7, *Gesetze* 1, 655; cf. Muir; Horn paraphrases it for posterity at *Munimenta* 636). A further statute in this portion states that London

> was long ago founded and built in the image and manner and in memory of the old Great Troy; and even today, it preserves the laws and codes, dignities, liberties, and princely customs of the ancient Great Troy.[58]

The physical form of the City, that inscribed on its seal, an object for legal use, models preserved succession, a memorial of origins; the law of the place, analogously, an appropriately written memorial. This passage presumably inspired part of FitzStephen's rhetorical description (108) and itself relies upon the historical record – Geoffrey of Monmouth 1.17–18. Ancient liberties and proper successions, indeed (cf. John Clark).[59]

But such 'situation', citation as siting, jurisdictional identification, bridges the historical, the imaginative, and the legal. The charge of such 'romance' analysis has always been laid against *The Mirror of Justices*, a work scarcely alien to Horn's interests, since the unique copy appears in his Corpus Christi 258.[60] This satire on the highhandedness and abuses of early Edwardian statute and royal justices initially (prologue and 1.1–3) argues for a return to 'ancient usages', but only insofar as these are specifically sanctioned in named biblical texts. And it does not seek a return to the most ancient British custom, but only 'puis le temps le Roi Arthur' (3).

The author has read and internalised the Alfredian code I cited in my prequel (p. xii) and finds in it the true onset of Law (15). Thus, his foundation cannot be legendary Britain, as I will indicate, dear to the king whose abuses he is attacking; the author describes British warriors as men of mere force, fortunately succeeded by right-loving Saxons 'more humble and simple than the peoples of all the surrounding lands' ('plus humbles e simples de tuz pais joygnauntz', 6). In the prologue to the climactic book 5 (outlining abuses, marked by a protracted and hysterically funny catalogue of Alfred's violent punishment of false justices, abuse no. 108, 166–71), the author identifies Law, not with royal initiative, but with a regular parliament operating by common consent and publishing written law (155–6). The legal teachings 'documented' in the book, although as usual said to be from ancient royal rolls (1.1, 2), are thoroughly imaginative, fictionalised legal history, presented in the interests of reform. The ancient practices that must be imagined to have existed (or that should have) would re-create England as promised land or New Jerusalem. One can see, easily enough, why such a work would have appealed to Horn, collector of local statute and custom as a guard against royal incursion.

Moreover, considering law in terms of 'romance history' cannot be construed as simply a literary device. Although prominent in London record from the early thirteenth century, it also functioned as a stark and widely shared aspect of British public policy, apparent in documents associated with The Great Cause, the issue of the lordship of Scotland. In 1301, Edward I was more or less forced into presenting to Boniface VIII a statement of his rights to the lordship. The historical record shows that he sought information to buttress this claim for something approaching a decade, in the main by requesting from various monasteries relevant evidence from their chronicles. (Horn was scarcely unique in his search for legal precedents and historical documentary evidences that would confirm the right to a jurisdiction in which he was interested.) Ultimately, *c.* 1297, the royal notary John of Caen wrote up, another act of legal textual memory like Horn's, the results of these inquiries on his 'Great Roll' (the original ed. Rymer 1, 2, 762–84). This material, an historical survey of the English claim to the lordship beginning in a securely distant Anglo-Saxon past with Edward the Elder, more pre-Conquest continuities, became the centre of Edward's response (*Anglo-Scottish* 96–109; on the process of assembling materials, see Stones).[61]

But preceding this demonstration, Edward's clerks wrote into his Latin letter responding to the pope a variety of earlier precedents. The materials were interpolated into the document at the head of John of Caen's account, and the Anglo-Norman draft for the intrusion still survives (PRO, MS Scottish Documents, Exchequer, E 39/1/18). These additions begin with Brut's invasion (including notice that 'he built the city he named Troynovaunt that is now called London', 'edificavit civitatem quam Trinovantum nuncupavit que modo Londonia nominatur', 97) and pass on to his division of the kingdom between his three sons, with the Scottish Albanactus subject to the supreme English Locrinus. And after other ancient precedents, Edward's letter continues:

> Also the most famous prince Arthur, king of the Britons, conquered Scotland, then rebelling against him, and destroyed nearly the entire people and later put a certain Anguselus in charge of that kingdom. Afterwards, when king Arthur held a most famous feast in the City of the Legions, all his tributary kings were present, among them Anguselus. He, performing due service in return for his kingdom, carried king Arthur's sword before him, and, in succession, all kings of Scotland have been subject to all kings of the Britons.[62]

The Brut material recalls the laws of the Confessor, and it will not be surprising that the Arthurian precedent comes from Geoffrey of Monmouth as well – in this case, accurate detail from *Historia* 9.6, 9, 12, and 13 (cf. Prestwich 1988, 492).

Although Edward's efforts certainly fall under the heading of English imperialism (see most recently Rees Davies), they do not form isolated examples of the appeal to romance-historical precedents in this international legal quarrel. The Scottish response to Edward's case, known from an Anglo-Norman letter sent Edward from an observer at Anagni, relies upon similar romance precedents, just a different narrative.

The Scottish diplomats at Anagni are not uncritical, and they certainly know well enough the fictiveness of Geoffrey of Monmouth: 'The Scots say that in this letter you ground your right in ancient writings that contain many lies and falsehoods'.[63] Yet they simultaneously take Geoffrey seriously as a source, and their reported reply implicitly corrects Edward's misreading of his text by alleging that all Brut's sons had been peers, not one superior to the rest.

But equally, the Scots respond to Edward's contentions with an alternative romance history. They have their own ancestor narrative: 'une femme Scocia par noun, fille Pharaon de Egipte' had occupied Scotland and driven out the Britons, who were then forced to seek Roman aid, losing their own independence (*Anglo-Scottish* 113). And ever since, the argument runs, English lordship had been in abeyance – Arthur's conquest was only temporary – and the English had thereby lost their right to claim sovereignty over the northern nation.

Indeed, from our perspective, the most fantastically inventive portions of the account prove to be the most generative. And certainly, if antiquity of record were to be central to The Cause, the Scots experts thoroughly trumped Edward's monastic librarians. Scota should have precedence over Brut, for at least the Egyptian ancestral story of the Scots is present in the ancient British historian Dumville despises, 'Nennius'. As daughter of the Pharaoh Chencres of Egypt and husband of the Greek exile Gaythelos, first king of Scotland, both exiles from an Egypt devastated by the Exodus (an origin more ancient and wiser than Troy), she appears as ancestrix in John of Fordun's fourteenth-century chronicle (see Walter Bower's fifteenth-century redaction, *Scotichronicon*, 1.9 *et seq.*, 27–9). And the story, as I will argue in a moment, does not end there.

Both sides, after all, put forward their claims on the basis of Horn-like documentary sources. And as the example of Horn's two-year search in

City archives for a document (pp. 59–60) will have indicated, absence of documents is tantamount to the destruction of right, however ancient. In this regard, Edward demonstrated the killer-touch; in Scotland, as he had done earlier in Wales, he exercised conqueror's 'rights', the new-found 'liberty' of subjection, and in 1296, removed to London chests of documents, as well as treasure (*Anglo-Scottish* 75, mentioned Clanchy 1979, 143). As a result, the Scots explain to the pope their difficulty in presenting their case, in the absence of their muniments (*Anglo-Scottish* 116).

This, of course, represents but one, in this case careful, example of the cultural pillage, historicist trophy-hunting (Roger Loomis's benign 'Arthurian enthusiasm'), in which Edward engaged. His *imperium* would be instantiated by possession or obliteration of any signs of independent nationhood in Great Britain outside England (see, e.g., Prestwich 1988, 120, 203–4, 474). All the London chroniclers notice this activity, perhaps most provocatively the Westminster continuator of the *Flores historiarum*:

> At Caernarfon, they found the body of emperor Maximus, the father of the noble emperor Constantine, and, with the king rejoicing, they set it honourably in the church. The crown of the renowned Arthur, king of the Britons, along with other jewels, were given to the English king. Thus, the glory of the Welsh has, through God's providence, been translated to the English, even though the Welsh have been unwillingly subjected to their laws.[64]

Possession of the tangible historical sign, document or relic, confers one form of legal (?) possession, a mode of extending the site of one's jurisdiction. But the value of the possessed relic is conferred by its documentary authentication (in the case of Maximus, ancient Welsh lore enshrined in the *Mabinogion*). And acquisition of the relic allows subsequent possession and assertion of an anciently confirmed jurisdictional power, in this instance, the construction of Caernarfon Castle, replete with architectural allusions to Constantinople and Rome, a grand, if not very Prester John-like, model of empire (see Prestwich 1988, 120, 214; and, in far greater detail, with attention to analogous earlier efforts in the capital, at Westminster, Binski 1990a, 32; 1995, esp. 93–110). In

sophisticated courtly circles, 'romance history' is again soberly deployed
to demonstrate legal right.[65]

Yet one might equally argue the absolute historicity of such modes.
For 'romance history' was to re-emerge in the same context, the lordship
of Scotland, thirty years down the line, in the 1324 truce negotiations
between the Bruce and Edward II. The detail of these discussions is transmitted in a factually meticulous chronicle, always heralded by modern
historians for its specific and unique information, the *Vita Edwardi
Secundi*. This was written by a sober insider historian, perhaps the magnatial clerk and civil lawyer John Walwayn (Denholm-Young 1956). In
Walwayn's account, the demands under which Bruce was prepared to
pledge a perpetual truce included, *inter alia*, unconditional recognition
of Scottish independence and the return of Edward's greatest trophy,
the Stone of Scone. The latter, Walwayn reports, was important not
simply as the coronation seat which symbolised Scottish kingship (and
ancient, non-Anglophonic tradition):

> Scota, the daughter of Pharaoh, brought this stone with her from
> the faraway Egypt when she arrived in and conquered Scotland. Also
> Moses had prophesied that whoever bore this stone with him would
> subjugate large territories to his dominion. Hence Scotland is called
> that from Scota, just as it was first called Albany from Brut's son
> Albanact.[66]

Edward, of course, rejected these positions and settled for a three-year
truce, not a perpetual peace; not only did he assert Scottish subjection
'ab adventu Britonum', a view Walwayn implicitly endorses by rewriting
the Scots' origin myth to make Scota a successor to Brut's son, but he also
reaffirmed the appropriation of the Stone. In a legalistic throwaway, he
bound himself, as inheritor, to his father's military power (presumably
in the hope it would obscure some of the more obvious and invidious
comparisons):

> It is not fitting for a son to invalidate what his father has decreed.
> I know also that my father, having conquered Scotland, carried off
> that royal stone as a token of his victory. Were I to restore it, I would
> perhaps appear to repudiate that right my father gained like someone
> unworthy as his successor.[67]

Just as Londoners have their perpetual City to defend through the vicissitudes of history, kings (and magnates) have something more personalised, inherited jurisdictional right to a property.

Most arresting in all this repetition is the one 'new' detail Walwayn provides about Scota, the connection of the Stone with Mosaic prophecy. This allusive appeal testifies to further Scottish canniness of a sort comparable to Andrew Horn's *Mirror of Justices*, in its evocation of rights enshrined in a deep history and the unimpeachably veridical text, Scripture. While, from our perspective, the Stone of Scone reflects ancient Celtic custom, it is archaic and pagan custom (although still in use in Ireland as late as 1601; see Nicholls 31–2), but one the Scots recast within sanctified law. Moses is the greatest prophet of The Law (cf. Deut. 34:10–12), and as Alfred acknowledges in citing Exodus 20 at the head of his code, the transmitter of an unquestionably binding Law. Equally, in its very stoniness, the Stone becomes associated with this transmission, the text appearing on 'a patente, a pece of an hard roche' (*Piers Plowman* 17.11). But God's inscription provides Moses a Law prominently associated with territorial aggression, quite specifically attached to a landscape to be conquered (seen by Moses almost as a map in Deut. 34), and uniquely pertaining to that land.[68]

Certainly, for once in his life, Edward showed a little nous at this moment and saw the Scots' prophecy as a serious threat. At the very least, it raised the prospect that the Stone's possessor might raise a legitimate claim to the 'ample terre' of large chunks of northern England. For the Scots, the allusion functioned otherwise, both as measure of antiquity and as a reference to a place in an incontrovertible, divinely sanctioned history, well beyond the reach of Geoffrey of Monmouth.

But most importantly, for Walwayn, who offers no overt comment or refutation of either position, this detail validates the historical importance of the Stone. One aspect of his *Vita* which modern historians do *not* appreciate (but which shows Walwayn as engaged in legal thinking like Andrew Horn's) is his persistent recourse to biblical and romance history. In fact, the chronicle is so scrupulously good a source precisely so that it can reflect, in its detail, divine and other historical writing, both the biblical narrative of Israel and such historically foundational moments as the Trojan War. Walwayn's favoured variety of historical explanation relies upon recourse to biblical moments deemed analogues to the present. Perhaps most striking to a literary scholar would be his criticism of the magnates for pillaging the estates of the banished Despensers in 1321 (115). He then cites, as an analogous bit of rapacity, as does the Westminster king's knight Conscience at *Piers Plowman* 3.259–83, Saul's disastrous acts in 3 Reg. 15. In fact, not just legal precedent (and Walwayn is every bit as apt to assimilate historical event and legal dictum, in any of the three laws, as he is Bible) depends upon the 'romantic', but scholarly historical scrupulousness as well (cf. Thompson 2000, 285–7).

By way of summing up, I cite a non-London author of the mid-fourteenth century. Probably from the North Yorkshire village Carlton Miniott (but see pp. 127 and 259), Laurence Minot concludes one of his poems and introduces another:

> Heres now how þe romance sais
> How Sir Edward oure king with croune
> Held his sege bi nightes and dais
> With his men bifor Calays toune.
> How Edward, als þe romance sais,
> Held his sege bifore Calais
> (edn 27)

Minot describes actual events, here an Edwardian campaign of 1337, and he may well have witnessed this and other events described in his poems. But the claim of personal experience and the reality of the events proves less important to him than ascribing them to written authority. Further, the authority that underwrites Edward III's militarism is not particularly veridical, but instead that discourse identified with heroic imaginative history. Nor is it accidental that Minot reports yet another imperial claim involving recovered rights to territory (and its own literature of historical/legal research and genealogical justification).

Later medieval English history-writing implicitly finds its founding model, not in Bede (whatever the immense respect he is accorded), but in Geoffrey of Monmouth. This, as Minot's example indicates, is not a matter of following Geoffrey in his notorious inventiveness (and imperviousness to fact), so much as one of intruding 'romance' language and analytic method into a narrative of *res gesta* (cf. Gransden 1974b, 186–218; Brandt 81–146). But Geoffrey is scarcely unique in providing such inspiration; as is well known, the nearly contemporaneous (*c.* 1140) originary Romance history of England, Gaimar's *L'Estoire des Engleis*, begins its account with Havelok as historical king of Lindsey (99–816). As Minot would again indicate, however, the evocation of romance in history also includes a veridical standard that romance, strictly speaking, lacks (cf. Damian-Grant, Durling 9–13).

Rather, given that history is always regal (*reges Brittanie*), or at least concerned with magnatial behaviour, romance provides its appropriate rhetoric. It demonstrates the high exemplarity of the events depicted, the capacity to assign panegyric/diatribe valences to secular actions (and can then be used, most typically ironically, in support of the City's anti-royal claims). But this process is surely facilitated by what I have been arguing, the persistent slippage between romance thinking and formulation of legal ideals.

The most basic magnatial activities, the unnarrated assumed of formal romance, all concern The Law. Fundamental to these is the administration of the 'lordship' or 'household' (Holmes 1957; Vance Smith 2003, 1–73). For example, prominent among those qualities Horn derives from Brunetto as identifying an appropriate civic leader are

> the nobility of his court and the virtuous works that he knows should be done in his household and in his other lordships.[69]

As Horn/Brunetto warns emphatically, riches (and concomitant power) are irrelevant qualifications. Rather than mere ownership of an estate, typically agricultural land, freehold (cf. Keene, p. 55 above), appropriate management skills that sustain a unit larger than oneself should be applauded. Law and romance focus upon the same ethos, gaining a heritable locale and exercising jurisdiction within it. Thus, romance language or incident properly underlies the secularised rhetoric of 'good governance', one capable of encroaching upon other discursive sites as an explanatory tool to assess noble action.

Equally, what one might be disposed to see as a 'perturbed boundary' between law, history, and romance might be perceived as doubly osmotic membrane. Not only does romance discourse infiltrate writing veridically historical or substantively legal, but the influence is mutual. Insistence upon the locale, the place where lordship may be exercised, or on the recognisable name, may equally confer the authority of truth or fact upon the fictive. Such a move insists upon the reality of the referent and thus, in a self-fulfilling mode, the successive connection of distanced historical ideal and specific local present, through processes of succession or descent. Moves like these form the mechanics of Norman historiography and the point at which it begins to impose upon romance (see, provocatively, Field).

This discursive acquisitiveness (or openness to appropriation) may explain often-noted features of Middle English romance, and beyond them of Auchinleck texts, to which I now turn. In contrast to John Finlayson's heroic labours at defining the Middle English romance tradition narrowly (for example, 1980–1), one might profitably attend to the expansive fuzzy-edgedness of this discourse. In the next chapter, I will suggest that Auchinleck romance interfaces with a variety of local London concerns, far from all simply 'literary'.

NOTES

1. For facsimiles of the enrolled version, see Skeat 1911 at the end and Palaeographical Society, 1st ser. I, 73; for the copy sent to Oxford, which eliminates a number of southern features felt to be 'Londonisms', Skeat 1880–1, a facsimile as the frontispiece to Ogle. For discussion, see Woodbine 1943, 420–3.

2. For Robert, see Brand 2000, 73–4, citing Treharne 120 n. 1. For the differentiation of script by language, a feature to which I will return in chapter 5, one might compare the Oxford copy, English only, with the more finished script of a contemporary (1257) Latin letter sent to Oxford, in the plate opposite Ogle 8 (likely a different scribe, which may in itself be significant).

3. 'stilo uulgari et uerbis curialibus utens ex industria ad eorum noticiam comparandam eis qui in huiusmodi uulgaritate minus sunt exercitati', Glanvill 3, cited Brand 1999, 54 (an essay with useful further references); cf. the discussion of university civil law techniques in the argumentative form of the text, Glanvill xi, xxviii–xxix, xxxvi–xxxix; Turner 103 *et seq.*

4. See respectively, *Statutes* I, i, 20–41; ii, 1–4, 19–39, 45–50.

5. Holt discusses the earliest politically important Anglo-Norman writing, a translation of Magna Carta, 1219 × 1226; on the language of the law and the persistence of Anglo-Norman, finally banned only in 4 George II, c. 26, see Brand 2000, esp. 64–6. As is well known, London legislation had already pre-empted the statute in the locale; see *Letter-Books* 7, 73 (1361).

6. The literature on Anglo-Norman and competitive linguistic usage in England is, of course, immense. I particularly recommend anything by William Rothwell (as well as Dean's bibliography); Rothwell's work is most impressive in demonstrating past over-estimation of the influence of continental French. See especially 1983, 259, on geographical spread and 1993 on types of usage. Also important are Short and Wright 1996, 2000 (the latter with a full list of publications at 151–2 n. 5).

7. For this last pair, see Brand 1996, lxxxvii–lxci, xci–xcv, respectively. Lansdowne resembles the Huntington MS in being composed of booklets, many now missing.

8. Most of the *Catalogues of Dated and Datable Manuscripts*, which should provide useful materials, have chosen to illustrate 'book-hands' and have excluded *Statuta* as simply documentary records. But see Watson 1984, nos. 556 (*c.* 1293), 22 (*c.* 1297), and 681 (*c.* 1297), plates 140, 144, and 145, respectively (and further, plates 154, 156, 160, 171, 172, 174, 185). Other examples occur in Watson 1979, plate 194; and Robinson 1988, plates 115, 123, and 129 (the first two of Robinson's examples are not *Statutes per se*, but copies of 'Glanvill' with writs; the plates show early examples of legal anglicana, 1261 × 1268, 1281 × 1289, respectively); and Robinson 2003, nos. 109 (1285 × 1292) and 40 (1285 × 1295), plates 33–4. I am very grateful to Pamela Robinson for showing me these, and a number of her other plates, in advance of publication. I should point out that 'X' differs from all those I have cited, as (quite unusually) being written in textura; see Robinson 2003, no. 130 and plate 38.

9. Two texts in the main hand added on fols. 153^v–54 (blank leaves left at the end of a fascicle) treat events of 1297 and 1300.

10. For lists of the large number of manuscripts including such texts, see the editions and Baker–Ringrose 64–5, 65, 64, 78–9, 55–6, 70, 78, respectively; for some idea of standard contents of the volumes, see Baker–Ringrose xxi–xxxii and Skemer 1999, 116–18. Genet emphasises (esp. 25–7) English pragmatic legal thought (and its eventual impact on vernacular authorship), as well as an associated historical exemplarism. For a general appreciation of Bracton, see Plucknett 1958, 42–60.

11. Cf. also Glanvill, in the main a discussion of writs, 12.2, 25 (137, 148), and its citation of the all-purpose 'writ of right/breve de recto', 12.3 (148). The final clause of this writ, 'Et nisi feceris', opens the way for transfer of any relevant case to Common Law/royal courts (see xiii).

12. One might note, as a foretaste of Digby 86, the 'anglicanised' *r*'s, with added descenders, of Cambridge, Gonville and Caius College, MS 234/120 (*Ancrene Riwle*, s. xiii med./xiii$^{3/4}$); see *English Text . . . Gonville*, with facsimile of p. 123 as frontispiece, and N. R. Ker's comments xi–xiii. Malcolm Parkes tells me the feature can also be found in books from the first half of the century.

13. Cf. Plucknett's passing reference (1949, 14) to 'those little manuscript collections of statutes which men carried easily in a pocket in the years around 1300'. In a random half-hour survey from various catalogues, I found fourteen examples with dimensions smaller than 118 mm × 70 mm and an equal number of larger, yet not full-sized, copies, all under 190 mm × 130 mm. For an example, see Clanchy 1979, plate xvi (298–9).

14. It mentions Ralph Hengham as one of the perambulators, a post to which he was demoted from Chief Justice in 1290; see Prestwich 1988, 292–4, 339–42; Brand 1992, 103–12.

15. Cf. 'in former innocent times estates of lands passed safely in few words (for these many entangling clauses are either intended at least to prevent or breed deceit)', John Donne in a letter of 1599 (1).

16. Although victualling always remained a major commercial necessity of towns, 'as a source of urban and mercantile wealth royal and aristocratic spending on textiles, furs, clothing, spices, wine, and other luxuries was more important' (*ibid.* 102); see further Keene 1990, 1999. Cf. also Brooke 30 on urban 'specialization of function' and 'variety of occupation and vocation'; this extends to a functional patterning of the agricultural hinterland necessary to feed the City, discussed Keene 1989, 104–5.

17. Cf. Davis 122–32 on this feature of Norman culture, the effort, already under way in pre-Conquest Normandy, to assimilate an alien past into a pattern of Norman

continuity, a tendency often viewed as germane to the romances to be discussed in the next chapter. See further Aelred of Rievaulx's restatement of such a claim in a different mode in his 'Vita S. Edwardi regis' 771–4, a text whose Anglo-Norman translation I will discuss in chapter 4; or Arnald Thedmar's citing, from Aelred, Edward's dying vision of hoped-for social harmony (edn 205–6, 'Liber de antiquis legibus', fol. 41ᴵᵛ).

18. For descriptions, see James 1921, 265–70; Liebermann, and Bateson. Facsimiles of fols. 3ᵛ–4 appear at Rumble figures 3.5–6 (46, 48).

19. Cf. Veale's findings (1969, 137, 142–3) that the great majority of those attached to guilds in the fur trade, itself a limited and prosperous population sample geared towards providing sumptuous royal/magnatial dress, were apparently not citizens.

20. On the ambivalence of City–Cathedral relations, see Barron 2003.

21. The City here resisted Edward's claim that the accused were his retainers, with whom he would deal, an example of that legal activity known as 'maintenance', reflected much later in the century in Langland's case of Peace v. Wrong, discussed at length pp. 263–72 below.

22. 'ueissele d'or u d'argent del oure salemun v piere preciuse v pailles de Costentinoble v de Renesburgh v cheinsel v walebrun de Maence' (Bateson 499).

23. Cf. Thedmar's account of the Aldermen's refusal in 1249 to be coerced into pleading before the King and outside the City, 'and if they should be required to plead in this cause, they ought to receive no judgement for it in the absence of their peers, namely the earls and barons of England' ('et si debuissent inde placitare, nullum judicium recipere inde deberent in absentia parium suorum, scilicet Comitum, Baronum Anglie', 17). See further Masters 108 for the often-cited example of Mayor Matthew Philip leaving a royal banquet in disgust because not granted precedence over the earl of Leicester (1463/4).

   Civic records persistently refer to another extra-urban right, signalled in Magna Carta's 'liber[e] consuetudin[es] . . . per aquas'. The City's rights extended to a role as 'conservator of the Thames' (as well as the Lea and Medway). For various examples of enforcement, see Thedmar 115–16 (1269), Riley 108 (1313), McDonnell 76–7. On the later institutionalisation of these practices, see Masters 101–3; on the intramural problem of comparable policing of the Fleet, Schofield 1994, 6–7.

24. Notice Horn's precision of reference – the justices were not going to be allowed any excuse for ignorance of the writ: 'in the rolls of the Justiciars for their session in the three weeks of Easter, 9 Edward II, the fifteenth roll' ('in Rotulis Iusticiarorum de tribus septimanis Paschæ, anno Regis Edwardi [II] nono, Rotulo xvᵗᵒ.'). Nor was the City to be forced to search its archives for the single sheet bearing the sealed writ again.

25. See 8 (twice), 10 (twice), 11–12, 13–14, 16–17 (the 1249 example), 21, 23, 34 (and Gwyn Williams 207; Nightingale 1995, 77–8). Although the Westminster Fair was granted, its effect proved vastly less dire than City leaders feared; see Rosser 1989, 97–106.

26. As Walter de Milemete was to counsel the youthful Edward III in 1326; see chapter 6, n. 35.

27. Gwyn Williams 256–68, 310–12; Nightingale 1995, 81–95, 118–23. Cf. Horn's discussions, *Munimenta* 205–11, 338–46.

28. See Nightingale 1995, 125, 152, 157–8, 167, 201, 203, 217–34 *passim*, 254, as well as her 1989 analysis of the effects on urban factionalism after 1377 – as the century wore on, support of closed trading was frequently construed as favouring oligarchic monopolistic practices of the major trade guilds.

29. See Walker and Theilmann; while the Ordinances may have functioned for some as a holy gesture benefiting a restored community, they were for others anathema, and near

the end of the century, Richard II would seek the canonisation of Thomas's tormentor, his great-grandfather.

30. On the onerousness of occasion, see *Munimenta* 381–2, 425, etc.

31. The fine also appears prominently in Thedmar's local history, passages that give some sense of how divisive the issue was, at 79–80 (1265) and 148–9 (1271).

32. A few examples: a letter from Richard of Cornwall (26–9, 1256); the royal and baronial letters before Lewes (63–5, 1263); the charter granted by Henry III in return for payment of the 20,000 *m* fine (80–2, 1265); the charges brought against Walter Harvey (168–70, 1273).

33. 'Gesta et opera bonorum in scriptis reddiguntur, ut ea ad eorum laudem et gloriam perpetuam possint posteris reduci ad memoriam; et ita debent crudelitates, malicie, perfidie, et nequicie iniquiorum in scriptis poni, ut ad eorum dedecus, vituperium, et scandalam ea possint toto mundo futuris temporibus notificari' (114).

34. 'Omnes de Civitate, tam pauperes quam divites, essent quasi corpus unum et vir unus, ad pacem Regis et Civitatis ad fidem suam fideliter observandum' (98–9, 1267).

35. Examples include 34 (1257), 43 (1259), and the ignominious assassination plot Thedmar claims was instigated against him by the evil FitzThomas (114–15, 1268).

36. 'per se fecerunt nova statuta et provisiones, que magis possunt dici abhominationes, et solummmodo ad commodum ipsorum, et ad intollerabilem jacturam omnium mercatorum venientium in Londoniis et in nundinis Anglie, et ad maximum dampnum universorum regni. Et tunc nichil actum fuit sive tractatum de communi utilitate Civitatis neque de augmentatione libertatum ejusdem' (56, 1262).

37. 'sine omni forma rationis ... de populo, filios diversarum matrum, quamplures nato extra Civitatem, et quamplures servilis conditionis' (35–6, 1256).

38. IMEV 322, ed. Brown 1932, 10–13; *Anglo-Norman* I–II, with a reduced facsimile of fols. 160ᵛ–61 as frontispiece; and *Medieval English* III–20.

39. Described MMBL I, 27–34; overall 220 mm × 142 mm, about the size of the Huntington Statutes, a total of 376 folios. On the expansions, see Catto's excellent study 370–1; on the decoration, Dennison 1990.

The book includes a set of *Statutes*, Henry III-Edward II, with 'tracts' (fols. 1–201ᵛ) and a large group of London documents (the remainder). Horn further exemplifies my earlier account of the formation of *Statuta Anglie*, since he found his Statutes in some loose form and subsequently authenticated and corrected a number of them against the sealed royally promulgated copies in the Guildhall (the copies marked as examined 'per ceram' or 'sigillatum per ceram'); see Ker, MMBL I, 28. The very explicit information on the preservation of one item, Ker's 78 (cxviii), 'in the London Guildhall in the second chest in the box/bag marked *T*' ('in Gildaula Lond' in secunda cista in tega cum Litera T', Ker I, 33) recalls both the City's search for its record of the 'explanationes Gloucestriæ' and the possibility of Thedmar using the 'scrinium' as historical source.

40. 'Ista statuta quorum prohemia superius hic intitulantur in libro isto non scribentur nec Registrum, quia *alibi habeo* et quia intendo *ex libro isto et aliis* impostrum deo dante magnum codicem componere, quia utile duxi posteris presentia temporum nostrum exprimere'; cf. Catto 373 n. 2. The book was not stillborn, since two derivative copies of s. xivⁱ/² survive: Corporation Record Office, 'Liber memorandorum'; and Bodleian Library, MS Rawlinson B.356 (cf. Ker, MMBL I, 35); cf. Cannon.

41. 'antiquas consuetudines et libertates in rotulis et libris cameræ civitatis fecit perscrutare et, congregatis sapientioribus, potentioribus, una cum aldermannis, coram eis fecit legi et pupplicari' (175).

42. For facsimiles, see the frontispieces to the two volumes of *Munimenta* and facing 117 ('Liber custumarum', fol. 6; Claudius D.ii, fol. 45ᵛ; and 'Custumarum', fol. 67ᵛ, respectively); Ker 1985, 134 (Oriel 46, fol. 169); Rumble figures 3.7–8 (50, 52; Claudius D.ii, fol. 4ᵛ; and Cambridge, Corpus Christi College, MS 70, p. 4); Robinson 2003, plates 43–4, 47 ('Liber Horn', fol. 5; 'Liber custumarum', fols. 3, 194, respectively).

43. The surviving Claudius MS has undergone a further legal extension, since Robert Cotton bound it up with an alien but relevant text; fols. 139–268 contain the *Vetera Statuta*, an only recently noticed example of work by the London/Duchy of Lancaster scribe Richard Frampton. For him, see Doyle–Parkes 192 (esp. n. 65), 196 n. 82; and Parkes forthcoming.

44. The title reflects an original plan, subsequently abandoned, for a four-book work, rather than the two ultimately produced. See Patrick Wormald 1994; 1999, 236–44, 411–14, 465–73; and Richard Sharpe 151 for dating (the Old English laws perhaps begun before 1100 and completed by 1106, the *Leges* 1108 × 1118).

45. For this model of transmission, see Rumble's analysis of the 'Burghal Hidage', figure 3.1 (37); another parallel line of descent occurs in copies made in Westminster for Exchequer use, s. xiiiᶦ. But the matter is complicated, and may reflect text-by-text decisions. For example, the older Additional MS conflates the two distinct textual traditions of 'Glanvill', while the other Guildhall copies follow the original recension (lv–lvii).

46. Cf. such a sloppy booklet juncture as that at fols. 69ᵛ–70, where the verso is virtually blank, with only six written lines and a catchword.

47. For the twenty central books, see Sandler 1986, 2, 64–82 (nos. 56–75). Her listing does not include Auchinleck, nor several other books potentially identified with the group by other scholars: Bodleian Library, MSS Auct. D.4.14 (Anglo-Norman *Apocalypse*) and Rawlinson C.292 (*Statutes*); Downside Abbey, MS 26533 (Psalter and Hours); and Norwich, Castle Museum, MS 158.926/4d (again *Statutes*). And she rejects (82–3, no. 76) Bodleian Library, MS Canonicus misc. 248 (illustrated computistical tables).

48. The texts are, in order, Dean nos. 632 (an explanation of the Creed in dialogue form), 629 (Edmund Rich, later to be several times translated into English), 722 (an explanation of the Mass), and the Latin abbreviated Psalter ascribed to Jerome (fols. 49–52).

49. And were, of course, still alive for those scribes discussed by Doyle–Parkes, a major point of whose study is to dismiss (correctly, I think) the possibility raised by Laura Loomis, of operative commercial 'scriptoria' in fourteenth- (or indeed early fifteenth-)century London.

50. Plenty of analogous copies of Aristotelian *libri naturales* appear in early fourteenth-century London clerical booklists, e.g. those of Geoffrey de Lawað, Richard de Gravesend, Ralph Baldock, William Tolleshunt, and Steven de Gravesend (see James 1905, 158–9; Cavanaugh 1980, 382–5, 64–9, 872–3, 385–7, respectively). Simon Burley (see p. 14) owned what was probably a French Giles of Rome.

51. See James 1903, 293 (no. 895). The current binding resists examination of the quiring, but as Crick makes clear, the book appears to combine at least four constituent parts, fols. 2–88 (Geoffrey), 89–175 (*Quadripartitus*), 176–81 (Marbod), 182–219 (orientalia, 'Prester John' at the head, Alexander beginning on the sixth leaf, after a blank, possibly suggestive of yet another division). Dumville 102 argues that the 'Nennius' excerpts depend upon a recension uniquely Kentish. Evidence for Horn's consultation of monastic libraries also appears in a booklist probably from the Cluniac priory of Bermondsey; see *Corpus* 4, 28.

52. Not only does Horn imitate the prefatory texts, but he also had recopied into his books some of the London documents here, e.g., the Flemish/Rhineland merchants at *Munimenta* 61–3.

53. Cf. for example, the Langlandian note, 'None among us lies, nor may anyone lie. And if someone begins to lie, he dies at once, that is, we consider him as if dead.... We all follow truth, and we love each other' ('Inter nos nullus mentitur, nec aliquis potest mentiri. Et si quis ibi mentiri coeperit, statim moritur, id est quasi mortuus inter nos reputatur.... Omnes sequimur veritatem et diligimus nos invicem', pars 51–2, 916).

54. 'Quare sublimitas nostra digniori quam presbiteratus nomine nuncupari se non permittat' (par. 97, 923). Cf. the double use of the cross, as threateningly opulent *vexillum belli* and as plain devotional object, associated with others designed to remind John of his mortality, pars. 47–8, 916.

55. 'ore uus uolum demustrer une partie des leis de la cité de Lundres e des franchises' (Bateson 505). The translation includes 1.1–8, edn 10–25. The following London legal materials, some of them printed by Bateson, were added by a second scribe, *c.* 1215 or a little later, and also recycled by Horn.

56. For idealising readings of Brunetto, see Gwyn Williams 196, Sutton 1992 *passim*, Catto.

57. They also need to be seen as carefully edited for the situation, not just a substitution of 'Meire' for Brunetto's 'li sires' (noted *Munimenta* 16 n. 2, but far from consistent). Horn presents as his chs. 1–3, *Tresor* 3.74–75, and ch. 4 = 3.102, ch. 5 = 3.104. 1–2, ch. 6 = 3.97–8, chs. 7–8 = 3.96 (edn 392–5, 420–1, 422, 416–18, 414–16, respectively).

58. 'fundata enim erat olim et edificata ad instar et ad modum et in memoriam ueteris magne Troie; et usque in hodiernum diem leges et iura, dignitates, libertates regiasque consuetudines antique magne Troie in se continet' (32 B 12, *Gesetze* 1, 657).

59. Appreciation of the full weight of the Trojan succession appears to belong after 1380; Auchinleck informatively includes no story of Troy, outside the historical account of 'The Anonymous Short Chronicle' 96–110 (note also the associated Westminster expansions unique to this version A475–82, 1135–1250). Eventually, the origin myth appeared on placards in St Paul's, with Diana's verses to Brut identifying his city as the second Troy (*Chronicle* 177).

60. Cf. Maitland's derision about what he took as non-legal formulations, e.g. 'He is quite able to do his own lying for himself, without any aid from Geoffrey of Monmouth or any other liar', or 'the romancer seems to predominate', *Mirror of Justices* xxvi, xlviii, respectively. See, more helpfully, Seipp.

61. The draft to which I refer in the next paragraph appears in facsimile facing Stones 81. Horn reproduced the entire brief, *Annales Londonienses* 104–27. Further, the Anglo-Norman of the inserted materials is not unique; it also appears in a verse translation, 'Political Letters' (Dean no. 67), perhaps produced by the chronicler of Edward's reign, Pierre Langtoft, an Augustinian canon of Bridlington (East Yks.).

62. 'Item Arturus rex Britonum princeps famosissimus Scociam sibi rebellem subjecit, et pene totam gentem delevit et postea quemdam nomine Anguselum in regem Scocie prefecit et cum postea idem rex Arturus apud civitatem Legionum festum faceret celeberimum, interfuerunt ibidem omnes reges sibi subjecti, inter quos Anguselus rex Scocie, servicium pro regno Scocie exhibens debitum, gladium regis Arturi detulit ante ipsum, et successive omnes reges Scocie omnibus regibus Britonum fuere subjecti' (*Anglo-Scottish* 98).

63. 'dient que en cele lettre vous fondez vostre droit par ancienetez qui contienent diverses fausetez et mensonges' (*Anglo-Scottish* 110).

64. 'Apud Kaernervan, corpus Maximi principis [var. imperatoris], patris imperatoris no-
bilis Constantini, erat inventum, et rege jubente in ecclesie honorifice collocatum.
Corona quondam famosi regis Britonum Arthuri regi Angliæ cum aliis jocalibus red-
debatur. Sic ad Anglicos gloria Wallensium, invite Anglorum legibus subditorum, per
Dei providentiam est translata' (59).

65. Cf. also Bodleian, MS Bodley Rolls 3; see Monroe, with reproductions; *Age* 200–1
(no. 10) and 152–3.

66. 'Scota filia Pharaonis hanc petram secum a finibus Egipti eduxit cum in partes Scotie
applicuit et terram subiugauit. Prophetauerat enim Moises quod qui petram illam
secum afferret amplas terras suo dominio subiugaret. Vnde a Scota est dicta Scotia que
prius ab Albanacto uocabatur Albania' (132).

67. 'Non decet filium irritare quod pater decreuit. Scimus etiam quod pater meus deuicta
Scotia petram illam regalem secum tulit in signum uictorie; quod si restitueremus,
uideremur forsan ius sic adquisitum tanquam degeneres repudiare' (133).

68. Cf. the great refrain of Deut. 4:1 etc., and especially Deut. 27:1–8; or such formulations
of specific precepts as Lev. 14:34, 19:23, 23:10, 25:2, etc. See further chapter 3, n. 17; and
on the Scottish origin myth generally, Broun 11–81.

69. 'la noblesce de soun quer et a ses vertuouses oevres q'il sciet faire en soun hostiel et en
ses autres seignories' (17).

3

Reading romance in London:
The Auchinleck Manuscript and Laud misc. 622

Every scholar who has seriously examined the Auchinleck MS has agreed that it is composed of twelve booklets (for these, see facsimile ix). Although certainly preserved in an intended order, fixed by the consecutively numbered texts, and imposed by scribe 1 at the end of the work, these pieces are almost certainly not preserved in anything like the order of their production (see pp. 75–9). That being said, it is possible to see in the book a somewhat more coherent structure, imposed by scribe 1, than merely the constituent production pieces.

Rather broadly, the book can be divided into three sections (cf. Turville-Petre 1996, 112–13, within an exciting extended discussion 108–41). At the head, Booklet 1 and the first text of Booklet 2 (item 10, the 'Speculum Gy de Warwick') stand apart. These are certainly separate from what follows (indeed, within the manuscript, the 'Speculum' is marked off by a change of scribal hand), and more unremittingly religious in emphasis than anything that will ensue. Moreover, the works are, in the context of this manuscript, unusually brief, and they share a general origin as being imports, not local London work. Analogues to these poems appear almost exclusively in a series of important thirteenth- and early fourteenth-century miscellanies from the Worcester–Hereford area: Bodleian Library, MS Digby 86; Cambridge, Trinity College, MS B.14.39 (323); and British Library, MS Harley 2253, or their later Western derivatives (e.g. the Vernon MS). However, item 13, the final text of Booklet 2, a *South English Legendary* derivative, returns to a Western ambit.[1]

The central core of the book, on which I will concentrate here, comprises the 'Auchinleck romances' that have ensured the fame of the volume. These extend from Booklet 2, item 11 (*Amis and Amiloun*) to item 39 at the end of Booklet 9. This portion includes the 15–17 conventionally designated romance texts, obviously the greater part of the volume. Although I later take up some important qualifications, a substantial amount of this material shows every sign of being local work. G. V. Smithers asserted that some very substantial poems, most in this portion (*Kyng Alisaunder, The Seven Sages, Richard Coer de Lion, Of Arthour and of Merlin*) are of common authorship, and common London authorship.[2] Interestingly, these works, with often substantial and learned historical interests, stand somewhat outside the usual concerns of the manuscript, with its profusion of later day English heroes (*Guy of Warwick, Beves of Hamtoun*, etc.), 'Breton lais' (*Freine, Orfeo*), or Charlemagne materials.

At the end, Booklets 10–12 include what Finlayson (1990) has identified as an 'historical' collection. Perhaps the pre-eminent text of this portion is the opening item 40, a hugely interpolated version of 'The Anonymous Short Chronicle'. Originally another Western text, here it has been deliberately tailored for London use (an episode on the founding of Westminster Abbey, for example), more precisely for London use in this manuscript context (extended Guy of Warwick and Richard Coer de Lion episodes). Its companion piece, with which the book now ends, *The Simonie*, examines the pitfalls of modern history, 'The Evil Conditions under Edward II', as the poem was once known. (In such a context, it interfaces with yet another interpolated episode in 'The Short Chronicle', a discussion of the dungeons of Nottingham Castle, used by Edward III to put an end to that 'evil' historical episode.)

One could, however, see at the boundaries of the last two sections a fuzziness that will recall themes of the last chapter. 'Romance' and 'history' interface and interpenetrate here, and not simply in the chronicle interpolations. Two poems conventionally designated 'romances', *Richard Coer de Lion* and *Horn Child*, follow *The Metrical Chronicle*. And at the end of the large second 'romance' section of Auchinleck, a corresponding blend occurs. The final Booklet 9, with *Tristrem* and *Orfeo*, succeeds the fragmentary *Kyng Alisaunder*, a text translated from a legitimately learned historical account.

Laud 622, now a seventy-two folio fragment, but from the page dimensions clearly once a very large book of which only the conclusion survives, might be perceived as offering an analogous structure of contents. Like Auchinleck (where Booklet 2 ends with a *South English Legendary* text earlier attested in Bodleian Library, MS Laud misc. 108 – and later in the Vernon MS), the surviving Laud 622 begins with three items from the *Legendary*. Inferentially, the compilers of this book also had access to Western sources for textual importation like those available to Auchinleck (this portion of Laud 108 was copied in western Oxfordshire).

The majority of the surviving fragment is filled by two large romances, *Titus and Vespasian* and *Kyng Alisaunder* (here surviving intact, as it does not in Auchinleck). While certainly in the ambit of romance, these display relatively learned historical interests of a sort analogous to those specifically London texts of Auchinleck. The London allusions of Auchinleck find an analogy in Laud 622 as well, in the two short texts intruded between these histories. Adam Davy's prophetic dreams, which must date *c.* 1308 (see Scattergood 1970), almost demand east London associations, since Davy identifies himself as marshal of Stratford-at-Bow, possibly indicating that he was an official of the nunnery of St Leonard's there (cf. Chaucer, 'General Prologue' 125). A life of St Alexius is likely derived from the early Anglo-Norman poem produced in St Albans, another proximate connection. These procedures, the intermixture of City productions with imported materials, will help focus my consideration of the situation in which these books were produced.

II

Carol Meale describes the romances as 'popular', a term she uses to emphasise two features, a later variety of cheap book-production and possibly a mass audience. Certainly the works' transmission histories, extending into the print period with Copeland's chapbooks, would confirm such a view. A quite large group of later manuscripts communicate Auchinleck romances or their congeners (see Thompson 1991), and this popularity did not slacken until well into the sixteenth century.[3]

The nature of such dispersal remains problematic in literary-historical terms, however. Meale's discussion of the transmission, although a fine piece of work, might nonetheless be taken as symptomatic of a persistent category confusion that has often hampered study of these and other romances. Transmission histories inherently attest to the literary value centuries of readers perceived in the poems, but Meale's second sense of 'popular', that the texts eventually appealed to a broad audience, often qualifies this story of continuous enthusiastic readings. Rather than being only demographically descriptive, in critical practice, 'popular' has tended to drag in its train the sense 'unsophisticated'. Because the romances appear verbally flaccid, overly dependent on the set phrase or rhyming tag, they are assumed to be narratively so as well. In a commonly repeated perception, they deserve about as much intellectual attention as fifties Western movies.

But Westerns, at least in the cinematic form epitomised by *Shane* (or the dialogically related *Pale Rider*), instantiate the great American national myth, not so very different from the medieval English legal imaginary. These narratives often describe a frontier, a locale open to be crafted into family properties, perhaps for others, by the typically damaged yet freeborn rambling man, a necessary adjudicator in a world of conflicting legal claims. Analogies to Horn's efforts, as well as the interests of many Auchinleck romances, would not seem far to seek.

The perception of Middle English romance as 'popularly' lacking in sophistication has sanctioned a long history of uninquisitive and unaggressive readings. I find this intriguing, since the 'popular culture' move that would applaud the texts precisely for their absence of high artistic pretension merely ratifies this perception, rhetorically making cultural exclusion into an over-determined alternate value system. Thus, cultural exclusion proves to protect the view of a 'high art' canon. But this move essentially repeats the canonical view:

> [Chaucer's] Rime of Sire Thopas was clearly intended to ridicule the 'palpable-gross' fictions of the common Rimers of that age, and still more, perhaps, the meanness of their language and versification. It is full of phrases taken from *Isumbras, Libeaus desconnus*, and other Romances in the same style.

Thomas Tyrwhitt here (lxvi) only re-presents the fourteenth-century view he purports to be describing critically:

> Men speken of romances of prys,
> Of Horn Child and of Ypotys,
> Of Beves and Sir Gy,

Of Sir Lybeux and Pleyndamour;
But Sir Thopas he bereth the flour
Of roial chivalry.
('Sir Thopas' 897–902)

Such views find their most meticulous discussion in Laura H. Loomis's impressive, if sometimes misdirected, studies of Chaucer's relationship, and possible access, to the Auchinleck MS or a book (or books) resembling it. For Loomis, study of Auchinleck and its texts only ratifies its cultural marginality. Although her provocative views about the composition of some Auchinleck texts have never been fully assessed, she tends to insist that the book was produced by a team of 'hack' or 'scribal' poets in a communal and commercial relationship.[4]

Yet Chaucerian parody, like all parody, depends upon the accepted status of its target and, equally, upon a reader's detailed knowledge of that product. The joke does not work without both knowledge and (perhaps undue) respect. Similarly, in Meale's most basic sense, 'popularity' indicates that Chaucer is but one reader among many. Whatever one may think of his 'poetic greatness' and/or canonical centrality, his is but a single reading – indeed, one very likely constructed precisely to displace his predecessors and to define a canon in which they would have no part. One might well offer in riposte a reading equally canonical, but supplied by a poet more sensitively attuned to the workings of romance, Edmund Spenser. Andrew King's impressive study indicates just how carefully and seriously Auchinleck romances may be integrated into Spenser's 'serious literary art' (see esp. 42–77, 129–45).

Yet even very careful studies, among which one should single out Susan Wittig and Carol Fewster (the latter discusses *Guy* at 85–128), often remain blinkered by the presumption that they are treating a 'popular literature' of swashbuckling action alone. They do not always properly attend to the texts' reliance upon the motifs of their (usually) Anglo-Norman sources and their conscious transmission of those narrative patterns these poems had inherited from an allegedly yet more sophisticated continental tradition.[5] Critics tend to associate the absence of psychological language in the poems with a disinterest in the hero's interiority (supposedly a mark of 'sophisticated' or 'literary' romance) altogether. But the poems, like all romances (and Westerns), display interiority otherwise, through stock narrative motif. Romance shows interiority allusively, through a narrative primarily legible only as quasi-symbolic action.[6] At the end of the tradition, Spenser systematically manifests what he had found inherent in earlier English writings, part of his sober Renaissance syncretism of diverse pasts.

As an example of such procedures at work, I bracket one episode from the central Auchinleck romance, *Guy of Warwick* (part I only), between its surely 'literary' source and its equally 'literary' Spenserian recuperation, the adventure of Red Cross Knight in *Faerie Queene* I. The Anglo-Norman *Guy* provides the Middle English poet with a smallish narrative itself derived from the title episode in the font of all medieval romance, Chrétien de Troye's *Yvain*, alternatively known as *Le Chevalier au lion*. In outlining Chrétien's handling, I hope to identify a fundamental thematic inherent in this episode and to demonstrate its continuing generative life for the *Guy*-poet and, beyond him, into the Renaissance. The Middle English romance thus may be positioned within a romance continuum. The example will be lengthy, re-enforcing my basic point that romance renders 'psychological analysis' through large and elaborated narrative patterning. But my imitative dilatoriness will indicate that denigrating the narrative sophistication of Middle English romance is a view far from well-taken.

When Yvain leaves Laudine behind, in order to go tourneying with Gawain, he is described as a body only (2639–66). He does not recognise that he is literally 'heart-less', without the heart he has left behind with his wife. Thus, he leaves deprived not just of his love, but of thought/emotion; he is reduced merely to the physical, to his strength alone. This should be sustained by Hope/Esperanche of his return (2659, 2662), but in the event is not.

In constructing the narrative in this fashion, Chrétien outlines the course the romance must take once Yvain, having over-indulged in physical prowess, overstays the date on which he had promised to return. With Laudine's subsequent rejection, he will be left as an empty shell. In terms of the narrative, he must reconstruct his interiority; he will perform this feat by a penitential series of tasks involving measured dealing with time, since forgetting his inner responsibilities has earlier been presented as a violation of 'dated time'.

But first, having been publicly shamed by Laudine's damsel as 'cist lerres' (2725, and following lines), a public criminal, not a man of prowess,[7]

Yvain enters a large-scale narrative regression. He returns to the forest where his adventure began in precipitateness (another misuse of time). But he regresses further, into madness, into the unformed and pre-civilised. He lives as if he were indeed an outlaw, like the thief Lunette claims he is. He tears off his clothing (2804–7) and eats uncooked venison (2825–6), 'Comme hom forsenes et sauvage' (2828). He has become something like the savage herdsman whom he met early in the poem and has lost the newfound identity which in tourneying he subconsciously assumed he still possessed.

Thus, when discovered by courtly people who know him, he lacks identity, is unrecognisable as the man he in fact is (2894–6). His rescuers can resuscitate him as a fighting machine, restore what one might consider 'noble heart', i.e. simple coeur-age/valour, not something like insight. When he defends them, he is applauded in language like 'vaillant sodoier' and: 'He charges among them like a lion among deer when hunger constrains and presses him' ('Tout autresi entr'eus se fiert | *Com li lions* entre les dains | Quant l'angousse et cache li fains', 3199–3209). This reference looks both backward to Yvain as savage woodland poacher and ahead to the subsequent adventure in which he gains his companion-lion by rescuing it from a dragon's onslaught (3341–3407).

As this narrative section begins, the warring Yvain and the lion resemble one another a great deal, a point signalled by the hero's adopting a new non-proper name 'le chevalier au lion'. The lion performs a gesture of homage in thanks for his release (3395–3401), just as Yvain has battled for women who saved him earlier. The beast is a companion hunter, but Yvain now can cook meat for himself (3461–5). Equally, the lion mirrors Yvain's continuing despair, Hope lost by the soulless body, in a scene of averted mutual suicide (3485–3521). And the lion continues with Yvain, like a faithful dog (cf. the early 3438–9 where he functions as Yvain's 'brachet' in a hunt), until the poem's end. But he becomes increasingly a grotesque adjunct, a one-dimensional prop used emblematically to measure his distance from, not similarity to the hero, and to mark Yvain's development/reintegration as a person who can, at the poem's end, deserve Laudine (and assume his real name) again.

At the Early Modern end of the romance tradition, Spenser's *Faerie Queene* I preserves this same association of lion, misplaced prowess, and abandoned love. Spenser's lion, although not rescued from danger by the hero, appears as a similar surrogate or alter ego for an overly bellicose figure who has abandoned his lady. Red Cross Knight, played upon by Archimago, believes Una to have traduced his love and consequently, he leaves her bereft, 'flying from his thoughts and gealous feare; | Will was his guide, and griefe led him astray' (1.2.12.3–4). He flees his own interiority into simple angry and frustrated prowess, and in his absence, Una receives protection when joined by the lion. Her lament, 'But he my Lyon and my noble Lord, | How does he find in cruell hart to hate | Her that him lou'd . . . ?' (1.3.7.5–7), recognises the essential similarity of her two protectors, both figures of modestly controlled ferocity. Red Cross Knight has abandoned, with Una (vera fides), anything approximating faith or holiness. He has become the faithless Saracen Sansfoy he will shortly meet, and they will engage in an even-handed battering, in which each mirrors the other. The lion is truly a surrogate, not Una's proper Lyon but only another 'cruell hart', just as Satyrane, another wild man/knight, who will later become her companion.

In *Guy of Warwick*, the echo of this sophisticated romance type-scene occurs just past midtext and clearly alludes to *Yvain*. Guy, like his predecessor, is described as lion-like, not simply in a passing simile, but throughout most of the poem (2072, 3125, 3600, 3960, 4054, 5341; the identification shared with an adversary once early on, at 2223).[8] Following a crescendo of such references, he rescues his lion from a dragon and gains its loyalty. The adventure here is, of course, designed to reflect the poem's climactic battle, Guy as St George preserving Athelstan's England, his first truly civil act in the romance. However, long before that encounter, Guy's lion is 'murdered', a variation on the motif to which I will return, and immediately following upon that crime, like Yvain (and the later Red Cross), he is revealed as unfaithful to the vows of love alleged to animate his action. Having (more than momentarily, I should think) forgotten his 'true love' Felice, he makes an ungracious at-the-altar escape from marriage to Another Woman, the Byzantine emperor's daughter.

But it is not just the similarity of narrative motif but the moral/psychological implications inherent in the scene that recur here. As hero, Guy is a diverting literalistic naïve, someone typically out of touch with his surround and merely 'man most of miȝt' (part II, 1/9; cf. 3570, 3596, etc.). He has been constructed in this way by his social superior and love, Felice, through a rather typical episodic sequence of three scenes. In these, the ignorant young man is implausibly offered instruction in knighthood by his 'cruel fair'.[9] He internalises this training to the extent that he strives constantly for prowess alone, somehow assuming that this pragmatic single-mindedness answers his emotional commitment to Felice. Indeed, at one point in this instructional cycle, the garbled lines 577–80, Guy appears to take upon himself the heart/body dichotomy of *Yvain*. The poem surely appeals at a raw level to enjoyment of the hero's efficiency at lopping body-parts off his numerous adversaries.

Guy is truly a lion-man. It is thoroughly appropriate that, like his romance colleagues, he should be blessed with a leonine companion who mirrors his force, his ferocity, and his murderous efficiency. Indeed, forceful risktaking is very much part of the experience of loving Felice, if not precisely a product of her instruction:

> Henne-forward ne reche Y me
> Of mi liif, whare it be,
> No of my deþ neuer þe mo
> No reche Y neuer where Y go.
> (593–6)
>
> *
>
> Into oþer cuntres Ichil go,
> For þi loue to wirche me wo.
> For dout of deþ nil Y nouȝt fle;
> ȝif Y dye, it is for þe.
> (1173–6)

If unrequited love exerts such a hold as to make one despair of life, it also bolsters courage, since Guy recognises that death, the worst danger can provide, is the fate he faces anyway. Guy thus becomes self-engrossed in raw acts of aggression. He is truly 'fole-hardy', idiot-brave, as he has been ever since first falling in love (382, 403). Hence, he is impervious to any further responsibility, entirely unaware of anything around him that is not a mounted adversary to hew or thrust at. In essence, then, reading the poem as 'popular', as the chapbook train of martial triumphs, is to read it wrongly, if entertainingly, as Guy himself would.

Morgadour, who will treacherously slaughter Guy's sleeping lion (the scene uses the companion to signal the hero's own obliviousness), is Guy's central adversary in another episodic thrice-repeated motif in the poem. He represents simply another version of the arch-villain Otto of Pavia whom Guy must face both early and late in the work. The two figures, evil stewards both, raise an issue that Guy never quite comprehends, that he has an effect on others. Guy can comprehend effects in the sense that he responds graciously to what he expects, praise for his derring-do, in its material form all the treasure and of-fers of maidens' hands that he routinely declines or redistributes. But Guy can't imagine what Morgadour and Otto exemplify – negative responses. In fact, his unrooted knight errantry might be perceived as socially and institutionally disruptive wherever he goes. He doesn't breed glory, only various forms of gratitude, for his various hosts; but, along with that honour he almost forces in return for his prowess, he equally breeds jealousy. Removed from his own home, he threatens persons already established in the households he visits, whether from jealousy of his achieved honour and the potentially intrusive social centrality he is awarded, or from frustrated longing for the various women he is promised.

Moreover, Guy cannot imagine how or why he evokes such 'trea-cherous' responses. He plaintively (and in ironic ignorance) queries his archenemy and deceiver Morgadour:

> Hou schuld Ich euer siker be
> Of ani bihest men hotes me?
> (3289–90)

In this befuddlement, and in his out-of-touchness with staunch English roots, it is scarcely surprising that the death of his lion, the sign of his compulsive martial obtuseness, and his forgetting his 'true love' occur coincidently in the narrative. In a poem that begins (at least in the parallel Caius MS, since the opening of the Auchinleck *Guy* has been lost) by applauding faith and truth as the cornerstones of wisdom (cf. 11–14), this represents a devastating commentary.

Almost simultaneously, immediately before the lion episode, the poet puts the issue about as bluntly as he can. Morgadour's accusations of Guy's 'treison' (3238, 3244) strike a tender nerve. While the unduly ob-sequious Byzantine emperor may not care about his daughter's chastity, so long as he can keep Guy by his side (cf. 3384), in dallying (if not sleeping) with her, Guy has already, with his typical unconsciousness, been unfaithful, to himself and to his Felice. Tellingly, he responds to Morgadour's treacheries by threatening to desert his fellow-Christians as oathbreakers and to cast his lot with their Muslim adversaries; valorous as he may be, a principled crusader he isn't. Nor can he be described as anything short of disingenuous in enunciating a similar logic for avoiding the Byzantine marriage and deserting that court (4404–22), rather than admitting, with embarrassment, that he has erred in never mentioning, or indeed considering, his previous (and now, he belatedly discovers, abiding) attachment to Felice.

Guy spends much of the poem feeling vaguely out of place, as if he should be returning to England. (He, of course, tries three times, at 1789–98, 4447–4502, 4931–2 and the continuation 7034–7105, only making it at the final attempt.) But he is remarkably prone to distraction, to tumbling upon yet another new adventure (and complication) that diverts him. The most notable of these, the decision to journey to Constantinople (2847–54) that precipitates him into the narrative I have described, takes him East, the direction precisely opposite that he should be travelling.

Guy begins to develop constructively only in the later stages of the poem. Here he shows himself capable of addressing Otto's guile with an equal guile (playing with his identity through disguise). Further, when he recognises the possible dishonour and pain his precipitate slaughter of Florentine's son produces, he shows some consciousness of the destruction he's capable of wreaking. Ultimately, he is only socially reintegrated at the climactic ending of *Guy I* with his return to England and his destruction of the dragon, an act that not only recalls the rescue of his lion but identifies him as national hero, loyal servant of the heroic Athelstan, and assimilates him to the saintly national patron George.[10] Instructively, on his final determination to return to England, he recalls 'fader and frendes', those who offered him early good advice, before he does 'mi leman' (whom he does not name) (7045, 7105).

Yet equally, as the denouement, the tail-rhyme *Guy II*, makes explicit, heeding his chosen woman has been the erroneous decision of a naïve:

> Seþþen Y þe seyȝe first wiþ ayn
> ('Allas þe while' I may sayn)
> þi loue me haþ so ybounde
> þat neuer seþþen no dede Y gode,

Bot in wer schadde mannes blode . . .
Ac for þi loue Ich haue al wrouȝt;
For His loue dede Y neuer nouȝt,
   Iesu amende mi fare!
þerfore Ich wot þat Ich am lorn.
(24/4–8, 25/7–10)

This is not, as Langland's reference to the poem (12.46, 'Felice hir fair-nesse fel hire al to sclaundre', cf. *Guy* 635–6) makes clear, simply re-trospective reading. When Guy first seeks to follow Felice's advice that he leave England to become 'greatest man of los and priis', every male authority figure in the poem seeks to dissuade him. Once he has ignored them and taken up continental adventures, like Yvain in his tourneying or Red Cross in the compulsive repetitions of meeting one Sans-boy after another, he spends most of the poem caught on a chivalric treadmill of triumph unmarked by introspection. One might compare the prayer to Love, part of a very Chrétien-like inner monologue and only answered, and then ironically, after his wedding to Felice in Part II, for 'lisse . . . þat Y miȝt meseluen knowe' (430–2), or the contemporaneous narrative comment on his behaviour, 'Now he haþ his witt forlore' (470).

Importantly, victory over the dragon can only occur in a fight in which Guy acknowledges limitations to his force. Unusually in his career, he here seeks divine aid, and in a mode that distinguishes him from his earlier lionishness:

'God', he seyd, 'Fader almiȝt,
þat made þe day and niȝt also
And for ous sinful þoldest wo
And heldest Daniel fram þe lyoun,
Saue me fram þis foule dragoun'.
(7222–6)

Moreover, as Spenser was well aware in adapting this narrative to *Faerie Queene* 1.11–12,[11] Guy here, for the first time, must actually develop a strategy, think his way through a complicated situation, in order to triumph in battle. But the payoff for this introspection comes only at the opening of *Guy II*; rather than make moony lyric utterances about Felice's tower, as he does at the start of his career (455–64), Guy now spies the grandeur of God in the night sky from a turret (*Guy II*, 21/1–23/3). As a result, he quite properly, given his earlier career, surrenders himself to penitential knighthood (see Hopkins 70–118, a study from which I have obviously profited). Whether this represents a truly desirable outcome, or simply a gesture as excessive as his commitment to military athleticism, in its handling *Guy* shares with *Yvain* and *The Faerie Queene* a comic-ironic vision of the hero-naïve who follows arms in the absence of a more abstract commitment. The poem relies upon similar narrative motifs and a similarly implicit quasi-symbolic narrative.

Such a reading obviously implies an audience of a good deal more sophistication than is customarily assumed. To be an appropriate reader of *Guy*, one must be capable of identifying relevant narrative motif, understanding it as constituting a type-scene, and intuiting the appropriate ethical referents. The poem is not without depth, although it may be couched in a language that does not readily express depth at the verbal level. (Yet simultaneously, a good many of the lines I have quoted above, however commonplace their diction, prove remarkably resonant as narrative signals.) There's evidence here to suggest that one needs to reconsider the readership of these poems, to see the audience as situated in relatively educated and literarily knowing contexts, ones prepared to read romance in the manner conventional in its great tradition, as exemplarising narrative addressing social responsibility. This conclusion implies that it will be profitable to seek further indications of how Auchinleck might be contextualised. Such study may point to specific London localisations where a book like this one (and Laud misc. 622) might be at home.[12]

III

In late 1326 or early 1327, while the adults tried to figure out what to do with his father, the young Prince of Wales who would become Edward III received a present. The royal clerk Walter de Milemete, perhaps his tutor, gave him two volumes, extra-illustrated 'handbooks for princes', both of which survive. The first of these, now British Library, MS Additional 47680, contains the most widely dispersed example of this genre, a Latin *Secretum secretorum*.[13] This work might well remind one of topics broached in the preceding chapter. The *Secretum* purports to be Aristotle's instruction offered to the youthful Alexander, what Milemete himself calls in his second book (fol. 8ᵛ) 'sciencia regalis'; the tutor has designed the work to construct in his princely student the virtues appropriate to a ruler. 'Romance history' once again underwrites – this at a moment of particular constitutional pressure, the verge of regicide – the most serious responsibilities of governance.

Yet Edward was only fifteen at the moment and probably not equipped to deal with a work that, if not truly Aristotelian, was at least the object of an appropriately serious intellectual interest by mature European rulers. As a result, Milemete provided him with a companion volume, now Oxford, Christ Church, MS 92, illustrated by many of the same hands involved in the production of Additional 47680. The book is not only visually similar but intellectually imitative; like the royal tutor Aristotle addressing his young prince, Milemete offers Edward a brief précis, explicitly a 'suplecio' (fol. 12ᵛ), of the *Secretum* for fifteen-year-olds, his own 'De nobilitatibus, sapienciis et prudenciis regum'.[14] As will appear shortly, this volume not only invokes a romance-historical model appropriate to Edward's political circumstances but draws directly on Auchinleck romance in ways visible elsewhere in contemporary London culture.

Milemete's discussion also implies that this second volume is a kind of stopgap:

> When you have come, lord, with God's grace, to manhood and to a state of greater power and dignity, as I foresee truly you will, I believe firmly and without doubt, if you perform resolutely following the doctrine I have recently composed for king Alexander, you will be deservedly able to have various successes.[15]

Edward will eventually be an appropriate successor to Alexander; but this will depend on his achieving both maturity and, with it, personal power. At that time, he will practise the then long internalised lessons of kingship, first adumbrated here (the book 'nuper editam') but fully realised in the larger, more difficult work.

This rhetorical trope does not simply engage romance, but also contemporary history, the stressful political situation in which young Edward received his books. Milemete here encourages Edward to consider himself in a pregnantly generation-skipping model of lineal succession. If his father is indeed dispensable, Milemete encourages Edward to consider himself as his grandfather's emulator and heir.

Longshanks, as the last chapter will have suggested, had been prone to imagine himself as chivalric inheritor. His range of reference was suitably encyclopaedic, but the best-recorded images, on the walls of the Painted Chamber at Westminster, involve an implicit self-presentation as heroic biblical warrior-king, perhaps especially Judah Maccabee (Binski 1986, 82–103).[16] In the aftermath of the old king's passing, similar imagery was reused, but now as direct representation of Edward's own triumphs. The first example we know appeared in the bishop's palace at Lichfield, its patron a former treasurer; Edward II in the early 1320s commissioned a similar wallpainting in St Stephen's Chapel, Westminster (Reeve).

One such evocation of Edward I seems to have been as Alexander. David D'Avray prints one funeral sermon entirely given over to a point by point comparison of the conqueror of Britain with the conqueror of the world (263–5). One might also see the popularity of *Kyng Alisaunder*, straightforwardly historical and strikingly uncritical (its hero is only undone by his human mortality, a theme signalled in the famous inset lyrics on the seasons) as another sort of heroic troping.[17]

Another piece of kiddie lit presented to the youthful Edward III in 1333 strikes a similar, if negative, note. In attempting to convince the king to avoid abuses instituted by his grandfather, William of Paull (known also as the Latin 'of Pagula') again evokes Alexander. But this is a different version, the vain conqueror obliterated by death; just as young Edward should end his grandfather's antisocial behaviours, so he should avoid a socially prominent trope of English royal succession. William constructs for the young king a new and provocative model, a purified genealogy (and a different jurisdictional claim), not Alexander/Edward but St Louis IX of France's instructions to his son.[18]

Milemete's work is a simplified *Secretum*, composed of hortatory generalisation. But however commonplace, its emphases seem strikingly resonant with the Prince's immediate situation, and many of these, corresponding to the need to convert romance image into political instruction, create a genealogy that would ignore the biological father. Such emphases might be construed as answering complaints registered in John Walwayn's contemporary *Vita Edwardi Secundi*. Quite substantial portions of the text address an issue Walwayn presents as Edward II's great failure, for example, the two lengthy chapters on 'national defence' (nos. 12, fols. 47–49^v, and 16, fols. 60^v–70^v). Two chapters (8 and 9) emphasise the king's pursuit of 'sciencia', explicitly to be trilingual, and his need to avoid treason through carrying on his own private correspondence. Edward was to be neither an unduly trusting Guy of Warwick, nor an image of his father (cf. Walwayn's attack on the downfall of prudence before avarice during the reign, 105–7).

Equally, Edward is to engage in 'otium' as well as 'negotium', to practise 'honestum solacium' (chapter 10), and not simply the expected aristocratic hunting and hawking. The image that precedes this chapter illustrates the command, 'sonos temporatos audire' (fol. 43ᵛ). This recommended engagement in harmony might be opposed to Walwayn's general view of the preceding reign as marked by 'sediotosa dissensio' and perhaps alludes to musical developments associated with the Prince's marriage to Philippa of Hainault (Wathey; for Edward's continuing enjoyment of music, Sherborne 17).

Most of the opulent illustration in Christ Church 92 represents what might be expected. Milemete's fifteen extant chapters typically begin with images that will recall Horn's books and Statute MSS – either enthroned royalty or God/the Trinity. The paintings illustrate the analogy Milemete shares with William of Paull, that virtuous royalty precisely imitates divine lordship. Throughout the manuscript, in richly ornamented borders lurk both images of aristocratic duty and a variety of grotesques, as well as an elaborate display of contemporary heraldry (for James's identifications, see Milemete lxiv–lxxii).

The importance of these blazons is signalled in the one unusual chapter-opening image, that to the longest and concluding chapter 16 on warfare (fol. 60ᵛ). Here Edward rides among a group of close counsellors, two identifiable by their heraldic devices. In the fraught, internecine partisanship in which the book was produced (at this point of more than a decade's standing), a king's best education might include recognition of loyal and trustworthy magnates. From this preselected lot, Edward might identify the 'virtuous counsellors' he would need in future, those described in chapter 11 as 'fideles, iusti, scienciis et moribus repleti secundum documentum philosophicum' (fol. 46ᵛ). This lesson the king certainly learned, through creation of the community of arms that sustained him through much of his reign – and through ordering the construction of heraldic images of this solidarity answering those of the manuscript, both in the Garter Knights' stalls of St George's Chapel,

Windsor and in the painted cornice of his Chapel of St Stephen in the Palace of Westminster.[19]

Somewhat less expectedly, the book includes both illustrative front- and back-matter, and in the latter imagery associable with the Auchinleck MS occurs. The materials at the rear mirror the painting spread across the full opening preceding the chapter on warfare – Edward leading English knights, with their blazons of three leopards, into battle. Rather than the melee there depicted, at the end a series of line drawings (perhaps the unfinished outlines awaiting painting) illustrate various acts of siegecraft. While a great many of these might be construed generic illustrations and following on Milemete's general instructions about preparing for warfare,[20] at least a few of these drawings, embodying some perhaps visionary techniques, imply that all are in fact illustrations of an Auchinleck text.

Most persuasively, one opening, fols. 74ᵛ–75, depicts a windmill-like machine, whose rotational motion casts beehives into a castle. On the facing page, the angry bees fly out to torment the defenders and render their efforts ineffective. While bee-casting as a siege-strategy does have a history, it is not a fourteenth-century technique. The depiction of the engine for this work as a windmill suggests that the illustrations here are representing the Palestinian activities (given the sources of the *Secretum*, rather ironically against Arabic-speaking opponents) of Richard Lionheart during the Third Crusade (1191–2).

The most proximate source for the depiction would be an English romance on this subject, one which lacks either Anglo-Norman or continental French analogue. This source, *Richard Coer de Lion*, although now mainly excised, was once present in the Auchinleck MS and there, as Smithers points out, in a language consonant with poems associable with London authorship. One may feel reasonably confident about this association of London vernacular romance with Latin royal book because the image fuses at least two separate depictions from the poem (see further Hebron 37–46).

When Richard sets off for the Holy Land, he carefully has 'þrittene schyppys ilade with hyuys' (*Richard* 1392), and they form part of his initial assault upon Acre, an effort to drive the 'Saracens' from the walls so that mining operations, depicted on the adjacent fol. 75ᵛ of the Milemete MS, can begin (2902–20, 2935–42). In the poem, however, the beehives are 'keste' by 'a mangnel', a more customary siege-engine than the windmill here illustrated. But the illustrator had in mind another device integral to the siege of Acre, one of Richard's theatrical self-presentations of terrifying severity. His regal identity as a Plantagenet, a line traditionally born of the devil, depends on expressing military power as a viciousness that paralyses adversaries.

As he personally opens the harbour of Acre by destroying the chain that has protected the Muslim defenders from naval attack,[21] the king announces his presence through a device 'of gret queyntyse' ('wisdom or ingenuity', the virtue Milemete strives to inculcate into his youthful charge Edward):

> Ouyr al oþere [devices], wyttyrly,
> A melle he made, of gret maystry,
> In myddys a schyp for to stande:
> Swylke on saw3 neuere man in lande.
> Foure sayles were þertoo,
> 3elew and grene, rede and bloo,
> Wiþ caneuas layd wel al aboute,
> Ful schyr wiþinne and eke wiþoute.
> (2655–62)

This windmill projects malice and death, not missiles; in addition to its coloured vanes, it is equipped with flames, grindstones that whirr and produce blood, and as the miller by the hopper, 'on | Al in blood ... begon, | And hornes grete vpon his hede'. The terrified Saracens 'get the picture', recognise the type-scene and Richard's demonic force, although including cannibalism (enemies as 'mete') here released in a Christian cause. They see that the millstones await, not sustaining grain, but their own bodies to be ground (2663–80). The Milemete artist has fused two discrete images from the romance, and the remaining siege images here may address somewhat less specifically other episodes.[22]

The illustrations might be seen as interfacing with other images prophetic of Edward's anticipated martial success. One *bas-de-page* illustration in Christ Church 92 (fol. 68) depicts Edward undoing Bannockburn, his father's greatest disaster, by driving a lance into the king of Scotland. Similarly, Walwayn heralds his birth (36–7, cf. 39, a reference to the Lionheart's renown in chronicles) with the hope that he will have the solid virtues of his ancestors, including specifically, 'that he will follow the famous prowess of King Richard' ('sectetur...regis Ricardi notam probitatem').[23]

The front-matter illustrations, in a quire bibliographically a cancellans, equally reflect *Richard*.[24] In the very striking image of fol. 3, identified by Michael (39) as 'the earliest depiction of St George as patron saint of England', the saint, in his crusading surcoat, presents Edward with the arms of England. Although a good many factors may have contributed to the mature king's choice of George as patron of his Order of the Garter, *Richard* may well be one. In a romance notable for its early (and perhaps initiatory) evocation of England as 'nacyon' (1848, cf. Turville-Petre 41), George appears, mounted and 'In armes whyte as þe flour | Wiþ a croys of red colour', as an intercessory figure whose inspiration (literally here 'þe wynd') saves the beleaguered English from a potentially disastrous dust-storm (4877–4900).

The siegecraft depicted at the book's end also finds an echo, in a different romance modality, at the opening. Fol. 4 depicts 'the storming of the Castle of Love' with ladies throwing flowers at the attackers. Edward later had this particularly courtly image woven into several tapestries, and it appeared in a pageant at a Valentine's Day feast in 1330. It ultimately derives, not from the sober English *Château d'amour*, Robert Grosseteste's religious allegory, but from continental sources, most notably, at some remove, *The Romance of the Rose*.[25] Although war and diplomacy are the centres of the Milemete treatise and the emphases of its decorative programme, this activity only exists to promote peace (cf. 'Prelium est pacis fundamentum', fol. 61).[26] The image idealises such activity, the 'otium' the wise ruler might achieve as the fruit of protracted martial busy-ness: after extended mock hostilities, the mutual amatory surrender of both parties, sapped attackers and perhaps not-so-reluctant (their flowers are, of course, their 'honours') defenders. The castle itself presumably represents one of Milemete's favoured 'obiecta proporcionata' and amatory dalliance a 'lusus honestus' (chapter 10, fol. 43ᵛ).

Christ Church MS 92 thus alludes in its contents and decorative programme to materials shortly to appear in Auchinleck. The book tropes Prince Edward as Alexander/Edward I in training and offers a further English royal/romance model, the Lionheart. But the very imagery shows further extensive London connections. Both Milemete's books are the product of the second of the three widely attested early fourteenth-century London collections of book-artisans (for 'the Queen Mary Psalter Group', see pp. 80–1). The Milemete limners, here observed in contact with something that resembles the textual community enshrined in the Auchinleck MS, are responsible for at least nine further volumes, in the main for aristocratic and episcopal patrons, the subsidiary hands who join them in producing Edward's *Secretum* with more books still.[27] But for at least part of their work, these illuminators may have derived inspiration from specifically London vernacular materials, at least the antecedents, and perhaps the text itself, of an Auchinleck romance.

The imagery of Christ Church 92 thus connects Auchinleck with royal books, as well as with Andrew Horn. And there are abundant artefactual examples (leaving aside the royal tournaments mentioned in chapter 1) displaying similar communality of interests between City and royal culture, as well as the involvement of local artisans in manufacture of these materials. These relationships may be signalled by drawing attention to another 'handbook for princes', in Edward III's hands early in his career. Philippa of Hainault is supposed to have presented him as a wedding present (the ceremony occurred 25 January 1328) Paris, Bibliothèque nationale, MS fr. 571 (Sandler 1986, 2, 103–5, no. 96; Butterfield 89–91). This volume includes, *inter alia*, the most sophisticated of the late medieval advice books, Giles of Rome's very academic *De regimine principum*. But equally, Philippa was presenting Edward a copy of Brunetto's *Trésor*, that text from which Andrew Horn was contemporaneously drawing his visionary description of a civic leader. Court and City, City and Court, share inspirations and aspirations.

One expects such materials in a royal context, and they appear there, dating back to Henry III's fascination with ornament depicting Richard and Tristram.[28] But one could identify with City, and not royal, owners or workmen a variety of objects, e.g. Richard on a binding stamp of *c.* 1275–1325 or a mirror case of *c.* 1300 with Tristram and Isolde (*Age* 386, no. 432; Spencer 327). Again, numerous badges or livery devices, heraldic or courtly, appear in City sites (Spencer *passim* 273–329), and City tapestries imitated central court models, e.g., the vintner William Brangewayn's hanging, depicting King Richard and Hector of Troy, bequeathed to his son in 1361 (Crowfoot *et al.* 69–72).[29] City church decoration often featured rich armourial materials, e.g. arms in stained glass; the earliest reference (1299) involves the blazon of a Bordeaux merchant involved in trade with the royal household as well as in collecting local duties on wine from fellow vintners (Schofield 1994b, 62, 64, 116). Or in 1366/7, Edward III seized from a London citizen three books of romances (Cavanaugh 1988, 315).

Specifically romance imagery appears, not just in the work of the Milemete decorators but in that of the third prominent fourteenth-century London association of artists. Among their other projects, they illuminated British Library, MS Egerton 2781, a Book of Hours for provincial magnates, with illustration reminiscent of *Titus and Vespasian*. The volume also contains a copy of the Anglo-Norman source-text underlying the *Complaint*-Nicodemus narrative in Pepys 2498. In addition, this group specialised in *bas-de-page* illustrations of romance episodes, including *Beves of Hamtoun*, among other subjects. This cycle appears in British Library, MS Yates-Thompson 13 (the Taymouth Hours, again for provincial secular patrons), but similar illustration also features in British Library, MS Royal 10 E.iv (the Smithfield Decretals). This volume, like a further commission executed by this group, was produced for a London canon.[30]

In short, at this period, it is difficult to conceive of mercantile-industrial City and royal Westminster as anything other than interconnected, not oppositional. City artisans are involved in royal projects – not just books, but other handcrafts like masonry and tapestry. And the Court persistently interpenetrates the City, not simply through such ceremonial as Edwardian tournament, but spatially. Courtly people were not necessarily residents of palatial Westminster, but within the City, where they would have met daily, perhaps even attended church with, Londoners.

One can be precise about identifying communities where such interpenetrative Court and City relations might have proved especially powerful. In particular, Barron (1995a) and Keene (1999) provide information suggestive and coherent about royal and magnatial communities within the City. The former finds (2) that, by 1520, at least thirty lay and forty-five religious lords (bishops, abbots, and priors) had established permanent City houses (the first figure an acknowledged underestimate). While ecclesiastical establishments followed the pattern early set by religious houses and concentrated in the periphery (see

p. 3), magnates set up almost exclusively at the west end of the City, both within the walls or sharing space with religious dwellings in the Westminster Strand (four examples, including Gaunt's Savoy) or Holborn (the later Farringdon Ward without, three examples). Keene's magnatial wardrobes, storehouses for City luxury products whose heyday spanned the century 1270–1370, show a similar distribution, particularly after Edward III moved the Great Wardrobe from Lombard Street to a site just north of Blackfriars.[31]

Establishments like these need to be seen as full communities and ones fully interpenetrative with their locales. They would have included not simply the magnate, the figure with London business, most likely parliamentary or other governmental service, but also his full household for some period. This group includes his domestic officers and staff, men accustomed to writing and accounts. Moreover, the urban property would have included the lord's supply house, if not formal wardrobe, facilities for gathering the luxuries appropriate to aristocratic culture, and thus necessitating exchanges with a City merchant and artisan community. It might, in this context, be worth recalling Myers's discovery that in the Richard Lyons inventory, the only books kept outside his chapel were preserved in his counting house.

One further contemporary development in this neighbourhood is also important, a growing concentration of sophisticated clerical talent. In one permutation, this can be seen, like Edward III's Great Wardrobe, as an extension of the 'familia regis'. For the area just over the Fleet, immediately west of the City, became at this time the site of royal offices. From at least 1307, the Chancery had become located in the Lane to which it gave its name (just outside the extreme western edge of the City); its headquarters were in the (Master of the) Rolls Chapel, originally the 'Domus conversorum (Judaeorum)' (Hallam–Roper 75).

A similar contemporary development is the growth of a more generally legal (Courtenay's term, 'Latin' represents the metaphorical, not the literal linguistic usage) quarter in much the same area. Beginning with the suppression of the Templars, many Fleet or Holborn private townhouses, especially those marginally suburban, began their long process of conversion into dwellings ('inns') for law or chancery clerks, the first stage in the quasi-collegiate shape they were later to assume. In addition to the Chancery itself, the New and Middle Temple, Clifford's Inn of

Chancery, and Gray's Inn, only the first pair in the City proper, probably predate the 1370s.[32]

In this regard, one might recall Bliss's statement that Auchinleck scribe 3 'shows the influence of chancery hand' (653). I doubt this view can be sustained, but it is clear that this individual was a great deal more used to some form of legal, business, or documentary writing than he was to text-production (cf. Parkes 1969, xvii). But this observation only serves to indicate the imbrication of the scribe in the same sort of domestic or clerical communities I have been describing. 'Inns' of all these sorts are particularly apt to have been communities generative of text-writers because situated in areas jurisdictionally marginal; City guild regulation only covered intramural London, and elsewhere, it was open season for writers to moonlight in literary productions.[33]

One variety of detail about Auchinleck texts may provide a fairly precise placement of this activity within the context I have been outlining. Maldwyn Mills has usefully qualified a number of Laura Loomis's still far from adequately investigated findings; he demonstrates that a substantial group of Auchinleck poems, large and small, may have been imported from a centre like York (*Horn Childe* 36, 39–43, 62–81; cf. Turville-Petre 1996, 114 and references). Unlike the Auchinleck borrowings from Western texts, fitful after the first section of the volume, this Northern influence is pervasive in Auchinleck and appears scattered throughout, examples distributed among at least six booklets.[34]

Here one can designate with some precision the probable mechanisms of inter-regional cultural exchange. Following Mark Ormrod (1997, 2000), one cannot over-emphasise York's importance as 'second capital' of the kingdom in the first forty years of the fourteenth century. But this is again to suggest the coincidence of London interests often considered separately. The most obvious conduits by which these romances might have passed between north and south include both mercantile figures (and royal bankrollers) like the de la Poles, originally a family of Hull shippers, but also individuals tangentially City people, royal clerks like Walter de Milemete.[35]

A large influx of royal clerks with Northern backgrounds first occurs in the reign of Edward I. In the Scottish troubles of 1298–1304, the king removed large portions of the royal administration to York and established a continuous interchange between London and York staffs, especially persons attached to the Chancery (Grassi). These patterns continue past the end of governmental perambulations to the North, perhaps *c.* 1340. Many of these individuals originated in a geographically delimited area, Howdenshire (not so far from William's Paull), the peculiar of the bishop of Durham on the north bank of the Humber and centred on the collegiate church in Howden.[36]

In addition to their royal service, these men retained their Northern links. The central government acquired their administrative expertise cut-rate by arranging their stipends to be paid from ecclesiastical positions within York diocese, where they doubled as archiepiscopal officials. Even places one might consider isolated backwaters were intimately connected to the capital by networks of government officialdom; thus, in Ripon Minster, the prebend of Studley Magna supported in turn, John de Markenfield, Chancellor of the Exchequer (prebendary 1309–23); David de Wollore, Master of the Rolls (prebendary 1346–70); and John de Sleford, Keeper of the Wardrobe in the Tower (prebendary 1373–1401).[37]

The affiliations of administrators like these neatly interlock with some plausible inferences about historical writing. The Anglo-Norman *Brut* chronicle, the history most immediately proximate to Auchinleck, was destined to well outlast the Middle Ages (Taylor 110–32, 146–7). This text was developed during the reign of Edward I, initially by appending to the Anglo-Norman versified version of Geoffrey of Monmouth, Wace's *Roman de Brut* (1155), materials derived from a London-area monastic Latin chronicle tradition. The extension most closely resembles *The Annals of Waverley* (a Cistercian house in extreme east Surrey). A further continuation carries the narrative through the reign of Edward I.

But more telling is the 'short version' continuation covering 1307–33. As Taylor points out, this includes 'detailed information on London affairs between 1307 and 1327, and on the campaigns against the Scots between 1327 and 1333' (146), the later portion relying upon Northern sources. Taylor suggests that, while there is nothing official about the *Brut* or its generation, the text appears to emanate from clerical and administrative writing teams, perhaps most specifically royal Chancery clerks. The division in local knowledges embedded in the *Brut* proves telling in these terms, for the Chancery went north to York with the rest of royal administration during the Scots wars (1332–6).[38]

Like Chancery clerical careers, and like the Auchinleck MS, the Anglo-Norman text shows interchanges between the disparate locales. But this did not represent a single oscillatory movement, and the work, even if completed in the North in the 1330s, had returned to London by an early date. There it served as source material for further historical writing – the London *Croniques* in the 1340s and, towards the end of the century, the Middle English translation (with persistent continuations) that was to be the most popular secular text of the Middle Ages.

Although clerical transmission of Yorkshire romances to the capital might fully explain Northern portions of the Auchinleck MS, another motive deserves examination. The de la Poles were not alone among Yorkshire merchants operating in London, often as drapery suppliers to the royal Wardrobe, or in central governmental offices (here more likely the Westminster Exchequer) as major underwriters of loans to the Crown. Further, their presence corresponds with a fundamental shift in royal relationships with the City under Edward III. Until the late 1320s, as I have shown, City authority was generally hostile to financing royal and magnatial projects, but in the dawn of the reign, perhaps a cooperative gratitude in the presence of a new charter, the situation changed.

Extensive City financial support of royalty appears from this time. A profuse series of City gifts is recorded from 1328 on (e.g., Riley 170–1, 185–7, 196–9, 350–2), perhaps to be read as a form of investment procedure or an insurance policy. Moreover, ample evidence shows City figures making their accrued wealth available and useful to magnates and royal figures (Nightingale 1995, 140, 154–5, 164, 182, 189, 199, 214). As a result, symbiotic mercantile–magnatial–royal relationships, in excess of those previously in place from the luxury trade, were created. O'Connor's outstanding case studies show both the ups and eventual downs of such relationships. Merchants profited from arranging royal loans, advancing funds to magnates, and receiving various forms of patronage in return.

By the end of Edward's reign, such behaviours were to become deeply problematic, however. John Pyel's relationship with John of Gaunt and cronies like Richard Lyons should have merited impeachment under the Good Parliament (O'Connor 1993, 31–2; 1994a, 31–6; 1994b, 22–7; on Lyons's activities, see Myers 302–4). In the next reign, much of the turmoil characteristic of early 1380s City politics, Bird's 'turbulent London', would reflect similar arrangements, City leaders manipulated by their clients/patrons (Nightingale 1989, revising Bird). But so long as it proved mutually fruitful, mercantile and associated informal banking interests provided a common ground for City and Court.

Just as the nation represents a congeries of regions, the urban locale is one of neighbourhoods (or parishes). London's original West End (the modern area so designated is a product of the Restoration) appears to have been a particularly vibrant place for cultural interchanges in the early and mid fourteenth century. Well stocked with intelligent, educated, and writerly bookmen, it also provided an entrepot for exchanges between a variety of elites, governmental, county, and City mercantile. The Auchinleck MS, with its Yorkshire touches and connections to royal and Civic governmental books, most likely should be conceptualised within this locale of interpenetration and cross-fertilisation.[39]

IV

Guy of Warwick, the sequence of three linked romances, may be, as is often claimed, the centre of Auchinleck. Yet Guy's story is also, in certain emphases, most especially its social detachment, atypical of the whole. The hero is a voluntary, not, as customarily, an enforced exile from his land. And twice, at the end of each part, in both instances virtually simultaneously, he is recuperated for and lost to English society and history. In part as a function of the disruption introduced to the text by its amatory emphasis, Guy perfunctorily supports Athelstan and his nation/kingship and then vanishes from the scene.

I have already alluded to the dragon fight of part I and its penitential aftermath at the head of part II; its corollary in the second instalment is Guy's battle against the African giant and Danish champion Colbrand. But, as Guy prioritises things here, this feat is undertaken 'for God in trinite | And forto make Inglond fre' (st. 248/4–5). Its parallelism with the first fight is signalled by another prayer invoking, *inter alia*, Daniel, implying a hero victimised by a lionishness not his own (st. 252/1–6, cf. Dalrymple). And this triumph (an echo of the extensive encounter with the heathen Amoraunt, sts 67–133, both recycled by Spenser in *The Faerie Queene* 1.7–8) is succeeded, as it can only be, by Guy's eschewing

Felice, but for a single sight, and his withdrawal to the hermitage where he will die a holy death.

Such a presentation remains unusual within the 'English' (i.e. both Anglo-Norman and later vernacular) romance tradition, early marked in *Horn* and *Havelock*. The former, of course, gets a reprise in Auchinleck, the North Country version in which the banished Horn Child regains his Cleveland patrimony. Further, versions of such a narrative pattern recur incessantly in Auchinleck texts, most impressively perhaps in the Winchesterised Greek harper Orfeo. He finds, through his self-imposed despair and exile, an unexpected fidelity in his Heurodis and steward that allows return to the unnarratable ordinariness of successful rule. Significantly, in the light of my earlier legal arguments, his climactic triumph requires, not just regaining Heurodis, but discovering that his kingdom has remained intact for his succession.

Inclusion of the work in Auchinleck might be seen as a particularly pregnant model of cultural appropriation. London circulation of the text enacts an important episode of administrative/legal history, the passage of central governmental function between locales. Winchester had been, since Alfred, the historical seat of government, only fully overtaken in the course of the thirteenth century by the movement of, first the Exchequer to the Green Yard by the Great Hall of the Palace of Westminster, subsequently by location of King's Bench in the Hall itself, and thus, their proximity to the City (cf. Hallam–Roper 76). And given its more widespread appropriations of dispersed local cultures, the entire Auchinleck MS might be seen as a self-conscious heralding of a new centre, one both absorptive and innovative, intruding conspicuously among its contents local London writings. These, not heretofore seen as so culturally powerful as the imported contents, might in this miscellaneous book take on something of their gloss.

The conventional Auchinleck ending, one of retirement to the lo-cale, the knight's home country, needs to be seen against a particularly legalised background of Right often not introduced into discussions. These have presupposed as a normative model a view of centralised, or perhaps royal, knighthood only fully applicable within a narrow and particular genre of Arthurian literature. In essence, critics have priori-tised the mode of Malorian prose romance, the company emanating from and returning to a courtly centre, as a model of romance generally.

But this is a particular, and a particularly restrictive, form of narrative perhaps simply foreign (as Malory's prioritisation of Lancelot over the native Gawain is foreign) to the general interests of English materials. (Cf. Hanning's comments on the French prose cycle that formed Malory's sources and their relation to other efforts, 234–42.)

In contrast, the Auchinleck poems re-establish the situations by which royally centred rule proceeded in the later Middle Ages. The knight's normative at-home retirement, his achievement of his patrimony and of his position in a historicisable territorial succession, constitutes the unnarratable horizon of English romance. Just as in Thedmar's history, retrieving patrimony asserts a prior right, not an innovation; the narrative, the individual's growth in 'fidelity and discretion', only affirms his capacity to continue what always has been. Of course, a knight at home, having pacified the place and removed usurpers, enforces the king's law. Central institutions decide the exact parameters of Law, in romance terms, apt simply to be preservation of the king's peace (cf. the description of the noble Athelwold at *Havelok* 27–105).

But whatever emerged from the centre, enforcement always depended upon the action of provincial barons, typically leading members of peace-commissions, in their dispersed locales. The knight/baron is the king's representative in his most prosaic, and thus unnarratable, labour of justice. Historically, over the long period Henry III to Richard II, kings who got into trouble (even generally successful figures like Edward I) did so because they intruded upon an understood prerogative, attempted centralised micromanagement, or allowed favourites to exercise it, in those areas where their authority should have been delegated. John Walwayn's sense that Edward II's reign was disastrous is predicated, after all, on the violation of an understood royal/magnatial cooperation.[40]

Moreover, the Auchinleck romances can scarcely be construed as anti-royal in even a weak sense. No text actually presents a royal villain. Indeed, the most culpable figures are in fact freewheeling royal servants who operate through manipulation of kings too prone to trust (cf. the *Mirror of Justices* or *Guy*'s Otto of Pavia). For this reason, Orfeo's climactic test involves proving his steward's loyalty; delegation is a fraught procedure, and wisdom, as Milemete seeks to teach young Edward III, a knowledge of the limits of trust. The same freedom to administer, to dispense justice, in a knight's home jurisdiction precisely admits, with the wrong delegation, the usurpation the hero must overcome to demonstrate his potential for success. Ultimately, the narratives that engage knights more normative and alert than Guy identify an administrative capacity.

Equally, *Guy of Warwick* is unusual in its portrayal of a second generating force of narration, Felice. While Auchinleck romances are typically doubly motivated – the hero not just usurped politically, but by his passion as well[41] – no other female figure shows Felice's engagement in dismissive *fin* (or perhaps more accurately, *haut*) *amour*. Quite the contrary. Indeed, the danger of female sexuality (or the alternative imperative of chastity, occasionally with a frisson of incest) appears repeatedly in Auchinleck romance as a destabilising motif. Rather than Felice's standoffishness, Auchinleck heroines are a great deal too prone to forwardness, indeed to engendering the narratively complicating claim of their own supposed lack of chastity, that they are 'forlein' and the typically befuddled hero hence subject to banishment. And a variety of woman-centred Auchinleck texts – *Degaré*, 'Lai le freyne' – play off such narratives in offering models of longsuffering and beleaguered chastity.

Not only is Felice unique in refusing to succumb to Guy, but the poem comes to lack that doubleness of development, both hero and heroine, more typical of these narratives. For if male figures move towards useful social roles through the activities of their banishments, the once-forward heroines are redeemed through their denial of that merely capricious sexuality of which they are frequently accused. One great female motif of the stories – Horn's ring/token appearing in Rimenhild's female chalice would be a locus classicus – is the heroine's resolve of fidelity, exemplified in her enduring the threat of forced marriage to the wrong man.

One testimony to the persistence of such doubled narrative patterns is Auchinleck's inclusion of a *Seven Sages* text (item 18, fols. 84[ra]–99[vb]). This is London work, to be associated with the historically inflected *Kyng Alisaunder* and *Richard*. It consists of a framed narrative sequence juxtaposing satiric attacks on evil counsel, bad service to (Roman) royalty, against analogous anti-feminist assays, testimony to the supposed instability and sexual rapaciousness of women.

To exemplify these various threads, I consider the most enduring of all Auchinleck romances, a text of ebullient narrative inventiveness and profusion, *Beves of Hamtoun*. Following from my comments about *Guy of Warwick*, a secondary purpose of the analysis will be to demonstrate that the work can be dismissed as 'popular' only through the crudest of readings (for provocative ones, see Barnes 1993, 61–123; Saunders). While the poem operates within those exile-return structures inherent in 'English romance', it proves far from sober. It shares prominent themes with a range of Auchinleck poems – *Floris and Blauncheflur, Orfeo, Amis and Amiloun*, and *Sir Tristrem*, as well as the associated *Lybeaus. Tristrem* (like *Amis*, a Northern import with similarly challenging themes), in particular, plays incessantly with a similar problematic, founded upon the necessity of contrivance and deception. The lovers' career ceaselessly refigures the ambiguity between the truth promised in legalistic oath and the differing embodied truth of passion (cf. Barnes 1984, Fewster 39–42, 50–81).

Beves of Hamtoun indicates in a variety of ways its involvement, both in detail and reception, with the topical and local. Associated strenuously with the South Coast, especially Southampton and adjacent west Sussex, it is marked with local references. Beves's Bucephalus-like steed gives his name to Arundel Castle, Sussex (3535–42). The poem further honours the lords of Arundel in a central episode exemplifying the hero's unique force, his slaying two lions; the lords of Arundel, eventually the Fitzalans of Clun, bore 'gules, a lion rampant or' (cf. Weiss 1979).[42] Episodes from and allusions to the poem appear in Southampton civic decoration (Fellows 1986, Rance); however, one should also recall the Dublin and Scheide manuscripts of the Prose Psalter (see pp. 17–18), an indication of London connections with South Coast.

The topical identifies Beves's homeland, the place of his 'kende eritage' (2940), the earldom of Southampton. Just as in all good 'English' romances, however, the hero will lose this locale through usurpation and will be forced to reassert his legal title as outsider. Yet *Beves* is particularly strident about foreign threat to and occupation of English soil, for the child's displacement leaves his locale in the control of his Scottish mother and her German paramour Devoun.[43] Beves loses his homeland through the complacency of his too aged father Guy, slain through the machinations of his sexy young wife, a bad presage for Beves's potential relations with women.[44] The hero berates his mother as a whore (302, 308–12), and he himself is compromised by her whoredom.

In a pattern of invective to be repeated through the romance, he is simultaneously identified and misidentified as 'scherewe houre-sone' by the porter of the castle that should be his own (398). Epithet in the poem invariably instructs; as a trope on the hero's proper name unspoken or unknown, it measures identity and defines a range of possible self-constructions demanding assessment by hero and reader. Here the child Beves accepts the epithet (410) – it is socially descriptive, yet simultaneously not so, bearing with it moral criticism for an action over which he has no control. In these latter terms, the insult functions as sign of impropriety, misrule, and identifies the local chaos Beves must eventually bring to order.

Similar invective identifies Beves as true heir, to become the adult ruler appropriate to Hamtoun. Insult links Beves with Guy as true son of the father, like him, a 'treitour' (as well as a 'foule', 438–41, 449). These epithets he properly earns for his outraged rebellion against his mother's authority. As such a rebel, he is expelled, no longer in his mother's eyes a fit heir but a lowly 'hyne' (497), and he spends the remainder of the poem in an effort at recovering his patrimony and his father's royally conferred office (eventually achieved at 3467–3510). With these externals, he gains a renewed sense of his identity. In this instance, the biological line of his 'eritage' compromised, Beves's renewed succession and jurisdiction must be, in part, a surrogate one, focussed in other lines, those of king Armyn's daughter Josiane, eventually to be his wife, and his faithful old tutor Saber of Wight.

Distinctive to *Beves*, however, are ironies of association inherent in the redemptive ending. The poem mainly treats leaving England for a(n Islamic) world of pure fantasy, or pure ingenuity, a bit ironically identified as Armenia/'harmony'. But the payoffs at the poem's end are manifold, reminiscent of Havelok as modernised Cnut governing a transoceanic empire. By the conclusion, jurisdictional succession has been assured to a new generation, in control of three kingdoms, stretching from Asia to England, as well as the local patrimonies of Hamtoun and Saber's Wight.

The ending provides another form of entrée to the poem, in a moment of deliberated whimsy:

An hous [Beves and Josian's son Guy jr] made of riligioun
For to singe for sire Beuoun
And ek for Iosian þe fre;
God on here saules haue pite!
And also for Arondel,
ʒif men for eni hors bidde schel.
(4613–18)

Typical of the general tone, the speaker dissipates the force of his expected pious conclusion. But he does so in order to place the three central characters, as he has persistently done, in parallel. One can learn a great deal about *Beves* and Auchinleck romances by examining the central episode of this type (1201–2200), if but a moment in the overelaborated, incident-packed time of this tale, a seven-year chronological space in any real history.

At this narrative juncture, all three figures find themselves imprisoned separately. Josiane, destined to be Beves's, although he is reasonably oblivious to her passion, is unhappily wed to the romance's great villain, Yvor of Mombraunt (only extirpated in climactic single combat at 4124–4242). Yvor is also in possession of Beves's miraculous sword Morgelay. For his part, Beves has been imprisoned by Brademond, an earlier candidate to coerce Josiane's virginity (lines 924–6 present his especially provocative statement of sexual sadism); captured while on embassy in circumstances designed to ensure his death, the over-muscled Arnold Swarzeneggerish hero, chained with an intricacy that might have challenged Houdini (1423–4, 1602–4, 1649), is being starved to death in a snake pit.[45] Finally, Arundel, like Beves, is chained and mistreated after having refused to let Yvor ride him.

As this narrative summary indicates, the reference to Arundel at the poem's end truly encapsulates important motifs. Unlike Guy's ironically self-reflecting lion, Beves's faithful horse functions within the narrative as a tertium quid.[46] Narratively, he shares with Beves physical imprisonment in chains and short rations (1529–32). But equally, he has sunk to that status because he shares Josiane's fidelity to the hero, the disinclination to be 'ridden' by anyone else, analogous to Yvor's possession of Beves's phallic sword, more of the poet's provocative cheekiness. (As I've implied above, English romanciers have no problem about letting readers see that they know what young lovers really want to get up to.)

However dire the characters' situation may appear, identified with hitting rock-bottom (cf. 'ibrouʒt to grounde' 1410, 1602; Beves's subterranean prison 'þis petes grounde' twenty fathoms deep, 1431), difficulties here are doubled. The poet chooses to associate this positioning of the central characters with a moment of potential disaster for the narrative. The poem presumes and provokes knowing readers, and, as such, we know that the lovers will, of course, be reunited at the end. We also know that their rejoining will depend upon the romance version of Aristotelian *anagnoresis*, their mutual recognition of identities (and thus, of their mutual passion) through exchanged tokens.

But it is precisely in these terms that the poet cleverly builds additional suspense into his narrative. The central trio will have to overcome various forms of analogous bondage. But equally, the actions constructed to ensure their parallel escapes will render their simple freedom an insufficient condition for the happy ending readers know is, somehow, in store.

Here, the acts that preserve self are foreseeably destabilising, carry within them the prospect, if not necessity, of further adventurous complication. For Beves and Josiane cannot achieve freedom, and with it, any prospect of a stable identity, without, deliciously and paradoxically, each making a gesture that will simultaneously destroy their identities. They are faced with situations in which each is constrained to make him/herself unrecognisable to the other (and thus constrained to underwrite, to readers' thorough narrative joy, the ongoing episodic proliferation of romance).

Josiane is, like all heroines, the universal object of desire; as the awestruck Beves says to her at an early moment:

> In al þis world nis þer man,
> Prinse ne king ne soudan,
> þat þe to wiue haue nolde,
> And he þe hadde ones beholde.
> (1101–4)

But to preserve herself intact for the hero, she must don a magic ring that renders her uniquely undesirable, 'To me schel no man haue welling'

(1472), not herself at all. (Similarly, in a later reduplicating moment of sexual threat, she will practise her skills as herbalist to make herself visibly a horrifying leper, literally a 'mesel' 3668–88.) But donning the ring already redoubles the device, for Josiane's overt state is as 'wife', thus a tainted sexual object unfaithful to (and inappropriate for) the hero.[47] The narrative coerces moments that, like invective rhetoric, dissipate identity, rather than consolidate it; Josiane remains beautiful, desirable, and chaste only by violating the overt signs associated with those standards.

Similarly, Beves can only break out of jail through a loss of self and identity. He has got himself imprisoned through a typically cocky act of unreflective self-reliance, thinking he was being tricky when in fact only a pawn in other characters' larger connivances. According to the imaginative laws governing the poem, he must be marked for, so that he may grow out of, his mistake. Hence, his escape involves an act of prowess that only an impeccably 'douȝti' hero can perform, thoroughly dismembering a flying adder using only a broken spear butt (1547–74). But the adder gets its own back by leaving Beves with a disfiguring torn brow; this injury (not to mention his standard-issue wild man guise, hair down to his feet, 1538) will render him physically unrecognisable as the person he is, unknowable to Josiane, just as she will be to him.

Thus, the poet constructs a brilliantly bifurcated attentiveness. By what connivance will they escape, and how will they reachieve identities that will enable each to recognise the other? Eventually, Arundel, rather than either human character, proves the vehicle of recognition; Josiane knows Beves because he can ride his steed, and thus, might appropriately ride her, were she suitable for him (2175–80).

But even this highly complicated narrative presentation fails to exhaust the sequence. For more important to the poem is another aspect of Beves's escape, his conversion to an active sense of himself as Christian knight, someone in a world of disturbing and ambivalent fiction yet nonetheless anchored in a sense of truth. As his situation in his dungeon becomes increasingly dire and dangerous, Beves turns to prayer:

> 'Lord', a seide, 'heuene king,
> Schepere of erþe and alle þing:
> What, haue ich so meche misgilt,

þat þow sext a þolen wilt
þat þe weþerwines and þe fo
Schel þe seruaunt do þis wo?
Ich bede þe, lord, for þe pite
þat þow haue merci on me . . . ,
(1579–86)

This is a language strikingly Davidic, a plea for help in extremity from a character alienated from appropriate power and perhaps from himself. In allowing Beves to enunciate such a discourse, and in these terms, the romancier displays again his playfulness and a destabilising openness about what is true (is Beves really a put-upon prophet? is Josiane really Josiane?).

Something more than just a vaguely biblical rhetoric suffuses the presentation of Beves in prison. Grotesquely chained in the deeps, in water up to his middle (a detail unique to the Cambridge University Library, MS Ff.ii.38 expansion of 1399–1430; see edn p. 74, 53–8, lines that more clearly visualise the scene), Beves quite unconsciously is re-enacting a common biblical image, and its associated text. This was certainly well known in Edwardian London. At the head of Ps. 68, the prophet cries out:

> Save me, O God: for the waters are come in even unto my soul. I stick fast in the mire of the deep: and there is no sure standing.[48]

This does not constitute a random verbal similarity, but rather, an allusion to a prominent and thus well-recognised moment in the biblical text. Following older monastic practice, devotional reading of the Psalter was conventionally divided into 'nocturns', associated with specific hours of the liturgical day (cf. Morgan 1, 40). In this system, widely used by lay people from at least the thirteenth century, Ps. 68 introduces a new textual division and thus typically is illuminated in manuscript copies. The picture at this point – in *Beves* transformed into romance type-image, like Guy and his lion – universally shows either Jonah being vomited from his whale (chapter 2:2–10 provides a great biblical reprise of this Davidic language) or David awash in a stream.[49]

The poet intends his readers to grasp this connection, a visualisation of man and snaky monster in the depths. Simultaneously one must remain aware that it is mainly a playful and provocative juxtaposition, another

of those labile gestures that characterise the text. Here one tantalisingly
confronts the unequivocal seriousness that inheres in Scripture inhering
also in the delights of ambiguously fraught romance fictiveness.

Yet equally, one can see the narrative of *Beves* as frequently constructed
from various verbal suggestions in this extremely long and rich psalm.
For however much complication is left for the central characters to endure, this narrative moment does change Beves, and he is never quite the
same after. Once he gets himself out of Brademond's dungeon (as recipient of a special chainbusting grace like that extended to Peter and Paul,
1645–9), Beves must flee a huge Muslim force. Weakened by hunger, he
cannot summon up the strength to fight his pursuers, and, following a
brief speech at the edge of a seaside cliff, throws himself over the edge:

> 'Lord', a sede, 'heuene king,
> Schepere of erþe and alle þing,
> þou madest fisch ase wel alse man,
> þat noþing of senne ne can,
> Ne nouȝt of fisches kenne
> Neuer ȝet ne dede senne ... '
> (1797–1802)

Of course, this gesture represents more narrative ebullience and duplica-
tion. Beves once again finds himself 'fallen to the ground', just as in the
dungeon, but in this instance, as an act of conscious voluntarism that
shows a good deal more providential faith than his prototype Jonah had.
Surrendering himself to God's fishies, of course, contrasts, not simply
with the 'heþene hounde' that pursue, but with the demonic serpents,
types of Jonah's whale, with which he has had to deal in the dungeon.

Moreover, the poet obviously intends his readers to understand the
scene multiply. It does not simply signal Beves's acceptance of providence
but identifies him sacramentally. Beves's rather Kierkegaardian leap is
into something like baptismal faith, a regained innocence like that he
ascribes to the fishes as natural birthright. Beyond that implication lurks
a rich archetypal pattern of 'rites de passage' associated with crossing
running water.[50] Further, the poet is inspired, as he is elsewhere, by his
chosen psalm, here the next verse, 'I am come into the depth of the sea:
and a tempest hath overwhelmed me' ('Venit in altitudinem maris; et
tempestas demersit me', Ps. 68:3).

Similar details of conversion are associated with episodes dependent on this moment. For example, on their reunion, but before their full recognition, Josiane removes what has been the running impediment to their relationship, from Beves's first moment in Armenia (561–8; cf. 699–700): immediately upon their mutual recognition, she announces her willingness to surrender Islam for Christianity (2181–6; she is actually christened only at 2590). Further, assessments of the causes for Beves's triumphs shift radically as well, routinely to include an acknowledgement that he is not just a warrior of strength, but one also receptive of divine aid. As King so ably demonstrates, such gracious sacramentalism is particularly notable (and was noted by Spenser) in Beves's battle against the dragon of Cologne (2611–2910), another moment when Beves is 'to grounde brouȝt' to be sacramentally released (2783). With typically almost by-the-by insouciance, the poet presents this triumph (rather than the return to England) as perhaps the hero's greatest claim to romance fame; he here provides comparisons with Lancelot, Wade, and Guy (and beyond them, implicitly, George; cf. Fellows 1993, 36–41).

Yet however sanctified the characters' careers, *Beves* remains a text devoted to *ingenium*, the knowing guilefulness of both characters and poet (Barnes 1984). If the poem might be thought educational or constructively entertaining, this turns out to be largely an education in double-dealing, in learning to manipulate that self-estrangement that the romance's persistent variety of incident (not to mention current political history) implies is living in the world. At least if one construes a passing tournament description as indicative – 'þar nolde no man oþer knowe' (3801) – even Beves's most straightforward doughtiness turns metaphorical. The poem describes assumed inscrutability, a deceptive cloaking of identity analogous to that performed by the poem's many epithets, and a labour in which the self-evident never reveals the totality.

This note is struck in the initiating episode of Beves's banishment, for central to his expulsion is destabilising misrepresentation. His treasonous mother feigns illness and her need for a boar's head to send old Guy to his death. Guy fails to exercise 'wareness' or prudence; in spite of the marked unseasonability of the request (it's May Day, 175, when one expects to bring in greenery to ensure fertility, not that deadly game properly associated with Christmas), he goes forth lightly armed (250–2).

In this context of 'tresoun' (190, 196), a word that reverberates through the whole poem and alludes to the studied misrepresentation of desire that drives the story, the hunter is the quarry, his head brought home instead of the boar's. The conflict is further enunciated in the exchange of Guy's normative, but impotent 'þow seist aȝen þe lawe', 'þow hauest no riȝt to me wif' (224, 238) with the murderer's accusation that he is 'treitour' and 'olde dote' (218). The charge puts forward an apparently verifiable claim that Guy has misrepresented himself as sexually potent, active, or interested, not superannuated (cf. 58–66).

This misrepresentation is doubled in the faithful Saber's effort to save Beves. The loss of station that will bedevil the hero until the poem's end is signalled in the loss of his rich clothes. Saber removes these to be smeared in the pig's blood he will present as the child's own. In this witty bit of guile, Saber appears to fulfil the 'appropriate' murder demanded by his superior, but actually expresses his fidelity to Beves through his untruth to the Mother who demanded infanticide. The pig-corpse he presents her alludes to Beves's proper status; the alleged victim appears as Guylike, a 'boar's-son'. But in the process, treachery, sly and artful dealing, loses any definitive sense of moral opprobrium; as a result, the variety of moral distinction inherent in the poem's later sacramentalism becomes particularly fraught.

This perception is sharpened by Beves's first independent action. Although a 'hende wiȝt', he is now declassé, off as a shepherd in 'pouer wede' (357–8), ostensibly not who he is. His complete exile from home and heritage – given to merchants to be exported to the East – follows, when the seven-year-old hero acts in accord with what he presumes his social identity. Drawn to the tower that should be his, he angrily invades his own hall and thereby rejects unaccommodated nature, the down he's lived on as a shepherd, the safety of his disguise (cf. 379–82). On the one hand, he is properly incapable of prudently swallowing outrage and dissembling, enduring the loss of his identity; on the other, he is expelled for trying to act out – too soon – the plot of the romance, the restoration of heritage. One can only fulfil the plot of desire through an education in appropriately deceitful dealing, by achieving that 'queinte gile' (3022, 3060) Beves will eventually use to pay out the usurper Devoun.

Christian guile in the poem thus potentially involves a disquieting collision of value systems. At one point, a Muslim adversary accurately labels Beves a 'fox welp' (1733), an insulting epithet that alludes to his status as offspring, and thus to an ancestry he attempts to regain; the identification jars against the narrator's awkwardly rhyming ascription of Beves's subsequent triumph to '*help* of Crist' (1770). Are these claims parallel and reinforcing, or simply at odds?

More troublingly, Christian guile is not bound by conventional religious categories. Although Beves, out of place in Islam, customarily expresses his antipathy for any native as 'heþene hounde' (first 692–3, an epithet imitated from his 'hosts' in 621), the poem is typically more even-handed. It includes both Muslims at least tolerable and villains who emerge from Christian contexts and who require appropriately guileful handling. Finally, about the only unsanctified guilefulness in the poem involves deceiving virtuous fellow Christians; Beves is precipitated 'to the ground' in the sequence I have earlier analysed by his refusal to allow his recognition by the faithful Thierry and to seek and heed his learned counsel (1289–1333). In their most imaginative moments, Auchinleck romances may express as laudable belief a self-invention capable of being read as seditious and sinister (like Richard's demonic Crusader windmill). In the next chapter, I examine one powerful set of London responses to such potentially troubling delight.

NOTES

1. I pass over these rather quickly; for further discussion, see 2000, 99–101 (with notice of similar texts used as filler later in the volume). Further books with some textual connections, in the main Western, or derived from Western sources, include British Library, MSS Additional 36983 and Harley 525; Bodleian Library, MSS Bodley 779, Rawlinson poet. 225, and Add. C.220.

2. Smithers, ed., *Kyng Alisaunder II* 41. Smithers's promised proof of common authorship never appeared, but presumably would have relied on identity of linguistic forms as described in EETS 237. I am grateful to Alison Wiggins for suggesting to me that, insofar as Smithers's perception depends on identity of rhyming forms, the first section of *Guy of Warwick* should be included among such works.

3. Manuscripts in one way or another derivative include, in addition to Hale 150 (see p. 16), British Library, MSS Egerton 1995 (London) and 2862 ('the Sunderland MS'), Harley 6223 (John Stow, London); Lambeth Palace Library, MS 306 (London); Bodleian Library, MSS Rawlinson poet. 34 + Douce 326, Douce 236; Oxford, Balliol College, MS 354 (London); Cambridge, University Library, MS Ff.ii.38; Gonville and Caius College, MSS 107/176 (London?) and 175/96; Naples, Royal Library, MS XIII.B.29. Of course, Sir Thomas Malory, presumably working in London (where he was buried), recycled *Lybeaus Desconus* for one original portion of his *Morte Darthur*, 'The Tale of Gareth'.

4. It would be more helpful to consider Loomis's 'scribal poetics' as something other than sports to concern editors seeking original versions of the texts. Rather, they might be seen as deliberate, if fitful, tailoring to create a textually integrated volume out of what the compiler would have been well aware were extremely diverse materials.

5. The most outstanding study of Anglo-Norman's literary sophistication, Wogan–Browne, concerns hagiography, not romance. On *Guy*, see also Mills (1992) and Price's interesting studies.

6. As Hanning's important study elaborately demonstrates (see 118–22, 136–8, 224–8, etc. on Chrétien's *Yvain*).

7. Yvain is properly a thief, for, not having a heart or any real interiority, he fails to see that he bears away from Laudine something other than the physical force that is properly his – her love, which he has ignored. Cf. the discussion of invective and insult in *Beves of Hamtoun*, pp. 133, 134, 141–2.

8. The cessation of the epithet in latter parts of the poem may well be significant; see further below.

9. These consume roughly the first 1,200 lines of the poem; cf. Benson 73–80 or Parker *passim* on romance dilation.

10. And to English history, in the discussion of the giant-killing at the end of *Guy II* at 'The Anonymous Short Chronicle' 596–602.

11. Cf. King 129–45, who concentrates on the more explicit description of the analogous fight in *Beves of Hamtoun*.

12. Cf. Riddy 1991, 317: 'Less clear-cut is the subculture evidenced by a book like the Auchinleck manuscript.... There ought to be ways of defining the subculture this book represents other than by negatives.' Below, I will only partially confirm Riddy's answer to these negations, 'well-to-do lay people literate only in English...whose tastes and interests are formed in the town or the manor-house rather than the court'.

13. The two volumes I here discuss are Sandler 1986, 2, 91–4 (nos. 84–5). For a very tentative and partial, yet still overwhelming, list of the manuscripts, see PAL 54–75 (no. 81), and for the several English versions, examples of quite extensive vernacularisation into most west European languages, *Secretum*.

14. Cf. also such statements as 'I have shaped two books, composing the present one from my own study, and another of the philosopher Aristotle, which contains great wisdom and human discretion' ('presentem librum proprio studio duxi componendum et eciam librum philosophi Aristotelis in quo magna prudencia et discrecio humana continentur', fol. 9ᵛ); 'I have fashioned and written the book word for word for your use' ('eundum librum de uerbo ad uerbum ad usum uestrum duxi scribendum', fol. 12ᵛ); 'These things are more fully contained in *De secretis secretorum et prudentiis regum*, which I have sent you' ('quo in libro de secretis secretorum et prudenciis regum plenius sunt contenta et per me uobis missa', fol. 70). And sporadic, if brief and fairly perfunctory, references to the Aristotle–Alexander relationship and Alexander's use of its fruits as his model for regal conduct recur through the treatise, e.g. at fols. 36ᵛ–37.

15. 'Merito et uos, domine, per Dei graciam cum ad uirilem perueneritis etatem et ad statum maioris potencie et dignitatis, ut michi uerisimiliter uisum est, credoque firmiter, opinor indubitanter, si secundum doctrinam regi Alexandro nuper editam ... firmiter operari ... [various successes] habere poteritis' (fol. 13).

16. Perhaps an early imitation of his crusading colleague, Louis IX; cf. Noel–Weiss, esp. 18.

17. Edward's Maccabean and Alexandrine pretentions were, to continue my narrative from pp. 89–94, eventually to underwrite the Scots vernacular literary tradition. In *The*

Bruce (1375), John Barbour engages in sporadic identifications of his freedom-fighter heroes as the true models he implies Edward I and II corrupt; cf. 1.465–76, 3.73–92, 10.708–40, 14.312–15 (and possible recycling of seasonal passages from *Kyng Alisaunder*, e.g. 5.1–13).

18. William of Paull's work (see Boyle), to which I will return in the discussion of Langland's Peace v. Wrong (pp. 268–9), displays further rhetorical similarities to Milemete's two handbooks. William's text exists in two versions, an 'epistola' and the *Speculum regis* proper. The first appears a rough draft composed of serious clerical notes, replete with legal citation and biblical reference. In contrast, the later version is more tautly organised, dispenses with learned references for rhetorical elaboration and general hortatory injunction, and centres around the two royal images. I'd consider it plausible to believe the second a scaled-down, non-scholarly version for a young king.

19. For St Stephen's, see Tristram 48–54, 57–8, 206–19, plates 1–6; the catalogue entry, last cited, includes extensive quotation from the late eighteenth-century antiquary John Topham. For the armourial decoration (and the two surviving warrior saints from the window jambs), see John Smith 232–50. For surviving paintings of the stories of Job and Tobit, see *Age* nos. 680–1 (498–501). The iconography, emphasising patient suffering rather than aggression, is nonetheless associated with William of Paull's heroic St Louis and thus Edward's claim to the French crown. For it is certainly a Parisian and Louisian allusion (not Henry III and Edward I's Romish imperialism), derived from Ste Chapelle (in its turn, from the north-west portal of Chartres).

20. Fol. 66ᵛ mentions the importance of preparing 'wooden castles raised on high' and 'other kinds of instruments for casting stones and cannon balls' ('castra lignea in altum erigenda', 'alia instrumentorum genera gressos lapides et pilas proiciencia'), with comparable illustrations in the lower margins through the chapter. Another bit of romance troping, the comment that in some places, kings include in their war provisions armed elephants, is also illustrated, recalling either Alexander's campaigns against the Indians or the wars of the Maccabees.

21. The image that precedes the romance in Auchinleck's fragmentary surviving opening (fol. 326ʳᵃ). Both bees and windmill episodes appear in an interpolation into 'The Anonymous Short Chronicle' unique to Auchinleck, A2065–2122.

22. Most provocatively, those of fols. 74 and 77ᵛ–78. Richard's fiery windmill fuses variously conventional torments of Hell, e.g. the hooked and fiery Catherine wheel used to punish the avaricious and the coloured flames emanating from the pit described in another Auchinleck poem, *St Patrick's Purgatory* ('Owayne miles', IMEV *11), sts 83–6, 105–6 (cf. the Latin, 133/449–62, 134–5/508–35: the poem has specified flame-colours approximating those of Richard's 'sayles'). See further Dante, *Inferno* 34.4–60.

23. In this account, the Prince has gained from Edward II only what a medieval thinker would describe as 'gifts of nature', 'He might ascribe to his father his strength and bodily beauty' ('uiribus et specie referat cum corpore patrem'). Cf. Walwayn's assessment of Edward's failures in the first half of the reign, 'If Edward had made as great an effort at arms as he devoted to rustic things, England would have been quite excellent' ('Si tantam dedisset [rex Edwardus] armis operam quantam impendidit circa rem rusticam, multum excellens fuisset Anglia', 40). For the charge, see Childs, esp. 160–1; *Great Chronicle* 27 (probably including elaborations from the Chronicle of Meaux; see Childs 150–2) reports that Edward 'lovyd namely suche cherles werkes'. More restrained accounts, not so insistent upon Edward II as a genealogical disruption, possibly a carter's changeling and not a truly royal scion, appear at Walwayn 86–7, *Annales Paulini* 282–3.

24. In Christ Church 92, the first quire, now the table of chapter headings and full-page illustrations, appears have replaced an originally planned text opening. The table of contents (fols. 1–2^v) promises a first chapter that does not appear in the current volume, which now begins with the second chapter in the table.

25. On the castle of love, see Veronica Sekules, *Age* 45; Camille 1998, 118–19 with plate; and for the pageant, Juliet Vale 42 and 122–3 n. 11. Grosseteste's lines 697–702, 823–42, in the Middle English version of the Vernon MS, ed. *Middle English Translations*, underlie *Piers Plowman* 5.618–29.

26. 'War is the foundation of peace', and continuing, 'since many kings preserve peace by making others fearful of their capacity for war. Therefore, the king who desires peace should prepare for war' ('cum propter belli timorem multi conseruent pacem. Ideo qui pacem desiderat, bellum preparet').

27. See Sandler 1986, 2, 87–9, 91–8, 123–4 *passim* (nos. 84, 86, 88) and the analogues there cited. Sandler also associates with these her nos. 82–3, and with subsidiary hands of the royal books, nos. 80, 85, and 111. To these volumes, Pächt-Alexander would add (3, 53, nos. 578–80) Bodleian Library, MSS Bodley 738 (Trivet on the Psalms, for bishop John Grandisson and donated to his Cathedral at Exeter) and Selden supra 38 (Apocalypse and Anglo-Norman infancy gospel).

28. *Age* 204 (cf. 127), no. 16. See further Staniland 1986, 243, discussing Edward III's decorations for the Guildford Christmas interludes in 1347 and for his 1350–2 bedding accounts including cushions 'stained with the history of King Alexander and other histories'; or Juliet Vale's descriptions (45 and 125 n. 53) of his two ewers with chivalric decoration.

29. For just a sense of what tapestries involve, see Riley 52–3, where Henry de Lacy, earl of Lincoln, has paid 300*m* for two large cloths 'embroidered with diverse works in gold and silk'.

30. For Egerton, see Sandler 1986, 2, 127–9 (no. 115), and Kathryn Smith's discussions; for Taymouth, Sandler 107–9 (no. 98) and Brownrigg and Brantley's; for Smithfield, Sandler 111–12 (no. 101) and Bovey's. Sandler 2, 109–10 (no. 99) (patristic prayers and Seneca) was produced for a canon of St Paul's. See further Sandler 113, 129–33. The Smithfield Decretals include illustrations from the romance of *Enyas*, not otherwise known to have circulated in England, but also on a pendant case from London, *Age* 458–9, no. 581.

31. Barron maps eighteen ecclesiastical townhouses immediately west of the City or in the Strand, ten in Southwark. On Southwark townhouses, see Carlin 25–30, and for Winchester Palace, Schofield 1994, 229, no. 193; on the palace area of Westminster only, Rosser 1989, 21–5; on the Fleet, western City, and Strand, his 'Latin Quarter', Courtenay 91–106, with further references; as well as Schofield 1994a, 33–8 and 210–11, nos. 157–61. Surviving buildings are thin on the ground: the best examples include the chapel attached to the Bishop of Ely's inn, now St Etheldreda, Ely Place (Schofield 1994a, 191–2, no. 106); part of the front and hall of the late fifteenth-century Crosby Place, Bishopsgate, moved and rebuilt in Chelsea, 1907 (161–3, no. 22); and a reused example incorporated into The Merchant Taylors' Hall, Threadneedle Street (223–5, no. 177).

32. See Keene 1999, 102; Schofield 1994, 37, 49–51. As readers of Hoccleve know, another major government office, the Privy Seal, was reasonably adjacent, in Chester Inn, i.e. property part of the Bishop of Chester's townhouse, in the Strand.

33. For information on the extent of London guild regulation, I'm grateful to Malcolm Parkes. Although Christianson's study tends to put as many book artisans as possible in

Pater Noster Row, alongside St Paul's, his showing only relies on the thickest and most continuous documentary evidence. For an informative example of another extra-urban writing community, in St John's Street, Clerkenwell, 1414, see Jurkowsky.

34. The relevant texts are *The King of Tars* (item 2 of the manuscript), *Amis and Amiloun* (11), *Guy II* (23), *Roland and Vernagu* (31), *Sir Tristrem* (37), 'The four foes of mankind' (39), and *Horn Child* (41). *Fragments*, the oldest 'extensive' piece of Northern Middle English, presents another *Guy* (not the Auchinleck version of the poem); as I suggest elsewhere, textual traffic was two-way, also evident in *Horn* being converted into *Horn Child*, a poem predicated on careful north-east Yorkshire lore and then circulating in the south again.

35. For de la Pole, see E. B. Fryde, in more detail Kermode, and, on a general Northern movement into the City, Gwyn Williams 129–31. On the development of clericism as state service, see Murray 213–314 *passim* and the intriguing twelfth-century case-studies presented Southern 151–218.

36. Quite tangential literary effects testify to this process, e.g. John of Howden, celebrated as a saint by a local cult there, addressing a religious poem replete with romance imagery to Eleanor of Provence (chapter 1, n. 38); or fifteenth-century London chronicles deriving materials from those of Humberside and York City monasteries, p. 35 and n. 23 above).

37. See Fowler's Minster 'fasti', 2, 185–8. Hughes, although requiring careful use, discusses the ecclesiastical-royal clerkly *familia* surrounding archbishop John Thoresby in the third quarter of the century.

38. At least two central manuscripts of the continuation – Leeds, Brotherton Library, MS 29, also including the *Anominalle Chronicle*; and Bodleian Library, MS Lyell 17 – actually belonged to the great Benedicine abbey, St Mary's, York, during the Middle Ages; see Ker MLGB 217.

39. The only real imponderable in such siting remains the persistently French quality of recorded royal and magnatial books (cf. pp. 10–11). This I consider, especially in the attenuated account of comparable English volumes in almost any context, finally a recording gap. Certainly, Loomis's arguments for Chaucer's knowledge of Auchinleck or something comparable, not to mention his entire interest in parodying it, would imply the continued presence of these texts in a similar environment later in the century, whether it was courtly or the entrepreneurial sort a Customs collector might encounter.

40. Cf. 'The magnates are the principal arm of the king, without whom no king may undertake or bring to conclusion anything great' ('[Barones] sunt enim membrum regis principale, sine quo nil grande poterit rex aggredi uel consummare', 28).

41. Cf. the (somewhat non-descriptive – the hero is relatively unaware just how he is wounded) double entendres at an early point in *Beves*:

> Lemman, þin ore;
> Ich am iwonded swiþe sore . . .
> And proue to hele, ase þow can,
> þe wondes of þat douȝti man.
> (713–14, 728–9)

42. The episode with the lions indicates the utterly unique and necessary status of Beves's war-fury through juxtaposition of his success with the failure of the poem's apparently most expert counsellor Boniface and the heroine Josiane's enforced non-involvement.

43. Similarly, during Beves's great battle in the narrow London streets, a form of 'local knowledge' of the metropole, while perhaps generally expressing an aristocratic disdain

for mercantilism, makes common cause with early fourteenth-century local interests – the hero's single great adversary a Lombard (4497–4508), a hated alien trader.

44. The rewritten couplet version here presents Beves's father Guy in the guise of the noble English lawgiver:

> He kepte well Englond in his da[w]s:
> He sett peas and stabelud the laws
> That no man was so hardye
> To do another velonye.
> (edn p. 2, 43–6)

45. This bizarre motif has presumably been imported from Scandinavian sources, e.g. 'Atlakviða' or *Ragnars saga*, one bit of the poem's thoroughly omnivorous syncretism and delight in alien(ating) systems of reference.

46. Rather like the fade frame of the sentimental Western, the virtuous gunman framed between hoss and heroine.

47. Cf. the instructions Beves is offered after confessing to the Patriarch of Jerusalem, who

> forbede him vpon his lif
> þat he neuer take wif
> Boute ȝhe were clene maide.
> (1967–9)

Being a 'mesel' appropriately describes Josiane's social bereftness, when she has lost both Beves and children. It is, as readers of Henryson's *Testament* will recognise, her exilic experience to parallel the hero's own (cf. 3701–8). On the third occasion when she is forced, with earl Miles (3161–3224), she indulges in a sanctified experience analogous to those Beves undergoes, plays guilefully warlike Judith and hangs her Holofernes, as Saunders sees. The scene involves yet another, in this case perfunctory (the English translator does lose interest after a while), non-recognition scene; when Beves comes to save her from burning, he finds Josiane in her smock (3289), earlier (2203–6) established as a symbolic referent for her (only potential) sexual infidelity.

48. 'Salvum me fac, Deus, quoniam intraverunt aquæ usque ad animam meam. Infixus sum in limo profundi, et non est substantia' (vv. 2–3).

49. Images appear prominently in Morgan, Sandler 1986, and Scott *passim*. In her survey of thirty-three fifteenth-century psalters (2, 378–9), Scott finds the David image in twenty-one, on five occasions Jonah and his whale, the more normal illustration here in the thirteenth and fourteenth centuries.

50. And perhaps, within it, a very deep reference to local historiographical models, Nicholas Howe's Anglo-Saxon narrative of migration.

4

Pepys 2498: Anglo-Norman audiences and London biblical texts

The depiction of Beves as a divinely 'helped whelp' speaks to one of the great paradoxes of romance. Northrop Frye encapsulates it in his provocative description of the form as involving 'fables of identity'. The poems build their exemplarism, the integrated individual capable of restoration to, and consequent restoration of, his paternal locale, through a process of successive and shifting representations. But not only do these shift; no one of the representations can itself be other than fragmented and plural (the hero's identity/his represented identity). Thus, the pluralistic narrative métier of the genre always plays against its larger foundational claims to singularity or identity, and, more importantly, threatens the social work the genre, as secular 'master-narrative', always claims it is performing. The first twenty lines of *Guy of Warwick*, for example, put the paradox forthrightly:

> Fayre aduenturis hadden they,
> For euere they louyd sothfastenesse,
> Faith with trewthe and stedfastnesse.
> Therfore schulde man with gladde chere
> Lerne goodnesse, vndirstonde and here.
> Who my[ch]e it hereth and vndirstondeth it
> By resoun, he shulde bee wyse of witte,
> And Y it holde a fayre mastrye
> To occupye wisedome and leue folye.[1]
> (Caius MS 12–20)

Like the similar opening of the later *Wars of Alexander*, *Guy* is presented as offering exemplaristic historical knowing, available in verse. Reading or hearing the poem is a wise occupation, and one that leads to appropriate moral knowledge, a sobriety in touch with the largest abstract verities. Yet these are to be discerned through plural 'aduenturis', with no explicit cumulative programme or progress for secure inference. My analysis of *Beves* would imply that the poems are just as apt to present things another way, in the words of Shakespeare's cataclysmic romancier, Leontes, 'All's true that is suspected' (*The Winter's Tale* 2.1.48).

The difficulty is that the genre, whatever its ennobling ideals of 'adventurous' conduct, too emphatically bares the device. In the name of enjoyment, it toys too openly with the fictive basis of very serious matters. And it shows them, as they always are, and yet may never too clearly appear, as susceptible to ongoing human manipulation. Yet to be a wiser Leontes, and not to believe the claims of romance, as I have argued in the last two chapters, might be seen as socially crippling. Romance fictiveness provides a basis for and is intertwined with the most powerful discourses of social identity and solidarity, those of history and of law. Like *Guy*, the poems always claim to reconstruct a past that underwrites and specifies unquestionable terms of social governance for the present.

In the face of such a discursive enigma, it is little wonder that many English poems of the Edwardian period (1270–1370) are marked by deep suspicions about romance. A long sequence of such works, all of them sober religious writings, begins with a rejection of romances (frequently named, *Guy* and *Beves* with pride of place). The poems propose other identity models, other ways of becoming, and provide variously alternative histories. These, because their discussions are frequently attached to an appeal for the language itself, argue for different models to underpin English social solidarity.

Such analyses and rejections occur prominently on at least five occasions during the period. The discussions introduce, in chronological order, *The South English Legendary* (*c.* 1275?), Robert Manning's *Handlyng Synne* (1303), *Cursor Mundi* (*c.* 1300?), the London prose *Mirror* (where the materials are translated from Robert of Gretham's Anglo-Norman verse, *c.* 1310–20), and *Speculum Vitæ* (*c.* 1348–70). The topos remained vital after 1380, indeed into the fifteenth century, e.g. in Sir John Clanvowe's 'The Two Ways' and one of the Lollard tracts of Cambridge University Library, MS Ii.vi.26.[2]

Of these accounts, the most simply legible is the earliest, in *The South English Legendary*. Near the end of the prologue, the late thirteenth-century Worcester or north Gloucester poet notes that

> Men wilneþ muche to hure telle of bataille of kynge
> And of kniȝtes þat hardy were, þat muchedel is lesynge.
> (61–2)

Like all romance poets, he has announced his intention to describe the attainment of a 'kunde eritage' (2) and accompanies this with a tree and fruit metaphor defining appropriate 'kindly' succession. This genealogical metaphor to identify the true child recurs at *Cursor* 33–46, and is, of course, biblically based (cf. Matt 7:17–19, *Piers Plowman* 2.20–35).[3] In its schematicism, reminiscent of the most common diagrammatic presentations of the Christian life, for example those in CUL Gg.iv.32, this metaphor counters the narrative divagations and redoublings of romance, and positions the poet to reject its promised mode of return from exile as pure falsification.

As master-metaphor for the project of rewriting romance, the fruitful tree is rendered non-natural, eventually in this account paradoxically the vital rood-tree of death, the foundation of salvific covenant. Hence chivalry itself (as so often in thirteenth-century English writings, e.g. the lover-knight of *Ancrene Riwle*) must be subjected to a metaphoric reversal to provide an account faithful to the true 'eritage' of spiritual heroism, e.g. 'þis oþer martirs eke þat oure Louerdes knyȝtes were' (19). The body of the prologue then can be given over to an extended metaphorical analogy in which holy sufferers perform those various tasks appropriate to a battle array, in this instance that of Jesus (23–66). In this figurative battle, one triumphs by apparently losing. Rather than aggressive victory, one seeks the defeat of death, and only thus does one achieve the 'kunde eritage' of salvation. The poet turns romance inside out, adopts its literal sense as if only a fictive analogue, a 'lesynge'. He reassigns the locus of narrative action to a plane with a sublime reality and fixed sense, underwritten by an unquestionable 'fei', not the wavery truth or loyalty of the *Guy* prologue, but The Faith itself.

The *Legendary* poet, in his direct formulation, typifies the general bent of anti-romance prologues. In contrast with other treatments (often in the spirit of later Puritanisms outlined by Robert P. Adams), his generic attack remains largely implicit and undeveloped. But like him, all these authors register an opposition to worldliness, which they take to be expressed in fiction and the less than sober use of time required for its consumption. They develop a lengthy string of vilificatory abstractions to attack the literary – the most widespread an identification with '(worldly) vanite', but also including descriptive nouns like ydelschipp, fantum, foly, trufle, lesing, ymaginacioun, and, perhaps most provocatively, wenyng (AN 'quidance')[4] – chiefly as a waste of God-given cognitive capacities as well as time. For example, the huge list of allegedly wasteful subject matters that opens *Cursor Mundi* attacks the claims of 'historical' topics (Alexander, Brut, Arthur, Charlemagne) much more than 'modern' English romance subjects; the poet overwhelms this comprehensive library of useless fleeting knowledge, committed to the vicissitudes of this world, by an even more expansive catalogue of the unfailing biblical *iestes* (115, 123) that will fill his massive poem (131–220).

While these prologues always argue that holy reading is better than any other occupation (man's wit should give way before God's word, whether bare or interpreted text), they variously unpack more sophisticated implications of romance. The Lollard writer of CUL Ii.vi.26 has his character Fool, the proponent of romance, allude to the argument from genealogy. In his account, one should follow truth to one's ancestry, so central to legal, historical, and romance thinking. He wants not just 'a mery tale of Giy of Wariwyk, Beufiz of Hamton, eiþer of Sire Lebewz, Robyn Hod, eiþer of summe welfarynge man', but associates hearing them with living as the true child of his ancestors, 'for þei weren wel iloued of cheters, wrestlers, bokeler-pleieris, of daunceris and syngeris, and þei weren wel-welled to haue hem to þe ale'. Lordly men arrange expressions of social unity as festive solidarity, in this account, expressed as over-determined and self-condemning frivolousness.[5]

This religious complaint, that literary discourse as perceived and received has become coterminous with romance, is thoroughly double-edged. In defining their poems as romance's productive Other, these poets ratify its discourse as what, by contrast, enables and empowers their own. And their arguments for a greater and more constructive social and literary power rely upon asking old romance audiences to accept metaphoric translation only, a new version of the 'champioun'. The rejection is in essence a statement that they too are writing romance, that the generic and rhetorical distinctions they insist upon lack any real force. This is true even of the most sophisticated such moments, for example Gretham's explanation of his title, as translated in the London prose *Mirror*:

> þe merour is made for to teche man and womman hou þat hij tyffen hem; þat [AN Cist, i.e. this mirror] is schewer forsoþe of vertues. Als tyffyng merour makeþ þise wymmon faire to be seen in þe werlde þat hij ben þ\e/ more coueited in þe werlde whan þat hij ben faire atyred, and þis schweþ þe fairnesse þat Iesus loueþ in treuþe and makeþ þe soules to dressen hem þat God wil coueite hem. þe merour onlich riȝtteþ þe body; þan þis [h]iȝtteþ [AN aurne; the previous usage = AN aturne] boþe body and soule . . . (Pepys 45ᵃ–46ᵇ, 7/4–9)

Following upon his association of romance with gabbing or 'quaint and delicious' speech, Gretham here identifies the genre as given over to the ornamental and vain. Romance is a lady cultivating herself for decorative physical allure, hiding pimples under a wad of cosmetics; the 'boustous' English speaker of *The Mirror* looks within, and uses his 'resurrected', if potentially indecorous, English for serious, doctrinal endeavour, the non-mendacious.

This shrewd, but again faulted, commentary attests to the confluence of romance narrative and rhetoric. Poems like *Beves* depend upon disguise and insult, essentially calling something by its improper name, a trope or metaphor. But this, as Clanvowe also sees, is a feature built into the very quality of romance- or aristocratic language itself. The honorific diction of romance, fundamentally encomiastic poetry, depends upon pleonasm, rhetorical figure, the refusal to use the banally denotative.[6]

But equally, one might see that Robert, and the range of London religious texts that accompany his translation in Pepys 2498, could be tarred by the very brush he uses on romance. The *Mirror* shares with Robert Manning the tendency to surrender to narrative impulse, to provide alternatives to romance by inset narratives. These take the form of *exempla*, and in them, detail becomes subjected to overt moralisation. This impulse towards the allegorical is yet another form of what vexes these writers about romance, the trope. Such explicit commentary retroactively renders particulars of narrative detail discardable annoyances or nuisances, as empty as rhetorical figure. Exemplum might be seen as a simplified or reduced subclass of the great métier of all Pepys 2498 texts, the commentary, in which any detail may be presented as trope, something that means other than it ostensibly says. Whatever the claims produced, religious writers cannot avoid being subject to the same critique as that they offer of romance; they can only alter the strategy of controlled reading/control of the reader and argue that their writings reflect a higher, purer, and more enduring Law than that embodied in the genre they are attacking.

II

So far as manuscript survivals allow one to tell, Pepys 2498 represents the most extensive project of English vernacular book-production undertaken before the close of the fourteenth century. While the older Auchinleck MS contains vastly more folios than Pepys, at least 420, when probable losses are taken into account, as against only 232, Pepys includes considerably more text. When one recognises that the actual written area of a Pepys page is about three times the size of the Auchinleck space (at a rough guess about 600 cm² to about 220), Pepys contains at least half again as much textual content and probably required a comparably greater expenditure of time in production. So imposing a volume seems explicable only as a lectionary or as a stationary reference volume, for group use in a household or a chapel.

I raise the chapel environment deliberately. Pepys, with an early copy of the translated Gretham's *Mirror* from which I have just been quoting, could well be seen as the anti-romantic response to a book like Auchinleck. Whatever the thickness of the book, Auchinleck pages present ribbony double columns of text, with extremely ample margins (even in the manuscript's current cut-down form). This substantial 'white space', facilitated by short-line romance verse contents, testifies, beyond the originally extensive illustration, to aristocratic opulence – here a form of superfluous waste. In contrast, the writing area in Pepys (*c.* 290 mm × 215 mm), exceeding in size the full surviving page of Auchinleck, is completely filled with sober religious prose, materials that, as the *Mirror* prologue promises, rebuff romance presumptions.

This fundamental contrast, the romance of recovered patrimony against the law of The Father, has long underwritten differing critical appraisals of the two books. Literary historians view Auchinleck as a central social document, in part because of possible Chaucerian associations (in this reading, a slightly disreputable centrality), but largely because they privilege its contents, imaginative romance. In contrast, Pepys, which is 'merely translation', has remained at the margins of critical notice. But the books are both products of the same London book-trade and very likely were produced for similar London audiences. In both, moreover, the same activities of literary appropriation occur, for both are imitative products which present English texts derived from aristocratic Anglo-Norman environments.

Yet Pepys 2498 differs significantly from any books with which it might be related on the basis of shared contents, those five other codices which transmit the Englished Gretham's *Mirror* (three of them early London), the eleven of the prose Apocalypse (another by the Pepys scribe), or three of the prose Psalter (all early London connected). These generally diverge from Pepys in two ways, partly related, comprehensiveness and size. First, a majority of the early London manuscripts includes only a single text. Second, a very large number of the codices, especially of the Apocalypse, remind one of early copies of *Ancrene Riwle*: the volumes are portable, in a number of cases pocket-sized, and minimally decorated. Only copies of the Gretham translation (a quite extensive text) approach Pepys in size; they are typically large quartos. But only a single early copy shows collection procedures at all comparable with Pepys: Dublin, Trinity College, MS 69 (which shares two texts and an excerpt with Pepys).

Yet however current these works may have been, the codicological evidence suggests that the Pepys scribe had to collect them and could not copy them all continuously. The manuscript was produced in three booklets of rather uneven size. These are identifiable by self-contained texts, short concluding quires at the ends of the separate units, and putative final blank leaves, now cancelled. It is possible, but I think less likely, that this division of the book may, like divisions in the later Vernon MS, reflect conveniences in the production of an extremely large volume, not necessarily difficulty of access to exemplars. (The copying of Harley 874 from the same exemplar as Pepys suggests that the scribe could count on continued recourse to the same copy for the Apocalypse at least.) Of these three units, Booklet II (pp. 45–370, originally 164 folios) provides the core of the manuscript; this begins with the translation of Gretham's *Mirror*.

The first booklet, which contains a unique set of gospel narratives translated from Anglo-Norman prose, appears a supplement or parallel to the prose *Mirror*, the initial text of the following booklet. The work appears, from its rubrics, a conflation of at least two sources; a more conventional gospel harmony or diatesseron has been supplemented by some use of the Bonaventuran *Meditationes passionis Cristi*.[7] *Mirror* and harmonies share a common subject matter but contrast in rhetorical mode: the gospel accounts are composed of direct narratives, rather than the sermon form given the Sunday liturgical readings in the *Mirror*.

The Pepys MS also includes the greatest English spiritual classic, *Ancrene Riwle*, at the head of its third booklet. The scribe has added relatively brief filler texts at the end – further translations from Anglo-Norman prose, a complaint of the Virgin and an adaptation of the popular Gospel of Nicodemus.[8] In a not quite successful effort at filling out the final quire, the scribe copied five prayers; this still left a blank leaf, now excised, at the end. The two Booklets I and III, although separated by the bulk of the manuscript, were at least decorated ('finished') together: although the same hand provided very nice large diapered initials wherever they occur at the heads of works (the book, whatever its contents, is not thoroughly plain), the texts of Booklets I and III share the same red and blue grounds for these, and thus differ from the red and violet grounds which appear twice in Booklet II.[9]

Further, one cannot be certain that the copying of the core Booklet II proceeded in an entirely straightforward manner. In the Auchinleck MS, which I again invoke as an analogy, booklets typically begin with large and self-substantial texts, followed by shorter bits (as occurs in Booklet III of Pepys). But both disposition of texts and problems of 'finishing' suggest the copying of Pepys Booklet II proceeded in at least two stages.

Initially, the scribe appears to have begun Booklet II without planning any further than his copying of the *Mirror*. To this text he added, in a relatively continuous stint of copying, the subsequent brief and typical booklet-ending piece, the unpublished 'Good Techinges of Wise Men' (also found in the Vernon MS).[10] At some point in the midst of this text and presumably while copying proceeded, the booklet as it then existed appears to have been broken into two parts and the fully copied quires 'finished', whether by the scribe or a separate decorator. The production break occurs between quires 11 and 12 of the booklet (about two-thirds of the way through 'Good Techinges') and is signalled by the absolute cessation of the 'finishing' process: no decorative capitals at text divisions were filled in after p. 220 (although the scribe continued to leave spaces for them).

After completing 'Good Techinges' in the retained, partially written quire 12, the scribe went on to copy two commented biblical texts, the Apocalypse and Psalter. The latter, the second longest text of the volume, thus was unusually placed, at the end of the booklet. Given the failure of any 'finishing' for this portion of the codex, neither of these texts was adorned with a decorative initial at the head, and the blanks have simply been filled with ink outlines.

This discontinuity during production implies that the codex as received reflects deliberate gathering procedures without specific preplanning of contents and extending over a fairly protracted period. Unlike virtually all other manuscripts which transmit the same texts, in far smaller format and usually providing only a single large work, the Pepys scribe is involved in collecting an extensive and, as I will show, in its major texts, an interrelated canon of spiritual texts.

Whatever the vicissitudes of its production, Pepys represents a deliberate and major gathering of texts, virtually everything we know of early fourteenth-century prose with the exception of Dan Michel of Northgate's *Ayenbite* and the great northern monuments, Rolle's Psalter and epistles. Further, with the exception of *Ancrene Riwle* and 'Good Techinges', all of these works are certainly translations. Beyond the fact that these two exceptions are not translated works, they differ from the remaining texts in the volume in two other ways: they are not directly biblical in inspiration, and they do not depend upon Anglo-Norman source materials.

In a context in which 'literature in English' was apt to have connoted 'verse', as in Auchinleck, the biblical emphasis of most Pepys texts is particularly important. These may have come to the Pepys scribe in a prose form precisely because they were biblical (and glossed), because for a group of London author/translators the Bible was perceived as requiring a fidelity to the sacred word that only prose would allow. That the texts reproduce such genres of the Latin tradition as narrative paraphrase, gloss, commentary, and sermon, all traditionally prose in that literature, may be responsible for the unusual form the works take in Pepys 2498.

Four texts – the *Mirror*, the prose *Apocalypse*, *The Early English Prose Psalter*, and a heavily interpolated version of *Ancrene Riwle* – consume something like 85 per cent of the full manuscript. Of these, the last will recall the preceding discussion of the Auchinleck MS; like the opening booklets of Auchinleck (and filler elsewhere), as well as the language of some Auchinleck scribes, the work testifies to the power of import-culture and the riches of thirteenth-century south-west Midlands work. The copy is further marked as 'western' by the distinctive title 'Recluse', shared only with the later Vernon MS, produced in northern Worcestershire. The other substantial texts are probably, given their manuscript circulation, London work. Yet at least two of these others have infiltrated the *Riwle*, one directly.

III

Pepys 2498 makes available to English readers some of the literary riches of past centuries, works composed in England but not in English. The texts propagated in English by Pepys and related manuscripts began, as all medieval biblical renditions, with the Latin Vulgate and its close associate, the tradition of learned Latin commentary. In the pre-university era in which these developed, they were texts of monastic origin and circulation. But from the middle of the twelfth century, they acquired, originally within the monastic setting, Anglo-Norman accretions, translations, glosses, and paraphrases. A little more than a century later, these Anglo-Norman versions emerged from a monastic milieu to become staples of a secularised Anglo-Norman book-trade. By the early fourteenth century, this Anglo-Norman material was rendered into English, the texts of Pepys 2498.

The manuscript thus provides a particularly neat example of what is often taken to be the standard English situation – the existence of three linguistic tiers. That one can identify this line of textual transmission as 'a standard situation' indicates the importance of a close examination. I would suggest that the widely acknowledged (yet very far from complete) linguistic separation I have outlined corresponds to separate social insertions bearing both on immediate textual production/reception and on later medieval literary practice. While intercalating some evidence for transmission of texts from Latin to English settings, I want to imagine the transpositions which such transmission – from Latinate monastics to French-reading monastics and aristocrats to English-literate Londoners – involves.

In the Middle Ages, all literary activity reflects a kind of sumptuary behaviour. It rests on what Keene rather blithely presents as 'return ... for the produce and income of the countryside' (1989, 99). This used to be called, more descriptively, but no less problematically, 'feudal peasant economy'. Literature depends upon the surplus value in one way or another extorted from a silent 90+ per cent of society, agricultural workers. As production, literature is thus never unproblematic, because always predicated upon extreme social exploitation. However much the display and beauty of medieval books may try to hide or romanticise it (as in the notorious example of the Luttrell Psalter), as Langland knows very well, books are always purchased – by someone else – with 'swinking' – stoop labour, red necks, and sweat in the field.[11]

One must always insist upon this agricultural underpinning of medieval literary production, since it is always silenced at the heart of texts and substantial efforts taken to hide its existence. Perhaps nowhere is this more true than in monastic book-ownership and -production, because once exclusive and unique the model appropriated in all other medieval literary situations. Monastic learnedness, the primary eleventh- and twelfth-century social model for an intelligent interest in man's state, presents itself, in all its aspects, as a labour and thus tends to obscure the existence of its actual support, a more physically demanding (yet economically less sustaining) labour which goes on elsewhere. Monastics compose texts, use them (both privately and as public liturgical act), and copy them as a part of their labour. Moreover, monastic reading and copying activities insist on a strenuousness and an effort one may minimise and thus ignore.[12] Yet however meticulous and physically enervating these activities, they must pale beside the efforts of those who actually sustain the monastic enterprise – the lay brothers and peasants who work the abbey estates. Like all medieval peasants, such people sweat to live; like all peasants, they are kept as close to a subsistence level as feasible by their landlords, the monks who read and write. As in any medieval landlord–tenant situation, any surplus the peasants accumulate gets withdrawn to support the hegemonic class which composes, copies, and reads.

If one can accept this given of medieval (and not just monastic) literary life, the actual parametres of monastic literary production can seem almost utopian:

> If heuen be on þis erþe, and ese to any soule,
> It is in cloistre or in scole, by manye skiles I fynde.
> (*Piers Plowman* 10.305–6)

The basis of monasticism is its status as a spiritual community, an enacted desire for and a prelude to an eternal spiritual community. Authors, scribes, and readers are all subordinated to a common, rather than personal, goal. Authorship aims at community improvement, edification (although it may not for all that be anonymous). Moreover, authorship may be a completely free gift: its very goal of improving others does not logically envision any boundary to instruction. Some works, typically ancient ones like those of Gregory the Great (the ultimate source of much of Gretham's *Mirror*), belong to the monastic tradition at large. But contemporary monastic authors certainly expect to be subject to the same communal appropriation: the house, to whom in some way the work 'belongs', may willingly impart the work to others by gift or as a loan for copying. Similarly, the monastic copying of texts is a selfless communal activity, as much as an act of personal devotion; reproducing the text supports the community by opening the text for use. And the monastic audience seeks the most selfless of goals, the praise of God (primarily through the communal act of liturgical glorification) and the self-improvement that will make individuals worthy to offer fit praise. This line of thought, which selflessly subordinates monastic author and scribe, in fact imposes that selflessness upon peasants exploited on the monastic estates; peasant labour addresses a communal need that monastic hegemony views as evanescent, this-worldly sustenance, and may consequently be perceived as a necessary sacrifice to higher forms of divine service.

The Latin of the biblical and patristic tradition was not the only monastic language in England: as Legge remarks, 'Latin and French were not rivals, but partners', even, perhaps especially, in the cloisters. Although many interested religious read biblical and exegetical texts in the original, abundant medieval evidence suggests that even those literate in Latin often preferred the ease provided by versions communicated in a less laboriously learned language. The stimulus to spiritual fulfilment that monastic texts were supposed to provide apparently led many to seek tools that would facilitate comprehension. And for many quite intelligent persons outside the monastery, French, every bit as much as Latin an acquired (rather than maternal) language, was the medium of choice. In their acquisitions, such non-monastic readers were, of course, facilitated by family connections – the monastic brothers and sisters were biologically the younger siblings of the lord, and did not necessarily remain detached from relations created by such ties of blood.[13]

The texts communicated in English by Pepys 2498 all begin with Latin versions. In this form, these biblical selections and pieces of biblical commentary are certainly intended for professional religious. The French translations (usually prose), where they are traceable, first emerge within such a professional community and are designed, at least initially, to increase the size of an in-house audience. The Psalter, which was, because of its liturgical prominence, perhaps the book of devotion par excellence in the period prior to the Book of Hours, survives in its earliest translated forms, all Anglo-Norman, almost exclusively in monastic copies (Dean nos. 445–52).

This Psalter circulation raises one issue that will point to the unusual status of Pepys 2498, its persistent vernacular biblicism. Magnates and country gentry commissioned Latin Psalters in abundance; the most glorious products of medieval English illumination, fourteenth-century East Anglian work, most typically ornament this text in its Latin form (Sandler 1986, 2 *passim*). Although there are early Anglo-Norman monastic Psalters, as a general rule French Psalters of known lay ownership are recorded only later in the fourteenth century (and there is no known English copy of the source of Pepys 2498's prose); these always represented a minuscule portion of those Psalters in lay hands during the period. In fact, the biblical text and its persistent liturgical use favoured reliance on the Latin original. Most of the opulent lay-patronised copies were probably always intended as acts of pious benefaction, donations either to domestic chapels or to parish churches where the donor was the patron. Such books might be perceived as a form of emulation, a carry-over of the monastic provision of ornate public service books. But they were intended to be handled and used by priests, not laypersons.

This pattern of translation and of use of Psalters also obtains for Apocalypses. As I indicated in the introduction (pp. 23–4), although Apocalypses appear in lay contexts from *c.* 1260, French versions (Dean nos. 473–8, no. 475 the source of the Middle English) are significantly belated. Until around 1300, illustrated Apocalypses provided a Latin text, with a late Carolingian monastic commentary, Berengaud of Ferrières's analysis of John's visions as representing seven ages of church history. When the belated French versions appear, they translate, not Berengaud (although inherited traditions of illustration may still refer to his exegesis), but a modernised clerical version. This derivative of the ordinary gloss on the Apocalypse is no longer monastic, but comes from the tradition of twelfth-century cathedral schools, as its prologue, ascribed to Gilbert de la Porrée, implies. These two examples suggest that the texts' status as 'biblical' retarded French circulation, but, as I will show, did not eventually have the same effect on London English.

The ultimate Latin sources of other Pepys texts should be sought in the same milieu, although the monastic survivals are much less clearcut. The Pepys diatesseron belongs to a genre commonly of monastic authorship or circulation, the most widely dispersed English product by the Augustinian canon Clement of Lanthony. Similarly, Robert of Gretham, who, according to Sinclair's arguments, had been an Augustinian canon of Brackley (Nhants.), relies on sources central to the monastic libraries and scriptorial efforts of the late twelfth-century generation which preceded him. His most frequent source is the great theologian of monasticism, Gregory the Great, and he also pillages other traditional authorities, Bede and 'Haymo of Halberstadt'. Finally, the majority of early copies of a non-translated Pepys text, *Ancrene Riwle*, can be associated, in one language or another, with thirteenth- and early fourteenth-century monastic establishments. Again, these are frequently Augustinian, testimony to the liminal status of these canons, their equal involvement in parochial as well as intramural devotion.[14]

As Legge demonstrates, Anglo-Norman instructional texts achieved considerable popularity in monastic situations. She traces monastic ownership of William of Waddington's *Manuel des pèches*, a text explicitly written for lay use, as well as of the French translation of Edmund Rich's

Speculum ecclesie. This text was addressed originally to monastics, but was of enormous interest to laypersons.[15] Both were eventually to have robust lives in English, Waddington in Manning's verse translation, with an anti-romance prologue. In sum, texts read in common by both enclosed and secular audiences were far more often items resembling the *Mirror* than non-Latin biblical texts. Such textual histories suggest some conclusions about the nature of the thirteenth-century Anglo-Norman literary audience. There appears to have been substantial interchange among two segments of this group which one may be inclined to consider separate – regular clergy and learned aristocratic laypersons. Authors who wrote with an immediate eye to one part of this audience routinely encountered no barriers in reaching the other portion. Just as texts intended for non-Latinate readers penetrated monasteries, so texts originally produced for religious houses passed from them, whether on the basis of family ties (many magnatial little brothers grew up to be professional clerics, whether regular or secular), communication of regular and secular clergy, or monastic educational outreach (like modern university extension programmes), to laity literate in French.[16]

But although a major impulse to Norman translation came from monasteries, the courtly milieu was far from idle. As has been widely recognised, the Anglo-Norman aristocracy formed the first organised literary public since late antiquity, and one invested in vernacular text-production.[17] The precociousness of such production depends, to a large extent, upon two factors. On the one hand, within Anglo-Norman culture, the connection between clerical and aristocratic interests may have been much tighter than elsewhere in Europe; with the Norman monastic 'plantation', family connections between persons in important ecclesiastical and social positions would have been extremely close. Moreover, unlike the rest of Europe, the two establishments, court and religious house, shared a common language, originally a 'learnéd' vernacular, then from the late twelfth century simply learned.

This close relationship would have intensified by a second factor. To an extent that was certainly unique in Europe, Norman aristocratic life in its socio-linguistic insertion closely resembled monastic life. Latinate monastic authors expect that their audience is restricted and excludes the great mass of society; they recognise the limited extent of their Latin readership, that they are linguistically isolated from the vast portion of the populace. But unlike most European aristocracies, the Anglo-Normans were equally isolated linguistically from their English-speaking subjects in the early twelfth century. The literary precocity of Anglo-Norman expresses aristocratic estrangement and alienation from a larger populace, over and above the expected sense of aristocratic identity as a special coterie audience. The second tendency, in particular, can only have intensified as Anglo-Norman became progressively restricted as a purely coterie language, a step followed by its becoming a purely learned language, then widely proliferating because of its use in legal and administrative contexts.[18]

Aristocratic book-production and interest in texts inherently place a negative value on the monastic conception of the book as labour. Monastic authors and copyists envision their labour as quite removed from actual social efforts, as purely spiritual acts. But the aristocratic reader, although he or she may ultimately perceive reading as similarly spiritual, has already performed a full and socially viable labour before professing any literary interest. For such figures, careers in estate management and service to local and national government precede literary endeavour; an ongoing effort at exploitation of the peasantry must generate the cash to produce such sumptuous volumes. The books express this hands-on exploitation openly; because the commissions of individuals, they indicate the value of real economic and political effort, a feature not the property of monastic books. Ornate books allow expression of a way of life presented as both more demanding and more socially central than that of monastics.

IV

The Middle English prose Apocalypse – arguably the earliest of the Pepys translations – is certainly the text most generative of London biblical thinking: its concluding scene of the New Jerusalem was to become, as Gordon Kipling has shown, integral to civic pageantry from late in the century. This visionary representation of a heavenly city lacking temple or priesthood may have attracted and incited interest for reasons other than royal compliment. London religious writers, most notably the translator of Gretham's *Mirror* and the reviser of the Pepys copy of *Ancrene Riwle*, derived from the Apocalypse commentary arguments for generalising religious functions customarily limited to learned clerical groups. These offered an analytical vocabulary reminiscent of conventional anti-romance sentiments; false Christians, those outside God's Law, became *loseniours* 'falsifiers'. Certainly, London English reception of the Apocalypse scarcely resembled that in England's other languages.

In its Latin and Anglo-Norman forms, the Apocalypse most typically appears as an extra-illustrated text – nor does it appear alone. It is both preceded and followed by an illustrative cycle depicting the life of the Revelator. This cycle, as Lewis indicates (1995, 19–30, 34–5, 38), is extrapolated from the discussion of John's career in the Latin prologue affixed to the Apocalypse, traditionally ascribed to Gilbert de la Porrée and eventually, in both Anglo-Norman and Middle English, replacing the first eight verses of the biblical text proper. Here Gilbert depicts John as the true priest suffering exile from his city (Lewis 1995, 189). Thus framed, the Apocalypse proper comes to form an episode, or the central episode, of a life. The available Anglo-Norman/Middle English narrative models into which this generic conception might be inserted would include the saints of *The South English Legendary* and the heroes of Anglo-Norman/Auchinleck romances. All these 'lives' are typically titled in manuscript simply by the name of the hero whose career is there displayed.

The pictorial cycle ostensibly depicts a story of exile and return, and thus conforms to the model narrative of Anglo-Norman/Middle English romance, but with a difference.[19] John does not through his vision gain some happy epic *nostos*, but must return to purge his City Ephesus. While in one sense, such a narrative is not alien to the climactic community-restoring violence of *Beves of Hamtoun*, John's remains a war that lacks the comfort of conclusive stasis. John returns to fulfil what he has achieved as visionary understanding, but his task is to be a continuing labourer in the Lord's field and to gain his ultimate end and *civitas*, the New Jerusalem of Apoc. 21–2 (cf. the schematic depiction, Lewis 1995, fig. 166, 193) only through a persistence that escapes this world.

Part of Gilbert's Latin prologue, not paralleled in the Anglo-Norman or Middle English (the sentences in the source follow *Apoc* 4/45–7), insists that John returns to Ephesus to fight two heresies. These have sprung up in his absence and between them, they deny an orthodox

Christian history encompassing all time and eternity. On the one hand, John must refute the error that Christ's origin is the Incarnation itself, not, as the bishop had earlier written and taught, 'In principio erat verbum'; on the other, the error that the tribulation of the Church represents merely an historical episode, that heretics will be overcome in time, and thus that spiritual warfare against them merits no eternal reward.[20] Hence John is required to live out the destruction visited on the Church and depicted in his vision, to engage in the process of spiritual combat, resistance, and persecution knowingly and voluntarily. To do this, he must fulfil – act out as deed, rather than let lie as precept – the very purpose of the Apocalypse itself.

In the standard prologue, Gilbert identifies the 'intentio' of the work as 'mouere ad patientiam' (cf. *Apoc* 4/49–50 'His entent'). Later, in a portion of the prologue not paralleled in Anglo-Norman or Middle English, he alludes to a verse from one of the generative texts under-lying the biblical work, Luke 21:19, 'In your patience you shall possess your souls' ('In paciencia vestra possidebitis animas vestras'), a widely quoted proof that patience is central to the Christian life: 'so that going from patience to contemplation of heavenly glory, we might pass to advantage and reward for our patience'.[21] John (and through him, the reader) should attain beatitude by a process like that romance describes, of travelling to arrive at reward ('peruenire possimus'). But the vision achieved at the end of the Apocalypse, later to be intruded as the climax of the Pepys *Riwle*, occurs in no worldly city, only out of this world. One might recall the later poet:

> Not sedulous by nature to indite
> Wars, hitherto the only argument
> Heroic deemed, chief mastery to dissect
> With long and tedious havoc fabled knights
> In battle feigned; the better fortitude
> Of patience and heroic martyrdom
> Unsung.
> (*Paradise Lost* 9.27–33)

Milton here echoes the traditional Ciceronian perception that the mar-tial virtue 'fortitude' is both active and passive, and that the latter provides no lesser triumph than the former. He, like the authors of commented Apocalypses, revises the potentially arrogant militarism of romance and epic, 'Fallen cherub, to be weak is miserable, | Doing or suffering' (1.157–8), itself echoing a perception of the heroic life ultimately Homeric.

In early London extra-illustrated Apocalypses, monastic outreach is apparent not only in the (still Latin) text but in the decorative style. In a number of early examples specifically marked as royal Westminster work, the formatting of the illustrations follows earlier monastic models. These books frequently have pages in which tinted or washed drawings appear in the top halves of the leaves, with textual materials displayed beneath them; they show the influence of earlier St Albans books, most especially Matthew Paris's historical narratives with accompanying tinted drawings. (An analogous local example would be Westminster Abbey's *Flores historiarum*, conceived as a continuation to Matthew Paris's histories.) Indeed, several prominent early Westminster Apocalypse MSS are illuminated in hands associated with those in a book that brings St Albans learning and illustrative style into a royal, Westminster ambit. This volume, Cambridge University Library, MS Ee.iii.59, was produced in a secular situation, outside the abbey. It contains the unique, and elaborately illustrated, life of Edward the Confessor translated into Anglo-Norman verse probably by Matthew Paris himself.[22]

The provision of Ee.iii.59 for royal patrons – the book has always been associated with Henry III or his queen, Eleanor of Provence – will recall a familiar narrative I have outlined above (although this is a late example). A monastic author provides a pious text for a noble patron, here in French, rather than the original Latin. Matthew Paris's effort with *La Estoire de Seint Aedward* imitates the earlier Latin prose monastic text that he here renders in Anglo-Norman verse. This source, itself derived from the earlier in-house account of Osbert of Clare, is Aelred of Rievaulx's 'Vita Sancti Edwardi regis'.

The Anglo-Norman translation again testifies to monastic/magnatial overlap of audience, but the imitation is more complete still. Aelred dedicated his life, through an abbot of Westminster, to Henry II as the first scion of a reunified Saxon/Norman royal line (773–4); in a similar spirit, he had also written for Henry II 'De genealogia regum Anglorum', an introduction to the king's noble pre-Conquest roots. Just as in both law and romance, history proves appropriative, a demonstration that Conquest represents neither cataclysm nor discontinuity, and that sacral kingship provides a powerful link to past native traditions. In the context of Henry III's absolutist pretensions, exhibited on the walls of the Painted Chamber (Binski 1986, 33–42) and at the very least queried by Montfortian reformist efforts, simply the existence of the text is a very powerful statement.

Aelred wrote following the translation of the saintly Edward's remains to Westminster Abbey; indeed, on that occasion, he had delivered the sermon. In turn, Matthew Paris versified Aelred's work in a similar context, Henry III's renovation of the church and the construction of Edward's opulent shrine at his orders (Binski 1995, 93–105). The text thus affirms, not simply the continuity of kingship but kingship of a particularly sacral stripe, committed to and carrying the blood of, one model pre-Conquest holy monarch and engaging patrons both of his church and his shrine (cf. Binski 1990b). But *La Estoire de Seint Aedward* contains some surprises, which might qualify some of the assuredness with which Matthew Paris presents his imitative text and might suggest interesting features both of its use and that of the Apocalypses derivative from its presentation.

La Estoire is particularly important, not just as potential artistic inspiration, but because, as Henderson realised (116), it includes poetic instructions for its own consumption as illustrated narrative. In his transition from the 'vita' proper to his presentation of Edward's posthumous miracles (those accounts that demonstrate his sanctity), Matthew Paris offers his labours upon the book as analogous to the activities of others seeking intercession:

> Now I pray you, noble king Edward, that you attend to me, a sinner. I have translated your story, so far as my talent allows me to understand its sense, from Latin into French in order to spread your memory widely. Moreover, I have depicted it clearly in painting in this book for laypeople who don't know letters; for one who desires and wishes it, the ear can hear and the eyes see.[23]

Although attached to a manuscript model and not to the Apocalypse itself, this description has particular relevance to the latter text, for 'ot, voient' echoes the injunctions, 'hear and see' of the Apocalypse itself (e.g., 1:3, 22:8). But such hearing and seeing is attached to a specific imagined and bifurcated experience of consumption. In Matthew Paris's account, a lettered person, assumed here (in a rather old-fashioned way) to be ordained and thus presumably a domestic clerk, reads the text while simultaneously his audience, 'lais ki de lettrure | Ne sevent', follow the pictorial account. Both words and pictures, the latter 'Figuree apertement', are integral to the consumption of the text, but they are addressed to different portions of the audience and to different effects.

The well-known ambiguities of 'figuree' are relevant here. Matthew Paris's 'en purtraiture' indicates that he uses the word in its most tangible sense, to refer to a depicted image. But the Apocalypse is renowned for being 'figural' in quite another sense, as, broadly speaking, an enigmatic and symbolic narrative. As Gilbert's prologue comments, 'John did not simply see images in his spirit but understood their meanings in his mind'.[24] John has an 'avisioun' and thus sees 'figuræ' in the spirit; but he is equally, always, and consciously engaged in intellectual, not visual, cognition, understands immediately the relevant 'significata'. In contrast, as Matthew describes it, Anglo-Norman users don't 'see in the spirit' but literatim, and they re-create 'significata mente' with the aid of a reader.

The distinction occurs again in a Middle English poem attached to 'The Croyland Apocalypse' (Cambridge, Magdalene College, MS 5). This text bridges the gap between an English prose translation and an Anglo-Norman illustrated example, an earlier production bound in to follow it in the book. The brief couplet prologue insists, on the one hand, upon the disparity between seeing a 'boke of ymagerie' (1) well stocked with 'beestis' (4) and, on the other, understanding 'þo gloose' 'as keye þat wil vnloken | þo dore þat is ful faste stoken' (8–10). The Middle English poet here argues that only seeing is a shocking act of blindness (11–13). Contextually, this view may be read back into the verse epilogue to the preceding Middle English version to yet more damning effect; there Antichrist's hordes persecuting the Church are depicted as 'deefe and blinde þat wil not se' (11).[25]

While one may wonder a good deal as to how these prescriptions would apply to the very lettered Henry III or Eleanor or their courtly companions,[26] the kind of reading experience Matthew Paris imagines for his illustrated book may be associated with a bifurcated experience.

In his conceptualisation, the non-learned audience gets John's visionary experience, but in a particularly sensory fashion, as bare image (in some books with tagged captions). As pictorial readers, such consumers resemble John as 'true priest in training' – but in a distanced way. Their experience as visual readers remains secondary to and dependent upon the explanatory voice of the clerical oral reader, who resembles John in seeing the pictures as well as both absorbing personally and passing on to a listening audience the figural text. That audience has direct access to the 'opened' (cf. 'apertement') figural text only as literal figures, pictures. As my last chapter would indicate, they are truly 'romance readers' who respond to type-scenes – which may or may not answer to exegetical interests in specific non-evident 'significata'.

This broaches a problem that often inheres in sumptuous visual texts. With books of this type, one can never forget the social underpinning of aristocratic wealth. Books like these presuppose profit, a concept foreign to the struggle for subsistence which comprises peasant life – a profit so large that it has no feasible practical use and can only express itself as sumptuousness. The elaborate decoration that in monastic book-production is sublimated as stimulus to affective devotion is visible in aristocratic books as that treasure that the powerful of this world properly seek to accumulate. The presentation of the patron/audience in such books therefore involves some uncomfortable stresses.

One problem, especially in late twelfth- to late thirteenth-century copies, concerns the form in which the sumptuous visual effects are provided. In a great many early copies of the Psalter and Apocalypse, a substantial part of the illustrative programme is not directly text-related; in others, while the text may remain Latin, the illustrations are provided with Anglo-Norman captions as if they were comic strips.[27] At least one way of interpreting such features (they do occur, albeit much less frequently, in books of monastic provenance) would be to suggest that the books may appeal less as texts than as sensory 'reading', that the owners are less interested in verbal comprehension than in being visually stimulated. The books resemble other visual forms of aristocratic sumptuousness (tapestry, wallpainting, or reliquary); the possibility that they are not to be read at all might be considered.

Here, Matthew Paris inscribes (and in-limns) a difference, in which clerical intermediation debars the lay audience from fully direct textual participation. In Apocalypse manuscripts, this consumption model might equally be seen as a way of reinscribing the text: the gloss, highlighting one possible recuperation of the biblical 'littera', not necessarily the narrative form of illustration, defines a status peculiar to the reader, not his associated audience. The Apocalyse commentary directly inscribes a clerical status, that of teaching and preaching, engaged in war against Antichrist. Yet implicitly, Matthew would seem to argue against professionally limited clerical responsibility in the overheard text expanding the narrative/pictorial 'littera'. Standing for truth against persecution has a relevance broader than the duties of the clerical reader and refers to the desired acts of Everychristian, but reading audience and seeing audience are nevertheless placed in a position where it is possible to perceive this responsibility in differing ways – especially since the iconography of Apocalypse illumination was frequently keyed to the old Berengaud commentary, and thus often 'out of synch' with the Anglo-Norman, or whatever else might be the orally provided explanation.[28]

This potential dual voicing, distortion and/or distraction, is completely lacking from Middle English consumption of the same text. Middle English Apocalypses are not illustrated, but plain books, and only 'Croyland' joins English and illustrated French. Thus, the only surface detail requiring textual consumption is graphemic, not pictorial, and, in essence, no 'surface' intrudes between reader and text. Access becomes immediate and ideational; the audience can pass directly, in a language not marked as 'clerical', to 'significata'. The available commentary aligns the reader with John, first, in terms of an experience which can only be, as Gilbert indicates, 'spiritu', in which the narrative can only be perceived through inner 'visualisation'. But further, like John faced with continuous narrative enigmata, the audience experiences directly, in the alternation of text with blocks of gloss, John's own search for clarification of what he sees. (With this entire discussion, cf. Camille, *Age* 32–6.)

Moreover, the commentary subsumed in the Middle English Apocalypse brings the reader directly to the Johannine response to his experience. (Whatever the involuntarism of vision, the prologue insists that the commentary explicates John's arrangement of the text to communicate 'his entent'.) John's arrangement, which allows the explanation of obscurity, makes of its reader someone immediately capable of access to 'significata'. He or she thus is potentially equivalent to the clerical reader who stands between Anglo-Norman visual audience and text. This procedure would include the overt claim that what was historically priestly task for the Revelator has become universal Christian injunction – that lay reader may be lay priest. Just as the English reader who wants to visualise 'figuræ' must draw upon his or her own imaginative experience, the text may be seen as enjoining an experiential and active model, one of lay spiritual busyness about the Lord's affairs.[29]

Such a reading experience is further supported by one characteristic feature of the Anglo-Norman and English versions, as against the Latin of illustrated Apocalypses. The 'materia' of the Apocalypse, Gilbert says, is 'status ecclesie' (cf. *Apoc* 4/47 'þe matier'). But it is possible to imagine several referents for such a theme. Typically, in thirteenth-century copies, the 'matter' was explicated through Berengaud's perception that 'status ecclesie' is historicisable. He explains the text as universal narrative by aligning the seven visions which he distinguishes as stages in world history. The Anglo-Norman and Middle English retain only a vestige of Berengaud's analysis. This is drawn from Gilbert's discussion, traditional in Latin academic prologues, of the 'ordo libri', here 'departed in seuen siȝttes so þat vche man may vchon by hym one onlich vnderstonden and tellen' (*Apoc* 5/61–3). Although this division is retained within the prologue, the visions are presented only as literal narrative breaks, not historical stages, and the breaks are neither here specified nor ever signalled in the commentary at large. Thus both the Anglo-Norman and Middle English attempt to remove the Apocalypse from time, to dehistoricise it, avoiding the contemporary references that provided the context in which pictorial presentations were developed.[30]

Such a presentation removes from the text a good deal of its opacity, those cryptic or occult identifications on which the historical readings depend. And it also denies one great luxury of historical reading, that events described remain distant (and potentially irrelevant), past, removed. Thus, Anglo-Norman and (even more so) English readers are allowed to address a text with its own confirmations. Moreover, this text has become one directed timelessly to the present, requiring rumination to process/comprehend in the immediate now and offering injunction to future action. But the cycle of 'life of John' illuminations historicises the Anglo-Norman, places it as past experience, something 'storial', in a way that the gloss, which suppresses the biographical verses at the head in favour of an academic prologue, does not entirely allow. Moreover, in the English rendition, without pictorial accompaniment, the very visual particularity of the Apocalypse cycle proper has been thoroughly suppressed. The bare text no longer insists upon the fantastic, perhaps romance, 'littera', distanced as part of some other, now departed world. Instead, the reader confronts a text that, through its commentary, insists on a truly spiritual reading experience, one detached from romance. According to its Anglo-Norman and Middle English commentaries, the Apocalypse outlines the role of the true preacher and thus constitutes a learned reading and learning experience.

The text is littered with the signs of clerical status, documents and books and characters (writing on bodies), objects requiring attentive reading and commensurate action. The book is truly apocalyptic/revelatory in its movement from quasilegal documents sealed and then made patent, and this is to be the ultimate fate of the Apocalypse itself as a book (22:10; cf. Rosemary Wright's discussion of legal documents). The two most significant such documents occur towards the middle and at the end. The latter, The Book of Life (20:12) contains, of course, the indelible inscription of reward for those who persevere.[31] But the terms of that inscription (and of the text at large) are established by an earlier example:

> And I took the book from the hand of the angel, and ate it up: and it was in my mouth, sweet as honey: and when I had eaten it, my belly was bitter. And he said to me: Thou must prophesy again to many nations, and peoples, and tongues, and kings.[32]

Made sweet in mouth by the word of God, John, the Lord's preacher, must explain in bitterness what he has absorbed. He is required to be the teacher persecuted in this world who endures patiently in his effort to expound and propagate the word. As the later appearance of the personification Verbum Dei (19:12–13) indicates, eating the book provides a tongue like a sword, evocation of God's Law through the voice of chastisement. This will not endear one to the world and thus ensures a bitter life to follow.[33] But The Book of Life promises the reversal of these worldly terms; the bitterness will be that eternal damnation visited upon the Antichrist and the sweetness the actuality of the new non-worldly city (John experiences it only as vision).

Such a formulation explains much of the serenity of Middle English commentary; the literally terrifying events described in the biblical text are subsumed in the joy of smashing evil, and torment includes retribution as well as merited joy for the just (cf. 18:20, 19:1–2 and 7). In adopting this thematic, the Apocalypse replays enabling texts from earlier Christian literature, connections ceaselessly played out in the commentary. The recipient text recalls Jesus's promises of false prophecy at the end of days, notably Matt. 24, perhaps particularly v. 11 'And many false prophets shall rise and shall seduce many' ('Et multi pseudoprophetæ surgent et seduceat multos'), as well as its synoptic parallels at Mark 13:22 (note 13:9–11 for the persecuted preacher of the gospel) and Luke 21:8 (I have cited the associated verse 19 above), as well as the derivative 2 Thes. 2:9–10. One might recall John's opening letter, to the church at Ephesus (2:2): 'those who say they are apostles, and are not, and [thou] hast found them liars' ('eos qui se dicunt apostolos esse, et non sunt, et invenisti eos mendaces'). The reading of the Apocalypse thereby becomes a massively confirmatory synthesis of Gospel promise.

Within the commentary, the Apocalypse ceaselessly appears as the battle of two preachments or prophecies, associated with its two Christs and their two Cities, Babylon and New Jerusalem.[34] Thus virtually any angelic appearance in the text may be glossed as the coming of a holy preacher (e.g. the commentary on 8:2, 14:6–7, 15:1, 18:1, 19:17); perhaps most striking is the discussion of 10:1–2 as the gospel-model provided by Jesus himself:

By þe face ben bitokned þe gode men of religioun þat ben likned to [Jesus] in hardynesse [AN aspreté] of lijf; þai ben as þe sonne, for þai liȝtten þe oþere þorouȝ gode ensaumple. By þe [feet] ben bitokned þe gode prechours þat gon from oo stede to anoþer for to prechen þe bileue. þai ben pilers of fyre, and þai owen to sustiene þe feble and vndernyme þe colde and hete hem þorouȝ þe fyre of loue. þat he had a book in his honde bitokneþ þat he seiþ in þe godspelle, 'I am nouȝth comen to breke þe lawȝe, ac I am comen to fulfillen it'. (*Apoc* 75–6/4–12)[35]

In contrast to this sun and fire, 'the mark of the beast', the number '666'/'dclxui' is interpreted as the parodic 'dic lux', 'for Antecrist shal be cleped falslich liȝth as Iesus Crist is seide sooþfast liȝth' (108/36–42). A precise language of vituperation appears associated with the numeral '666'. The Middle English commentator, expanding upon the 'merc de parenté ou avoerie par servise' he found in his Anglo-Norman source, comments:

> [They] haue merk of þe kynrede, þat is to seie þat he be comen of grete kynde oiþer þat he be in grete lordes seruise oiþer þat he come þerto þorouȝ symonye, oiþer þat he goo to þe ordre for to haue bodilich delices. Alle þise be Antecristes prophetes and his ypocrites and his eretikes. (*Apoc* 107/26–30)[36]

Throughout the commentary, Antichrist's army is characterised by a preaching false in its spirit, hypocritical and heretic (in one of the unspecific loose senses, 'cut off from the law of God' or 'erroneous in its understanding of Scripture'). This preaching has been undertaken for the wrong cause and intended to seduce, rather than enlighten:

> þai shullen ben dampned þat corrumpeden holy wrytt and han tourned þe suetenesse of gostlich vnderstondyng into þe filþe of flesshlich wytt [AN sens '(literal) sense']. þoo ben þise heretikes, and þoo þat prechen for werldelich þinges, and þai þat tournen þe godspelles for to pleden wiþ hem [AN in pleiderie]. (*Apoc* 127–8/13–7, glossing 16:4 'sanguis')[37]

Antichrist's troop take up this high responsibility for worldly gain, not devotion. They look for worldly power and praise, and they gain it precisely through pleasing their audiences, not correcting them according to the Law of God. To preserve their position and perquisites, they drive out salutary clerical chastisement, persecute those who would seriously offer instruction in the faith; the gloss to 6:14 'the heaven departed as a book folded up' ('celum recessit sicut liber involutus'), prophesies Antichrist's coming in terms of 'þe defaut of soþfast prechyng þat þan shul be' (*Apoc* 52/12–13).

Such a language of false prophecy/preaching, hypocrisy, and heresy, recurs with frequency throughout the commentary. In a form derivative from this source, such vituperation will have a hardy life in London devotional literature. But the commentator's most incendiary epithet is another term that, in its identification of falsification, recalls the anti-romance prologues:

> Ac þe loseniours ben werst of alle þat maken hem holy and for drede oiþer for loue oiþer for ler [OE lyre 'fear of loss'], þat þai hopen þai ne shullen noþing haue of hem ʒif þai seiden þe soþe, þise haue taken vnder honde to speken þe deuels langage for to disceyuen goddes childer and bynymen God his eritage, and swiche ben strengere and wers þan ay deuel in helle. (*Apoc* 170–1/15–21)[38]

The pursuit of popularity – and with it, apparently, the fear of lost donations – produces namby-pamby clerics, ones afraid to offer rebukes. They falsify by pleasing parishioners, but, in so doing, they mislead them. 'þe deuels langage' conveys spiritual adequacy to those who lack it, and in so doing, simple Christians, believing themselves virtuous only because not truly instructed, lose their souls.

In this context, the non-pictorial and textualised Middle English allows the possibility of routinising the text in this world. As Lewis points out (1995, 240), in the customary Sarum Use, the readings for the Feast of the Dedication, the service honouring the local City of God, the parish church, include Rev. 21:2–5 (along with the gospel, Luke 19:1–10, Zacchæus in his tree). By 1318, this date had become the occasion of a new image of corporate community and mutual spiritual responsibility, the feast of Corpus Christi (moveable, but generally falling in late June) with its processions, so ably discussed by Miri Rubin.[39] On a routine basis, liturgical event recalls the faithful to the Apocalypse as ecclesiastical mode, and the text has become attached to the routine rhythms of parish observance.

But this conclusion only restates the unglossed 'littera' of the Apocalypse itself (replaced by the translated Gilbert prologue and thus excluded from the Middle English and Anglo-Norman versions):

> Blessed is he, that readeth and heareth the words of this prophecy; and keepeth those things which are written in it; for the time is at hand. John to the seven churches which are in Asia. Grace be unto you and peace from him that is, and that was, and that is to come . . . and hath made us a kingdom, and priests to God and his Father.[40]

Significantly, the Revelator does not write 'Beatus est sacerdos qui', and he addresses the churches of Asia, the believers at large, as 'sacerdotes'. One should compare the gloss explaining Apoc. 1:10 '[I] heard behind me a great voice, as of a trumpet' ('audivi post me vocem magnam tamquam tubæ'), as: 'þe buscyne [AN busine 'trumpet'] þat amonesteþ hem þat þai done in werk al þat þai seen in holy writt and techen þe oþere þoruȝ gode ensamples to done wel' (*Apoc* 6–7/3–5). That clerical instructional role associated with reading the Anglo-Norman illustrated text has now become an open injunction directed to all comprehending English readers, in their local 'ecclesia'.[41]

The commentary re-enforces this tendency to generalise priestly parochial work. Persistently, yet generally without explicit rhetorical marking (as in his handling of the seven visions, the commentator sees no need to signpost his argument), 'significata' assigned the biblical text associate it with commonplace, allegedly timeless, catechetic processes. These, it is implied by other London texts, e.g. the instructional lists of St John's 256, or the diagrammatic presentation and Anglo-Norman septenary (see p. 10) in the priest's book, CUL Gg.iv.32, are the business of simple parochial instruction. Thus, the reading of Apoc. 5:1 'sigillis septem' (*Apoc* 38/6–8) identifies the seven seals with the sacraments and the gifts of the Holy Spirit; and, as had been conventional since Peraldus a century before, the seven heads of the beast from the sea (13:1) represent the Seven Deadly Sins (*Apoc* 92/2–3). As is catechetically suitable, and in accord with the basically oppositional character of the Apocalypse (the Lord v. Antichrist), these vices are traditionally extirpated through the seven virtues instilled by the seven gifts.

Most strikingly, the commentator associates the enemies of the Church with a usually fixed triad of sins. In a succinct example, glossing 14:9–10, the English follows the source in identifying Antichrist and his disciples as 'þe fals prelates and þe fals clerkes'. But the English uniquely continues to qualify, 'þat ben proude and coueitouse and leccherouse and losengeours' (*Apoc* 115/10–12). The formulation points the traditional division of the Seven Deadlies among sins of the devil (pride–wrath–envy), the flesh (sloth–gluttony–lechery), and the world (avarice).[42] This particular focus of the argument finds answering detail at 19:14, where the Lord's 'exercitus' is glossed:

hem [AN adds de seinte glise] þat willen fiȝtten aȝein þe *fende* þurȝ lowenesse and wiþ [queyn]tise [ME coueitise, AN cointise]; aȝein þe *werlde* and with pacience aȝein aduersites, and richeses fiȝtten wiþ queyntise; aȝein þe *flesshe* and wiþ discrecioun and abstinence and sternesse of penaunce and in clenesse [AN nesté en vesteüre] stonden in vertu of gode werkes. (*Apoc* 164–5/9–13, my emphasis)[43]

Such an argument, emphasising ceaseless ongoing battle against sin, recuperates the text for a use absolutely universal, reliant on the most basic kinds of brief instructional materials. As the anti-romance prologues enjoin, the London English Apocalypse eradicates the 'losengeries' associated with romance and brings religious knowledge to potentially the widest audience, parish Christians.

V

Only partially edited, the sermon-cycle *Mirror* is the most extensive text of Pepys 2498.[44] In producing the Anglo-Norman, as I have already noted, Robert of Gretham relied upon authoritative monastic texts, notably Gregory the Great's forty sermons on the gospels. As a result, Robert preserves a homiletic form alien to the most sophisticated and well-recorded thirteenth-century preaching. Rather than a contemporary 'sermo modernus', with its elaborate divisions and ordered exposition of carefully established *distinctiones*, Robert, although he intercalates about a dozen lengthy exempla (reproduced by Aitken), follows his patristic sources in presenting old-fashioned 'sermones antiqui'.[45] Such a sermon offers a paraphrase of the day's gospel, followed by an explanation of the text. This typically begins with the assignment of allegorical significations ('X betokens Y'), reminiscent of the Apocalypse commentary, and passes on to a hortatory explanation of the Christian habits inherent in and enjoined by these identifications. As the Middle English says, 'þe godspell ȝe schull fynde hereinne, first þe tixte and þan þe vndoyng schortlich' (Pepys 45[ab], 5/4–5).

As one immediate result of this treatment, Robert's work closely resembles the prose Apocalypse in its repeated themes. John the Revelator is the true priest, but the gospels represent nothing except the biography of the model 'pastor bonus' (John 10:11). 'þe vndoyng' invariably connects the activity both of the prophetic Jesus and of his disciples with clerical functions, and the subsequent moralisation ceaselessly

provides explanations of clerical responsibility, especially the requirement of preaching (Latin homiletics are nothing if not self-referential/-
congratulatory), and analyses of clerical performance, good and
ill.

But more than bald thematic connects the two pieces of English biblical prose. For, on a sporadic basis, much analytical language in the
Mirror has been derived from the Apocalypse commentary. In Middle
English interpolations or original sermons, examples are direct, precise
quotations of the text I have just discussed; a few analogous examples
in Robert's original may imply his access to the Latin source behind the
English Apocalypse. For example, at the head of the 'second prologue'
to the Middle English *Mirror*, following upon a distinction of the estates I have already discussed (pp. 21–2), the translator elaborates upon,
and specifies through invective, a discussion of clerical performance
(Gretham's 263–86):

> And assailours – þat ben men of holy chirche þat schulde techen boþe
> [magnates and labourers] wiþ far speche and wiþ reddure. ʒif þat hij
> duden any synne and trespasseden aʒeins God, hij it schulden adressen
> and turnen hem to Godward, ac as þe werlde schapeþ now, hij ben
> þe moste deel rauysschours and rauisshen þe poeple from Godward,
> boþe wiþ her ensample ʒiuynge and wiþ her werk.

He continues this interpolation:

> Ac all þat ben proude or coueitous oþer leccherous, þise ben Antecristes
> chesynge and han þe cure [Holk toure] of holy chirch aʒeins Goddes
> wille bot þat he suffreþ it . . . þan to þe men of ordre it is ful hard whan
> þat hij schullen ansueren tofore God of her office þat hij han taken
> on honde, and hij nyllen noiþer techen hemseluen ne non oþer men
> oþer þat he leteþ for loue or for wynnynge or for drede. (Pepys 46^b,
> 9/14–28, in part)

While the translator has drawn the term 'ravisher', a new epithet of
opprobrium foreign to the Apocalypse, from elsewhere in Robert's
French,[46] his specifications of 'ravishing' as the covetous longing for
lordship, rather than saving one's flock, are derived from the English
version of the Apocalypse. Thus, the second passage I cite alludes directly to the Apocalypse and includes its standard rendition of the three

sins to be associated with Antichrist's members. And my citation concludes with fairly direct quotation from portions of *Apoc* 170–1/15–21
(see above, p. 175).

Robert was thoroughly capable of such invective. For example, his
discussion of the parable of the tares (Matt. 13:24–30; sermon 10, for
the 5th Sunday after Epiphany) conventionally identifies the sleeping
men who allow the field to be despoiled with non-feasant priests, un-
committed to spreading the word of God.[47] In their indolence, they
are replaced by the fiend's limbs, those who entice others to evil, including, not simply the expected 'ypocrytes' and 'priue heretikes', but a
rich array of false teachers unimagined in the Apocalypse commentary:
'baudestrotes . . . charme[r]s . . . wicked nigromauncie[ns]', and, echoing
the anti-romance prologue, 'trowauntes þat maken seggeynges of [Holk
songes and] stories forto lete Goddes werkes' (Pepys 71[b], 115/25–33).
Robert includes similar invective and a further reference to bad priests
as the notorious heretics of the Apocalypse in sermon 37 (Pepys 139[b]-40[a],
AN 135rb).

But such an analysis is considerably more intense in Middle English
additions/interpolations. For example, the Middle English intrudes a
reference into sermon 53 to 'þise wicked men and wymmen and ypocrites
and fals prophetes and eretikes swiche þat han so gret likyng in her
yuels þat hij nyllen nou3th leten hem' (Pepys 180[a], no parallel at AN
170[rab]). The extra sermons (not included in the Nottingham MS) are
redolent with such materials; the 55th (for Christmas, on John 1:1–14), in
describing those who, unlike the Word made Flesh, were not sent, quotes
from the analysis of the Mark of the Beast as involving 'gret lordes seruice'
(*Apoc* 107/26–30, Pepys 191[b]); and the next sermon (for the common of
several apostles, John 15:12–16) defines the pseudoprophets of last days
as those who 'maken hem as hij weren holy and han oiþer coueitise oiþer
proude oiþer leccherous oiþer losangeres' (cf. *Apoc* 114–15/10–12, Pepys
196[a]). And a massive Apocalypse interpolation in sermon 48 includes
an attack on false learning in similar terms (see below, pp. 198–9).

Robert's self-presentation as devoted true priest is conceived in opposition to such apocalyptic figures. In the second prologue, he detaches
himself from the invective of Apocalypse commentaries to explain his
authorial interests:

I ne make it nouȝth for losengerie [AN losengerie], ne for pride, ne
for to be praised þorouȝ [AN pur mustrer ma] clergie, ne for to haue
worschip in þis lyf; I þenche to onoþer londe þere better ȝeldynge of
mede is þan in þis werlde, and I make it for to aquiten me body and
soule from encoumbrement and for to staien [Holk speke] for me
þere I ne may ne can. (Pepys 48ᵃ, 15/20–4)[48]

Or again: 'No man schal praise me for þise sawes þat hereþ it, for of me
is it nouȝth, ac of þe spirit þat al wisseþ [AN guie 'directs']' (Pepys 48ᵇ,
17/12–3). The text is not the Anti-Christian vehicle for Robert's self-
display, and its only motive is salvific – for an author who does not care
for worldly gain. The act of having written it is the only meaningful
investment, and the writer denies to himself any possible authority
which might inhere in presenting the work.

Although he uses none of the technical terminology which Minnis
associates with medieval authorship, he presents himself as compiler
of his work only, its personal benefit the hope of salvation. Indeed, at
one point, he promises not to give his name (although twice in the
course of the text, he relents). Robert associates this clerical fidelity –
and the point is more forceful in the English rendition than in the
Anglo-Norman original – with a specific conception of vernacularity.
In his prologue, he argues that the specific linguistic surface of the text
is an irrelevance:

Ne ȝiueþ no kepe to þe lettre ne to þe speche, bot vnderstondeþ wel
to þe resoun. God ne ȝiueþ no kepe to þe faire speche, ac to þe spiryt
he ȝiueþ kepe. Better it is for to saie soþ bustouslich þan for to saie fals
þouȝth queyntlich, for al þat acordeþ wiþ soþenesse is wel seid byfore
God. (Pepys 45ᵇ, 5/15–9)

In the French (105–7), the opening concludes an apology to Robert's
addressee Aline; Robert defends himself against possible objections to
the use of 'Franceis' (on the excision of the term from the English, see
further p. 183 and n. 51) and to the presentation of the text in rhyme.
'Resoun', communicable sense, provides the centre of the translator's
effort. As I have suggested in pointing towards the translator's reliance
on the language of Apocalypse, unveiling God's law in gospel narrative
underwrites the basic clerical function defined in the *Mirur*. On several

occasions, Robert defines clergy as the literate understanding of the two laws, from which is derived the entire basis of human conduct:

> For boþe owe þe preest to do, ȝiue hym penaunce for his synne and teche hym hou he schal kepe Goddes lawȝe, for boþe þise fallen vnto þe preest. And þerfore þere schulde non take þe ordre bot ȝif he couþe boþe þe olde lawe and þe newe and kepe hymseluen out of synne (sermon 8, for the 3rd Sunday after Epiphany, on Matt. 8:1–13; Pepys 66ᵇ, 95/22–6).

Translation itself serves the most basic clerical duty, a knowledge sufficient for instruction. In the grossest sense, this occurs simply by providing a content, the dominical gospel selections; these may be identified as the useful sum of scriptural knowledge because assigned for public liturgical reading and explanation. The Old Law turns out to be inherent in the New, since 'sermones antiqui' are frequently typological junctures of the testaments (e.g. the repeated linkage between Jesus's leper healings and Levitical imperatives which underwrite the power to absolve sin, a subject of the sermon from which I quote, as well as of sermon 43).

Such statements form more than simply a retread of the ancient topic of translating for the precise sense, since their major purpose is to graft onto Robert's text the Pauline contrast between letter and spirit. Translation for the plain sense gives the reader the 'resoun', but 'þe lettre' here is associated with an effort at verbal embellishment, in anti-romance prologues linked with 'lesynges' and construed as always misleading and distracting. The effort to achieve stylistic excellence is imagined as inherently an act of misrepresentation; for 'bustouslich . . . fals þouȝth queyntlich', the French reads: 'par rustie . . . mesprendre par curteise' (111–12). Robert's evocation of 'curteisie' immediately recalls the stated antithesis between his work and romance. He shrewdly identifies the language of courtesy with misconstruction; aristocratic discourse is courteous precisely in that, as an act of stylistic elevation, it is ceaselessly engaged in the creation of honorific synonym or figure, in that it refuses resolutely to call a thing by its proper name. This rhetorical mode runs counter to all the impulses of the French *Mirur*, primarily that insistence on meaning inherent in the form of the 'sermo antiquus'.

Scripture requires 'undoing', translation of literal narrative into a sometimes non-obvious spiritual 'resoun', a clear instructional programme; Robert seeks to make of the text he has constructed a reproduction of Pauline rhetoric.[49]

But stylistic bluntness accommodates the other basic clerical function of the *Mirur*, signalled by the penitential reference in the passage I have just cited. A few lines earlier, Robert has asserted:

> Latin ne wil Y sette non þerin, for it semeþ as it were a pride for to telle anoþer þat he vnderstondeþ nouȝt. And so it is ful gret foli to spek Latyn to lewed folke, and he entermetteþ him of a fole mester þat telleþ to hem Latin. For ich man schal ben vndernomen and aresoned eftter þe language þat he haþ lerd. (Pepys 45[b], 5/7–11)

Implicit in Robert's transferred language is the basic process of 'assailing', 'underniming and aresoning' – the function of penitential chastisement. The priestly duty of 'correptio', of not pulling punches and identifying sin forcefully, resembles the exegetical interest in the Pauline 'spirit'. Both are equally resistant to the misrepresentations inherent in romance discourse. The priest seeks to identify sin, to call it by its proper name, and to 'assail' – a transformation of romance militaristic metaphor into Christian sacrament – its adherents while showing neither fear or favour. 'Boustous' speech in the *Mirur* is the stylistic analogue to penitential encouragement of contrition through correction. 'The work' of penance will then follow, the actualisation of the word through an appropriate fulfilled confession (another important thematic concern). Such language precisely fulfils the mien ascribed to the Apocalypse's good priest, who does not desist for love or dread or fear of loss (a topic also quoted here from the Apocalypse).

The Middle English translator might be perceived as having taken this constructive stylistic resistance yet a step further. His decision to effect a 'derimage', so far as one knows unparalleled outside his London context at this early period, eschews the last romance feature Robert did not escape, the search for rhyme.[50] Moreover, it allows precise reproduction of 'resoun' through its reliance on a broadened and potentially common 'bustous' (a local, although probably not in London English, Robert's rustic or peasant) lexicon, freed from the selective choices by which the honorific discourse of romance is constructed.

Simultaneously, the reference to writing Latin points towards a fundamental reticence of the English *Mirror*, perhaps deliberately in keeping with the translator's understanding of the anti-romance prologue. For in rendering Robert here literally, the English elides any reference to its actual source in French. The English reader is allowed to believe that his text is direct from learned originals, without intermediary, that it reproduces what was in fact Robert's source directly and not at a linguistic distance. Thus, the potential distractions of romance French, part of the text's history, are removed. That this reticence represents the translator's deliberate suppression is probably affirmed by another direct appropriation into the English of a position properly Robert's alone; in the second prologue, the translator comments (Pepys 49[b], 21/5–7): 'And al hij mowen sen in þis wrytt þat þe Latyn spekeþ [Holk spelleþ] and seiþ suffischauntlich; [Holk inserts: hij mowen] heren here al þat nedeþ to hem'. And this answers a further duplicitous promise of the first prologue (Pepys 45[b], 5/5–7): 'And wite 3e wel, þere is nou3th o word inne þat it nys in holy wrytt and out of þe bookes þat þise holy men þat weren toforne vs han made ydrawen'.

In rendering this claim for textual exactitude, the translator suppresses the standard claim – that not only has nothing been added, but equally nothing omitted – always associated with canonical texts (cf. n. 37). This statement Robert had made, 'Jo l'ai excerpe e estrait' (77). Whatever its pretences, the English *Mirror* is not a full literal rendition of its alleged Latin source materials: it has been through both a selective process (a trace remains in 'al þat nedeþ to hem', a reproduction of Robert's French) and a complete redaction in an intermediate language.

The promise of direct reproduction of unimpeachable texts customarily serves a textual positioning one might identify as authoritative, typically a clerical one. Yet *The Mirror* has in fact been composed for a very different non-Latinate audience. Although the sermons typically address their responsibilities, *The Mirror* has not been composed for clerics, and thus is not, as 'published' medieval sermon collections routinely are, a trot for imagination-starved preachers to use in drawing up their sermons. Although the text routinely affirms and discusses 'ordre', the clerical status, it exists to fill a gap within the very context of potential clerical failure, that indifferently engaged priesthood so often imagined in the text: it in effect replaces public sermons. But the work also exists for private consultative use without clerical supervision.

In some respects, Robert had ensured that such supervision would be provided within the text itself, and he had already in the French offered an attentive sequence of instructions on the use of the book. It is its own gospel, spread in the world, and the prologue, reproduced in the English, becomes progressively more explicit about the procedures required for this dispersal. Initially, Robert's instruction for textual use is the broad and general, 'Whan ȝe han will for to reden, draweþ forþ þis book' (Pepys 45ª, 5/3–4). Robert assumes not simply a literate but a libraried audience. The instruction occurs, however, within the context of the attack on romance; the book-owner is required to exercise personal choice about texts, to put aside his or her romance manuscript and instead, to get into something edifying.

The next book-reference takes the discussion out of the realm of whimsical personal choice and into a more fully socialised situation:

> *Destruxisti eum ab emundacione.* 'Lorde, þou hast destroyed þe vnclene'. Vnclene is he þat God wil nouȝth chastise; þerfore I amonest all þat hij wil [AN uolent 'wish to'] chastise hem in God. And þerfor ich haue made þis book, þat vche man may haue delite forto here and rede openlich what apendeþ to God and to hem: hou þe clerke schal prechen and kepen [AN sermuner e guarder] hymseluen in good, and hou þe lewed schal wel wirchen [AN oir 'hear'] and loue his techer, and hou al schul wirchen and done Goddes commaundementz, and what merytt hij schull han þat seruen God wiþ good wille. (Pepys 48ª, 15/1–8)

The book has replaced the priest who composed it. Robert imagines its use for public reading, where some portion of an audience, all apparently lay, will hear and some will read. This activity occurs 'openlich' (AN vuertement), a semantic pun. The text represents its own overt/open form of chastisement, a recall to the will of God and a programme fundamentally penitential. But it is equally 'open' in the lay use of the book, its public communication. Moreover, in the one deliberate mis-representation of the source here, 'wirchen' for 'oir', lay readers are called out of their passivity; they are to work, rather than preach like clerics or merely listen like the laity of the Anglo-Norman. But this labour, as the passage develops, becomes fused into a practice indistinguishable from the clerical; all shall work/perform God's commandment.

The Christian responsibilities of cleric and lay person are identical; the former has merely provided the information that allows the latter to behave properly, as he has done. As the *Mirror* says elsewhere, in an emphatic crescendo of this repeated theme:

> Understondeþ now vnto þis lessoun, ȝe þat louen God and skyl and resoun, what þat it is to menen. For wite ȝe wel, he þat vnder-stondeþ it wel and doþe þereafter, it wil profyt hym gretlich, for litel oiþer nouȝth it is worþ to heren it þat nylleþ nouȝth wirchen þereafter. For wordes beþ ordeined þerfore for þat man schal ȝiue vn-derstondynge þerto, and of vnderstondynge ne comeþ no good, bot ȝif it be done in dede to Goddes worschipp. No man may neuer see þe kyrnel of þe nutte bot ȝif þe schelle be broken first; no more ne mowen Goddes wordes ben vnderstonden bot hij ben y-opened open-lich vnto mennes vnderstondynge. (sermon 10, for the 5th Sunday after Epiphany, Matt. 13:24–30 [the parable of the tares]; Pepys 70ᵃ, 113/14–22)

In this imagined situation, the clerk whose work is to break the shell, to unpack spiritual meaning, in some measure disappears. Insofar as he resembles Robert, he is an invisible translator, and he addresses willing lay users of the text. The translator will undo the letter, 'þat men wel vnderstonde hem, and forto schewe vche man his lyf and hou he schal take ensample of holy men hou he schal ȝelde God his soule and reden his book for to amenden hemseluen and for to techen oþere' (Pepys 48ᵃ, 15/10–13).[51] At least one lay work in accord with God's law becomes that of instructing other lay people through the literary absorption of the text.

In this regard, one might insist that the Norman audience for the original *Mirur* differs from that imagined for the prose Apocalypse. In contrast to those visual literates I have discussed above who only hear, Robert wrote for a select lay audience. Most immediately, he addressed a pious woman, Aline de Quency; perhaps more generally, he wrote for people like her, for members of a lay confraternity attached to his Augustinian hospital/canonry, or for similar aristocratic persons of par-ticular devotion, ones seeking or requiring more than a merely parochial attention, and for whom he performed as a domestic chaplain. The

English *Mirror* is much less clearly sited, certainly much less exclusively so. And it opens the way for a different, and potentially more sweeping, variety of textual interchange. But the contrast with the Apocalypse underscores the general point – that interlingual relations, relations between learned and vernacular, and thus between different cultural sites, cannot be reduced to a single form of analysis, squeezed into a single template, but remain always subject to individual/local negotiations. Here, although in the same language and manuscript, the texts each construct and hail their readership differently.

Finally, Robert comments:

> Now I beseche wiþ good herte to all þat þis wrytt han, þat hij lenen it wiþ good will to alle þat it willeþ writen. For þe custume is of Goddes word [AN sermun], þe more þat it spredeþ abrode, þe better it is and þe more hij quemen God þat it owen [þe better—quemen = AN plus est cher]. For he þat heleþ Goddes worde, it semeþ þat he haþ envie to God and to soules he doþe gret harme, for he bynymeþ hem her fode. Wharfore he moste ȝelde rekenynge þat may helpen and wil nouȝth; of als many he schal ȝelde rekenynge as ben lorne þorouȝ his conseil, for þorouȝ his conseil it is whan he haþ a þing þat he may helpe soules wiþ and nyl nouȝth. God nyl nouȝth þat non wiþdrawe hym þat he ne schewe his wordes to alle. He þat can and may, schewe hem wiþ worde, and he þat ne may wiþ word, schewe forþ his bokes. (Pepys 49^b, 21/13–23)

At this point, Robert extends his argument for the lay responsibility to offer one's neighbour spiritual counsel. His final sentence perhaps implies that the book may be secondary. 'Schewynge wiþ worde', perhaps clerical preaching, but equally lay oral reading, seems here prioritised. But the sentence also implies something in excess of oral instruction, reading one's book to others. Robert now insists upon textual promulgation, lending of the book as an exemplar which will spread the word of God by repeated copyings, multiplication of an unsupervised text to ensure its presence in lay hands.

Yet perhaps the logic for transmission, itself gospel derived (cf. Matt. 5:15–16), is more telling than the injunction itself. Robert argues that it is positively sinful to retain the book as private commodity, rather than publicise it. In so doing, he relies upon a biblical text he invokes only a great deal later, in sermon 59 (see further pp. 192–3):

þe more þat a man can, þe besier he mote be to kepen hym in good lyf and techen oþere þat he can wiþouten mede-takynge. For Salamon seiþ þou ne schalt nouȝth selle þi wytt, for God it ȝiueþ þe. And look wel þat hij ne leten nouȝth erþelich þinges ouercomen her wytt, þat hij ne ces\c/en nouȝth for to prechen for no werldeliche þing ne for to techen þe wytt þat God haþ sent hem, ne for doute, ne for pouste, ne for no werldeliche enemy. (Pepys 212ᵃ)

Robert alludes here to Prov. 23:23: 'Buy truth, and do not sell wisdom, and instruction, and understanding' ('Veritatem eme et noli vendere sapientiam et doctrinam et intelligentiam'). This text has a lengthy history in canon law; it is customarily invoked to enjoin the responsibility of cathedral chapters or university canonists to offer free instruction to the willing (Post *et al.*). Evoking it here represents, just as the Middle English translator's claim to authoritative sources does, a translation of specifically clerical imperatives and responsibilities into literate lay culture. As a canon of St Paul's might be held to provide instruction to London priests and appointed to a mastership, so a lay owner of *The Mirror* is enjoined to similar acts of learned dissemination. Indeed, these could be construed as more extensive than clerical teaching, since they potentially involve releasing an expensive (spiritual) investment, the book, into alien hands.

Robert's command for textual dissemination appears to have been heeded. For example, a similar argument that the refusal to instruct is sinful underlies a definition of properly 'gostlich men and wymmen ... Goddes childer' in the Pepys 2498 copy of *Ancrene Riwle*:

Ne holde no gostlich þing fro no man þat may do anoþer man good als wel as ȝou, þat ȝe ne be redy at helpe hym wiþ al at his nede, wytt oiþer any oþer þing. For Salamon seiþ þou ne schalt nouȝth sellen þi wytt, for God it ȝiueþ þe and leneþ for to parten wiþ oþer ... For God haþ made þe his reue and his spenser for þou scholdest dispenden it to his worschipp and to note of þi soule. (112/30–13/6)⁵²

As the *Riwle* reference, 'reue and spenser', makes abundantly clear, the injunction against hiding knowledge rests on further gospel arguments Robert does not here cite so openly. He thinks specifically of parables of non- and mal-feasant stewards, exegetically associated with those called to the priesthood. And most especially perhaps, his phrase 'ȝeld rekenynge' recalls the summons to judgement always associated with the unjust steward of Luke 16 (and the subject of a famous and widely reproduced St Paul's Cross sermon, delivered by Thomas Wimbledon in 1388). Lay and clerical status begin to blur; both are held to analogous acts of instructing in scripturally based responsibilities.[53]

The final sentence of Robert's command to copy the manuscript must also be seen as re-enforcing the potentially powerful appropriation of clerical positions I have mentioned. The lay reader who 'shows with word', through literate reading to others, significantly resembles the priest and his equally oral sermon activity. But priests in fact rather rarely 'show with books'; as Robert is aware, sermons communicate book-lore indirectly, in edited form. Moreover, these conventional literates typically share their books only with each other, as reference volumes to aid in the care of souls (cf. the later complaint discussed by the Rouses 1987). 'Showing with books' refers to acts of the literate book-owning lay person. He or she may be neither a public speaker, nor indeed even literate (recall the universal Middle English 'lewed' for Robert's 'lais'), perhaps someone who keeps the book for others to read to him/her, as the London skinner John Claydon kept the Lollard *Lanterne of Li3t* in 1415. In this formulation, the sermoning priest – although he is expected to be literate in Scripture – in fact has come to work in the mode of oral knowledge, while the layman stands as a figure specifically 'textual'.[54]

One might see this reversal as always inherent in the form and language of the English *Mirror*. The text is composed of old-fashioned 'sermones antiqui', with about a dozen lengthy intercalated exempla. But in their original form, as composed by Gregory the Great, these sermons were, at best, addressed to a mixed audience, and often one composed only of deacons. It is for this reason that they so often construe the prophet Jesus as a priestly model, a 'pastor bonus'. The translation allows what may have been an originally excluded laity to hear exhortations to proper clerical performance and, simultaneously, allows them to draw judgements about the local service they receive. Moreover, because the sermons habitually outline the nature of adequate priestly behaviour, the lay audience can judge what this entails, and, at the most basic instructional level, they can be aware of their own capacity to comprehend, or indeed to perform a similar office. Further, in the situation of a mixed audience, both lay and clerical, ancient sermons can never quite shut down a spillover of injunctions literally clerical onto lay hearers. That increasing turn to generalisation inherent in this sermon form, the text followed by a progressive 'undoing', means that precepts developed from allegorical readings of the gospel and specific to priestly duties become loaded onto a lay audience as well.

In the *Mirror*, one such overt moment occurs in sermon 42 (the 13th Sunday after Trinity, on Luke 10:30–7, the good Samaritan). The homilist begins (Pepys 152^b) with his customary allegorical identification, 'þe stableer bitokneþ þe preest þat [God] ʒiueþ vnderstondynge of þe elde lawʒe and of þe newe'. Once again, as in the citation on p. 181, this biblical knowledge, joined to a life of sanctity, constitutes priesthood. But as the sermon approaches its hortatory conclusion, it continues as if a precept for all Christians, who are to be the exemplary Samaritan, rather than the secondary stabler:

> Riʒth so we schull loue oure neiʒbour as Ihesus loued vs þat so mychel lowed hym for vs, and we schullen also lowen vs forto helen [so Holk, Pepys beggen] oure neiʒbour . . . Crist suffred deþ forto ʒiue lyf, and we mowen don also. We ne schull nouʒth douten þe deþ for to bringe oure neiʒbour vnto heuene. Biþenke we þat Crist seide þus, 'Do þou also'. ʒif þou wilt haue mede of God, do as dude þe Samaritan, for nouʒth þou clepest þe for Crist[en] [so Holk] ʒif þou late anyþing of þis. For Ihesus Crist þat neuere ne liʒeþ saiþ, 'Do also'. Lokeþ wel þat non do amys þat doþ als he dude. (Pepys 152^b–53^a, AN 146^{rb-vb})

Not fearing death in the interest of correcting sin, 'healing neighbours', forms, of course, the act of the Johannine priest of the Apocalypse and significantly resembles the injunctions to active priesthood elsewhere in *The Mirror*. The sermon imagines for its ideal audience more than just the customary hear/teach or the experience of private reading for edification. It allows and encourages routinised lay activity in a priestly mode, although, unlike later formalised Lollardy, it still enjoins clerical respect as a basic Christian responsibility.

Throughout the *Mirror*, Robert testifies to a fundamental distinction between cleric and 'lewed' layman. Sermon 36 (for the 7th Sunday after Trinity, on Mark 8:1–9), states the issue precisely: 'His deciples ben þe lettred to whiche God schewed wytt and vnderstondynge and haþ ʒiuen

[Holk vndon] hem holy wrytt for to reden forþ [Holk ȝeuen fode] to oþere'. But equally, the emphasis in the sermons on performance, 'work', 'doing in deed', often produces statements which imply that learned clergy does not form an utterly exclusive status. For example, twice in sermon 33 (for the 4th Sunday after Trinity, on Luke 5:1–11), Robert comments, 'His deciples alle ben þat heren his wordes and done hem in werk', 'Alle þat ben goode Cristen men ben his disciplis' (Pepys 131[b] and 133[a], AN 128vb). And similarly, a little later in sermon 36 than the passage I have cited above, Robert comments:

> It ne falleþ nouȝth vnto my matere [this clause not in AN], ac oft good lyf makeþ a man þe holyere þan grete clergie, ac whan þise two comen togedre, hij þat it hereþ [AN l'oent, i.e. 'hear him (preach)'] beþ wel payed þereof. (Pepys 139[a], AN 134va, for both passages)

Querulousness about clerical failures may open the way for considering developed lay piety, a perhaps silent exemplary performance, as a more efficacious teaching device than the most successful book-derived sermons.

Early in his second prologue, Robert enunciates such a view. In a passage that ostensibly protects the clerical function, by arguing a view categorically opposed to the developed Lollardy of century's end, he nonetheless leaves logically a place for lay instruction:

> And þeiȝ al he [Holk adds be] of yuel lyf þat bereþ forþ Goddes wordes, men owen ful wel heren his wordes, nouȝth for hym, ac for þe spirytt þat spekeþ in hym . . . þerfore no man schal take kepe to hym þat spekeþ þe word, for out of þe bordel may come a good man and out of þe castel a wikked man. What þat þe persone is, he is good þat hereþ it and doþe it in dede. (Pepys 48[b], 49[a]; 17/26–8, 19/9–11)

In context, these statements claim that an evil priest may be an efficacious bearer of God's word (recall Robert's own earlier modesty topos). The virtue of the preacher is irrelevant to the truth of his message, and the word of God will spread itself. Yet simultaneously, and especially in the context of Robert's socialised contrast of whorehouse and castle, the argument tends towards justifying a teaching function for anyone, regardless of his morality. And interestingly, the only potentially unqualified locus of virtue in the passage is that of the pious auditor; the layman who hears the word – and actuates it – is beyond the balancing the remainder of the argument requires.

Thus, the *Mirrour* routinely urges respect for those ordained and holding clerical office. Moreover, the text centres in the penitential need for chastisement, and Robert almost invariably argues, often as a silent given, that such fulfilled chastisement requires a traditional confession to a priest. The sacramental system remains in place. Moreover, Robert routinely endorses translating respect into open-handed financial support of priests:

> *Dignus est operarius mercede sua etc.* Wel he owe to haue werldelich mete [so Holk, Pepys mede] þat bringeþ þe mede of heuen; wel he owe to haue werldelich þinges þat byhoteþ þe godenesse [Holk godes] of heuen. Out of heuen he schal be putt þat leteþ his prechour haue nede. Seynt Poule it seiþ for soþe, þat vche man þat oþer lereþ or techeþ, he schal ȝiue him of al his good wiþouten askynge. *Communicet* [so Holk, Pepys Conueniunt] *autem his qui catezizatur verbo etc.* (Pepys 49^{ab}, 19/25–31)[55]

'Al his good' goes well beyond the minimal requirement – soon to be contested by Lollards – of paying one's tithes.

On the other hand, Robert is never far from putting forward a conception of lay ministry. In the main, he envisions a non-sacramental instructional fellowship, probably corresponding to that 'spiritual work of mercy' which enjoins one to counsel the sinful.[56] Thus in sermon 26 (the Ascension, on Mark 16:14–20), having aligned the miraculous powers promised the disciples with the duties of the priest, Robert continues, in a universalisation of these powers, 'Lewed may done þise toknes ȝif þat hij bileuen wel in Ihesu þat is oure lyf, for þe gospel seiþ al þing he may do þat bileueþ wel in Crist'. He then cites a series of four actions lay persons can undertake that will parallel those he has previously outlined as priestly powers, concluding:

> þan he spekeþ newe langage whan þat he scheweþ his foule willes [AN sun fol curage] whan he scheweþ his synnes and askeþ mercy of God ... Vnto seek he schal do grete good whan he helpeþ man out of synne wiþ word oiþer wiþ dede, and hij þat contenen [AN cuntendrunt] hem þus wiþ Crist hij schull stiȝen vp into heuene. (Pepys 112^{b}, AN 112rb)

While avowedly sinful (and needing confession, not here presented sacramentally), lay people, Robert argues, might equally attain salvation by counselling others to leave their sin.

At another point, Robert offers a prescription less overtly aligned with clerical powers, and overtly secondary, yet more sweeping in its claims:

> First owe man to heren mekelich his techer, and þan wel vnderstonde and hold [AN adds fermement e salf] þat he hereþ þat he may after, whan myster is, schewen it to þat oþer, so þat þai mowen kepen hem fro harme and to wirchen wel þereafter and chastisen hemseluen and oþere. (sermon 41, for the 12th Sunday after Trinity, on Mark 7:31–7; Pepys 150ª, AN 144ʳª)⁵⁷

The clerical sermon is both inspirational and informative, and the layman a secondary purveyor of its wisdom. Rather than focus on the book, here Robert invokes memory, the power of recall, and a 'showing' of textual data that is clearly conversational, but equally clearly, free lay teaching, involving particularly lay chastisement of the errant. This lay instruction and chastisement may not, in this context, be expected to involve anything particularly 'learned'; it sounds very much like the kind of activity one London guild stated in its regulations to be its remit: members were to behave 'in meyntenance of good loue and forto norische good and trewe companye in destruccioun and amendement of men of wikked fame and of euel berynge be wey of almesse and of charite'.⁵⁸

So Robert of Gretham. But late, uniquely English portions of the cycle, often more clearly Apocalypse-based than the original, are marked by an expansive stridency on this point as well. For example, sermon 59, in all the manuscripts, but with no known Anglo-Norman source (in Pepys, it is identified as for the nativity of a confessor), discusses the parable of the talents (Matt. 25:14–30).⁵⁹ It plays out the implications of Luke 16, when conjoined with Proverbs 23:23; the preacher argues that the man who buries his besant should be read as someone given to worldly goods, not to spiritual multiplication, and the sermon becomes an impassioned exhortation to free preaching by all people and to all people:

> And als manye as swiche on miȝth saue þorouȝ his cunnynge and ne dooþ nouȝth, als many o he schal be dampned fore. And summe seien, 'I nam nouȝth lerned, I ne haue no speche, and I ne can nouȝth'. Ne

> excuse no man hym so, for þat he can, þat he seie: þat litel can, litel
> seie; þat mychel can, mychel seye. He þat can o godspel and haþ on
> ensaumple of vertue, teche it forþ to oþere, ne loke nou3th aftere þe
> tyme ne þe age ne þe persone, bot teche to men and to wymmen.
> (Pepys 211[b])

The talents/abilities of the servants are construed as levels of knowledge.
And even the most minimal lay knowledge, a thoroughly unlearned,
non-clerical command of but a single gospel, even a single example of
(?non-biblical) virtuous activity, will be efficacious. Moreover, such oral
instruction is defined as thoroughly open, restrained by no conventional
category of audience appropriateness – all are equally souls to be saved,
and all merit hearing the word in virtually any self-anointed form. In
his enthusiasm, the Middle English author enjoins teaching to anyone,
anywhere, and at any time; he continues, 'to wymmen, 3onge and
elde, to riche and pouere, in welþe and in pouerte, ny3th and day, and
morowen and euen, in chirches and in waies, in stretes and in feldes,
and in þe cee and in þe erþe and in alle stedes and in alle tymes'. As his
argument proceeds (Pepys 212[a]), the preacher adduces the now familiar
Apocalypse-inspired claim that only false servants will not preach – those
who dread rich men, love their friends too dearly, or dread losing their
goods.

Similarly, the 61st sermon (on its status, see n. 54), both blurs and
retains a lay/clerical divide:

> *Cristus idem est quod sacerdos crismate vncti.* Crist is as muchel to seyn
> on oure tunge as prest and no3t [presumably for 'anoynt'?] wiþ creme,
> and so is euerich man þat is cristned Goddes prest. But euerich prest,
> þoru3 his ordre and þoru3 his dignete, haþ more power and more is
> worþ þan anoþer and more endette forto teche and forto preche þan
> anoþer, 3if þat he liue þerafter as he au3te forto don. (Holkam 125)

The homilist's expansion of his source text (even if he has not deliberately
mistranslated it) manages to obliterate any distinctive feature of the
sacrament 'order'. All Christians through baptism are equally priests and
thus presumably share the clerical functions, teach/preach, live a life that
exemplifies your teaching. Equally, this author, like Robert, reaffirms the
distinction of states; yet his distinction has now become relativised ('*more
endette forto teche*') and has become dependent upon the sanctity of the

preacher's life. Implicitly, the priest can forfeit his greater power through a non-virtuous life, but no clear parallel disenfranchisement hinders a lay person, presumably because he has made no similar sacramental vow. Thus when the sermon's author turns to the now-familiar constraints of Luke 16 and Proverbs 23, he asserts:

> For I seye ȝou forsoþe whoso can and may helpen anoþer out of his synne and ne doþ noȝt, he is coupable of þat iche synne tofore God, be he lered, be he lewed, but þe lered more þan þe lewed. But non ne be so hardi for to preche ne for to teche for wynnynge of worldliche þinges ne for to be preised of man ne of womman.

The preacher, whose responsibilities fill the remainder of the sermon, still has priority. Yet the final sentence, while it certainly evokes the bad priest of the Apocalypse, lacks any vocational qualification and thus presumably imagines limits upon the instructional function that include both groups. Without 'order', lay persons are just as apt as clerics to teach for the wrong reasons, for self-aggrandisement, rather than love and fulfilment of God's law; in this effort at limiting a lay sense of vocation (not ordination), one might see the roots of the querulous animosity stimulated by unanointed lay instructors like Margery Kempe – and Longe Wille.

But, just as sermons 59 and 61 have been variously appended to Robert of Gretham's original, the *Mirror* translator is not a passive figure, but intrudes bits to very similar purpose into the material he had received. For example, even the 22nd sermon, on the good shepherd, has not been immune to such tinkering and reformulation of the notion of clerical office and function:

> Alle ben kepers of holychirche þat entren into any dignite oiþer any ordre þat falleþ to holy chirche [AN Ki rien en unt par dreit assise], popes, cardynales . . . persones and preestes, and vche man þat God haþ sent more cunnynge þan anoþer. He is endette to [so Holk, Pepys in doute] teche his broþer and wiþnyme hym of his synne in als mychel as he can and may, oiþer elles is he out of loue and charite, [Holk adds: and ȝif he be out of loue and charite], all his werkes beþ nouȝthe. (Pepys 104[b], Panunzio 209–31, lines 245–8)

Robert of Gretham had stopped his explanation with 'preestes'; the remainder, with the customary injunction to teach and chastise, as well as the customary warning of the dangers that will ensue on failure to perform, is a Middle English addition.

Some small adjustments to the received text offer possible qualifications of the Middle English translator's actual orthodoxy. These interestingly are focussed, so far as I can see, in a single topic, the clerical right to administer the sacrament of penance. On the whole, the *Mirror* appears to me to encourage perfectly orthodox behaviours in this regard, to insist on the right of the priest to hear confession and on the priest's capacity, even if a sinner, to offer appropriate absolution. But, for example, in sermon 21 (for the 1st Sunday after Easter, on John 20:19–31, Panunzio 189–206) the translator suppresses some twenty lines (197–206) which elaborate on the clerical power to bind and loose. Such an excision might remain a fairly unconvincing argument *ex silentio*, were it not that the preceding lines appear to have been subjected to deliberate mistranslation:

> þis forȝiuenesse falleþ to hem þat haue taken þe ordre [ki force unt del ordeinement], and nouȝth for þan ['nevertheless', altering AN e pur quant 'and therefore'] parfytt orisoun of holy man haþ ofte forȝiuen synne. (Pepys 102ᵃ)[60]

In the source, the holy man is the priest, whose prayers are seen as inherent in the process of absolution; the Middle English manages to suggest a thoroughly non-sacramental absolution, in which a holy neighbour's prayers might suffice to clear one's account with God.

Similar adjustments, less ambiguous in their nature, occur elsewhere in this specifically penitential context. On at least two occasions, the *Mirror* addresses the question of confession to a sinful priest. One even appears in the 43rd sermon, which I have already cited as taking a fairly orthodox position on the sacrament. The translator, in a general way, follows Robert in urging respect for such a priest:

> ȝif we despise þe preest, we despise [AN Hunte e tort ... fesum] God hymselue, ȝif þat he be swiche as he auȝtte to ben [the clause not in AN]. ȝif he ne be, *kepe we vs oute of his compaignye, ac despise we no man be he neuere so synful,* [Holk adds *for ȝif we dispyse prest oþer ony man*], we so dubble [AN dubler | ... e multiplier] oure synnes. (Pepys 154ᵇ, AN 148ʳᵃᵇ)

I italicise in this quotation a sustained refusal to transmit what Robert had written: 'Let us preserve God's commandment; we ought not refuse what God wishes to command us'.[61] The Middle English advocates 'shunning', not only not participating in a tainted sacrament but actively avoiding an unrepentant sinner, an activity reminiscent of that written into the guild statute I have cited (p. 192). Robert's comment is a thoroughly orthodox pronouncement – it's too bad if one has a bad parish priest; it's God's command to confess (and one needn't worry, must assume the sacrament is efficacious). But the translation, at its most benign, has converted this into the more general statement that it is prideful to despise anyone, lay or priest, and has essentially denied any specific virtue to 'order' itself.

Sermon 33 (for the 4th Sunday after Trinity, on Luke 5:1–11) includes a Middle English interpolation that is surely in its strictest sense heretical:

> þe blynde ledeþ þe blynde whan þat o blynde chastiseþ anoþer blynde. Forþi þai owen to holden hem clene þat schullen chastisen oþer, and nameliche men of ordre... [followed by examples of priests giving light penances for sins resembling their own]. For ȝif þe preest be in any oþer synnes, he may do no sacrement, schrift ne oþer of alle þe seuene sacrementz, but ȝif he do dedlich synne. And þerfore who þat schryueþ hym at swich on, ȝif þat he wote hym swiche, þai fallen boþe in þe diche, for þe blynde ledeþ þe blynde. (Pepys 133[ab], AN 128vb includes no such statement)

The insistence upon consciousness of the priest's fault implies that parishioners must shun the services proffered. The suspicion that a bad priest would offer easy penance undermines the system, and to visit such a cleric would be deliberately to seek not to be appropriately chastised. The text remains silent about the lay person's alternatives, but one would be to seek another priest, known to be of good life. Such a step is customarily deprecated in canon law, on the assumption that one confesses to someone not one's 'proper' priest for precisely the reasons the lay person would here seek to avoid. Or the frustrated lay person might avail him/herself of what sermon 21 has already suggested, the prayers of a pious friend.

The *Mirror* thus tends to view clerical status within a broader framework. The universal gospel imperative requires Christians to translate

196

God's word into God's work, and such a performance of divine law will save all. Within this general injunction, priesthood forms a special category, a dangerous one since it offers greater penalties for nonfeasance, the indolence that violates the promises of 'order' and corrupts the clerk's special skills. In such a context, the dutiful pious Christian may assume responsibilities equal and analogous to those of the priest, conferred on him or her by gospel precept, not ecclesiastical practice. Fulfilling these responsibilities may grant to laymen powers conventionally deemed learned and clerical – Kempe's 'holy conversation' (cf. 125/7–126/20, including her captious distinction between mere talk and preaching), chastising the sinful, perhaps praying for a sinful friend's conversion from sin, in lieu of the priest's absolution.

This corrective responsibility appears strikingly in a passage actuating that democratising impulse that sees the priest as but a fellow follower of God's law. In sermon 4 (for the 4th Sunday of Advent), Robert had offered an exemplum designed to show that God's service is not compromised by the wickedness of a bad priest and that such a priest deserves the respect of the laity (51/5–32). The Middle English at once intrudes a qualification: 'Vnderstondeþ nouȝth þis tale bot for ensample; soþ it may wel be bot holy wrytt nys it nouȝt'. And the author immediately proceeds to explain one's responsibility to the sinful priest as precisely the same as one owes any sinful neighbour, and equally subject to the constraints of Luke 16:

> ȝif ȝe wyst [the priest's sin] and miȝth amenden hym [but did not], it were wers unto ȝou, for ȝe dude dedly synne for ȝe meyntene hym in his synne. For he is conforted in his synne whan ȝe bere hym as good felawschip as anoþer man. (Pepys 56[b], 53/3–6)

In offering this advice and universalising the power of lay correction, the translator ignores Robert's far less tendentious advice (1580–7), to use the priest as mirror and see in him what are potentially one's own faults requiring correction.

Perhaps most striking of all, sermon 48 (for the 19th Sunday after Trinity, Matt. 9:1–8) includes a massive interpolated diatribe (unparalleled at AN 158[v]–59), an attack on the very basis of clergy, its learning. In the key of the prose Apocalypse, the scribes who chastise the healing Jesus are identified as:

Antecristes prophetes þat wil coniecten Goddes wordes and hem þat
speken hem, ȝif þai mowen in any manere, for hem þencheþ it is aȝein
her libbyngs and þencheþ it al scorn in her hertes þat any schulde
speken of God, but he were a riche man and a grete clerk. And God
haþ euere ȝutt taken mo vnto hym þorouȝ symple lewed folk þat were
tauȝtte of hym þan of þise grete clerkes þat comeþ [for conneþ?; Holk
adds to her] gret clergie þorouȝ gret stodye. Ȝa, I dar hardilich saie
he haþ taken mo þorouȝ on þat is of his techinge þan he haþ don for
fourty swiche grete clerkes [Holk adds: þat com to her clergye þoruȝ
studye. And þat is o poynt why þat þei ben litel preysed of God oþer
noȝt, for hem þinkeþ in her herte þei schulde be worschiped þerfore,
and for o poynt þe Pycard les his eiȝe: be war þat þei ne do noȝt so].[62]
Witnesse of Poule: he biȝate mo to God þan now don a þousande
clerkes for her gret clergye, [Holk adds: Seint Dominik and Seint
Fraunceys þei turned al Lumbardye into good bileue, þat is al a lond;
and alle her successours may noȝt tur\n/e a toun] and þat is for þai
lyuen nowth after her techinge [Holk adds: and þat is for þei wolden
han los and goode and God, and for þei desyre alle þre þei ne schul
haue neuer on. And ȝif þei desyred on riȝtfulliche, þei schuld han alle
þre]. þei prechen of pouert and þat man schulde forsake his delites,
and þere nys wel neiȝ no man þat secheþ so mychel after her delites
and after ese as hij don. And alle swiche ben Antecristes prophetes.
(Pepys 166ᵇ)[63]

Antichrist's team is identifiable through two partially distinct, partially
coalescing charges, signalled by the introductory 'a riche man and a gret
clerk'. On the one hand, and in keeping with *The Mirror*'s persistent thematic, learned 'clergie' does not automatically qualify one for sanctity; as
the very existence of the text indicates, true action, a proper individual
response to a publicly opened gospel, is a real possibility for lay persons.

In pursuing this goal, the individual in essence learns directly from
the model teacher, Jesus himself, and becomes 'on þat is of his techinge'.
Not only are scholarly paraphernalia, learned books, unnecessary (if
not thoroughly redundant and distracting) for such skill, the Middle
English preacher argues implicitly that learning involves undue subtlety
('studye' may concern itself with the inessential), certainly that it may
as readily instil pride of mastery as proper behaviour. Rather than taken
up for the love of God, 'gret clergie' may feed love of self; thus, it may
be construed the 'hypocrisy', the pursuit of a wrong end, against which
the Apocalypse rails.

But with the mention, in the more extended Holkham account, of Francis and Dominic as unlearned Pauline teachers, the argument shifts slightly. Certainly, latter-day friars, those ubiquitously urban figures, are renowned for their desire to haunt places of learning on their own terms. And a heady load of anti-mendicant satire, stretching back to Parisian difficulties of the 1250s, would identify them with the pseudo-prophets of the Apocalypse (Szittya offers a useful overview). But their hypocrisy, in this account, has been doubled; consummate town-dwellers, once capable of converting 'a lond' by their example, they have uniquely disqualified themselves for their chosen task, degenerated into even local incapacity (and thus are thoroughly disqualified for citizenship in the Great City).

Not only do friars personify that same arrogance generally ascribed to clerics, but the higher claims of gospel poverty inherent in their foundation render them suspect. In forgetting evangelical poverty, they have doubled their hypocrisy, confused 'goode' and 'God', and thus damned themselves. In the last analysis, the only trustworthy teachers may be those ostensibly least qualified, removed from the distractions of unnecessarily learned texts, without a formalised learning in which to take pride, labouring as a performative parallel for 'working' God's word. In short, they are the audience the *Mirror* translator had always imagined and whose presence in Robert of Gretham's text he sought to emphasise.

This discourse of sanctifying lay piety and of holy correction seems to me susceptible of social placement. A few pages ago (192), I alluded to the regulations of a London parish guild; such documents are redolent with injunctions towards Christian fellowship. Such an emphasis includes stipulations for Christian correction analogous to those encouraged by the Middle English *Mirror*. These organisations, although remarkably diverse, were most typically neighbourhood religious corporations insistent on good fellowship and including a strong element of a private insurance group. Both activities merge in their most prominent activities – maintaining a chantry dedicated to a patron saint with a paid priest to perform stipulated masses (but in no surviving regulation, to preach). Also prominent among their functions were attendance and offering alms at members' funerals, as well as arranging, out of corporate funds, memorial masses for all departed members.[64]

Organisations of this type appeared in London as early as the reign of John, but their recorded profusion dates only from the later 1330s. Their appearance is contemporary with a widespread movement to record trade guild statutes (e.g., Riley 153–62), and like the regulations of trade organisations, all of which include features shared with parish guilds, the actual recorded appearance may be belated, the codification of behaviours already well established.[65] The initial appearance of these organisations in the legal record was followed by an exponential jump in numbers after mid-century, stimulated by the increased mortality of the Plague and a newly perceived need for intensified bonds of community. Whatever their specific functions, parish guilds express a desire for a free sustaining fellowship (best exhibited in universal provision for an annual feast, cf. Rosser 1994). These are voluntary associations, and they have a conception of fit members, again often shared with craft guilds. The guilds exist to join persons of virtue and probity, of 'good fame', with those likeminded; the guild gains its strength from their conjunction in an organisation committed to virtuous community among neighbours (cf. Barron–Wright 127, 141; for trade guild analogies, Riley 148–9, 277–8, 281–2, 371).

These organisations were particularly committed to converting their worldly fellowship into an eternal one. As spiritual documents, guild regulation imagines a continuity between charitable Christian living here and the eternal fellowship depicted at the end of the Apocalypse. As a result, parish guilds attend to publicly perceived virtuous behaviour not simply as a requirement for admission, but also for continued membership. If the guild should foster the good name of its members, the failures of one may reflect upon all. Hence, most statutes identify behaviours that will merit expulsion from the group; regulations typically confer on elected wardens (and sometimes a wider group of the more virtuous members) the responsibility of admonishing the errant. They offer an opportunity for both correction and for reform. An unusually specific example comes from a guild in what was perhaps Langland's parish church, St Peter's, Cornhill, founded 1403; expulsion will follow refusal to respond,

> if it may be founde prevyd that ony of the same fraternite be ony comune contectour, hasardour, lechour, chider, fals usurour, or usethe

ony othir shrewed tacches, and thanne therof be resonabilly warned
and repreved onys, twyis, thriys by the wardeyns... withe vij. or viij.
the more discrete and wele consciencyd mene. (Horwood 414a)[66]

While this list is broadly inclusive and the guild unusual, but not unparalleled, in the number of chances for reform it offered, its prioritisation
of 'contek' is revelatory. These organisations are committed to virtuous expression of social amity; in that context, verbal crime, especially
engaging in slander and quarrel, often attacks on that centre of spiritual and commercial probity, another's 'credit', are especially damning.
Yet if such sharp speech is a crime against community, the corporation
retains the right to reciprocal sharpness. Chastisement, the repeated ad-
monition to reform, will produce either renewed Christian fellowship
or dismissal (cf. pp. 33–4).

One distinction between this commonplace sense of fraternal correction and the version in Pepys texts, however, needs to be insisted
upon. Parish guild regulations are unremittingly conventional in their
imagination of virtuous behaviour and of properly fraternal religious
usage. All are clerically cooperative, not antagonistic. But these organisations are, at least liminally, in a position to bring lay-inspired standards of behaviour to bear upon clerical appointees. St Peter's guild
explicitly acknowledges the possibility of choosing the wrong chantry
priest. The statutes specify what behaviours will require repeated correction and the possible termination of the priest's services.[67] But this
apparent limitation to a single guild and to a single area of clerical
critique may be only artificial. Many guilds, more engaged in regulat-
ing the wardens' behaviour (since it involved responsibility for the corporate assets), may have thought that such control went without saying;
the chantry priest was a corporation employee, and thus a contributor
to the fraternity's good or bad fame, to be treated like any other member. In contrast, a parish priest, responsible for sermons and confession,
would have been appointed by the bishop and beyond the fraternity's
control.

Although parish guilds are diverse, most of the surviving record reports on neighbourhood guilds, the membership limited to a community centred in the local church. Parish guilds were open to all of
'good fame', regardless of gender, and apparently had a large component

of women members. These persons are apt, in the broad sense, to be 'middle class', if perhaps at its lower end. The benefits of burial and requiem masses extended to all members would have been unattractive to reasonably prosperous merchants; they could draw on arrangements established by their wealthy trade guilds or establish elaborate, and often expensive, trusts in their wills for these purposes. Yet at the other end of this urban continuum of wealth and power, the required dues, usually about 2*s* a year paid as 'quarterage' (but with an admission fee, often larger), plus additional funerary alms, would have excluded some range of actual proletarians, manual workers. On this basis, one might wish to associate Pepys with a parish chapel frequented by a different clientele than one imagines using Auchinleck: pious literates with serious devotional interests, actively committed to imposing high standards of devotion and conduct on their community (cf. Barron 1985, 30; Hanawalt 1984, 24–5; Hanawalt–McRee 166–9).

VI

As a final exhibit of early London devotional writing, I turn to 'The Recluse', the Pepys copy of *Ancrene Riwle*. Like many early London texts I have mentioned, the very transmission of the *Riwle* testifies to non-local antecedents, and interest in a thirteenth-century Western English text. Like many earlier examples, this manuscript version of *The Riwle* has been revised for an audience differing from that of the original. But while most earlier *Riwle* MSS imagine an audience of regular clergy, the Pepys revisions, intrusive to a degree unparalleled elsewhere, have been designed to accommodate the text to its manuscript context, both in form and theme, and to facilitate its lay usage.

The overall effect could well be compared with Anglo-Norman adaptation of monastic texts for lay aristocratic audiences. The *Riwle* was originally composed as a conduct-guide for women in a quasi-regular status that depended on their special devotions. Just as monastic instructional literature, delineating the communal incarnations of basic Christian behaviours, appealed outside the cloister, this text has become, in Pepys 2498, a devotional text for lay people. However, given the texts accompanying it in Pepys 2498, this is a different adaptation, intended for insertion into the same devout urban parochial contexts outlined in my discussion of *The Mirror*, one of the reviser's major inspirations.

Consonant with Pepys 2498's other appropriated aristocratic texts, 'The Recluse' is frequently presented as if a prose biblical translation with commentary. The Pepys scribe adjusts the original *Riwle* to bring the *mise-en-page* into accord with that of other manuscript contents, the prose Apocalypse and Psalter. The *Riwle* appears divided into paragraphs and given a form typical of translated biblical texts, with an ornamented Latin lemma at the head of each unit. Such a *mise-en-page* only becomes possible through substantial changes in the structure of the original, changes which accommodate it to the form of a text plus commentary. Colledge describes very well these local revisions:

> The reviser has taken the first Scriptural or patristic citation in each paragraph of the original, and has placed it first (very often supplying the Latin original or an English translation, if either has been omitted) and has then given a shortened version of the paragraph. Usually he omits whole sentences or clauses (3).

Moreover, biblical translation with commentary has been inscribed into the Pepys text, in one of the frequent interpolations that characterise this version. The reviser who creates 'The Recluse' suppresses the anchoritic specifics of Part 8 and in their stead (177/30–182/29) inserts a substantial chunk of the prose Apocalypse with its commentary.

Limiting his additions to the text of and commentary on Apoc. 21:9–22:9, the description of the New Jerusalem,[68] the reviser enhances the somewhat anticlimactic 'outer rule' ending of the original; he replaces that material with a hortatory vision of the New Jerusalem, the promise of salvation and eternal bliss. This vision is an urban and corporate one that reshapes the celestial imagery of the original *Riwle* with its emphasis on an isolated woman's direct personal love of Christ. Other interpolations in 'The Recluse' support this new emphasis. On the one hand, the reviser insistently relies upon the analytical vocabulary of the Middle English Apocalypse, e.g. repeated references to false Christians, those outside God's law, as *loseniours* (e.g., 28/21–29/15, 40/14–25, 49/32–50/10, 73/1–4, 84/17–85/26). And he tendentiously and repeatedly foregrounds in interpolations themes associated with lay instruction that he has imported from the *Mirror*. Through these, the originally anchoritic text has been transformed into a work of general lay piety. The reviser assumes that his audience includes 'vche man of þe commune poeple', and that his audience does not, as the original 'ancren' did, have continual access to the text (apparently its members are to hear it read aloud, 149/23–6).

The most striking features of 'The Recluse', the tone of which I believe Colledge misinterprets,[69] all stem from its rewriting of inclaustration into a purely metaphorical concept. In a very long interpolation at the opening (4/19–5/12), the reviser argues that the world brings only wickedness and sin. Hence, the act described in the original as inclaustration here refers simply to the individual's custody of the senses, to not allowing worldly corruption to intrude into the self. While self-custody and self-discipline form a central metaphorical extension of inclaustration in *Ancrene Riwle*, in the revision, this becomes a generalised responsibility for every mature Christian who hopes for salvation. In a particularly explicit passage, the reviser comments:

> Now vnderstondeþ þat a mannes body is cleped in holy wrytt sumtyme an hous, and sumtyme a citee, and sumtyme Goddes temple and holy chirche. þan riȝth as ȝee see þat an ancre is bischett in an hous and may nouȝth out, riȝth so is vche mannes soule bischett in his body as an ancre. And þerfore vche man, lered and lewed, ȝif he wil queme God and be his deciple, helde hym in his hous, schete his dores and his wyndowes fast, þat ben his fyue wyttes, þat he take no likyng to synne ne to werldelich þynges. And þan he is an ancre. (44/2–10)[70]

Self-custody is no longer a specialised programme for a solitary but, as in the *Mirror*, part of a virtuous act of apostolic imitation. Further, the reviser gives this passage additional force by insisting that the source text, even where retained, can never be read literally. References to the anchorite throughout the text should be taken with this metaphorical transposition in mind: 'Vnderstonde þat wel, vche man, whan ich speke of onelich men oiþer of ancres, takeþ it on non oþer maner þan I speke it here' (43/29–31).[71]

It hardly needs to be pointed out that 'The Recluse', because of the continuous collision of received literal and asserted figurative readings, often approaches incoherence. Because simple signification is called upon to do so much varied work here, the text persistently falls apart. The passage I have cited above actually involves further (and more potentially vertiginous) metaphorical possibilities. As the reviser (accurately) indicates the meanings of Scripture, the possible readings and implications of his account proliferate. While the central sense remains surely the last mentioned, the body as God's temple and image of the apostolic/apocalyptic church (cf. 1 Cor. 3:16–17, a central metaphor in Grosseteste's handbook *Templum Dei*, once part of the Psalter manuscript Additional 17376), other projected *significaciones*, reminiscent of Thedmar's reliance on the 'body of the City' metaphor, cannot be expunged from the text. Associating body and city might ceaselessly remind a reader of Pepys's emphatic conclusion, the priestless and templeless *civitas* of the Apocalypse, the actualisation of the amicable City in which the readers currently work, disport themselves, and pray. Alternatively, associating body and house, while it recalls the 'ancre', equally might evoke civic domesticity – the home as site both of parental, as well as potentially fraternal, correction.

In 'The Recluse', the reviser accommodates the central view that avoiding sin altogether is the most important human act through a second revision. This nearly obliterates from the text the literal inclaustrated life. He assimilates the word 'ordre', which the original author uses to define anchoritic vows, to a more routine sense of Latin 'ordo': it here most normally refers to priesthood. If avoiding sin is the highest goal, then the most selfless and laudable human behaviour fulfils a basic clerical function, to teach and bring others out of sin. Here the reviser builds upon a passage from the original *Riwle* (4/10–18, cf. *English Text Nero* 4/14–28 and *Ancrene* 3a/10–25); his interpolation on 'ordre', with many other additions, renders instruction, a behaviour forbidden to the anchoresses addressed in his source, a central topic in 'The Recluse'. (See further 56/33–57/2, 101/26–31.)

Insofar as this educational effort is associated with clerics, the reviser insists on the necessity of providing an example for parishioners. This feat the cleric accomplishes first by a blameless life of good deeds (cf. 60/34–61/19, 66/21–67/4). But in the view of the Pepys reviser, the disparity between clerical and lay responsibilities is minimal. Both groups strive for the single reward of salvation:

Als gret myster haþ o man come to blisse as anoþer. Whi, ne haþ
nouȝth a lewed man als gret myster come to God as a clerk? Als grett,
ȝif he looke to hym, for als dere bouȝth God on as anoþer. (43/31–4)

Although educating one's neighbours and drawing them from sin form
a 'clerical' function, for the reviser this function is not necessarily one
reserved for persons literally in a clerical status. His emphasis upon
deeds implies that priests can fail at their proper labour; in contrast, laymen, who lack the nominal sign of 'ordre', the sacrament of ordination,
can nonetheless perform as successful Christian actors (cf. 5/4–12). In
pursuing this argument, the reviser follows *The Mirror* and reinterprets
a statement he receives from the original *Riwle*, that it is improper and
dangerous to vow what one cannot achieve (3/18–22, cf. *Nero* 3/5–19, *Ancrene* 2a/20–2b/6). Clerics promise a special performance similar to that
of anchoresses – the reviser follows the *Riwle* in calling this 'heiȝe lyf';
as a result, clerical failures and lapses are especially disastrous because
they reveal the presumption of the vows that preceded them.

Anti-clericism in the text is constantly governed, as Colledge fails to
see, by this premise of non-performance:

> þan [the virtuous layman] is an ancre, and wel better quemeþ God þan
> hij þat byschetten hem and taken hem to heiȝe lyf and ben werldelich,
> þat is setten her hertes vpon werldelich þinges. For hij quemen litel
> God oiþer nouȝth. (44/10–14; see further 28/21–31, 51/17–22, 70/22–34,
> 71/18–73/9)

Even more stridently, the reviser argues, in the spirit of the Apocalypse
and *Mirror*, that good Christians resemble true apostolic priests and
require nothing like an 'ordre'. In describing the highest degree of life,
he associates it with any Christian who risks him- or herself by engaging
in educational pursuits:

> þise ben þe good men þat speken fast of her Lorde and many scornes
> and many schames han þerfore, and þat is al þair gladnesse. And
> þerfore hij nyllen nouȝth leten it for non harme þat man may don
> hem, þeiȝ hij deden hem to þe deþ þerfore.

And he continues this counsel of perfection in a gesture that obliterates
any distinction of cleric and lay as pedagogues:

þis staire is þe hei3est staire of alle þe oþer, and þis a man may haue
þat liueþ in þe werlde and trauaileþ for his mete, as Poule and Petere
duden, 3if hij willeþ. For hij nere in non oþer religioun bot lyuede
among þe commune pople and wrou3tten for her mete and 3eden
aboute and tau3tten þe commune pople. (153/13–22)[72]

Thus, the virtuous lay person may prove more adequate than a priest.
Because attempting less in making no special vows, this person is more
likely to achieve a virtuous life without endangering his soul than is a
priest (cf. 89/23–90/3 and the examples twice repeated, at 60/34–61/9,
71/18–72/4). For the Pepys reviser, like the author of *The Mirror*, a lay
person cannot perform as a priest sacramentally, but can give a neighbour
similar spiritual comfort. Such respect for the potentially salvific activity
of common Christians informs the entire text.

In the discussion of Pride in the *Riwle*'s part 4, 'The Recluse' reviser inserts a long overt digression ('Now go we a3ein to oure matier',
he says at its end, 91/9–10), identifying the outstanding perpetrators
of the species-sin of presumption as 'þise clerkes . . . þat seien þat no
man schulde preche of God bot 3if he were ordred' (89/24–5). In the
Pepys *Riwle*, virtue, not ordination or education, makes one an appropriate teacher/preacher. Of course, as the Apocalypse and *Mirror*
illustrate, virtue is as available to a lewd person as it is to a cleric, a
claim strikingly enunciated in a citation from *Confessions* 8.8: 'Austin
seiþ þat we clerkes lerne for to go to þe pyne of helle, and lewed
folk lerne to go to þe ioye of heuene' (90/2–3). The reviser here paraphrases the text Langland cites in Latin at 10.461, to describe 'Plow-
men . . . and oþere lewed iuttes | [Who] percen wiþ a Paternoster þe
palys of heuene'. And this writer appears to know it in the same form
of inexact citation as Langland does, since Augustine says only that the
learned 'wallow in flesh and blood'. (See further pp. 289–91.) Accompanying this emphasis on probity is a detraction of specifically clerical
learning:

And summe wil saie where lerd he of diuinite? Hou bicomeþ hym
forto speken of God? Herto liþ gode answere. Where lerned Peter and
Poule diuinite? Ierome and Ambrose and Gregori, of whom lerned
þise men? Wheþer comen hij to her wytt þorou3 þe holy gost, oiþer
þorou3 stody of gret clergie? I saie þat hij hadden it of God, and

207

nouȝth þorouȝ her stody ne þorouȝ her lernynge, and ich vnderstonde þat þise were good men, for by hem is holy chirche yreuled now. (90/10–17)

If all men may be saved, then all can perceive the salvific spirit. And, just as in the reference to discipleship in the passage identifying man's body with an anchorhold (p. 204), all good Christians implicitly answer an apostolic model of inspiration.

This interest in presenting responsible religious potential in lay persons has rhetorical corollaries throughout the text. The Pepys reviser provides numerous generalising interpolations. He intensifies the tendency of the *Riwle* to exemplify its argument by adapting popularising sermon methods; the text includes numerous new *figuræ* and several added full exempla (see 52/8–15, 15–19; 53/10–11, 14–5, for the first; and 103/19–36, 112/26–31 for the second). Through such additions, the reviser expands the original author's reliance upon worldly situations to provide models for Christian action. The labouring life in the world gives a training useful for the perception and performance of the highest Christian truths (cf. 56/20–7, 85/5–17, 86/8–27, 150/16–27). These materials drawn from daily life – how one would go about hiring a servant (87/4–15), for example – are linked with the reviser's high evaluation of practical knowledge. 'The Recluse' contains lengthy additions extolling wisdom and prudence; further, it argues that the Christian will gain that knowledge requisite for salvation through exactly the same procedures by which he or she acquires worldly information (see 50/32–51/29, 113/1–13). The reviser offers an alternative to that clericism responsible for the original *Riwle*; viable spiritual forms of knowing and living in the world exist apart from the clerical educational system.

The reviser who creates 'The Recluse' considers the lay status of his audience as basic and confers on that status the highest value. In his acute consciousness of worldliness, the contamination brought by sin, he adopts an ostensibly pragmatic point of view: a low-risk lay effort at salvation may appear preferable to the specialised appeal of orders, whether those of secular or regular clergy.

The reviser expresses two constraints on lay adequacy as instructors, however. In the first place, lay persons are held to the same standards of performance as priests. I have already cited (p. 187) a passage from the *Riwle* pointing towards the absolute requirement to share one's spiritual gifts with fellow Christians, whether or not one is ordained. This note is struck elsewhere in the text (e.g. 136/23–137/8), and includes the same strictures as are apparent in the *Mirror*. A good person is not simply obliged to teach, but, if he or she refuses to chastise a neighbour's sin, will merit the same condemnation. Secondly, lay persons can overstep, although not quite in the same way as a priest might. Lay theologising may represent the same prideful assumption of learning for self-aggrandisement attacked in the Apocalypse (e.g. 4/32–5/12, 27/26–28/17). Such prideful efforts at showing oneself popeholy merit severe condemnation. However, the general tenor of the Pepys *Riwle* implies that clerical failure remains a more likely prospect than out-of-place lay theologising.

The Pepys reviser thus sees the power to teach as dependent on personal probity: the Holy Spirit confers both virtue and the power to communicate it (although the reviser once expresses hesitation over whether women should preach, 28/18–20). However, even discredited, malfeasant clerics still retain a religious function. *Ancrene Riwle* remains, after all, at bottom a penitential tract, and the reviser firmly believes in the necessity of sacramental penance as a function of due obedience to God's law. Moreover, the confession required can be made to a priest, even if he is not a follower of God's law; just as the Spirit animates instruction by the laity, it equally animates the sacrament, irrespective of the person administering (the orthodox view also held by *The Mirror* but vehemently attacked in developed Lollard writings).

Moreover, in Pepys the ideal of the lay instructor is thoroughly imbricated in the apostolic models evoked in Matt. 10:8, as inflected by the mid-century discourse of labour David Aers has so powerfully associated (1988, 20–72) with *Piers Plowman*. On the one hand, the reviser early on defines 'ordre' as extending beyond priesthood to include the community of all the working faithful:

For seint Austyn seiþ a gaderyng of wicked folk, þat he clepeþ þe werlde þat God biddeþ vs forsake, ac nouȝth þe goodes of þe werlde. For none ne may wel lyuen and seruen God bot ȝif hij han her sustenaunce, and better is to ernen it þan to bidden it. (4/21–5)

Or again, '[God] wott best þat vche man auȝtt to trauaile for her sustenaunce and nouȝth bidde it' (72/29–31). To labour for one's necessities,
and thus not require added recompense for any spiritual avocation, is to
follow God's law and demonstrate one's sanctity. The only exception the
Pepys reviser immediately allows is an itinerant preacher, not necessarily
ordained.[73] But this exception must follow from both the injunctions
of the gospel and of canon law; such a person will be without benefice
and thus deserving of support from those he serves. Yet even about this
exception the reviser admits doubts: 'Neren nouȝth Peter and Poule
[both of whom, he says, worked] prestes? ȝis, forsoþe, als gode, I trowe,
as any were siþen. þan miȝth anoþer preest wirche' (72/34–6).

The reviser goes beyond this conventional view and enunciates opinions I have earlier argued inhere in aristocratic attitudes towards monastic labour. At this point his work might be most clearly distinguished
from views about clerical support enunciated in the *Mirror* (see p. 191).
Among other interests the Pepys reviser shares with *Piers Plowman*, as
well as with other early London texts, is an interest in 'huyre', recompense for one's labour. He worries a great deal over pay for clerical labour;
in the oldest vernacular discussion Anne Hudson and I can recall (*Piers*
15.546–67 comes next chronologically), he offers an explanation – to
say the least, idiosyncratic and counter-historical – of the Donation of
Constantine (68/32–69/27).

The pope was endowed, he claims, under an interlocked pair of conditions. First, his clergy had to abandon any tincture of worldliness, by
which he understands marriage (and the familial responsibilities that underlie labour); and they had, in return for endowment, to give themselves
totally to study and especially to teaching. Lay people, who are responsive to God's law (since for them, toil and sexuality are licit), can thus
be perceived as Christians superior to many priests, worldly, avaricious
and most especially concubinous – all which may explain why the *Riwle*,
with its emphases on chaste devotions, might have seemed to the reviser
a vehicle appropriate to his ideas.

Given the possibility that clerical pretension may not match the claims
of clerical life, the reviser argues that the most substantial form clerical good works can take is participation in a worldly labour. Ideally,
the cleric should become a working man like his parishioners. 'The
Recluse' adds to the *Riwle* extensive arguments against non-labouring

clerical possession: the reviser repeatedly alleges gospel precedent for the injunction that a cleric 'earn his living' by self-supporting labour (cf. the extensive discussion at 68–73). This suspicion of indolence does not simply pertain to clerics but to almsgiving as well. In the passage I've been citing, all, including perhaps priests, are held to work, 'bot ʒif he ne myʒth erne it for sekenesse oiþer for elde oiþer croked' (cf. Scase 1989, 63–4). And the reviser does worry this question in the spirit of the Piers–Hunger conversation of *Piers Plowman* 6, although to different ends. He ends up sounding a good deal more like Hunger than Piers, for example, 'And ʒutt it were for hem bettere þat hij erned [their sustenance] þan þat hij badden it ʒif hij miʒth, þeiʒ he were a preest'. Similarly, a later discussion of good works allows the *Riwle* reviser an opportunity to outline the Works of Mercy (146/3–147/8). But this turns into the caveat that one should be scrupulous not to give 'any [that] is þe crasker for wel fare for to done synne'. In this case, one sees the obverse of not helping a sinful neighbour out of sin; aiding the indolent actively supports sin and thus constitutes doing evil oneself.

The injunction reflects adherence to the fundamental rule, God's law. If spiritual counsel – unreimbursed instructional involvement with one's culpable fellow-Christian – provides the most basic rule of life, with this goes a notion of good stewardship. Mirroring the requirement that one share one's spiritual gifts is a second, not to spend one's gifts in an evil cause. If others resist one's best effort at spiritual counsel, they finally must be shunned. Not doing so in fact makes one a bad steward, outside God's law, and endangers one's own salvation (cf. 2/16–29). Abetting sin undermines the true Christian's probity, as well as communal integrity:

> He nys nouʒth þi neiʒbur þat lyueþ in yuel lyf, ne þou ne schalt hym
> nouʒth loue bot for to helpe hym out of synne, ʒif þou may. And ʒif
> þou ne may, kepe þe out of his compaignye and ne helpe hym noþing
> to bodilich sustenaunce wharþorouʒ þat þou be susteyner of synne.
> (66/36–67/4)

Similar views also typify London guild regulations. In addition to their interest in pious correction, these stipulate charitable relief of indigent fellows as a guild responsibility. But such almsgiving always carries with it the proviso that true indigence reflects natural (or providential) disaster, age (some guilds supported their superannuated chantry priests), or injury.[74] In keeping with the conduct-centred emphases of the statutes on 'good fame', mere improvidence, the failure to perform astutely, does not confer the right to tap community resources:

> ȝif any man be of good stat and vse hym to lye longe in bedde and atte risyng of his bed ne wil nat worche to wynne his sustenaunce and kepe his hous, and go to þe tauerne, to þe wyn, to þe ale, to wrastelynge, to schetynge, and in this manere falleþ pouere and lest his catel in his defaute for socour and trust for to be holpe of þe fraternite, þat man schal neuere haue good no help . . . (Barron–Wright 123)[75]

In this set of rules, not only will the indolent be excluded from charity, but from the fraternity and lose the right to share in its death benefits (and thus to join its apocalyptic heavenly community).

Grafting these particularly strong lay claims onto an accepted masterpiece of English spirituality firmly places this audience within the mainstream of devotional culture. The author of 'The Recluse' is particularly clever in showing in that new audience a potential and inherent dignity. In the context of my speculations above about the origins of Pepys texts, 'The Recluse' testifies to the active desire of a middle-class London parochial audience for a statement that would verify that audience's conception of itself as composed of responsible religious agents. In this manuscript created for metropolitan use – perhaps in a chapel – the provision of a text originally intended for an inclaustrated community gives to this new audience a canon of English works which can challenge those available to both Franco-Latinate regular clergy and French-reading aristocrats. Such longstanding early London views would be especially influential in the future, not only upon William Langland, but later practitioners of Lollardy.

NOTES

1. The Auchinleck MS here lacks a leaf, but was surely similar, since the lines accurately reproduce the French. In line 17, I correct MS myke, following AN mult.
2. See Görlach 7, 134, 221 n. 6, and 263 n. 13; he cites Legge's discussion of Anglo-Norman parallels (1963, 195–6). In the texts I discuss, these materials appear, respectively, at 'Banna sanctorum' (IMEV 2304), edn 1, 1–3; Manning 41–56, *Cursor* 1–130; Pepys 45a, 45b–46a, *Middle English Mirror* 3/1–21, 7/4–9; *Speculum Vitæ* 35–56; Clanvowe 485–501, edn 69–70, and Hunt 2, 346–7/226–60.

3. The Matthew verse appears in an attack on 'falsæ prophetæ', a context I will shortly show as profoundly generative of London religious ideas.

4. For this term – Leontes's 'suspected', cf. the *Mirror* 3/14–15 (see *Piers Plowman* 20.33), 87/32–3, and a further use in sermon 37 (AN 135ra).

5. With this unduly revealing evocation of romance joy, cf. Manning's location of these despised narratives 'Yn gamys and festys and at þe ale' (47), and cf. Langland's Sloth, 5.394–6, 402–8, or his poetic figure Wille at C 5.93–101.

6. Cf. also Manning's provocative term 'troteuale' (48) or *Cursor's* 'truandis' (253), the first 'vain talk or chatter, gab'; the latter a metaphoric extension of the root sense '(false) beggar' to identify that counterfeit talk associable with sloth (the term recurs in the *Mirror*, see p. 179). Among the provocative extensions in *Piers Plowman*, cf., besides the obvious (and deliberatedly shocking) inversions at 13.172 ('a dido . . . a disours tale') and 18.143 ('a tale of waltrot'), the lunatic lollers of C 9, beggars of no certain status but with unique prophetic (poetic?) powers.

7. For evidence of a French source, see *Pepysian* xv–xviii. Evidence for Bonaventuran indebtedness comes from the concluding rubric, which apparently considers the passion narrative (chs. 95–101) separate from the remaining 106 chapters, and from the form of two chapter headings (75, 87), which reflect the *Meditationes'* provision of a weekly cycle for contemplation.

8. On this pair of texts, which appear together in all three of their manuscripts, see *Comp* and Drennan's two earlier studies. For their Anglo-Norman source, see p. 124.

9. Påhlsson already noted these variations in finishing; see *Recluse* vii–viii. One further change, probably of minor importance for the production, occurs in Booklet III, where, after about five pages of *Ancrene Riwle* (in the second column of p. 376), the scribe shifts decorative schemes to highlight the initia more than was originally planned. This new scheme supports the view I argue at p. 203, that the *Riwle* has been accommodated to its manuscript context, that of glossed biblical texts.

10. At least one reason for insisting on the discontinuity of copying in Pepys is that text order in the manuscript as received does not necessarily correspond either to order of copying or to disparate source of materials. Although 'Good Techinges' is separated from *Ancrene Riwle* in this codex (in contrast to the presentation in the Vernon MS), it need not have come to the scribe separately.

11. See Turville-Petre's ideological reading (1988, 20–2) of the Luttrell Psalter; and at far greater length, and with attention to professionalised medievalism, Camille 1998.

12. On monastic reading as labour, see Leclercq, esp. 22–6. A mid-fifteenth-century Northampton secular scribe still writes a colophon of complaint with venerable monastic antecedents: 'Three fingers write, and the other limbs labour. | The person who doesn't know how to write thinks this no labour, | but while the fingers write, the other limbs are scarcely at peace' ('Tres digiti scribunt et cetera membra laborant. | Scribere qui nescit, nullum putat esse laborem. | Dum digiti scribunt, vix cetera membra quiescunt', Dublin, Trinity College, MS 432, fol. 155[v]).

13. I cite Legge 1950, 48. Knowles makes similar comments, although mainly about monastic culture of the early twelfth century (495, 501). English monastic (as well as later collegiate) usage allowed conversation in either Latin or French; in statutes of 1325 and 1334, the province of English Augustinian canons, often perceived as ill-disciplined, explicitly forbade English conversations in their houses (*Chapters* 14, 17).

14. For the Psalter, see Legge 1963, 176; the exact French source of the Pepys text survives in only a single fifteenth-century copy, Bibliothèque nationale, MS fr. 6260. For the source

of the commentary accompanying the Norman Apocalypse and transmitted in English in Pepys 2498, see *Lambeth* 25; Freyhan 223; Lewis 1995, 203 (on connections with *Bible moralisé* MSS produced at St Victor, Paris); cf. Breder. The prologue – it replaces Apoc. 1:1–8 – is a fine example of Minnis's 'academic prologue Type C' (19–27, with a bit quoted at 27) and appears in *Glossa* 4 (see 'Die mittelenglische' lxii–iii). See Berger 88; Deanesly 1920, 142–3; and, on similar Latin texts, *Apoc* xxxii. For Robert's reliance on Gregory's selective *XL Homeliæ in Evangelia*, see Aitken 39–46 and Panunzio, in his Gretham edn 58–80.

15. Lay readership is inscribed in both the *Mirror* and the *Manuel*; cf. Robert 83–6: 'E si est ço mult grant folie | A lai parler latinerie; | Cil s'entremet de fol mester | Ki vers lai volt latin parler' (the Middle English cited p. 182); and William 113: 'Pur la laye gent iert fet'. Legge cites (1950, 115–16) nine monastic copies of Rich's *Mirour de seinte eglyse*, six now lost; and eight or nine monastic copies of the *Manuel*, five now lost, lists capable of considerable extension. Gretham manuscripts are virtually devoid of information concerning provenance (in a great many copies, excision of initial folia suggests depredation for opulently decorated pages, perhaps including owner portraits or arms). The only monastic copy (also including a *Manuel*) is Huntington Library, MS HM 903, from St Mary's, York, in the light of my arguments at pp. 126–7 a provocative provenance, particularly since this is the only known copy with the additional sermons included in the English version.

16. Doyle 1953, 1, 120n. provides a neat example: a French Apocalypse manuscript, British Library, MS Additional 42555, was lent by Abingdon (OSB) to Queen Joan of Scotland in 1362 (cf. Lewis 1986). Such social solidarity also appears in the elaborate heraldric decoration of Madrid, Biblioteca nacional, MS 6422, a Psalter produced for the Benedictine nuns of Carrow priory, Norwich, *c.* 1250–60; the arms probably depict a perhaps unseemly family pride, representations of those genealogies from which the house drew its sisters. See Morgan 2, 90–1 (no. 120), and compare the slightly older Psalter, Stockholm, National Museum, MS B.2010 (1, 113–14, no. 68), perhaps originally monastic but in secular hands for about a century before ownership by the Cistercian nuns of Tarrant Keynston (Dorset).

17. Bezzola (esp. 1, 238–9; 2, i, 391–461; 3, i extensively) collects expansive materials for such a view. Auerbach (203, 269, 289–93) makes the point quite explicit, and Parkes develops (1973, 556–7) Auerbach's views. Legge 1965 emphasises the early contributions of Anglo-Norman literature.

18. Salter's interrupted final book, 'An Obsession with the Continent' (1988, 1–100), argues, I think inaccurately, that the Anglo-Norman coterie audience eventually became reduced to rural magnates (esp. 29, 76–7, 95) and that central court production, her major interest, had always been more cosmopolitan and looked to continental French and to Latin for its literary materials.

19. 'Romance' has persistently been associated with the illustrative cycles, following Freyhan 225 and Henderson 116; see *Lambeth* 12–13, Wright (esp. 260 for parallels with Alexander romances); Lewis 1995, 50–5; most extensively yet abstractly Klein 171–84.

20. Both errors are confuted by the repeated 'ego sum alpha et omega, principium et finis' of his vision (1:8, cf. 21:6 and 22:13). Neither error corresponds to the apparent identification of specific heretical practice in the text; cf. the glossa's explanation of 2:6 'Facta Nicholaitarum', 'communem vsum mulierum et commestionem idolothicorum', gleaned from the 'edere et fornicari' associated with the other reference to this sect as modern Balaams at 2:16–17.

21. 'ut de patientia eundo ad contemplationem celestis glorie peruenire possimus ad vtilitatem, ad remuneracionem, scilicet patientie nostre'. Gregory the Great had established the importance and resonances of the verse from Luke in his great *Homelia in Evangelia* 2.35, *Patrologia Latina* 76, 1259–65, in the Middle Ages the single most widely cited discussion of patience.

22. Henderson first asserted (116) the connections between *La Estoire de Seint Aedward* and three or four Apocalypses, as well as with the romance-inflected biblicism of the Painted Chamber wallpaintings. Morgan identifies (2, 103) London as the centre of Apocalypse production before 1270; he comments at 2, 12 and 18 on the four copies associated with the royal family (nos. 124, 125, 153, and 154 in his catalogue). Books with similar styles and provenances include his nos. 122 and 123 (Ee.iii.59); see 2, 92–101, 141–7.

23.

> Or vus pri, gentilz rois Aedward,
> K'a moi pecchur eiez regard
> Ki ai translaté du Latin
> Selum mun sen e mun engin
> En Franceis la vostre estoire,
> Ke se espande ta memoire,
> E pur lais ki de lettrure
> Ne sevent, en purtraiture
> Figuree apertement
> L'ai en cest livret present,
> Pur ço ke desir e voil
> Ke oraille ot, voient li oil.
> (3955–66)

24. 'non enim figuras tantum vidit [Iohannes] spiritu, sed earum significata mente intellexerit' (cf. *Apoc* 3–4/39–41). The Anglo-Norman (and consequently, Middle English) significantly lack any equivalent for 'spiritu' and 'mente'.

25. For the poems, see Robbins 93–9 and 259–60. For this translation of the Anglo-Norman, independent of the London text I will discuss at length, see 'Mittelenglische'. The verses are unique to 'Croyland' (of the three manuscripts total).

26. For Eleanor of Provence as patron, see Gee 148–9 and the index entry 212; for Eleanor of Castile, considerably more intellectually engaged than her warrior-Alexander husband, Gee 145–6 and 212, and esp. Parsons.

27. For discussion of aristocratic 'picture books', see esp. Kauffmann 17; Morgan 1, 15–16; 2, 18–19; and Sandler 1986, 2, 37–8. For examples of Anglo-Norman captions, see Kauffmann, plates 221–2 (in a volume produced for a bishop of Winchester and thus within a Latinate tradition); and Morgan 1, plates 109, 232–3. The earliest version of the Apocalypse cycle is usually thought to have been a picture book without full text; see the surviving representatives of this archetype, Morgan, nos. 97 and 137 (2, 52–3, 119–22). Edward I's queen, Eleanor of Castile, often is taken to be the patron of one of the most picture-booky of all copies, Cambridge, Trinity College, MS R.16.2 (Morgan 2, 73–6, no. 110). This book still has the marginal instructions for the painter, all printed James 1900–4, 1, 297–300. The book has frequently appeared in facsimile, e.g. *Trinity*. Rosemary Wright reproduces thirteen illustrations with Anglo-Norman inscriptions, and further colour examples appear in Klein.

28. On this issue, see Henderson 116–17, Freyhan 223–5, *Lambeth* 30, 94–6; Rosemary Wright 239, 247 (the potential disparity of image and significance). Cf. the Parisian evidence cited by the Rouses, 2000, 1, 254–8, a reference I owe to Anne Hudson.

29. Contrast the usual discussions of Latin and Anglo-Norman Apocalypses, which rely on models of particularised social insertions, e.g. Rosemary Wright (and implicitly Klein) on regal power, Lewis on bishops, 1986 and 1995, 33–5, 221–4.

30. On historically specifying impulses inherent in the development of the extra-illustrated presentation, see Freyhan 213–21, *Lambeth* 31–5.

31. Cf. Margery Kempe's vision, 206/27–207/14, simultaneously a depiction of the miracle of uninstructed reading ability and of salvation itself.

32. 'Et accepi librum de manu angeli, et devoravi illum; et erat in ore meo tamquam mel dulce, et cum devorassem eum, amaricatus est venter meus. Et dixit mihi: Oportet te iterum prophetare gentibus, et populis, et linguis, et regibus multis' (10:10–11).

33. In the commentary, Apoc. 19:15 is glossed 'hij þat ne receyuen nouȝth þe prechyng of þe riȝth bileue shullen ben dampned in body and in soule' (*Apoc* 165/13–6); cf. the gloss at 1:16, indicating the sword-like tongue as one promising double punishment, two deaths (17–18/11–17); or 11:5 'ignis' glossed 'þe gostlich swerd þat is goddes word þat is fyre' (83/13).

34. Cf. such glosses as 11:8 'civitatis magnæ . . . Sodoma', 'þe werlde þat is cleped Sodome, þat is anoye for to heriȝen god' (*Apoc* 85/5–6); 14:8 'Babylon', 'þe werlde' (114/3; similarly 17:18, 146/50–2), but at 21:2 'magnam civitatem', of course holy church (179/5). Similarly, the great whore's antithesis, the woman who withdraws into the desert, is the Church, cf. 12:6 glossed 'þat þe womman fel into desert bitoknеþ þat holy chirche departeþ hir fro þe delices of þis worlde and þe noise into lijf of penaunce, and þere fede God hir wiþ gostlich bred' (93/13–15).

35. I have taken some liberties with Fridner's textual presentation. I adjust capitalisation and punctuation silently, and I have generally ignored the repetitive sentence openings 'Here is/are betokened', 'This/They betoken/eþ'. I have throughout read the text in conjunction with its Anglo-Norman source, and I use the latter to emend obvious English scribalisms, here, for example, substituting 'feet', AN piez, for the senseless 'face' of the English.

36. For the third charge, cf. 18:11 (*Apoc* 155/1–3), with an identification with 'gauelers' (AN symoniaus).

37. Cf. the attack on canonists in the gloss to Apoc. 22:18. This verse, a claim for the necessary completeness of the text inspired by Deut. 4:2, resonates with *Piers Plowman* 11.303–10a, with its detraction of skipped or interlineated charters as models for not heeding the sanctity of the liturgy.

38. Cf. 'þe maistres heretikes' (*Apoc* 19/1) and similarly 42/14, 46/1, 65/5–7, 68/2–4, 73/16–18, 131/3–4; for hypocrites, see 22/1–2, 48/1–2, 70/2–4; for both together, see 99/4–5, 173–4/7–9. For 'losengeours', see 115/10–12 (partly cited below) and 170/15–17, 182–3/41–7 (where 'heriȝers' presumably is scribal for either this word or 'liȝers', AN mençongers, Vulgate mendacibus).

39. Zacchæus, according to the glossa, represents 'Gentile believers who, through their preoccupation with worldly things have been cast down, and people little in the eyes of this world but sanctified by God' ('credentes ex gentibus qui per occupationem temporalium depressi erant, et minimi sed a domino sanctificati'). It comments further, 'the little person, by leaving worldly things behind and climbing the tree of the cross, rises above the obstructive mob of the vices' ('pusillus terrena relinquendo arborem crucis ascendendo turbam ostantem [sc. vitiorum] transcendit'). Having left

sin through confession, the prerequisite to the Eucharist, and identified oneself with the *bonus arbor* of anti-romance prologues, one may join the Christian community and partake of Him.

40. 'Beatus qui legit et audit verba prophetiæ hujus, et servat ea quæ in ea scripta sunt; tempus enim prope est. Johannes septem ecclesiis quæ sunt in Asia. Gratia vobis et pax ab eo qui est, et erat, et qui venturus est . . . et fecit nos regnum et sacerdotes Deo et Patri suo' (1:3–4, 6; echoed in 1:9).

41. Cf. further such readings as 3:7–8 'ostium apertum' explained as 'our Lorde openeþ heuene and holy wrytt to hem þat han litel cunnyng [AN petit science] and kepen his comaundement' (*Apoc* 24/2–4), and the gloss to 21:21 'plateas' (193–4/3–8, reproduced in the Pepys copy of *Ancrene Riwle, English Text . . . Magdalene* 180/23–7).

42. Cf. 'Pryde, wraþþe, and envie ben synnes of þe fend; coueitise and auarice ben synnes of þe world; glotonye, slouþe, and lecherie ben synnes of þe fleisch', the opening of a widely dispersed instructional tract (Jolliffe F.21, here from Huntington Library, MS HM 502, fol. 87). Similarly, at the point *Piers Plowman* most closely approaches catechetical instruction, only to expose its limitations (see Aers 1986), 'the sins of the fiend' appear at 5.609–17, followed by the appearance of 'the remedial virtues' (those given by the Spirit and banishing the seven sins) at 618–29.

In the Apocalypse, this identification begins, somewhat waverily, with the gloss on 2:17 'manna absconditum' as 'þre maner of synnes þat ben in many þat han receyued þe bileue and ne holden it nou3th. Vche [AN Les uns] fordooþ oþer þorou3 yuel conseil þat þai 3iuen [text adjusted to answer AN doner; les autres]; [þe] oþere, þorou3 ensaumple of leccherie; þe þrid, þorou3 ensaumple of glotonye' (16–17/1–6). Cf. another early example, the gloss to 6:8, citing covetousness, gluttony, and lechery (48–9/4–10), with the large number of parallels to the formulation I cite: 73/10–15, 131/3–4; 'her ydolatrie [þat is maumetrie, a ME gloss, not in AN] and couetise and leccherie' (137–8/2–4); 148/5–7; 170/15–17; 175–6/3–4 (lechery, the last term, a Middle English addition).

43. At least some of the passage's multiple *and*'s are probably scribal, the result of misdivision of the sentence; I retain them as potentially sensible, if oddly placed, efforts at rendering a 'both . . . and' construction.

44. Given the unpublished texts, I cite more extensively than elsewhere. The English, so far as possible, represents the text of my central manuscript exhibit, Pepys 2498, accompanied by identification of its page and column, with a few bracketed readings from 'Holk', Bodleian Library, MS Holkham misc. 40; those portions published in *Middle English Mirror* (from MS Hunter 250) are cited by page/line. I cite the Anglo-Norman preferably from the published selections of Aitken, Panunzio (although see Marshall–Rothwell's caveats), or the parallel version in *Mirror*; otherwise I cite, as 'AN' by folio and column, from Nottingham University Library, MS Mi(ddleton) LM 4, the copy taken by earlier scholars as a standard version. There is a brief description (as a 'deposit', the book does not appear in Ker, MMBL), with plate, at *Middle English Mirror* xxi–xxiii.

45. On the distinction, see Charland. Like the older 'Kentish sermons' (IPMEP 140), *The Mirror* analyses the gospel in a tripartite format, which moves from bare narrative to allegorisation and moral exhortation. On the form of Maurice of Sully's sermons, the source of the Kentish set, see Robson 31 and the texts he prints. Aitken discusses (24–6) Robert of Gretham's similar form.

46. See, for examples, the extensive definition of 'ravisher' and 'ravishing' in sermon 14 (Pepys 80^a), following Gretham's 'la rauine | D'auarice' (AN 85ra). The term 'rauysour'

itself is almost certainly inspired by 'lupus rapit' (John 10:12), as this is explained in the discussion of the good shepherd (sermon 22), Panunzio 209–31, lines 203–8, 233–4. Cf. sermon 8, where the sinful priest is 'a rauisschour and no keper' (Pepys 57ª, 95/28, not paralleled at Gretham 2944–50).

47. See 115/17–21, 117/23–31, following the glossa on Matt. 13:25 'homines', 'Who have been assigned to others, for their instruction and care, i.e. priests/bishops in the church' ('Qui aliis ad tutelam et custodiam deputati sunt, prelati in ecclesia').

48. In the citation, the unpointed 'and for to – can' reproduces Robert's lines 465–6:

> De la folie que ai parle
> E del bien que ai entrelasse,

i.e. '(from being encumbered) by the folly I have spoken and the good I have neglected'. Pepys appears to say, 'and in order to get for myself an ascent (i.e. to heaven) to where I have neither permission or power (i.e., of myself, but only through grace)'.

49. Although one might note Robert's reliance on romance address, e.g. *Mirror* 71/9 'Loke, lordinges...'; 77/17–18 'Kepe we, lordinges...', 133/2 'Forþi lordynges þat ben cristened...', all usually answering 'Seignur' in the original. Whatever the translator's claims for plain English, such often includes a heavy retention of French lexis and idiom.

50. As late as 1348 × 1370, the Yorkshire author of *Speculum Vitæ* was doing the expected, converting Lorens of Orleans's prose *Somme le roi* (the original text of St John's MS 256) into verse. In contrast, the earliest prose rendition of this text, indeed the next oldest Middle English prose translation after these London examples, is the Canterbury priest Don Michel's *Ayenbite of Inwit* (1340).

51. The Anglo-Norman for the last clause here reads:

> (Ke hom le ewangelie puisse entendre)
> E li nunlettrez bien aprendre,
> E chascun ki siet lettrure
> E de Franceis la parleure,
> Lire i poet pur sei amender
> E pur les autres endoctriner.
> (433–8)

Once again the translator omits that detail which indicates his source in Gretham's francophone world, to protect the fiction of his own direct access to the Latin. The discourse of 'opening' here presumably has influenced the more famous discussion of textual openness in chapter 15 of the 'General Prologue' to the Wycliffite Bible.

52. The Pepys *Riwle* also includes more elliptical instructions implying a need to reproduce its text, a form of chastisement more efficacious than prayer, at 184/10–23, a reference I owe to my graduate Marisa Libbon. Beyond these passages, cf. *Piers Plowman* 5.554–8, 7.53 (and cf. p. 278).

53. Cf. 3/24–9:

> He haþ ȝeuen vs bodi and lif, sen and heren [AN Veer, parler, implying 'and speken'?], wit and hereing and vnderstondinge in hert [AN menbres e curage], and al forto kepe þe fram harm. We ben al his spensers [AN despensers] to serue him of his ofices; ȝif we serue him wel, an hundredfold schal ben oure mede, and who þat doþ iuel be his wil, ful gret [AN dur] schal be þe veniaunce þat schal be taken of him. (Pepys 45ª);

or sermon 38 (for the 9th Sunday after Trinity, on the unjust steward, Luke 16:1–9):

> [God's] reue [AN prouost] oiþer his spenseer [AN despenser] is vche man þat
> is born in þis werlde [for the phrase, AN de muiller] . . . . þis reue bitokneþ vs
> alle þat God haþ ȝiuen will and lyf and vnderstondynge and felynge [Holk
> has the different list: witt and wisdom, heringe and vnderstondynge and
> felynge], þorouȝ whiche we owen to seruen hym'. (Pepys 142ᵃ, AN 136ᵛᵇ–
> 37ʳᵃ)

54. However, the priest as book-learned (yet not, on that account, book-lending, but rather
    orally popularising) does emerge with a vengeance in materials derived from Gratian,
    Decretum D.38.5 in sermon 61. This exposition of John 21:15–19, in Sarum Use the
    gospel for the vigil of Peter and Paul (28 June), is not part of the *Mirror* proper but
    appended to it in three copies, the London Harley 5085 and Holkham misc. 40, as
    well as John Rylands Eng. 109. I am grateful to Anne Hudson for (among many other
    things) drawing my attention to this passage.

55. The passage appears in the Prologue; cf. also sermons 1 (Pepys 50ᵇ, 27/18–20), 8 (Pepys
    67ᵇ, 99/3–5), and 22 (the good shepherd): 'Ac [God] biddeþ þat ȝe schullen ben buxum
    to ȝoure keper and fynde hym his sustenaunce þat he ne haue no meschief ne þat he ne
    be nouȝt letted for none erþelich þinges to do Goddes seruise' (Pepys 105ᵃ, Panunzio
    209–31, lines 289–96, citing Heb. 13:7).

56. In a general way and usually as a subordinate part of larger instructional patterns, a
    commonplace injunction, e.g. *Speculum Cristiani* 2/5–13, *Speculum Vitæ* 4563–84, or
    Hoccleve's *Regiment* 2485–99.

57. The French here is reformulated (both cut and expanded); the section paralleling 'þat
    he may after . . . ' runs:

> Ke lom puisse puis bel mustrer
> Quant bosuigne surd e encumbrer
> E ke lom eit entendement
> De bien urer escordement
> De sei e altres enseigner
> E de tuz mesfaiz chastier.

58. From the regulations of the fraternity of St Anne's chantry, St Lawrence, Old Jewry,
    Barron–Wright 121.

59. In the Sarum lectionary, a gospel for feastdays of confessors and bishops.

60. Cf. Wille's self-defence (*Piers Plowman* C 5.84–5):

> Preyeres of a parfit man and penaunce discrete
> Is the leuest labour þat oure lord pleseth.

61. Guardum le deu cumandement;
    Nus ne deuum pas refuser
    Ço ke deus nus uolt cumander.

62. This proverb, although it appears elsewhere (cf. MED picard, and note the apparent
    echo at Pepys *Riwle* 33/24–8), must refer to a specific anecdote I have been unable to
    discover.

63. A similar diatribe appears in sermon 56. Here 'Antecristes prophetes' are the expected
    villains of the Apocalypse, who 'maken hem as hij weren holy and han oiþer coueitise
    oiþer proude oiþer leccherous oiþer losangeres, ne seien nouȝth þe soþe þere þai comen

for drede of deþ oiþer of bodilich sustenaunce' (Pepys 196ª). But the end-time is, for this homilist, now, and one detail suggests that he is thinking of friars, like all other traducers of God's law to be shunned: 'And þis werlde is now ful of hem and han ben now þre hundred wynter and more. And þerfore vche man þat wil queme God keep hym out of her compaignye oiþer hij schullen gon wiþ hem to her lorde þat is þe fende'.

64. On specifically London examples, see Thrupp 34–8, Thomson 82–146, Barron 1985; more generally, McRee (with useful summaries of past discussions), his 1993 article an important assessment of the charitable functions; William Jones, Hanawalt 1984, Hanawalt–McRee, Rubin 1987, 250–9. For the London regulations, see Barron–Wright, *Parish Fraternity* 1–4, Horwood (the manuscript there described now is Corporation MS 4158); I have limited myself to the published examples in English, but Westlake 180–8, 236–8 provides summaries of all the London responses to the 1389 inquiry. Most City parish churches were victims of the 1666 fire. St Helen Bishopsgate (originally with an attached nunnery) is perhaps the most interesting survivor, some furnishings transferred from St Martin Outwich; see Schofield 1994b, 104–7, figs. 8/44, 42–3 (37, 70–1, respectively).

65. Cf. Veale 1969, 137–9; 1991; the regulations of the whittawyers (Riley 232), for example, begin by asserting the company's responsibility for a light in a parish church, before passing on to regulations specifically associated with the guild's craft function.

66. For similar examples, stipulating various faults and sets of procedures, see Barron–Wright 122, 123, 130, 132, 134, 139, 144; *Parish Fraternity* 3. The London regulations identify antisocial behaviours, not the spiritual limitations enunciated by St Leonard, King's Lynn, which would expell any member 'rebel ageyne þe lawe of holy chirche ... tille he come to amendment' (cited William Jones 650).

67. St Peter's guild worries over a priest 'if he be ony tyme, that God forbeyd, on notorie lechour, or an nyghte-wandrer, or oute of mesure, or taverne or [al]hous [MS althous] haunter, or otherwyse criminous or mysproude or debate-maker in chirche or elleswhere' (Horwood 412b).

68. In this portion, there are occasional signs that the reviser used a copy of the Anglo-Norman original, as well as the English Apocalypse, e.g. at *Apoc* 193–4/3–8, where the original 'sterres' here appears as 'stretes' (cf. Apoc. 21:21 platea) (*English Text Magdalene* 180/23–7). The end of the addition (182/19–29) represents a phrase (and the commentary it elicits) from Apoc. 22:15.

69. Although Colledge conveniently lists the more than thirty major interpolations (13–14, some of them simply movement of passages from late in the *Riwle* to earlier positions in the text), his summary view of the *Riwle* revision requires the qualifications offered here: '*The Recluse* [is] Anti-Petrine, anti-papal, and opposed to the religious orders' (131).

70. Cf. the extraordinary comparison of self-custody with the incarnate God enclosed in the Virgin's womb at 164/13–27.

71. The positioning of this passage, near the head of part 3 of the *Riwle*, is peculiar: one would expect these metaphorical instructions to stand at the head of the work. In this regard, Anne Hudson tells me that the late Eric Dobson remarked in conversation that he believed the Pepys *Riwle* to have been subjected to two different acts of revision and that the second began at this point.

72. Cf. the added example at 139/32–140/1 and the subsequent pietistic expansion 140/14–31.

73. The passage cited continues: 'bot 3if were a prechoure and preched Goddes woord fram toun to toun so þat ne my3th nou3th for stody ernen it. And 3utt Peter and Poule

erneden her mete wiþ her hondes and preched fram cite to cite. For Poule seiþ þat he ne ete neuere mannes mete, bot ʒif it were his vnþonkes' (4/25–9).

74. Cf. such a stock formulation as 'ʒif it so befalle þat any of þe bretherhede falle in pouerte or be anientised thorwʒ elde... or thorwʒ any other chaunce, thorw fyr or water, theues or syknesse, or any other happes,... he schal haue in þe wyke xiiij. *d*' (Barron–Wright 136). Cf. *Piers Plowman* 6.218–21a.

75. Similar examples appear at Barron–Wright 126, 130, 131–2, 135, 136, 138, 143–4.

5

Anglo-Norman's imagined end

The period from the late 1360s, that context in which the Pepys MS was copied, already saw many sweeping cultural changes, foretastes of the future. Among these, one might reckon the death of Anglo-Norman. Of course, Anglo-Norman's historical end lies well outside the period; as a well-known, mostly south-eastern *lingua franca*, it survived the Middle Ages, eventually, as 'Law French' to be euthanised by statute in 1731.[1] But its last two poets are John Gower and, the focus of this chapter, Sir John Chandos's Herald. The latter describes the period *c.* 1370–85 as one of crisis and disorder, both as event within his strongly retrospective narrative and as the social context into which he presents his text. His discussion, beyond pointing to the similar sense of crisis that turned a London hanger-on, William Rokayle, into William Langland, the poet of *Piers Plowman*, exemplifies Anglo-Norman's imagination of its own (preordained, I'm afraid) end as a literary culture.

The Chandos Herald (who signs the last line of his work) is not precisely an English figure at all. As his great editor, Mildred K. Pope, demonstrated, he came from Hainault, the same region near Valenciennes as his colleague, perhaps friend, Jean Froissart. He may be identical with the herald Haneray (Henri?), brought by the Black Prince's companion Sir John Chandos from 'outremer'; Haneray received a payment from Sir John Wingfield, the Black Prince's administrator, in 1355. After Chandos's death in Gascony (1370), his herald apparently became a royal servant, perhaps the first designated English King of Arms; he wrote, probably late in 1385, *La Vie du Prince Noir*, 4,200 lines in octosyllabic couplets recounting the military career of England's fallen hero.[2]

The Herald's work survives in two manuscripts, both, I would suspect, from the 1390s. Although a foreigner, writing in his native French dialect, his work is certainly Gascon/English and known only in Anglo-Norman transmission. The two books – Oxford, Worcester College, MS 1; and University of London Library, MS 1 – are remarkably similar presentations of his work. They have identical contents; both present two appendices to the Herald's biography – a verse listing of the Black Prince's household officers in Gascony (headed by John Chandos) and an accurate rendition of the Black Prince's epitaph (Tyson). This, chosen by the Prince himself, copied in his will and inscribed on his tomb, is an excerpt from an Old French translation of Petrus Alphonsus's *Disciplina clericalis*, known in Anglo-Norman form for at least a century, e.g. at Bodleian Library, MS Digby 86, fols. $96^{vb}/27-97^{ra}/21$. Moreover, in both books, there are analogous signs of separateness of intent or receipt of these ancillary texts: in Worcester 1, much of fol. 59^v, where the *Vie* ends, appears to have been blank, with the heading for the subsequent listing of the Gascon household now added in and the text beginning on the following folio; in London 1, the colophon to the *Vie* is written in double-sized display script, preceded and followed by four blank lines.

Resemblances between the manuscripts extend beyond contents to near physical identity. The two books are virtually the same overall size (235 mm × 140 mm), have the same writing area (185 mm × 80–5 mm, to the bounding lines) and almost the same number of lines to the page (forty in London, forty-two in Worcester College), the same page preparation (prickings and yellowish brown ink rules), and the same absence of signatures and catchwords (although perhaps cut away in both – one original catchword exceptionally appears at London, fol. 27^v – which would still testify to a similar placement well beneath the writing area).

Their common size suggests that the parchment has been prepared in the same, slightly unusual way: each quire is composed of a single smallish vellum sheet folded in octavo, as opposed to the technique more usual in contemporary English books, a quired pair of sheets folded in quarto; a typical example of the latter would be Cambridge University Library, MS Additional 3035, Gower's *Miroir de l'omme*, overall 302 mm × 200 mm. Both copies also resemble another Anglo-Norman manuscript, in this case from the early years of the fifteenth century, the 'Trentham MS' of Gower's *Balades* (British Library, MS Additional

59495), although that book is significantly 'squarer', about 10 per cent broader, and these as a consequence appear 'oblong'. In addition, the original text portions of both copies are bibliographically identical, each composed of eight eight-leaf quires – Worcester fols. 1–63 (the whole), London fols. 4–67 (fols. 1 a flyleaf, fols. 2–3 front matter, with a fifteenth-century inscription of ownership/use to which I will return).

However alike, these books differ in two significant ways – in decoration and in script. Their production reflects analogous decisions, I should think actuated in reasonable proximity, but executed for different levels of formality and costing. The two manuscripts have a common sense of how to present and decorate the poem. Both have red headings in the text-script to divide the poem into sections, and both an illuminated opening page, with flower and leaf border. Likewise, both set off the heads of individual sections of the poem with a decorated *littera notabilior*.

But where Worcester has a demivinet at the start and blue lombards with red flourishing at the heads of the sections, London has a full vinet at the opening and the lombards at the section headings, while adding painted champes for the first lines of the text units proper. Moreover, the London MS shows superior, indeed elegant, planning: one reason for the scribe's spaced heading between *La Vie* and the ancillary texts is to ensure that the poetry ends precisely on the last line of the last surviving recto, fol. 67; fol. 67^v is blank but ruled (as may have been the now-cancelled final leaf).

Consonant with these elaborations, the London MS also has a more ornamental opening. Its initial champe is inhabited – with arms, England quartering France ancient. Although some scholars have read from this armourial signature a royal provenance, such a view is mostly scholarly wish-fulfilment, a desire to inscribe anointed presence. This decoration may simply identify the subject of the text, a person associated with the royal claim to France; it answers a painting across the opening, on the verso of the second front-matter leaf, fol. 3^v.[3]

The left page is thoroughly flamboyant, but also documentarily accurate and acutely intelligent. The illuminator, a bit unusually, actually knows the text(s) he is illustrating and here represents the pious Edward in his prayer before his great triumph, the Battle of Najera (1367).[4] The lower half of the illumination depicts the Black Prince, fully armed with sword and gold spurs and wearing a surcoat bearing the arms that inhabit the champe at the opening of the text opposite; these arms are a statement of genealogy, filial piety, that the driving force behind the Prince's militarism is his father's claim to the double monarchy. The heraldic display is completed by two of the Prince's ostrich feather badges, each with his motto 'ich dene'.

Above this chivalric display, the artist has depicted the Trinity on a golden ground. The Black Prince – as *La Vie* notes, committed specially to Trinitarian devotion – kneels below in prayer on a cushion; a scroll from his mouth bears the legend 'hec tres unum sunt'. The documentary basis for the depiction – and a text being illustrated here beyond the poem itself – is what its author knew as a herald. The Black Prince had died prematurely on 8 June 1376 (ironically, his special day, Trinity Sunday) during the Good Parliament. In keeping with his devotion, he was buried in the Trinity Chapel at Canterbury Cathedral, the epitaph he requested and wrote into his will inscribed on the tomb (as well as included in the manuscripts), a depiction of the Trinity comparable to that of the manuscript painted on the tomb's tester (for the Prince to stare at until the Judgement), and the costume and heraldry depicted here displayed at the tomb.[5] This illustration provides, as I will show, a truly prescient reading, in which narrated triumph and death are superimposed.

An even more persistent distinction between the two copies of the poem concerns their scripts. In these terms, Worcester College 1 is pretty unproblematic; it is written in the great script of Edwardian England, a neat anglicana formata. However, the hand of the London MS is rather splasher: while it retains features proper to anglicana, for example its double-looped *d* and complex *w*, as well as anglicana *litteræ notabiliores*, it regularly uses a different selection of letter-forms:

(1) rather than a two-compartment, rather tall *a*, a single-compartment form written as three strokes, the last a transverse movement that often leaves protruding 'horns';
(2) rather than the 8-shaped *g* of anglicana, one with a sweeping lower stroke and open lobe;
(3) instead of the distinctive anglicana below-line *r*, one constructed with a rounded foot on the line and a peaked horizontal stroke

at minim height (this contrasts as well with the Worcester scribe's frequent reliance on the *r* of textura scripts, basically formed of a minim and dot);

(4) finally, rather than sigmoid final *-s* (sometimes bent into an 8-shape), a kidney-shaped form, its initial stroke beginning at a position different from that of the anglicana letter.

In the London MS, the script also appears 'elevated' and 'bookish', one modelled on formal textura. With that style, the hand shares a propensity for broken strokes, rather than anglicana curves. Likewise imported from textura is the 'biting' of adjacent curved strokes. This is a quite flamboyant early example of the script called 'secretary'. This hand would achieve a swift (within thirty years) ascendancy and would become the dominant English script for something like two centuries, the period roughly 1450–1650. (Anglicana would survive even longer – but as 'court hand', a retreat to its origins as a legal script, e.g. as the display hand of formal deeds.)

The origins of secretary are certainly legal/documentary. In the Bible of book-hands, Malcolm Parkes gives as his first examples documents from the Chancery of the archbishops of Canterbury, i.e. Lambeth, just about 1377 (1969, xix–xxi and plate 9). When the Prerogative Court of Canterbury began enrolling wills in 1383, they were first recorded in secretary.

But the 'dawn of English secretary' may be pushed back somewhat further. Pierre Chaplais identifies 1372 as a date from which the offices of the Privy Seal and Signet developed a distinctive script; this he describes as 'the result of a break-away from English writing traditions rather than the outcome of a gradual evolution' (52), and he reproduces a document of 1377 illustrating the hand (plate 16c). But Chaplais's earliest example of an Englishman using the script is a text from English-occupied France, a Privy Seal writ executed for the Black Prince in Gascony in 1370. This document was copied by one John Fordham, who eventually became Keeper of the Privy Seal for the Black Prince's son Richard in 1376 and Keeper of the royal Privy Seal on his little boss's accession to the throne in 1377.[6] That this government office had conducted its normal documentary business in Anglo-Norman since 1290 (Chaplais 27–8) makes this importation of French chancellorial styles seem almost inevitable and equally explains the association of the script with late Anglo-Norman literary texts. In this instance, as a poem applauding overseas adventurism, the text is written in Gascon chancery script, the second or third oldest such book I know. It testifies to cross-Channel cultural continuities, a nostalgic allusion to old solidarities, carried hopefully down the family line.

Such a hand can be paralleled in manuscripts from the other node of late Anglo-Norman literature, John Gower's French poetry. The unique copy of *Miroir de l'omme*, CUL Additional 3035, uses a somewhat more cursive version with less attention to decorative broken strokes; Malcolm Parkes has identified parallels which would allow a narrow dating of the book *c.* 1379–81, very shortly after the poem's composition. A more telling parallel is provided by the Trentham manuscript of Gower's *Balades*, Additional 59495; Parkes finds this scribe also responsible for 'versional' adjustments in a central manuscript of Gower's English *Confessio Amantis*, Bodleian Library, MS Fairfax 3.[7] In Trentham, again copied very shortly after composition (1402 × 1408?), the scribe shows extreme specialisation of script, and uses two stylings of anglicana for English and Latin, a script like that of the London Herald MS for the French items only. He has a rather uneasy go of it; for nearly a full leaf at the point of transition (fols. 11^v-12^v), he inconsistently tries to convert his script from its Anglo-Latin anglicana to his Anglo-Norman secretary letter-forms. Both script and the texts it communicates are distinctly 'modern' – Anglo-Norman poems almost contemporary and presented in an innovative writing style. But equally, their cultural bases are old-fashioned, and their script's lengthy history is appropriately a French one, associated with Edwardian imperialist adventure.

In form *La Vie du Prince Noir* is a throwback, something between chivalric chronicle and romance biography. Perhaps its closest congeners, e.g. the Bridlington canon Pierre Langtoft's verse chronicle (Dean no. 66), might be associated with the idolisation of Edward I as quasi-imperial figure. Certainly, the emphases of the work would bear out such a presentation of a true genealogical succession, for as all past critics have pointed out, *La Vie* provides an unbalanced representation of Edward, the Black Prince's career. More than half of the poem, from line 1639, treats his Castilian adventure, and the climax of the work details the triumph of Najera in 1367. At that moment, the

Prince, if not gaining a kingdom, should at least have expanded the ambit of English influence.[8] At the formal opening of this narrative portion, the Chandos Herald links Prince Edward's pursuit with unquestionable royal virtues, most particularly legal power, shortly to be associated with proper succession:

> Now begins a noble *matière*, one about a noble military endeavour, for, as you may hear, pi(e)ty, love, and the pursuit of Right all sustained it. (1817–21)[9]

Although one might see this as an evocation of sober English values, *La Vie* is very much a continental poem, and its model for its noble lord is most usually not an English figure, say Arthur, but a French. Like Roland and the *douce pers*, the Prince traverses Roncevaux, and his journey is, at least apparently, a vastly more successful one than theirs had been. Indeed, on the field of Najera, his men explicitly exceed their noble predecessors of the *chanson de geste*:

> What should I say? In the Prince's company, there was no man, however lowly, who was not every bit as bold and fierce as a lion. One cannot compare even Roland and Oliver to them. (3377–83)[10]

If Edward I might be connected with an imperious Alexander in Great Britain, his great-grandson follows appropriately local continental antecedents, also a contemporary subject for English appropriation.

Interestingly, the portrayal of Najera isn't everything. Critics have typically complained about the Herald's 'chronicle'-like effort to work a Najera poem into a full *vie*. From about line 100, the text begins with the Crécy campaign, where Prince Edward first distinguished himself; and it includes a very substantial discussion of the battle of Poitiers. But, especially in its appendage on the Gascon household, the poem is about a retinue and the reciprocal relations of lord and retainer, rather than simply the Black Prince's person. Indeed, this interest in relationship, or a leader in his social context, extends to the family, the Black Prince's lineage, the English royal household. This feature is evidenced in the quite ahistorical equanimity with which the Herald has Edward III greet his son's impolitic love-marriage to Joan of Kent.

The poem constantly emphasises the impressive ability surrounding the Black Prince, his comrades, and it is replete with the full naming of historical persons. Here the Herald most obviously deploys his master, Sir John Chandos, as exemplary, e.g. in his taking the banner at Najera (lines 3113–56). The Prince's closest companion, and about ten years older, participant at Cambrai (1339) and Sluys (1340), knighted on the eve of an abortive effort to stage a battle at La Capelle (1339), Chandos came from a relatively obscure non-armourial Derbyshire family. His reward – one shared with the remainder of the companions the Herald names – was his inclusion as the twentieth among the original twenty-six Garter Knights – as well as the gift of very extensive Cheshire and Lincolnshire properties after Poitiers (as I will show, a major subtext to the poem is the profitability of warfare).[11] In this regard, the one discernible indication of the manuscripts' medieval provenance is important. The London copy of *La Vie* includes in its two folios of 'front matter' the crowned motto/signature of the fifteenth-century Smithfield scribe John Shirley. The poem suggests very clearly why Shirley should have had this book and where he would have gotten it.

Among those important in the extended narrative of retainership the Herald provides is Thomas Beauchamp, 11th earl of Warwick (1314–69). He appears prominently, indeed might be taken as the central retainer, in early portions of the poem; he was at Crécy, later in Gascony and at Poitiers, another memorable moment for him in the poem – the occasion for his let's-get-ready-to-rumble speech. Historically, he was a founder-knight of the Garter, indeed the third knight, after the Prince himself and another late Anglo-Norman author, Henry of Grosmont, then earl of Derby, later duke of Lancaster (and father-in-law of John of Gaunt). At the opening of the poem, the description of the French invasion in 1346, Beauchamp has pride of place; the account begins:

> There king Edward had many a good and aristocratic knight: the noble earl of Warwick, about whom someone should write a poem. (122–4)[12]

Beauchamp's son Thomas, the 12th earl (1338/9–1401), was also Knight of the Garter (1373). Although he does not appear in the poem, William Worcester, writing a century later, believed he had been part of the English force at Najera (14–15). His son Richard, the 13th earl (*d.* 1439), was, of course, John Shirley's long-time employer (GEC 12, 372–82 *passim*). One would suspect that at least this manuscript of the poem, if not the entire endeavour, reflects Beauchamp patronage.[13]

Whatever one may say about the English social solidarity *La Vie* expresses, the poem remains a life of the Prince because it enunciates that solidarity as overseas adventurism – and as a notion of territorial solidarity. The London MS illuminator properly showed the Prince's surcoat as England quartering France, and Najera is properly central to the poem, because it is a trope for a 'Rightful' true claim Death prevented the Black Prince from making. Edward, in the Herald's most usual (but significantly not his only) formulation, supports the exiled Pedro of Castile from 'nobility'. One might compare the Black Prince's most explicit self-representation, to God (the moment the London frontispiece illustrates), in his pious prayer before the battle of Najera:

> True sovereign father who has created us, you know truly that I have come here only to sustain Right and bravery, and you know that *franchise* propels my spirit to gain a life of honour by conquest. (3172–81)[14]

In the Spanish adventure, Right and noble honour are intimately linked. Pedro deserves support because he is a legitimate king, not a bastard like the evil Enrique who has usurped his throne (2909–50). And as the poem initially describes this adventure, supporting Pedro's assertion of proper inheritance interfaces with Edward III's dynastic claim to France, a claim the Black Prince, readers are to believe, would surely have pursued, had he lived. Before the battle of Poitiers, for example, Prince Edward explains to a truce-seeking cardinal:

> You know well, and it's no lie, that, at the time when Philippe de Valois was crowned, my father, King Edward, was certainly the heir with the greatest Right to hold France, the person to whom each should have done homage. (828–34)[15]

But equally, the poem is elegiac: the Black Prince's heroic triumph is his failure and death; both manuscripts end with his tomb inscription (and as I have argued, the London manuscript implicitly illustrates the tomb and its accoutrements). Indeed, the poem is quasi-critical, for the prince's nobility is ultimately out of touch with a more corruptible and decaying world that surrounds him. The Herald is always conscious of writing twenty years later, from hindsight, and he goes about as far as he can to expose the Prince, to show that his piety, nobility, and prowess are (and were) compromised both by modern political realities, as well as by the nature of things. Like Kyng Alisaunder, Edward is done in by mutability itself.

The Najera campaign has an ignoble aftermath: the Black Prince does not get paid by his allies. This is an after-the-fact acknowledgement of one of the poem's usual reticences, that 'nobility' and Right have to pay, that heroes are mercenaries. Yet the Herald lacks Terry Jones's satiric view of this issue and remains thoroughly accepting of the economic underpinnings of warfare. Thus, his insistence on the Prince's debilitating idealism, destructive enough, provides a way of not addressing Edward's real political failures, hard-headed financial exploitation in Gascony. The Herald implicitly approves of this behaviour, although it produced revolt and slaughter, disordered lordship in France.

War as a form of personal finance is one thing, but welshing on debts, a refusal to acknowledge one's Rightful obligations, bothers the Herald a good deal. Prince Edward's downfall stems from political naïveté; he discovers that noble genes don't necessarily lead all people to noble practices. Having reseated him on the throne – and urged him to show mercy to the vanquished Enrique:

> The Prince now saw well that king Pedro was not so faithful to his promise as he had believed he would be. (3703–5)[16]

For Pedro won't pay up for the military aid he has received. Moreover, the Black Prince doesn't leave Spain, although his men have no food – and he contracts his eventually fatal dysentery while campaigning. Further, his mercy, however noble, appears faulty: he won't pillage the population and starves because of his nobility (3635–76), retrospectively revealed as a tactical sense that only works on the battlefield. Back in Gascony, the Prince pays his men, munificently (cf. 'grantz douns' and 3789–3814), but at his own cost.

This chivalric cover-up – as it were – presages the string of disasters which close the poem. Disorder and revolt follow the not so triumphant return to Gascony; with them come, in 1370, the deaths of Edward's mainstays, Chandos and Audley. The Herald does not note, but certainly knew, what another veteran of Spanish campaigning, Geoffrey

Chaucer, tells: that Edward had extended mercy to a Ganelon, that his Castilian candidate was eventually murdered by his brother, and that bastardy, not an honourable line, triumphed in the south.[17] Further, the Spanish expedition is framed by a double reference to the Black Prince's (legitimate) progeny: the birth of Richard is an omen of his expedition's success (2091–2102), but following the return to Bordeaux, Richard's older brother, Edward, dies, an ill omen that foreshadows the unfortunate ending (4057–66). The Herald's comment, 'Mais nulle poet la mort fuyer' ('No one can avoid death', 4064), establishes the terms for the Prince's own mortality; he is ultimately done in by sickness, ostensibly unblemished in military and political terms.

This conclusion answers the extraordinarily downbeat opening of the poem, the proverb, 'everything withers' ('Mais homme dit, et si est de ceo voir, | Qu'il n'est chose que ne delzeche' 8–9). The Herald's opening is impressively familiar, resembling that of another poem associated with the Black Prince and his retinue (notably the administrator John Wingfield), *Winner and Waster* (19–28); from this source it passed, *c.* 1377 into *Piers Plowman* (13.409–59; in C frontloaded to 7.69–118a), and after the Lancastrian usurpation, it was further disseminated through such works as *Mum and the Sothsegger.* The Herald depicts himself saddened by the death of an ancient minstrelsy ('du temps jadis' 1) that transmitted true stories and allowed the minstrels to be invested with authority ('tenu pur aucteur' 3). Past poets did not simply work from historically present models but were authoritative figures of counsel, part of a communally understood system of retainership. But such old minstrels of truth 'are not welcome at court nowadays' ('Car cils ne sont saunz contredire | Mie bien venuz a la court | En le mounde q'ore court' 24–6), and they have been replaced by janglers, liars, and jesters.

II

La vie contains many allusions that imply what the Herald was probably thinking about here; these illustrate the disparity between the world in which his poem appeared and that which it describes. There are any number of ways of showing this, e.g. Simon Burley as character represented by the Herald and the Simon Burley known to modern scholars as an extensive book-owner, but only because he was the victim of an attainder lodged by the Lords Appellant of 1386.[18] Yet for me, the most telling example concerns the Count of Denia.

In his dispatch to Joan of Kent following Najera, the Black Prince tells his wife of his great triumph. And he lists a number of known prisoners. The first of these, Sancho, was Enrique the bastard's brother; the second, an Aragonese nobleman, Alfonso, the count of Denia; the third, that long-time thorn in the side, Bertrand de Guesclin (Barber 1986, 83). The Chandos Herald provides similar information:

> There Bertrand was captured, and the capable Marshal of Audrehem, who was very bold, and a widely renowned count, the count of Denia. (3401–5)[19]

This information was obviously important, not just poetically but bio-graphically, one of those things which made going to Najera worthwhile and heroic. One customary profit of warfare was ransoms in exchange for prisoners, and indentures of military service routinely included clauses stipulating how the proceeds of such triumph were to be handled.

Thus, this should have been a convenient and noble financial trans-action, except that it wasn't. At this point, I segue ahead eleven years to the days leading up to 11 August 1378, and allow a master narrator, Thomas Walsingham, to take up the account (1, 376):

> At this time, there were two knights, Robert Haulee and John Shakel, nor might more vigorous knights easily be found in either England or France. Ten years before, during the war which the most noble Prince Edward had pursued against the Spanish, in which he conquered Henry the bastard and restored Peter his brother, unjustly expelled, to his kingdom, they had captured the noble count of Denia. At the judgement of the Prince and of John Chandos, their master, he was made their prisoner. And, on the basis of their verdict, Haulee and Shakel had obtained charters, with the seals of both the Prince and Sir John affixed, so that no one might later impede them or prevent them from obtaining the ransom due from such a person. The count of Denia had given them his oldest son as a hostage in his place, while he, with these two knights' permission, had gone back to his own country and affairs. However, the count, after he got to Spain, set his pledge to the knights at naught and abandoned his son as a hostage in England.

[My interjection: it was not simply the Black Prince who found how ignoble those Spaniards were about paying you what they had promised. Walsingham resumes:]

> Now those two illustrious Edwards, the father a King and the son a Prince, had paid their debts to nature, and the counsellors of the new King presumptuously demanded the hostage. As some people think, this was done in the interest of the Duke of Lancaster, who had a right in the kingdom of Spain. If he were to possess the count, he might more easily pass to the conquest of that kingdom. But others asserted it was done for lady Matilda, the king's sister . . . But neither the King nor the Duke might extort this prisoner from the knights, however hard they tried; indeed, the knights hid him and kept him far from their clutches. For this reason, they were seized and thrust into the Tower of London. But escaping from this imprisonment, they fled to Westminster.

The full ramifications of what ensued occupy Walsingham for five pages. In order to get Hawley and Shakel back into closer custody (and, it's implied, greater pressure to release the hostage), fifty armed men – the York *Anonimalle Chronicle*, the other leading source for this incident (121–3), notes that they were led by Alan Buxhill, constable of the Tower and Ralph Ferrers, member of the continual council governing during Richard's minority[20] – went to Westminster Abbey on 11 August, as Walsingham alleges, 'secretly, for fear of the Londoners, lest the mob should riot'. The troops got Shakel out, but they murdered the resistant Hawley (and a priest who got in the way) at the high altar.

At issue in both Walsingham's and the anonymous Anglo-Norman chronicler's accounts is the abrogation of normal rules of war and piety in the interests of other political goals. The continental infection has hit England, and not just Spaniards (or Edward's recalcitrant Gascon vassals), but English turn out to be contract-breakers, in the interests of gain. This is, I should think, the kind of 'withering' the Chandos Herald describes, the loss of that solidarity in the Right that to his mind constructed Edwardian activities, the cohesive retinue *La Vie* celebrates. The *Anonimalle Chronicle* comments on the situation in a similar spirit:

> The king, through bad counsel, wanted without either wisdom or justice [*iugement ou resoun*] to have this prisoner and bear him away

from them; they did not want to give up the prisoner in answer to the king's command, but, in accord with the true Right [*verray droit*] which they had in him according to the law of arms, they put him away secretly. (121)

Now one does need to insist that both these comments and Walsingham's account are entirely representational, not fact. Since it involves money, war spoils, there's a large documentary record on this case, indicating *inter alia*, that only Hawley had actually captured the Count (Shakel had bought his share from the second captor as an investment, a very bad one in the event).²¹ But equally, this violation of sanctuary produced a nasty political explosion, at its centre unpleasantly personalised, yet susceptible to fractious global readings. At one extreme, both arch-bishop Sudbury and bishop William Courtenay of London repeatedly promulgated sentences of excommunication against everyone involved. They excluded (and thereby damned by association) only the king, the queen-mother Joan of Kent, and Courtenay's old adversary, the locally unpopular John of Gaunt, in whose interest, Walsingham claims, the whole episode may have begun (see Walsingham 379).

In Sudbury and Courtenay's terms, the Right at issue was not simply that of arms and honour, but a sacral one. The chroniclers are equally broad-bore in their condemnation; while they assert the Rights of arms, they implicitly also ratify the piety *La Vie* shows the Black Prince always observing. Walsingham introduces a bravura 'luget Syon' passage to describe the desecrated sanctuary (378, cf. Lam. 1:4), and the St Mary's chronicler describes Hawley 'slain by Ferrers and his *fautours et tourmentours* who despised both God and Holy Church' (122).

But on its part, the Gaunt-dominated regency asserted other views. The Parliament of October–November 1378 was deliberately removed from the incendiary metropolitan locale (and from its traditional site, the, in this version, offensively stiff-necked Westminster Abbey) to Gloucester. And the government (i.e. Gaunt) arranged for the gathering to hear a debate on the merits of sanctuary, answering archbishop and bishop's outrage head-on; the designated expert witness cum political spin-doctor summoned to present the case was the Duke's once and future adherent, John Wycliffe.²²

His response on behalf of the regency is now buried in the revisions that created his tract *De ecclesia*, although signs of its separate textual life are still extant (see Hudson 2003, 61–2, esp. 62 n. 27, 65). Wycliffe attacks ecclesiastical privileges directly. In addition to his customary aversion to clerical 'possession', in this case he urges that sanctuary only protects sin and thereby engages the Church in evil. But his arguments have considerably more troubling implications. Wycliffe visualises the secularised jurisdiction that would replace ecclesiastical liberty as centralised royal power. That rendition of the (to him) primary issue draws in its train a very different reading of Hawley and Shakel's behaviour than the chroniclers would suggest. The two men are, as the York chronicle says Council accused the Abbey chapter of being, 'inobedientes' (142/9–11), failing to heed an appropriately global royal authority; but beyond this, the knights' acts may be deemed treasonous resistance ('perturbacio sive prodicio', 144/19–20, 145/11). They are criminals against peace and realm, disrupters of a desirable national policy.

In Wycliffe's account, Gaunt, with his pretensions to be not only the Black Prince's inheritor, but his better, not just kingmaker but King of Castile, is no longer central. Submerging his possible involvement allows Wycliffe to urge that the two knights' private interests have impeded an appropriate public good, 'through their captive the kingdom might ransom many English knights held captive in Spain'.[23] Thus, what might be construed private property (held with due legal Right, sealed charters) has become, in practice, simply a public asset, capable of whatever ad lib appropriation the moment demands. And customary pieties of equally long standing can be dispensed with in the process; 'possession', whether secular or religious, has come to be dependent on royal/magnatial whim.

However one wishes to read it, this episode in the saga of the Denia ransom (outstanding issues remained unresolved for another twelve years) might be taken as depicting the crisis towards which the Herald gestures, the end of the Black Prince and his culture. Within a year of Richard's accession, things had changed; the law of arms and those procedures understood as appropriate by all aristocratic men of valour and all pious Christians had been abrogated. Military property won heroically and Rightfully possessed has been converted to the (?seedy) ends of personal ambition and factional politics, obfuscated in Wycliffe's account.

Equally, the chroniclers obscure the nitty-gritty finances behind ransom. Similarly, the Herald's poem obscures the Black Prince's status as paid general and elides quite completely another aspect of his impolitic nobility, his merciless and mercenary extortions as Lord of Gascony. These actions are responsible both for his sobriquet and for the revolt that ends his Aquitanian adventure (and *La Vie*).[24] Like the Chandos Herald, the chroniclers choose to emphasise the perfidy attending an arrangement now considered purely economic and valid only at political pleasure, as well as disdain for larger fidelities, the honour due the Church. Arrangements once perfectly understood are now renegotiated, and policy overwhelms chivalric gesture and clerical privilege. Perhaps in the episode one can see something of Felicity Heal's reading of a transition in the politics of the household, from a theatre of mutually sustaining reciprocity to a relatively closed locus of centralising magnatial Magnificence.

At this point, one might also view the Herald's mordancy as the return of the repressed, of that 'seditiosa dissensio' John Walwayn had described (4) in the *Vita Edwardi Secundi*. Walwayn had seen the disruptions of the 1320s as the failure of cohesion around a powerful royal figure, faction 'inter dominum regem et barones' (4); the fallout of the Denia ransom raises the prospect of no centre whatever, every *baro* who can alleging that his private interests represent the public good. Of course, the whole affair ironically foreshadows the worst political crises of the 1380s and 1390s (to continue in some form or another until after 1485). Gaunt's logic, as expressed by Wycliffe, ultimately underwrote the royal confiscation of his own estate, as well as the opportunity for his son to enact *Beves* or *Horn*, the plot of the banished youth returned for his inheritance. As Walwayn trenchantly puts it, 'Amor magnatum quasi ludus in alea, et uota diuitum pennis similia' (in the vernacular, 'Pursuing the favour of magnates is a crap-shoot, and the vows of the powerful take wing and fly away', 8).

Whatever one may think of militaristic expropriation, in the mid-fourteenth century, as the Herald sees it, it signifies cultural cohesion around a heroic and pious monarch and his line. In a world of New Men – at his death, Edward was surrounded by a magnatial staff thirty years his juniors and with none of the triumphs (and profits) the Black Prince and Chandos had enjoyed – the cohesion has departed, although the lust for similar profiteering remains. One sporadically revisits the excesses of the 1320s, what had been the second unusual blip (1297 was the first) in a general pageant of Edwardian triumph.[25]

One might return at this point to consider those 'janglers' the Chandos Herald mentions in his opening (the *Winner*-poet calls them 'child[ren] appon chere withowtten chyn-wedys', 24).[26] The Herald presumably alludes to the 'new poetry' that surrounded him as he wrote, for example Geoffrey Chaucer's *Troilus*, a work almost exactly contemporary with *La Vie*. The Herald's story of decline and loss, of the end of Edwardian warfaring culture (the longue duree, stretching back to Edward I's conquest of Wales in 1282), is the replacement of his Hainault/Gascon culture by Middle English.

This story is partially inscribed in what became of the script used to present *La Vie de Prince Noir* in the London manuscript. So far as I know, the first serious and substantial English literary manuscript written fully in secretary is the Campsall MS of Chaucer's *Troilus* (New York, Morgan Library, MS M.817), an elegantly decorative form, heavily indebted to textura, produced for Henry V as prince of Wales 1406 × 1413 (see Krochalis's facsimile).[27] Shortly afterwards, secretary appears prominently in the two Ur-manuscripts of Hoccleve's *Regiment of Princes*, advice on good governance dedicated to Henry V just before his accession. In these books, British Library, MSS Arundel 38 and Harley 4866, both *c.* 1412, the script is a fully established book-hand, if used inconsistently (recall the Trentham scribe's hesitations) in the latter by a scribe plainly more used to writing anglicana. In fact, the scribes of this work may well be imitating the hand of authorial papers; Hoccleve, as a Privy-seal clerk, had been brought up in this script and routinely uses secretary in his surviving autograph manuscripts.[28] The Gascon script, with its expressions of continuity, has been (guiltily?) subsumed in other, here royal, interests by subsequent book culture.

Such a reading – which may well be epiphenomenal, an insistence on superstructure while ignoring base – gives a different purchase than is usual on that other Najera campaigner, Geoffrey Chaucer. His reference to King Pedro of Castile, after all, is closely conjoined with the narrative of Ugolino, one of his most overt bows to his usually silenced precursor, Dante (as John Fyler argues persuasively, the Virgil to his Ovid). One might also recall his snidenesses about Stratford French, which construes Anglo-Norman as nun-speak associated with the suburbs (McDonnell 143–4, cf. 68–71); or about 'moral Gower' (another Anglo-Norman poet

with an ostensibly sober Edwardian commitment to homologies between realm, ruler, and self). A 'cosmopolitan' view far removed from
the Herald's community of arms and Right underlies those features
usually appreciated in Chaucer's work – his eye for 'individuality', his
insistence on (re)negotiated contracts (necessary because so regularly
broken), and his jester's evasion of coherent social authority. (Biographically, Chaucer was a survivor, not a counsellor, someone who knew how
to keep his head down and negotiate court faction.) He might well be
the New Man for the Herald's withered world of modernity, in which
the situational has overridden the principled. To a very large extent, this
too is social mythmaking (the Black Prince, and particularly his agent
John Chandos, solidified their Gascon lordship only through plenty of
negotiating with the local aristocracy).[29] Yet however centred in a cult
of military personality, *La Vie du Prince Noir* affirms, in its passing, a
particular type of community with coherent and legible rules.

The narrative I outline in another way represents a return to origins,
for the period from *c*. 1280-*c*. 1377 might be described as the 'Edwardian [i.e., Edwards I–III] dominance of Anglicana'. Indeed, this writing
style began to emerge as an acceptable text-hand, out of its legal and
documentary origins, precisely with the profusion of Law and Right
associated with 'Longshanks', Edward I – that same agreed Law and
Right I have shown the Herald as both applauding as ideal and, in its
passage, lamenting. Thus, this might be considered a period bracketed
between Hengham and Herald – Ralph Hengham, justice of the King's
Bench and author of two popular introductory legal *summæ*, and the
Chandos Herald, the chronicler of its end.

NOTES

1. On the regionalisation, see Rothwell 1983; and cf. chapter 2, n. 6.
2. See the fine introduction to *Life of the Black Prince*; the more recent edition, *La Vie*,
   updates the scholarship, and adds references to the Herald from Froissart (esp. 16,
   34). See further Palmer 1982; and the numerous references Palmer 1981 *passim*. On the
   possible royal appointment, see Wagner 36. But one might note in this regard *Calendar
   of Patent Rolls 1385–1389* 128 (11 January 1386): the king grants John Marche, Noreys
   King at Arms 7 1/2 *d* daily and robes, to be paid by The Keeper of the Wardrobe,
   'notwithstanding that heretofore no herald has been accustomed to receive any wages
   in the king's household, yet this grant is not to be a precedent'!
3. Although, in fairness, I should point out that related Westminster artists, active from
   1383, appear in a manuscript certainly Richard II's, Bodleian Library, MS Bodley 581; see

Sandler 1986, 2, 175–6 (nos. 151–2) and plate 406, with one of the workshop's armourials from British Library, MS Cotton Nero D.vi, a historical compilation produced 1386 × 1399.

4. For reproductions of this image, see Rye's catalogue and Barber 1986 frontispiece. Depictions of the Black Prince, perhaps comparable to and certainly recalling early portrayals of Edward I (see p. 118 above), appeared in his lifetime, e.g. the tapestry bequeathed by a canon of St George's Chapel, Windsor in 1376 (Sharpe 2, 190, cited Schofield 1994a, 128–9).

5. As they are still; see *Age* 479–81 (nos. 626–33) and Juliet and Malcolm Vale's comments 24–6.

6. He was subsequently bishop of Durham, then of Ely, 1381–1425 (!); for an instance of his continuing fellowship with Gascon officials, see Labarge 178.

7. See 1995, 99 n. 8 on the *Miroir*; 89–91, 95–6 on 'scribe 5', responsible for the Trentham MS; 94 and 103 n. 7 on 'scribe 10', who made additions to Trentham; and plates 14–15 (110–13) for scribe 5 at work (from Trentham, a leaf illustrating his English and Latin scripts, but not the French).

8. On the centrality of such topics in the analogous fifteenth-century 'biographie chevaleresque', see Gauchier, esp. 24–5.

9.   Ore comence noble matiere
    De noble et puissant mestiere,
    Car pitee, amour, et droiture
    Mist ensemble sa noriture,
    Einsi come vous purrez oier.

10.   Quei voillez vous qe vous die?
    Il n'avoit en la compaignie
    Du Prince homme, tant fuit petitz,
    Qe ne fut bien auxi hardis
    Et auxi fiers come un lioun.
    Homme ne poet comparisoun
    Faire de Oliver et Rolant.

Cf. the first touch of this treatment, at 161–4.

11. Most information about Chandos seems to be based upon Froissart, e.g. 1.38, 41, 50, 127, 160–3, 241, 278 (his death, and Froissart's praise for him, as the man who could have prevented the loss of Gascony). See also Barber 1978, 33–4, 40–1, 89–90; on the Garter, Juliet Vale 76–91. Chandos is still taken as chivalric paragon in William Worcester's book encouraging Edward IV to invade France (1475), 46–7.

12.   La ot maint bon chivaler fin –
    De Warrewik lui noble counte
    De quoi homme devoit faire counte.

On efforts to provide just such a representation of Beauchamp, an echo of family veneration of Guy, see Ferris 27–9.

13. On Shirley's books, see Griffiths 1992 and Connolly.

14.   Adonqes le Prince de valour
    Devers le ciel joindi sez mains
    Et dist, 'Verray Piere soverains,
    Qe nous avez fait et creez,

Si verraiment come vous savez
Qe je ne sui pas cy venuz
Fors pur droit estre sustenuz
Et proesce, et pur franchise
Qe mon coer semonte et attise
De conquestre vie de honour . . .'.

15.   Bien savez qe ce n'est pas fable
Qe mon piere, roi Edwardz,
Certes estoit le pluis droitz heirs
Pur tenir et pur possesser
France, qe chescuns doit amer,
Au temps q'il fuist coronez rois
Lui roi Philippes de Valois.

Cf. the opinion advanced in the London *Croniques*, that Philip was 'coward et recru chevaler' (81) following his avoidance of battle with Edward III in 1340: 'And from that time, Philip de Valois lost his title, King of France, and all Christian chivalry granted our king, the Lord Edward, the title the Rightful king of France and of England' ('Et a celle heur Philip de Valois perdi le noun d'estre appellé le roy de France, et a Sire Edward nostre roy fust donée le noun d'estre apellé droiturel roy de Fraunce et d'Engletere, et fust graunté de tot le chevalrie de Cristienté', 72).

16.   Lui Prince ad bien aperceu
Qe le roi Petro ne fu
Pas si foiaux come il quidoit.

17. See 'The Monk's Tale' 2375–90. The bastard Enrique assassinated Pedro 23 March 1369; Enrique's daughter was, of course, John of Gaunt's Constance, whom he married in 1371 and who provided his claim to a Spanish throne, a topic to which I turn in part II. Pedro was betrayed by Bertrand de Guesclin, and Chaucer's account includes an image mirroring the Herald's in its derivation from Roland materials – de Guesclin as Ganelon, not Oliver. Chaucer was certainly in Castile at the time of the campaign, and may even have been at Najera.

18. For Simon Burley's heroism in Spain, see *La Vie* 2450–77, 2525–42. For Burley as Richard's tutor, see Saul 15–16 (he succeeded Guichard d'Angle, also a character in *La Vie*) and on Burley's influence, 112–20. For his booklist, first identified Clarke 119–21, see Scattergood 1968. This includes twenty-one volumes, not very clearly identifiable, but mostly 'Romans', i.e. French and what we would call 'romance' (eight of them), but also 'bruyt' (no. 20), 'de gouernement de Roys et du prynces' (no. 7), and a single English book, mentioned above, p. 14.

19.   Illoeqes fuist pris monsire Bertrans
Et li mareschalle sufficeantz
D'Odrehem, qui tant fuist hardis,
Et un counte qui eust grant pris,
Counte de Dene fuist nosmez.

This follows an earlier reference to Denia as a leader of the Spanish infantry at 3060–8.

20. All these events also appear in popular accounts, the *Brut* and the *London Chronicles*: Najera at *Brut* 318–19 and 320/*London* 170–1/*Great Chronicle* 42; the violation of the Westminster sanctuary at *Brut* 335/*London* 172/*Great Chronicle* 45. For Najera (as indeed

for the extension to 1377), the *Brut* is drawing on the standard continuation of Higden's *Polychronicon* to 1377, 'Adam of Merrymouth' 174–227, here 203. See also Saul 36–8.

21. For the documentary evidence surrounding these accounts (not equivalent to what the chroniclers allege), see Perroy, with information on the further ramifications of this contretemps.

22. Cf. *Anominalle*: 'The king and his council intended, because of the contempt they had shown in refusing to deliver these squires to the king, to remove the entire royal franchise from Westminster and to seize from the abbey all its temporalities' ('Le roy et son counseil furount en purpos de defaire toute la roial fraunchese de Westmoustier et toller del abbé toutz ses temporaltes pur contempte qils ne vodroient deliverer al roy les ditz vadlettes', 123). And the chronicler, more detailed about the Parliament than is Walsingham, describes Wycliffe as having already 'shown in an academic presentation that the king might seize the possessions of regular clergy in order to aid him in his war and that no church possessed the liberty of sheltering a man charged with debt' ('determyné qe le roy purroit prendre les possessiones des possessioners pur luy aider en sa guerre et qe nulle eglise avoit tiel fraunchese qe purroit recetter une homme pur dette'). Such views had already been bruited in Parliament, by two Augustinian friars in 1371; see Aston 51.

23. 'per quem captivum regnum redimeret multos milites suos in Hispania captivos' (142/15–16).

24. Cf. the *Brut*'s references, associated with the 1370 sack of Limoges, to his 'grete taxes, costages and raunsoms . . . charges . . . unportable and to chargeable' (323/30–2), here quoting Adam's Higden continuation 209. See further Labarge 141, 159, 164; and *La Vie* 4036–42, a tolerably bland account of the sack and slaughter of Limoges, in response to Gascon revolt (although modulated by its positioning as an example of the decline of Edward's Gascon fortunes).

25. For the magnatial demographics of the 1370s, see Prestwich 1980, 285–6; Waugh 223 (and more generally, 19, 221–30), Sherborne 18, Ormrod 1987, esp. 416–21. Against such views, contrast the *Brut*'s threnodies for the Black Prince and Edward III, 330 and 333–4, in both instances translating Adam (220, 225, respectively).

26. Cf. the Green Knight's taunt to a fictionalised new/first age, 'Hit arn aboute on þis bench bot berdlez chylder' (280).

27. The original scribe of Fairfax 3 (the *Confessio Amantis* corrected by the Trentham scribe), *c*. 1390?, knows the range of secretary forms, but rarely displays the full lot in conjunction.

28. See Chaplais plate 22a for Hoccleve's engrossing hand (here dated 1415, not identified as Hoccleve); it differs from his absolutely cursive in-house hand, seen in the Privy-seal formulary he copied in British Library, MS Additional 24062. Doyle–Parkes plate 53 (183) shows him in Cambridge, Trinity College, MS R.3.2 (Gower, *Confessio Amantis*); plate 57 (202), a leaf from Arundel 38. For a full reproduction of the autograph poetic manuscripts, in his most formal and studied secretary book-hand (mostly 1422 × 1426), see *Thomas Hoccleve*.

29. On Chandos's 'tact and firmness' in dealing with recently acquired Gascon towns in 1361–2, see Labarge 150, 154, 155. Indeed, he seems to have been the politic brake on the Prince's worst, most excessive impulses.

6

'Ledeþ hire to Londoun þere lawe is yshewed': *Piers Plowman* B, London, 1377

Whatever one may feel about the ambivalences of 'Whan Y woned in Cornhulle' (C 5.1) or about Langland's attitude to the metropolis,[1] his poem, particularly in its B inflection, is a London work and the culmination of Edwardian literature in the City. Evidence for such a siting appears prominently in the manuscript record, as well as inferentially in specific contemporary references inscribed in the poem and surrounding it.

The immediate evidence for Langlandian publication has long since disappeared, and one must recuperate it from books in the main contemporary with early manuscripts of Chaucerian works. The surviving books represent the end of a tradition; for example, as defined by Russell-Kane, at least four or five intermediary copying generations intrude between the poet's C Version and the extant manuscripts. The B Version is much less problematic, embodying some suggestive evidence that at least two copies are second generation.[2]

Initially, firm placement in London depends upon Doyle–Parkes's identification of the hand responsible for an early C Version copy, University of London Library, MS S.L./V.88 ('the Ilchester MS') with their Scribe D, who participated in the Gower of Cambridge, Trinity College, MS R.3.2 (174–82, 206–8, illustrated plate 51 [180]). On the basis of Jeremy Smith's linguistic researches (1983, 1988), which show progressive removal of what may be this scribe's native Worcestershire spelling system, the book probably represents his oldest surviving copying. It thus dates presumptively from some point in the 1390s, an indication of the poem's popularity and speed of dispersal, four or five copying generations in under a decade.

Scribe D will recall, of course, some earlier London scribal careers and textual appropriations. Chapter 1, n. 7 signals, for example, the Worcestershire language ascribed to Auchinleck scribe 2 (LALME LP 6940) and scribe 1's reproduction of south Worcester forms in *Otuel*. Similarly, Auchinleck often relies upon texts otherwise attested in western books such as Digby 86, Harley 2253, or Cambridge, Trinity College, MS B.14.39, some of them filler, and the Black Prince's epitaph can be paralleled in the first of these codices as well.

Further C Version copies can be connected with Ilchester and with London. In similar Worcester language, and from the same exemplar as Ilchester, come Huntington Library, MS HM 143 (X) and the fragment now owned by Martin Schøyen (H) (the former appears in a full, but usually unavailable facsimile; the latter, Hanna 1993, plate facing 1, with information on dialect and affinities at 3–13). Both these hands at least resemble yet another scribe of the Trinity Gower, Doyle–Parkes's B, although more closely each other, raising the possibility that the hands have been commonly influenced by the forms of their shared archetype. The two scribes' mutual attentiveness to details in their archetype is also signalled by their agreement in a sequence of distinctive spellings. As I argue above (p. 74), copyists' imitation of their exemplars may extend well beyond transmission of textual content and include the reproduction of very small details indeed.

With these C Version copies, one might join a later, mixed text. Huntington Library, MS HM 114 (Ht) was copied in the 1420s, by a known metropolitan scribe (to the evidence of Hanna 1989 one should add his stints on London civic documents *c.* 1420). Ilchester and HM 114 show evidence, necessarily, on the basis of these books' production there, London based, of an early effort (given the date of Ilchester, *c.* 1390?) to accommodate an A version to the longer ones (see esp. 1996, 204–6, 212–13).

The B Version manuscripts offer a particularly rich and early trove of evidence for London circulation. Cambridge, Trinity College, MS B.15.17 (W) is certainly in London language, and a script style, particularly in its presentation of the Latin, very reminiscent of Doyle–Parkes scribe B (Turville-Petre and Duggan provide a full facsimile; for a stronger claim that the hand is in fact scribe B's, see Mooney–Horobin).

With W may be associated its four genetic affiliates, at least in part testimony to protracted retention of these archetypes in the metropolitan book-trade:

(1) Huntington Library, MS HM 128 (Hm): although produced up-country (LALME places two scribes in South Warwickshire as LPs 8040 and 6910), its production team was clearly in touch with the City book-trade, and acquired a further London exemplar, close to that available to the scribe of HM 114 in his production of Lambeth Palace Library, MS 491, for the copy of the alliterative *Siege of Jerusalem* here;
(2) Crowley's prints of 1550 (Cr);
(3) the similarly belated Toshiyuki Takamiya, MS 23 (formerly at London, Sion College, S); and
(4) genetically related only in parts of the poem, British Library, MS Additional 35287 (M), parts again in a script Doyle notes as comparable with Scribe B.[3]

W and M share one peculiarity of reproduction. They mark the verse paragraphs of the text not simply with paraph signs, but also set them off with blank lines. This was an important and serious decision, as my student Brian Morgan points out to me; in the usual presentation of *Piers Plowman*, it cost more than half a quire of extra vellum to include those spaces. Beyond its aid to early readers of the poem, it is also an important gesture historically; the earliest *Canterbury Tales* manuscripts, e.g. Hengwrt, adopt this model for spacing – although they restrict it to a situation for which it had earlier been deemed otiose, the presentation of poems in stanzaic forms. (Earlier in the century, the paraph at a stanza head constituted sufficient punctuation.) This feature is recessive everywhere within the tradition of *Piers Plowman*, but appears outside W and M in three further copies, all inferentially of London manufacture:

(1) Bodleian Library, MS Laud misc. 581 (L): still in London *c.* 1540, when either the property of or used by Ralph Coppinger, a customs collector, and integral to the Bale ascriptions to 'Robert Langland' (most of which rely upon Nicholas Brigham, Coppinger's colleague in the Customs) (a full facsimile, Duggan–Hanna, is forthcoming);

(2) Bodleian Library, MS Rawlinson poet. 38 (+British Library, MS Lansdowne 398, fols. 77–80, R), with a layer of London language, but with a Suffolk layer atop that; and
(3) Cambridge, Newnham College, MS 4 (Y).

In addition to this common treatment of paragraphs, R and L share a layer of spellings, in largely identical distribution (Samuels 1985, 241). Since these relationships are distinctive and regular, the two manuscripts must share a common source; yet, since the two copies represent different branches of the B transmission (see *B Version* 25–7, 61–9), this source can only have been Langland's scribal fair-copy. On this basis, one can confirm Kane–Donaldson's view of the state of this archetype, yet simultaneously one might believe that B manuscripts include clearer evidence for constructing a text than either of the other versions. These shared spellings would re-enforce what is evident in the C copies X and H, that the shape of the exemplar influences matters of production, down very small details. On that basis, one might well believe that the paragraphs with blank lines, along with certain other details, further reflect Langland's authorial papers.

Four of the spaced paragraph early London B manuscripts (WMLY, not in this case R) share a further feature, a colophon that identifies the poem as 'dialogus Petri Plowman'.[4] Given that at least two manuscripts with access to authorial papers (L and M) include it, this identification may be inherited from the archetype, in contrast to its subsequent lateral diffusion (like a virus through Y's genetic companions).[5] The colophon responds to one function of paragraphing in the five early London copies that is neither inevitable nor well-precedented (but was again to become a model, e.g. for producers of *The Canterbury Tales*). The five books all use paraphs, typically in rough agreement, to indicate a change of speaker (for these purposes, I've simply surveyed some passages I've recalled as significantly stichomachic).[6] Wherever this procedure originated, and the evidence would suggest that it is likely to be authorial, I think it understands better than many modern commentators what Langland's text was about. One might consider equally prescient the heading to passus 8 in M (it also occurs as an ignored guide for a heading at this point in L, lies behind a heading at the same point in the B-conflated A+C copy Aberystwyth, National Library of Wales, MS 733B, and was still alive in London to be picked up for the same use *c.* 1550 by S and Cr), 'incipit inquisicio prima de dowell'.[7]

These two generic markers, 'dialogus' and 'inquisicio', show the production teams either responding to or passing on Langland's indication of the unfixed and non-visionary properties of the text. On the one hand, the copyists emphasise the inherently talky and oppositional (i.e. 'opposing' in the grammar-school/Oxford sense, engaging in disputation; cf. 7.144) nature of the poem – about the only thing plentiful in Langland's world is talk. But this designation also attends to the poem's persistent refusal to settle upon the monologic closure of conventional dream poetry, and its equal refusal to reveal a way of shutting off its discursive openness (cf. Middleton 1982). ('Dialogus' is, of course, not a widely attested English title, but it's worth noting that it does designate a legal/clerical work, on Exchequer procedure.)[8]

Simultaneously, some scribes found at least later stages of the narrative an open-ended 'inquisition' (and no B copy calls it a 'vita') – certainly it's predicated upon search procedures. Perhaps, given the legalistic background that hovers all around the poem (and includes its transmitters and audience, as well as its author), the copyists sought to draw attention to the work as baldly 'inquiry' or even 'judicial inquiry, an inquest'. That Langland's whole production might have been a 'visio', with all the extraterrestriality that implies, is foreign to the early London book-producers (who generally restrict that terminology to the headings for the first two dreams).[9] Such language certainly sets copies of this poem apart from the Literature by this time circumambient in London – developing Chaucerianism – and indicates the necessity, in contemporary terms, of overmarking the text by any means at one's disposal. This act would (hopefully) ensure the legibility of its procedures.

I'll return to the implications of the 'dialogus' and 'inquisicio' headings, but for now, consider some early local knowledge of the text in London. As has become apparent in the last decade or so, the usual placements of Langland have significant chronological blindspots. In spite of his great services to *Piers Plowman*, John Burrow's powerful arguments for a 'Ricardian poetry' have not well served the poem, in his reading treated as if a *fin-de-siècle* production. Langland is only incidentally and peripherally 'Chaucer's contemporary', as J. A. W. Bennett would have it; his career had, in the main, ended in autumn 1377 when

247

he published (a locution the evidence above allows me to use deliberately) the B Version. The C text, always taken as the product of some portion of the (Ricardian) 1380s, suggests a desultory, if sporadically intense, engagement with the work.[10]

Hence, any putative dialogue between Chaucer and Langland, as I will indicate shortly, is at best a monologue, Chaucer's effort to escape the Bloomian shadowing cherub of his predecessor. As Langland carefully suggests early on, he looks towards some normative state of things back past 'þe pestilence tyme' (Pro. 84). Thus, *Piers* might more profitably considered a work more distinctively 'Edwardian' than 'Ricardian' in its focus. As Nevill Coghill pointed out more than half a century ago, in Langland's precursor poem from the fifties, *Winner and Waster*, Edward III is virile and powerful.

It's very easy to demonstrate the Edwardian situation of *Piers* B in another way – the latest incontrovertible historical reference in the text. This passage, inserted into the old A prologue – if it were Chaucerian, one would follow Barry Windeatt in calling it 'ineching' (and one might consider where Chaucer discovered that compositional technique?) – places the poem at a specific social faultline. The discernible end of Langland's poetic composition is very precisely the end of Edward III. Langland did not even revise out in the C version (3. 164) a reference (or indeed a full characterisation) that clearly identifies Edward as The King. The latest historical references to which all can agree concern the death of the old king and the political turmoil of his last year, the Good Parliament and John of Gaunt's quarrel with the City of London.[11]

A concatenation of such detail appears scattered through Pro.112–45, for example:

> . . . iustus es, esto pius!
> Nudum ius a te vestiri vult pietate . . . .
> Si seritur pietas de pietate metas.
> (134–5, 138)

The passage resembles an account of a ten-year-old boy, nude to his shirt, being instructed by a bishop as he is being anointed and before he is reclothed in the regalia which will mark his office:

> Lord, cause this same blessing to penetrate even to the inner places of his heart, to the extent that by this visible and tangible gift he may

perceive invisible things, and having administered his worldly realm with justice and moderation, that he may earn the right to rule with you in eternity.

The child is seminude and vulnerable, shielded from watching eyes by magnates holding rich cloths. This symbolic collation is intended to ensure that he will remember not to use *nudum ius*, for he should not render his subjects equally vulnerable. While verbally not so exact as one might wish, the echo becomes compelling in its narrative context. For Walsingham's account includes a king constantly 'ladde' by 'knyȝthod' (Pro.112, cf. Walsingham 331, 337); entertained both by an angel offering him a crown (Pro.128ff., cf. Walsingham 332) and by an episcopal sermon 'to the people, concerning the king and the realm, how the king should comport himself towards the people, and in what things the people were obliged to obey the king' ('de materia Regis et regni ad populum, qualiter Rex se haberet in populo, et in quibus populus sibi debuit obedire', *ibid.*); and preceded in his return to Westminster Hall by 'a great number of performers of a diverse sort' ('magno numero diversi generis histrionum' – I would imagine the lunatic and 'Goliardeis' of Pro.123, 139; cf. Walsingham 337). These correspondences, first noted long ago by J. A. W. Bennett (1943, 57), are to events surrounding Richard II's Westminster Abbey coronation, 16 July 1377.[12]

Moreover, the Goliardeis's address Langland reports includes some rather antique echoes. 'Dum rex a regere . . .' (Pro. 141–2), for example, finds a corollary in John Walwayn's discussion of Edward II's tyranny, supposedly quoting a letter sent the king by one of his confessors:

> As long as a king may be said to rule as one might expect, to govern his people by laws and defend them from enemies by the sword, so long as he rules well, he is appropriately called king; so long as he plunders his people, he is rather judged to be a tyrant.[13]

While the Goliardeis may be urging strict justice, Walwayn's citation would combine his counsel with the milder angelic instruction received by Langland's king. Simultaneously, this passage in Walwayn appears juxtaposed with one relevant to the succeeding discussion of royal justice in passus 4, a Walter Map-inspired court satire, ascribing to excessive engagement with *munera* the conclusion that 'tota iniquitas originaliter exiit de curia' (74). Not only does the account allude to Richard's coronation, but it invokes discourses deeply embedded in Edwardian culture.

But of course, this is not Langland's only depiction of 'founding the commonwealth'. I pass over 6.7–58 (Piers in the halfacre, yet another piece of B 'ineching' in the interests of clarifying themes and connectives) to the reprise of both passages, at 19.200–337. Here Grace shares his gifts with different social orders, and founding this commune is closely associated with the four cardinal virtues, as it is in the Prologue. There, the virtues appear immediately before the 'foundation' passage (at Pro.100–11). The description of B 19 represents an allegorical advance on the Prologue precisely because, among other things, it integrates what the earlier passage merely associates.

But this description also might derive, as historical allusion, from the same moment described in the Prologue, Richard's coronation. For at that point in the actual *ordo* of the service when Richard was anointed, not only did archbishop Sudbury pray that he would rule 'with justice and moderation', he offered this prayer in the name of the Paraclete and, once he'd smeared little Richard, the entire clerical party sang – as Conscience instructs the commune to do at 19.209–10 – the hymn 'Veni creator spiritus'. (See Simpson 1993 for a different effort at associating the passage with London, in this case with events of the early 1380s.)

Thus B's conclusion and its revised opening can be viewed as precisely contemporary. The poem was finished, both in terms of its inner chronology and of its imaginative structure, at a single moment. And while, in strict logical terms, summer 1377 might be only a *terminus a quo*, it is the point at which the B Version achieved imaginative stasis. As the last datable references in B, the two passages indicate succinctly Langland's chronological affinities with the reign of Edward III, his productive career bracketed neatly between 'þe pestilence tyme' and the old king's passing.

However, Langland's B Version, at least, had a literary public. The earliest evidence for it is not that customarily cited, most especially in Steve Justice's fine study, but is local, London, and perhaps to circulating pre-publication materials. As part of 'ineching' and expanding the A Prologue into the B version, Langland retells the fable of the rats' longing to bell the cat (146–210). These materials cannot have been written any earlier than 1372 or 1373, since both

Ther þe cat is a kitoun, þe court is ful elenge...
Ve terre vbi puer Rex est [et cuius principes mane comedunt]
(194, 195a, the concluding 'etc.' expanded from Eccles. 10:16)

and the reference to 'þe cat of þe court þat kan yow ouerlepe' (200) refer presciently to events I have highlighted in the last chapter – to a moribund Black Prince, a minority succession, and magnatial (here the hated John of Gaunt?) machinations for personal advantage in a now inevitable interregnum.[14] The locally allusive efficacy of the passage will only have increased as the Black Prince's death became more certain (moving towards the event, 8 June 1376).

As is well recognised, there is a second outstanding contemporary use of the same fable. This occurred in a sermon delivered by Thomas Brinton, bishop of Rochester, on 18 May 1376 (2, 315–21). Brinton, a supporter of reform, was urging his audience to be 'doers of the work', not 'forgetful hearers' (phrases from his sermon-text, James 1:25). From the perspective of this proof-text, his mice prove a negative example; they have all the right intentions, but they give up when it comes to doing the deed.

Immediately upon concluding his version of the fable, Brinton continues:

> People frequently use the proverb, 'Do well and have well' (prouer-bialiter solet dici, Benefac et bene habe'). Every sermon is spoken to this end, that the audience learns how it should work well, and after performing good works, should hope for a reward.[15]

This is yet a further allusion to Langland:

> 'Peter' quod þe preest þoo, 'I kan no pardon fynde
> But do wel and haue wel, and god shal haue þi soule'.
> (7.115–16, but cf. also A 8.97–8)

Moreover, it is an allusion precise and contextually apt, for the pardon from Truth ostensibly discusses the reward Piers's workmen are to gain for their good works, their aid in the field. Further, the cleric and the poet are not quite 'frequent users' of a common folk-source, for this is not, whatever Brinton says, a common proverb in English,[16] and the preacher's reference involves a cloaked (perhaps charitable) reticence. The only earlier use of the English proverb I know appears in British

Library, MS Egerton 613, fol. 5 (s. xiii med.), in a mainly Anglo-Norman (but in fact trilingual) tract for nuns, where it is cited in a similar context of eternal reward for (and divine sustenance in) avoiding sin.[17]

It is hard to see how Brinton might have known this argument, unless Langland was a parliamentary or royal clerk, or unless his circle of patronage was somehow among those clerks attached to episcopal townhouses along the Strand. But in any case, Brinton is engaged in an implicit refutation of Langland's poem at a politically fraught moment of confrontation, in many ways more dangerous than the comparable Denia affair (cf. 'What þis metels bymeneþ . . . | Deuyne ye, for I ne dar', Pro.209–10). Brinton's was not an open address, say at St Paul's Cross, but one delivered to a private audience, the Clergy in convocation before the Good Parliament. He was actively engaged in urging restraints on court power and the purging of royal cronies profiting from their familiarity during Edward III's dotage. Brinton's side won temporarily in the spring of 1376, but they could not press their advantage; John of Gaunt had undone their perceived reforms within fifteen months – one should think to the satisfaction of the poet.

Although he is the accused, not the respondent, here, Langland's reading of the fable devastatingly exposes Brinton, whatever his stock as moralist (and his sermon contains a bold and unveiled attack on Alice Perrers),[18] as at best an unrealistic fabulist. Both writers can agree on one thing, that the rats are unrealistically stupid and short-sighted. But Langland offers a critique that eludes Brinton, that the rats are (as Given-Wilson's analysis, cited n. 14, implies might have been the case) incriminatingly self-motivated. Their anti-feline oppositionalism is predicated only on their own desire to partake of limited social perquisites, and they seek only the free right of pillage others now enjoy. In such a context, centrally imposed disorder, random but dispersed predation by a single cat, should be preferred to complete deregulation, every rat for herself, no law at all. While perhaps a bow to cynical *Realpolitik*, this cooperative conservatism redounds through the poem. And however one chooses to assess this moment of political crisis, it lies near those impulses that created *Piers Plowman*, a poem that in its B Version begins and terminates on a London afternoon in July 1377 and had been known in some form in London for more than a year previously.

II

As a final foray into Langland/Chaucer relations, I begin discussing *Piers* at – or very near – the beginning:

> Persons and parisshe preestes pleyned hem to þe bisshop
> That hire parisshe were pouere siþ þe pestilence tyme,
> To haue a licence and leue at London to dwelle,
> To syngen for symonie for siluer is swete. (Pro.83–6)

One can inflect this with a second well-known text:

> He sette nat his benefice to hyre
> And leet his sheep encombred in the myre
> And ran to Londoun unto Seinte Poules
> To seken hym a chaunterie for soules,
> Or with a bretherhed to been withholde;
> But dwelte at hoom and kepte wel his folde.
> ('General Prologue' 507–12)

The first detail one learns of the next Canterbury pilgrim, of course, is that he is the Parson's 'brother' ('General Prologue' 529). This is, of course, the Plowman, usually accepted as a Langlandian rip-off. Here Chaucer 'does Langland': the portraits are overtly tautological because they are thoroughly exemplaristic, a deliberate flattening out of Chaucer's normal Prologue rhetoric, courtly diction, 'the beste style I kan' misapplied (paraphrasing the 'Thopas'–'Melibee' link 2117). This intertextuality can run only one way: Chaucer 'does Langland' and not the reverse. The lines from *Piers*, after all, go back without change to the earliest, perhaps 1360s, state of the poem (cf. A Pro.80–3).

Chaucer's portrait of the Parson, of course, is immensely successful. It works by combining two features foreign to *Piers Plowman*. On the one hand, there's its wonderful specificity, the poet's ability to imagine where, if you wanted them, you would find your really neat, cushy London chantry spots, their pleasures underlined by the delicious metrical expansion of 'chaunterie'. And this oscillates with Chaucer's exemplarism, the universalising rhetoric of pastor, sheep, and wolf. This I would see as that typical bow to the universal, 'the effect of the Literary' – which allows Chaucer to deliberately programme the success of his own reception.

But it's easy to miss the comparable variety of Langlandian specificity. Chaucer assumes with the anti-Parson, as he does for all his pilgrims, his characters' independent agency – here, as most frequently, *pace* recent readings of Canterbury community, antisocially expressed. His character can ramble, *leet* 'abandon' his sheep in the rural *myre* the Plowman – diking, delving, and mucking – knows only too well. And he can do so because he's a Parson, the *persona* with right of appointment to his church, capable of 'setting his benefice to hire', signing on a cheap curate for the job, without *lette* 'hindrance'. But Langland's lines are equally knowing and specific, if not about things the tradition Chaucer has established as English Literature teaches one to admire.

One thing Langland knows is that you can't, with impunity, just up and abandon the flock in Bromsgrove for the Bright Lights. To leave, you must have 'a licence and leue', formal papers. And to get those, you must follow a fixed code of procedure: you have to supplicate – and convince – your 'ordinary', the bishop of your diocese. Chaucer may, in the Parson's portrait, pick up on Langland's aversion to wandering, but he doesn't appear to have a clue about the legalities involved. Langland lives in a world with books like episcopal registers (not Dante) and knows things in a differently intimate way.

Chaucer's bad Parson, the shepherd playing false to the flock, misses out yet a further Langlandian specificity. Chaucer's effect, Literature, situates abandonment in the context of transhistorical Christian duty, something of a piece with his Monk's evocation of the textual *locus classicus*, Benedict's Rule chapter 1 ('General Prologue' 177–88). Langland's malcontents, in contrast, respond to a specific historical moment, 'siþ þe pestilence tyme'. Disaster does not concern any very longue duree but the last twenty-odd years. Through this reference, Langland creates a readily assimilable memorial space within which one might apprehend normative social relations, a space extending back to the blush of Edwardian triumph, Crécy in 1346.

As it continues in the B Version, the passage further specifies the disaster of 1348:

> Bisshopes and bachelers, boþe maistres and doctours,
> That han cure vnder crist and crownynge in tokene
> And signe þat þei sholden shryuen hire parisshens,
> Prechen and praye for hem, and þe pouere fede,
> Liggen at Londoun in Lenten and ellis.
> Somme seruen *þe king* and *his* siluer tellen.
> (Pro.87–92, my emphasis)

Note the jarring effect of that third non-alliterating stave. The A Version, much more compact, is thoroughly explicit about the process, e.g. 'I sauȝ bisshopis bolde and bacheleris of deuyn | *Become clerkis of acountis þe king for to serue*' (Pro.91–2, the same construction repeated with 'clerkis of þe Kinges Bench' in 93–5). Among the effects claimed for 1348 Langland presents an undesirable polysemy which has intruded upon a proper clerical 'service': priests leave the *cura animarum* to be administrators.

This move, typifying of *Piers Plowman*, I would identify as the Langlandian nostalgic imaginary, a legally and historically informed one. For while one might somehow believe that everything was just ticketyboo in the 1340s, it wasn't so because there were no ecclesiastical administrators in royal service or because the ubiquitous late medieval crossover of governmental and ecclesiastical careers had never occurred. In chapter 3 (pp. 126–8), I discussed the families of Yorkshire clerks who entered royal service as early as the 1290s. As I have indicated, such people were useful, not simply because they came 'free', supported by their diocesan endowments instead of royal grants, but because they knew the job. They had run efficient chanceries of their own (dealing, for example, with those petitioning parish priests, the antitype of Chaucer's Parson), on whose careful practices royal administration could be modelled.

But the word 'clerk' itself is the real focus of this imaginary and of its nostalgia. Langland badly wants to inflect this word in the direction of Latin *clericus*, to fix it back within that etymological sense – and implicitly, to inveigh against a social neologism – 'clericus id est clark', if you will. But just as the history of English administration would argue that *Piers Plowman* misrepresents the revolution of 1348, so also Langland's etymology runs defiantly against the grain of all previous Middle English usage. Before Langland, Middle English 'clerk' most normally means 'administrator'.

This quibble, out of which, in some way, Langland generated the first major non-translated Middle English narrative poem, precisely addresses the disaffections inherent in discovering the profitability of being learned. However things should have been, smart guys ended up being interchangeably 'clerical' *and* enmeshed in the world of 'business'. The problem isn't – as in Old Historical versions – that of an unbeneficed clerical underclass, but precisely of employments themselves.

255

This emphasis should be perceived as an especially local response to a universal curial problem. I use the adjective 'curial' designedly, for the word embodies an ambiguity of romance (curia = court) and religious (cura animarum) implication similar to that of clark/clerk. In a situation of spiritual need/dearth, Clergy, that capacity to guide discourse, to order and to transmit the world of knowledge, has uncomfortably shifted its bearings. Langland contemplates what ensues when the most qualified respond simply to dearth, limited resources, the 'pouere parisshe', and pursue material fulfilment alone. In so doing, clerks abandon the discursive, leave it to proliferate without regulation, almost as a randomly generating engine. Passus 20, the poet's farewell to his project, provides one obvious version of what might ensue in such a state – to paraphrase Eliot, the ruins the poem's dream-fragments try in every way to avoid.

Certainly, preceding chapters have passed among a variety of comparable visions of history. Like Arnald Thedmar (or indeed, Auchinleck romanciers), Langland visualises proper historical innovation as essentially 'ineching', a filling in of what has always been implicit yet heretofore unstated or unrealised. It rounds out, fills the cracks in a (perhaps as yet unperceived as incomplete) discursive whole. Other modes of innovation will, from such a perspective, appear catastrophe, abuse, enormity.

Thus, Langland stands quite against the Chaucerian projective, the imagination of a literary future. This goes so far as to attempt (as *Piers* never does) real prophecy, as Chaucer imagines extending his authority/iality beyond the grave to literary Fame. In contrast, readers of *Piers Plowman* need to recognise and define the interests of this self-bounded and retrospective Langlandian Other.

Langland was very nearly a full generation older than Chaucer, perhaps as old as seventeen or eighteen at the younger poet's birth. And he had already experienced adult frustrations; by the time he writes the C Version, 'siþ þe pestilence tyme' has segued into 'seth my frendes deyede' (5.40) and the apparent failure of his expectations. Further, he may have been active as a poet in London from sometime in the 1360s, before, so far as is now apparent, little Geoffrey had ever written a line. But equally, he may have begun writing only in his forties, and thus, with very different conceptions of procedure than those growing up to write around him.

I merely point to one further example of shrouded indebtedness, hidden under a different modality. Chaucer may in actual fact have been podgy, but even if he wasn't, he would necessarily have had to be in his poetry simply to indicate that he wasn't a 'long lean Langland'. When the Host reveals Chaucer's well-shaped waist, he begins his inquiry, 'What man artou?' (Prologue to 'Thopas' 1885). But, in one of those passages Middleton has singled out as an 'authorial signature' (1990, 38–41, 80), the question, 'What/who art þou' signals the earlier poet's failure to recognise his self-image, Thought, 'a muche man, me þou3te lik to myselue' (8.72, 74, 70). This echo suggests reopening the issue of *Piers Plowman* and its contribution in a different context, an antique pre-Chaucerian one.

In this situation, the old Bloomfield dictum, '*Piers Plowman*...a commentary on an unknown text', points to the conditions of Langlandian textuality as incomprehensible. But to it, one might poise an alternative siting, Muscatine's 'poetry of crisis', the confrontation of various discursive possibilities, as put in play in the critical historical juncture 1376–8. In the remainder of the chapter, I examine confrontations in the poem that enunciate discursive collisions, particularly confrontations between and within the two nodes of early London writing I have been discussing, romance and devotional literature.[19]

At least one guiding principle is that the poem offers an adequate commentary on its own effects and was intended to communicate. Consequently, Langland's frequent inexplicitness about his own procedures implies a knowing audience, individuals who respond to a shared sense of implication, not to the more overt markings which characterise familiar Chaucerian and later medieval English poetry. If the poem describes a crisis, it was written precisely because, in a situation of emergency, its audience represented a disappearing cadre.

But equally, the poem may only have been intelligible to a similarly trained and disposed audience, one equally in touch with the curial, the religio-/administrative clergial. Langland's target readers had to have been too much like Langland himself. The poem's demise as a central English text, under the pressure of developing circumambient 'Ricardian poetry', may reflect the cadre addressed, men of similar age and experience, like the Chandos Herald, a predictably antiquated and dying breed.[20]

III

If *Piers Plowman* is a 'dialogus', one prominent dialogic nexus in the poem is provided by the confrontation of the two centres of early London writing. Langland accepts the presumptions of anti-romance prologues (cf. pp. 149–52), but only insofar as he sees master genres, a religious discourse predicated upon bible-history and the secular history of romance, in confrontation. He rejects, however, the prioritisation of earlier instructional efforts and subjects religious discourse to the world's fictions – or attempts an economy, discursive and spiritualised, that would include both. His writing thus represents a mix derivative of Edwardian curial Anglo-Latin, e.g. Walter de Milemete, John Walwayn, or William of Paull, figures who perceive no difficulty in aligning bible and romance. Yet writing in a political situation in which he must acknowledge the confrontational nature of 'dialogus', the difficulty of this mixture provides a centre of contention, initially played out in the collision of Conscience's sober biblicism with the allure of Meed, the perhaps too accommodating *grande dame*.

Not only 'dialogus' but also the quasi-legalistic 'inquisicio' comes into play here. The latter, of course, addresses the claims of government and the Common Law, the romance involvement with heritage and succession. Langland is unwilling to commit himself squarely to the conventions of the London discourses of religious instruction, nor completely to deny their possible efficacy. Rather, in both these and in the discourse of romance he finds confirmatory challenges to notions of responsible Christian action.

Among her many seminal contributions to understanding the poem, Anne Middleton has highlighted its affinity to romance narration (1982a, 95–8, 103–8; 1982b, 114–17). In her account, the poem's basic form is the *roman d'aventure*, the note struck as early as 'a ferly of fairye' (Pro.6) (cf. Vance Smith 2001, 85–6, 89, 144). The line alludes to the accepted Ur-romance narrative, the knight and the elf-queen, exemplified in *Launfal* (Marie's or its translation), 'Sir Thopas' (more constructively 'The Wife of Bath's Tale'), and *The Faerie Queene*. But there's a twist in Langland's 'knight's tale' here, the dreamer's shock and distaste when he sees his local dream version – 'I was afered of hire face þei3 she fair weere' (1.10) – indicative of a disjunction to be accommodated.

I here consider Langland's bout with the 'romantic' within one particularly influential formulation, the alliterative tradition, a topic with, of course, a venerable history. Ever since Oakden, distinguished critics have sought to assess the debt of *Piers Plowman* to the alliterative movement. It is simply too large a poem (and too major an intellectual statement) to pass up. And yet virtually every study has ended in frustration; *Piers* seems too aberrant – too much out of touch with the stylistic and historical imperatives of the 'central works' – to really fit into going models of what Middle English alliterative poetry is about.

But past associations of Langland and his poem have significant geographical and chronological blindspots. Unlike the poems to which it has usually been compared, *Piers* is both a southerly poem, however one wants to define that, and an early one. Langland is variously placeable either in the old home of continuous alliterative composition, the diocese of Worcester, or in western Oxfordshire, or in London. Most helpfully, as Nevill Coghill pointed out more than half a century ago, the poem might be considered distinctively Edwardian, its origins intimately connected with using as model *Winner and Waster*, a mid-century poem with some signs of Western circulation.

Thus, *Piers Plowman* is significantly older than any other alliterative poem scholars have taken as usefully comparable. The relevant comparison class cannot include those 'Ricardian' poems most typically invoked – the *Gawain*-group, *Morte Arthure*, *The Wars of Alexander* – while it should include, in addition to *Winner* (in its surviving Yorkshire form probably no more than one step removed from a copying near the Severn) and the north Gloucestershire *William of Palerne*. Significantly, *Piers* has more in common, stylistically and metrically, with the latter work than with any text of the later 'central tradition'. This will seem dispiriting to many, because it removes *Piers* from comparison with 'literary monuments', works deemed of comparable grandeur (cf. Hussey 1965). But there is worse news still, for the other relevant comparisons would be to alliterative poems distinctly ephemeral – the fragmentary 'Wit and Will', the 'historical poems' of Harley 2253, or the alliterative poems praising Edward III's military achievements composed by Laurence Minot (known only in British Library, MS Cotton Galba E.ix, a manuscript associable with the family of the Yorkshire, and Exchequer, clerk John de Markenfield; see p. 127).

Langland may have begun writing his poem in the sixties. But 'begin' is the operative term: *Piers Plowman*, from modern historical retrospect, is what was promulgated in 1377. Yet the poem obviously started as something considerably less grandiose, and probably something more typical than the aggregate eventually became. I imagine this as an effort initially considered just a one-off, a single-vision poem (one of Langland's great innovations, after all, is his profusion of linked visions). And the most obvious such vision to consider is the first, Pro.-passus 4. This episode, leading up to the equivocal banishment from Court of the character Lady Meed 'reward', is typically alliterative in subject. All the relevant Edwardian predecessor texts (the atypically escapist Frenchy romance *William* needs to be ignored) fall into one category, 'discussions of contemporary conditions' and of wars and politics.

The Meed episode has long implicitly been recognised as the poem's 'alliterative' centre. Old-fashioned positivistic searches for the 'alliterative Langland' have focussed upon 'alliterative diction', and their examples have tended to derive, in the main unconsciously, from the description of Meed's activities (e.g. Burrow 1957, 380–2; Vance Smith 2001, *passim*). Indeed, given his usual métier, Langland overmarks the narrative as 'alliterative' at the head of passus 3: e.g. 'murþe and mynstralcie' (11, cf. 220), 'busked hem to þe bour' (14), 'men on þis molde' (80), 'And brou3te hire to boure wiþ blisse and wiþ ioye' (103), 'menske þee wiþ 3iftes' (184), 'kyng of þat kiþ' (204), etc., etc.

But at a verbal level, the debate between Meed and Conscience is marked by rather more commonplace alliterative usage, scarcely ornate enough to draw into the ambit of *The Wars of Alexander* (although in fact *Wars* 11–14 uses similar phrasing to identify its central subject). At the start of *Winner and Waster*, Langland's most accomplished predecessor identifies a modern world of disaster:

> For nowe alle es witt and wyles that we with delyn,
> Wyse wordes and slee and icheon wryeth othere.
> (5–6)

The poet of *Winner* here plays off the conventional opposition of 'wit' and 'will'. In modern conditions, the former, which should mean something like 'reason' (the basic clerical virtue), has degenerated into sharp practice, the activity of 'wise guys'. This collocation underwrites the ubiquitous vision of disaster in alliterative texts of the generation preceding *Piers*; untrammelled personal interest, what should be an oppositional 'will' to be squelched, has overwhelmed, indeed come to pass for wise behaviour. For example, in the Harley 2253 'Song of the husbandman', an important model for Langland's character Peace, and later his Piers:

> þus wil walkeþ in lond and wondred ys wene,
> Falsshipe fatteþ ant marreþ wyþ myht.
> (31–2)

Or in the Harley prophecy of 'Thomas of Erceldoun', which sees an apocalyptic millennium

> When wyt ant wille erres [ayres 'travel'] togedere.
> (5)

Or in 'Wit and Will':

> By Witte þe wise kyng wele mai we trow
> Ilkane wey in þe werlde þat wilnes þe right,
> þat bothe leute and loue louies with herte
> And leues on þar lefte hoende alle lither redes.
> (fragment G/3–6)

From early in his narrative about Lady Meed, Langland exposes the reader to a category dislocation like that described by his predecessors. Theology expresses what should be the conventional equation, 'Wercheþ by wisdom and by wit also' (2.134). In (momentary) contrast, False and Meed's chartering is the documentary instantiation of wille 'desire' (2.67). But in Langland's poem, such clear-cut probity is only momentary; later in the sequence (4.70), the wise guys Wit and Wisdom will soberly counsel Wrong to offer compensatory payment, because 'Whoso wercheþ by wille, wraþe makeþ ofte'. This mixed diction should remind one of that coalescence of categories like Truth and Guile in *Beves* and other Auchinleck romances, where it marks tensions within the aristocratic life.

Further, the passage from *Winner and Waster* I cite above eventually defines Langland's C text depiction of his persona. The *Winner*-poet continues:

Dare neuer no westren wy while this werlde lasteth
Send his sone southewarde to see ne to here,
That he ne schall be holden byhynde when he hore eldes.
(7–9)

At least in the retrospective version of his career, Langland/Wille has become the ill-fated son, bereft of the supportive provincial lineage *Winner* wishes were normative. In C passus 5, being 'holden byhynde' has become the dreamer's fate, his major effort to demonstrate that he is put upon, not profligate Prodigal Son in a world of want, and that his poem results from the failures of older proprieties.

In apparent contrast to *Piers, Winner and Waster* is a *jeu d'esprit*, a debate between two equally powerful imperatives for magnates: (1) to manage your estate efficiently and expropriate as much as you can out of land and tenants; (2) to spend and demonstrate your standing through sumptuous show (cf. Vance Smith 2003, esp. 62–107). The judgement this poet's king, Edward III, offers (456–503) comically ratifies one version of Edwardian policy (it resurfaces in Meed's discussion of the Brétigny campaign of 1359–60 at 3.189–208): to pillage folks on the continent in order to support domestic sumptuousness, the pleasures of Cheap. The poet, as well as an alliterative writer like Laurence Minot, may have been amused, but I'm sure some of Edward III's continental acquaintance, e.g. Norman peasants or the Bardi bankers off in Florence, did not find such a shrewd policy a laughing matter.

The debate between Conscience and Meed is, of course, central to Langland's first vision. It has quite typically not been read against its alliterative background, as a debate, but over-moralised by critics into straightforward venality satire. But it becomes considerably more interesting, if one sees it through the rules of Middle English debate poetry (and those of *Winner*), rules consonant with Langland's generic identification of his poem as 'dialogus'.[21]

This term identifies a form more conflictual than does one like 'lecture' or 'oration'. Implicitly, in such a text, finding Truth is a property of dialectic, of reading logically between statements and attending to their contextual siting – a discursive confrontation voiced within a dramatic situation. Dialogues are supposed to be reasonably equal contests, the interlocutors evenly poised and evenly self-interested. As such, the form directs one towards a Truth conditional, rather than absolute. Most frequently, dialogues emphasise the very machinations of argument – how to use rhetoric, how to co-opt your opponent's best arguments for your own side, and how to score points. Thus, debate is intellectual play and its interests most typically speculative, rather than definitional or definitive. It is precisely given to the occasional, in the case of *Winner* – and I would think the Ur-*Piers* – the demands of the moment, including the historical moment.

A postmodern version of this poetic would say that debates treat bipolar opposites whose identities are fully constituted by and depend upon the other half of the opposition for stability. Thus, each side must ceaselessly ratify (if not in fact turn into) the other. The medieval statement is Waster's:

> Whoso wele schal wyn, a wastour moste he fynde,
> For if it greues one gome it gladdes anoþer.
> (390–1)

And *Piers Plowman* equally toys with this feature in the irritated initial resolution (couched in an alliterative language of conciliation) proposed by Langland's Edward:

> Cesseþ; . . . I suffre yow no lenger;
> Ye shul sauȝten forsoþe and serue me boþe.
> (4.1–2)

Following *Winner*, the Meed-Conscience debate relies upon concerns about noble behaviour integral to Edwardian alliterative poetry. Langland addresses magnatial activities and responsibilities in their relation to the discourses of two laws, the Bible and Common Law. Early in this vision, Holychurch has attacked finance and a money-based economy; she argues that coin/money is not a divinely created necessity but, citing Matt. 22:21 *'Reddite Cesari'* (1.52), a convention of the secular state. Logically, Holychurch must thus always oppose Meed, as outside the spiritual economy (and in the overwrought language of 2.20–35, the genealogical lineage) she administers; she speaks the univocal language of earlier anti-romance prologues, or the London *Simonie*. Yet equally, she has acknowledged the presence of a sphere, not her domain, in which coin might have power.

The subsequent debate analyses her querulousness, its terms posed by two questions. The first of these is indirect, 'and whos wif she were' (whose wife should Meed be?, 2.18), and the second of dominion: who is 'wel worþi þe maistrie to haue'? (3.239, Bx).[22] These are different formulations of the same issue – is Meed to be considered a tractable dependent, securely governed by a trustworthy husband? And if so, who – False or Conscience? Or is she simply a 'loose woman', independent and thus of dubious morals, an ungovernable and disruptive force to be excluded utterly from considerations of state?

As Langland proposes it here, the issue is one internal to aristocratic life and one of the great social topics of the fourteenth century. It is adumbrated in the opening vision of *Winner and Waster* – retainership and other relations of protected dependency. At the opening of *Winner*, the sleeping poet sees two private armies, lords leading their retinues, on the verge of war; within England, such an act was inherently treasonable, encroaching a prerogative reserved to the king and violating a 'peace' viewed as a royal property ('the king's peace'). In one leading social perception of the period 1320–50, the most flagrant forms of lawlessness were perpetrated by those in fact responsible for law and order, local lords, 'fur collar crime', as Barbara Hanawalt has put it (1998, 53–69).[23]

The language of retainership suffuses Langland's entire account of Meed. The sleeping Wille is instructed to observe 'whiche þei ben alle | That longen to [Meed and False's] lordshipe, þe lasse and þe moore' (2.44–5). He immediately notices 'al þe riche retenaunce þat regneþ with Fals' (2.54–5). And retinue language constantly recurs in the passage: 'þe route' (2.62), 'al þis meynee' (2.185), 'þe tail' (2.186), 'his felawship' (2.210). But, of course, all retinues exist and are sustained by monetary relations, fees (most typically in Meed's account presented as 'free gifts', e.g. 2.147–50) paid in recompense for services rendered. Thus, Meed asserts a common fourteenth-century perception when she claims that her rewards are the very glue of social life:

> The kyng haþ mede of his men to make pees in londe.
> (3.220, cf. 209–10)

As has long been recognised (see p. 37), Meed to some extent reflects the contemporary political scene. Her real-life referent is Alice Perrers, a villain for the Good Parliament. The episode, although cast in more general terms, uses Meed/Alice to analyse the outrage that, in the crisis of

1376, greeted royal favourites, political grafters and influence peddlars. Discussion of coin, ultimately to be focussed in a monetarised justice system, presents factional problems created by magnatial power.[24]

Yet Conscience is equally a party to events of 1376, not the unequivocally privileged speaker customary in over-moralised readings. His introduction as 'a [king's] kny3t . . . cam late fro biyonde' (3.110) associates him with failed English military efforts in France, 1372–4 (including those of John of Gaunt). For Holmes (1975, 21–33, cf. 51–62, 155–6), these form an 'essential condition' underlying the June 1376 outrage of City merchants and shire knights. In his role as king's knight, Conscience might, as much as Meed, be a subject of critiques the Good Parliament levelled at the court party (not to mention the suspicion of Langland's king).

Further, past failures might motivate his clear sense of probity and his enmity towards Meed. In 1376, a king's knight might feel abandonment: Alice and her ilk's search for personal profit could be perceived as producing a cash shortfall that hamstrung royally sponsored militarism (cf. Holmes 1975, 78–9 with pp. 128–9). Thus, Conscience enunciates royalist views one might find attractive but also compromised. One might see these as just as befuddled as his French campaigning had been, his outraged messianic idealism never quite addressing the contemporary conditions out of which Meed emerges, only wishing they were (?cataclysmically) replaced.[25]

One problem with the debate here is the relative, rather than absolute, status of the issues discussed. In 3.220, Mede identifies herself with those 'gifts' that bind all retinues, royal as well as magnatial. But the difficulty she ignores is the fine line that divides confederacy, social bonding, from conspiracy, fellowships pledged to an extra-legal act. Ultimately, the Meed–Conscience debate slides into examination of the second of these problems, an easy slide signalled by:

> Yet I may as I my3te menske þee wiþ 3iftes
> And *mayntene* þi manhode moore þan þow knowest
> (3.184–5).
>
> *
>
> I wolde be wroken of þo wreches þat wercheþ so ille
> And doon hem hange by þe hals and alle þat hem *mayntneþ*.
> (2.196–7)

The Middle English term 'maintenance' is not just, as Meed uses it, a colourless noun referring to 'support', but a legalism. Coke defines it as 'a taking in hand, bearing up or upholding of quarrels and sides, to the disturbance or hindrance of common right' (Alford 1988a, 94–5). A 'maintainer' is one who supports others in their legal cases, ones to which s/he is not properly a party; such a person implicitly violates one of the most basic rules of Langland's communal foundation –

> Shopen lawe and leaute eche lif to knowe his owene
> (Pro.122) –

for maintenance is not knowing (or wilfully ignoring) the boundaries of one's own legal interest. Meed's action (the one Good Parliament charge that stuck against Alice Perrers; see Holmes 1975, 137) thus echoes rat-parliament behaviours, 'many mannes malt [not our own] we mees wolde destruye' (Pro.198). Most typically in the fourteenth century, superiors pursued 'maintenance' as central to their responsibility to show 'good lordship' to their dependents. What mattered was fidelity to one's retinue, and the display of one's power by achieving a legal result favourable to one's crew, not what might ethically have appeared 'the rectitude of the case'. Factional favouritism might be construed a law of retinue life.

This is a problem in the main specific to a particular Edwardian moment of Langland's youth, a behaviour which seems first to have attracted public notice in the 1320s (cf. Natalie Fryde). Edward II's favourites (most especially Langland's father's lords, the Despensers) were of course vilified for their oppressive and tyrannical governance. Their retainers were, in popular perception, allowed to run rampant in the provinces without legal restraint, and connived lordly 'maintenance' shielded them from the punishment appropriate to their crimes.

But such 'good lordship', now re-emergent in the 1370s, cut both ways and expressed itself as proliferating social discord. A thoroughly classic instance is associated with the assassination of Edward II; it is no accident that he was imprisoned, and done away with, at Berkeley Castle. Edward's Despenser henchmen, *père et fils*, with their *caput* in Tewkesbury, thirty miles north, had been 'legally' expropriating Berkeley lands and perks for the previous six or seven years, and this was payback time.

Controlling such behaviour was one of Edward III's major concerns early in his reign (in this instance, often curtailing the excesses of other possible Langlandian patrons, the Mortimers of Wigmore). Finally, in 1346, 'maintaining' the quarrels of others, supporting one's retainers at law, was outlawed by statute.[26] After a gap in accusations of maintenance until the crisis of the Good Parliament, the problem resurfaced under Richard II, in this case as a complaint over 'liveries', and Edward's statute was repromulgated (13 Richard II, stat. 3, 1389/90, *Statutes* 2, 74–5). Whatever the promulgation would indicate on its face, it represents only further factional quarrelling; it was presumably an attack on the Lords Appellant and support for *centralised royal* maintenance, since Richard was renowned in the nineties as the greatest giver of liveries, scattering White Hart badges (and with them his personal support) round the land.

Langland's first major revision of *Winner* (another important example will appear in the next section) concerns the resolution of his debate. On the face of things, as the king sees at the head of passus 4, Conscience v. Meed resists resolution: Conscience's complaints against Meed, while they draw attention to real social abuses, equally oppose engrained, and often constructive, social practices. Although certainly aired in Parliaments, his views are simply Brintonesque, those of a precisionist. His most apparently damning charges only draw attention to fourteenth-century business as usual, the normal activities by which lords *and kings* conducted their affairs, and his outraged responses are often politically naïve, not statements of unquestioned moral probity:

> She copeþ þe commissarie and coteþ his clerkes (3.143);
> Sir Symonie and hirselue seleþ þe bulles (3.148);
> Wiþ hire ieweles youre iustices she shendeþ (3.155);
> She ledeþ lawes as hire list and louedaies makeþ.
> (3.158)[27]

As a result, Meed can only be expelled, not through argumentative refutation, but by narrative demonstration of her ill effects.

In *Winner* (as for example, in *The Owl and the Nightingale*), debate poetry, *dialogus*, applauds verbal dexterity ('Wyse wordes and slee'), not any relationship between words and behaviour. In a revision of the rules, Langland has Meed rejected on the basis of deeds, not her argument (where she at least holds her own against Conscience). She is finally expelled for her efforts at 'maintenance' in the case of Peace v. Wrong, when she intervenes to protect one leading member of her retinue (cf. 2.108).

Wrong's activities, as described in 4.51–8, are certainly reminiscent of the rapacious taxman about whom the Harley Husbandman complains. That is, of course, not a magnatial act, but a royal one. Wrong's abusiveness, perhaps a product of having been sent off to London, is of another order, 'foregoing', the provision of supplies for a mobile lordly retinue (cf. 2.180–8). Yet, at least in literary production, this abuse might be perceived equally as much a regal as a magnatial one. I have mentioned before (p. 118) William of Paull's *Speculum regis*, written for Edward III in the early 1330s. William, a priest in the Windsor area, addresses the king precisely to protest against excessive forced appropriation of peasant goods to accommodate demands imposed by residence at the Castle. This abuse he sees as specifically royal and Edwardian, a pernicious innovation of the king's grandfather, datable precisely to the year 1290 (115). Rather than a sustaining sacral lordship, like that practised by St Louis IX in France (or in England, by a better Edward, the Confessor), the Edwards through this practice were exercising an Alexandrine tyranny.[28] Indeed, in William's presentation, no lordship, the royal absence sought by Langland's rats, is locally construed as preferable to royal visits to Windsor.

Both versions of William's text, scholarly 'epistola' and the conciliatory exhortation of the *Speculum* proper, arrive at the same climax. This answers the opening citation of the 'epistle', derived from ps.-Cyprian's 'Twelve abuses', 'Justicia regis est pax populorum' (83). Ending abusive foregoing, enforced removal of peasant assets for royal castle use, will restore the honour of the crown and renew the countryside:

> 'I am the Lord that love ju[stice], and hate robbery' (Isa. 61:8). And if in this verse you will hear your people and grant it to them, you will have *peace* with your subjects in this land. Hence Cassiodorus says in a letter, 'A king's grace is extolled and preserved, if he directs his people in *the equity of peace* and preserves them in the vigour of his justice, and it is fitting for a king to preserve *concord* because a nation will achieve praise, if *peace* is loved by all. What better suits or

describes a king or prince than a *peaceloving* people, *concord* preserved, and the entire commonwealth clothed in virtuous behaviours?' But, if you will not hear your people in this verse, great affliction will befall you.[29]

In identifying his hapless peasant victim as Peace, Langland follows the emphases of an earlier appeal to royal justice, but against royal, not magnatial, abuse. Edward III, even before Paull's tract, had made efforts to restrain such *royal* purveyance, first in 1330, statute injunctions repeated, presumably because they had failed to squelch the practice, on five further occasions during the reign (4 Edward III, cc. 3–4, *Statutes* I, 262–3; cf. 265–6, 276–7, 288, 301, 319). This collocation might be seen as telling, for it indicates – as the expulsion of Meed will further – the thorough imbrication of monarchy in possibly questionable magnatial practices.

In spite of Conscience's moralising gestures, Langland's debate resolves itself in a manner ironic and equivocal, reminiscent of *Winner*. The savaged Peace is in some measure vindicated as royal property, rather than subjected to Meed's typically transformative logic. She would re-create the querulous petitioner as her own, as a desired silenced tranquillity, but one non-royal (not 'the king's peace') through a cash payment (cf. 'make P/pees with his pens' 4.64, 75). It is indeed precisely these conflicting possible proprietarial recuperations that should give one pause at the end of passus 4.

Royal judgement links *Winner* and *Piers*, since Edward is the judge of cases in each. The *Winner* poet entertains the notion that royal power provides the regulatory solution to modern disaster:

> And all prayed for the pese till the prynce come,
> For he was worthiere in witt than any wy ells
> For to ridde and to rede and to rewlyn the wrothe.
> (55–7)

In Langland's most problematic echo, his Edward III promises to forgive Meed 'if she werche bi wit and my wil folwe' (3.7); I'd translate the line, 'If she'll behave reasonably by doing just what *I desire*' (cf. 5.587, 8.129, etc.). This desire should prepare one for an eventual royal judgement every bit as whimsical and self-interested as that of *Winner*'s Edward:

þoru3 youre lawe, as I leue, I lese manye eschetes;
Meed ouermaistreþ lawe and much truþe letteþ . . . .
I wole haue leaute in lawe . . . .
(4.175–6, 180)

While the lines acknowledge the disruption Meed as a 'maistre' might create, the logic for the rejection is scarcely compelling. 'Lost escheats' are not analogous to Wrong's freedom, since they are not felonious crimes escaping punishment, but rather a form of tax evasion. 'Lost escheats' thus speak, not to criminal justice, but to Meedish impulses, the loss of (royal) revenue.[30] The king manages implicitly to equate 'lawe', 'truþe', and 'leaute' with his private financial profit, the final extension of 'working his will'. And Langland seems disposed to break off here – having displayed royal 'just-dealing' as simply an internalised version of Meedishness. Just as in his vision of the rats (or indeed, Wycliffe's 'solution' to the Denia ransom), centralised plunder, the king as Biggest/Fattest Cat, under the guise of Law, proves more disinterested and efficient than ceaseless dispersed social negotiations.

This view, as Stokes, the most distinguished analyst of this problematic has indicated, redounds throughout the poem. For example, the royal resolution of Peace v. Wrong forecasts one breakdown in the renewed fair field of passus 19, the king's definition of *spiritus iusticie* as the licensed right of plunder, for 'I am heed of lawe' (466–76). In that context, the assertion only engenders dispersed social spoliation – and not just by magnates. Royal Meed echoes and proliferates, as William of Paull promised, through the 'comune'. The brewer so central in Stokes's presentation echoes the king's view, and in Wille's last temptation, Need encourages him (e.g. 20.6–9) to invoke *spiritus temperancie* and convert Piers's patient poverty, 'swynke no3t so harde' (7.122) into simple 'swynke no3t', morally licensed theft (aptly discussed Robert Adams 1978).

At least one problem implicitly evoked, in both passus 4 and 19, is social justice, 'leaute'. As Alford (1988b) points out, Edward's newly favoured counsellor Reason is preeminently a measurer, an accountant.[31] Indeed, in the C revision his role is designated as the master of royal finance, 'my cheef chaunceller in cheker' (4.185). By couching matters as a due return of (financial) authority to royal control, centred in a case of criminal trespass, the narrative manages to omit as much as it might be seen to resolve. Reason's line, 'Reed me noȝt . . . no ruþe to haue | Til . . .' (4.113–14), in a fallen world, insists upon mercilessness. Justice, at the conclusion of passus 4, rests upon a criminal jurisdiction that is foreseeably the perpetuation of 'nudum ius', not 'vestita pietas' or William of Paull's commonwealth 'honestate vestita'.

In contrast, those acts of Meed's here deemed abusive might be perceived as both socially more pervasive and more constructive than the royal centrism here enunciated. Utterly neglected at the narrative's end is the plaintiff Peace. The restored King's Peace is an abstraction; the wronged peasant Peace with 'his heed and his panne blody' (4.78) is not. The king's law simply wants fines and seizures for himself, but Meed would address what are now called 'victims' rights', provide Peace with recompense for his injury, 'a present al of pured golde'. She also strives to bail her boy Wrong, with an accompanying promise the King can't offer, of his future good behaviour: 'I wol wage for Wrong, he wol do so na moore' (4.94–7).³²

This frustrated act of compensation leads back to one of Conscience's complaints against Meed, the last I cited on p. 267. At 3.158, he inveighs against her involvement in 'lovedays'. Such informal efforts at dispute arbitration typify a situation in which, as Conscience says, 'Lawe is so lordlich and looþ to maken ende'. But this, as Langland is surely aware, is a normative description of the dilatoriness of the contemporary royal judicial system (not as Conscience has it, in 3.161, of Meed). In such a context, arbitration, viewed as settlement by 'love' rather than 'law', was a well-established procedure for resolving complaints and one of wide social dispersal. For example, many London parish guilds enjoined compulsory arbitration of disputes between members; social fellowship required adjudication and informal settlement, rather than the acrimony and aggression associated with legal action. The anti-feminist sniping at Meed as loose woman, typical of the three passus (cf. esp. 3.336–48), redefines, so as to overlook, ways in which she gestures, however imperfectly, towards 'love' and conciliation as an integral accompaniment to 'law'.³³

The C revision, with Reason as Chancellor of the Exchequer, also speaks to this lacuna in the narrative and serves to further qualify whatever resolution is achieved here. Following out what is already implicit in B, it draws attention to a further bit of allegorical sleight of hand, another loose end to Peace v. Wrong. Reason and Edward may fulfil demands of the Common Law:

> Mede shal noȝt maynprise yow, by the Marie of heuene!
> I wole haue leaute in lawe, and lete be al your ianglyng;
> And as moost folk witnesseþ wel, Wrong shal be demed.
> (179–81)

Formulating the case in this way merely speaks, once again, to royal Meedishness. Reason and king construe Peace's complaint as charging a simple felonious act, assault and/or larceny; upon conviction under such a charge, Wrong's assets will revert to the crown. But Peace should have had an alternative action, for damages consequent on 'trespas de bonis asportatis'; in this case, the king would not be a party and Peace entitled to full compensation (cf. John H. Baker 1990, 445–6 and 572).

Equally, both Reason and king overlook what is known as Equity. Having Reason as 'chaunceller in cheker' both alludes to and obscures the existence of a second Chancellor, the household officer in charge of the Great Seal and royal secretariat, Chancery (until recent reforms, Lord Irvine and not Gordon Brown). One later fourteenth-century legal innovation concerns the development of equity jurisdiction. The Common Law, while adept at handling issues like property and crime, might be perceived as slow to address civil law issues (e.g., a modern notion of contract). Apparently in response to such a perception, the Court of the King's Chancellor began, in the last quarter of the century, to function as what was considered, pregnantly in the context of passus 4, as a 'court of conscience'. Its jurisdiction was specifically designed to address, and in its early years, overwhelmingly did address, questions of reparation in situations where the Common Law offered none. It thus supplemented, by offering compensation, the Common Law insistence upon penalty, but not remedy, that same function provided by Meed's proffer to Peace (cf. John H. Baker 1990, 112–21; Avery).

Peace returns in the poem, of course, and in a context that might indicate how law needs to be transformed. Associated with Mercy, this woman will speak to the need to dissolve strict legalistic thinking into a different discourse. And with this transformed personification named Peace, the character as conceived in passus 4 returns as well; bloody pans will be redeemed only through a new conception of affinity, law, and legal metaphor, one founded in universalising love and grace, in eternity:

> And my mercy shal be shewed to manye of my haluebreþeren,
> For blood may suffre blood boþe hungry and acale
> Ac blood may noȝt se blood blede but hym rewe
> *Audiui archana verba* . . .
> (18.393–5a)

The lines follow on a rejection (at 18.390a) of Reason's jingle enjoining strict justice (4.143–4).[34] But in passus 4, allegory, the pursuit of a morally appropriate outcome, an answer to the husbandman's complaint in Harley 2253, is qualified. Langland, in the last analysis, shows the same speculativeness, gamesomeness, and suspicion as that underwriting *Winner*. This perhaps ironically recapitulates Theology's hapless optimism 'Ledeþ hire to Londoun þere lawe is yshewed' (2.135, Bx).

Thus, although Langland appears to resolve debate in a way foreign to *Winner*, such resolution as he offers shares with the earlier text a qualified bow to *Realpolitik*. His vision ends awkwardly poised between according possible value to magnatial jury-tampering (and other forms of extra-legality) and a suspicion that The Royal State may only be the same tendencies writ large – but presented with better spin. To get past this cynicism, Langland had to return to his alliterative roots in another vision, a different (and nearly equally frustrating) take on the same issues of Christian social justice. There beginning at 5.537, ' "Peter", quod a Plowman', he was to imagine a new voice for the Harley husbandman, one that translates complaint into that variety of instructional and penitential thinking I have shown prevalent in early London devotional writing – and a new direction for his poem.

IV

London may appear a divagation in the poem, brought about by efforts to deal with Meed. Langland's narrative returns, in the second vision, to the rural fair field with which the poem began, with Piers Plowman's main actual (as opposed to referential) appearance in the poem. This is pretty much limited to passus 5–7, a significant appearance in another cultivating context in passus 16, and the brief reprise of the agrarian issues I will broach here, in another mode in passus 19. Yet Piers remains very much a London character.

In part, this continuity of presentation reflects longings for something like a Piers enunciated in the poem's own London language. In the B version, this is exemplified in the messianism of Conscience the king's knight:

> Ac Kynde Loue shal come ʒit and Conscience togideres
> And make of Lawe a laborer . . .
> *Conflabunt gladios suos in vomeres etc.*
> Ech man to pleye with a plow, pykoise or spade,
> Spynne or sprede donge or spille hymself with sleuþe.
> (3.299–300, 308a-10, cf. 5.539, 6.9–56 *passim*)

The language promises a society predicated on bible-lore, Piers as in essence an embodied and active textual gloss, subsuming the sense of all texts. He is someone who might make a knight with a sword eager to 'pleye with a plow' (cf. 6.21–3).

Similarly, at the end of the C autobiography, Cornhill Wille pre-empts Conscience's final command 'ʒe! and contynue' (C 5.104). Rather than perpetuity in the specifically sober 'lyf þat is louable and leele' his interlocutors imagine (103), the poetic figure has already ima-gined or projected continuation in his usual mode, the visionary rather than the penitential, one that appears 'louable and leele' only to himself:

> Suche a wynnyng hym warth thorw wyrdes of grace:
> *Simile est regnum celorum thesauro abscondito in agro.*
> (99–a)

If this gracious treasure from Truth is not Piers himself, it is at least a pointed reminder, for the parable appears intermixed with those identi-fying agricultural metaphor and Heaven in Matthew 13. For any trained medieval exegete, equality of reward might be construed as promising equality of metaphorical vehicle.[35]

But although forecast in a London language of desire for what is ab-sent, Piers is much more powerfully a local figure, an instantiation of the holy vernacular layman heralded in the devotional materials discussed in chapter 4. Such a conception drives and governs the character from the moment he appears until he vanishes:

'I knowe hym as kyndely as clerc doþ hise bokes';
The preest and Perkyn apposeden eiþer ooþer,
And þoru3 hir wordes I wook . . .
(5.538, 7.144–5)

As the priest, much to his vexation, sees, Piers is the unlearned and
natural divine, the true teacher texts like *The Mirror* and Pepys *Riwle*
encourage. Clergy, learning its own self, reaffirms this view in the 'two
infinites' speech (brilliantly discussed Middleton 1972):

> For oon Piers þe Plowman haþ impugned vs alle
> And set alle sciences at a sop saue Loue one
> And no text ne takeþ to mayntene his cause
> But *Dilige deum* and *Domine quis habitabit.*
> (13.124–7)

Clergy expresses the same vexation as the priest, that distaste for a virtuous lay holyness that can conceive right belief from a few unconcorded
and unglossed textual scraps (the single example of virtue that might,
for the *Mirror* translator, make one a worthy preacher, for example; see
pp. 192–3).

The insistent association of Piers with 'kynde knowyng' presupposes
the non-institutional power of the individual to access, understand, and
actuate God's law. While in the long haul, as customarily in London
devotional literature, this insistence does not operate to the thorough
denigration of learned knowledge, it places that knowledge as potentially
unnecessary to Christian action or salvation, open to all.[36] This note
is struck early in the poem, in the foundational non-communicative
conversation between Wille and Holychurch:

> 'Yet haue I no kynde knowyng', quod I, 'ye mote kenne me bettre
> By what craft in my cors it comseþ and where'.
> 'Thow doted daffe!' quod she, 'dulle are þi wittes.
> To litel Latyn þow lernedest, leode, in þi youþe:
> *Heu michi quia sterilem duxi vitam iuuenilem.*
> It is a kynde knowyng . . .'
> (1.138–43)

Holychurch unsatisfactorily (as it were) answers by tautology – I have
no kind knowing/It is a kind knowing. But there are equally gestural

acknowledgements of basic difficulty – the dreamer's 'by what craft in my corse it comseþ', an effort to draw the discussion down to the physical, or to sensation itself.[37] His misunderstanding is, in its turn, matched by Holychurch's apparent suggestion that book-learning, acquiring Latin, has something to do with it all and that some greater attentiveness, stipulated by the quotation as textual, might straighten everything out. (If she means to instruct metaphorically – 'any child knows what I mean' – the very citation vitiates the metaphor and emphasises learned language acquisition.) This represents, of course, another temptation ceaselessly played out in the narrative, e.g. the dreamer's last gasp joust as 'oon of Prides knyȝtes' (15.50), intent on intellectual achievement.

More normatively in Langland's poem, however, learning typically represents the belief that, to progress, one must supplement the self. In contrast, both Holychurch and Piers imply a duty to accept that there is nothing to progress from, that all the needful was there to begin with. In this formulation, to learn can only mean to remember, to recall what was already present; it's no accident that the C autobiography is defined as 'romynge in remembraunce' (C 5.11).

There was once an innate understanding – biographical, spiritual, political – that required no explanation. Just as in Thedmar's discourse of law, or the return to the home locale in Auchinleck romance, his-torical/biographical progression represents merely an extension of what always was and has been. The poem is the effort to remember that innate understanding, to recall what, in modern crisis, is no longer self-evident, apparently has not been explained. Thus, the fits and starts of *Piers Plowman* reflect an effort to unscrew the inscrutable, to explain what was, before the Plague, axiom – and thus, logically, beyond ex-planation, what provided the grounds from which explanation might proceed. At some level, such an axiom must be both obvious (It Is) and, equally obviously, because lost, questionable from any variety of positions. Failure to understand, manifest just about anywhere the poet thinks to look, is the cause of the crisis provoking his activity.[38]

The London reception and rubrics with which I began my discussion indicate the difficulty of the *amplificatio* that succeeds in creating a poem. Langland chronicles the vertiginousness of trying to discover what it was one supposedly knew all along, what is now socially resisted as a knowledge (most basically self-limitation, and a consequent need for a now-lost social cooperation and cohesion, along with penance for past and continuing personal failure). Piers speaks the passage exemplary of the difficulty, in which elaborate road-maps and progressive narrative metaphors eventually turn back into:

> And if Grace graunte þee to go in in þis wise,
> Thou shalt see in þiselue Truþe sitte in þyn herte
> In a cheyne of charite, as þow a child were,
> To suffren hym and segge noȝt ayein þi sires wille.
> (5.605–8)

At the end, one returns (with Matt. 18:3) to the 'kynde' place of loving and to the child, here not babbling his declensions but silently obedient to the still undefined 'truþe' that has always been present and that has always possessed him/her in love.

This visionary moment ('see Truþe sit') underscores the simplicity of the poem's arc, from the start:

> [Truþe] is a kynde knowyng þat kenneþ in þyn hert
> For to loue . . .
> (1.141–2)

through the first truly normative definition of Dowel, that of Patience (at C 15.140 quoting Piers, but acknowledging the triad as a reflection of Piers's patient poverty by citing 'Pacientes vincunt' at the head of the speech, 137):

> '*Disce*', quod he, '*doce, dilige inimicos.*
> *Disce* and Dowel, *doce* and Dobet, *dilige* and Dobest:
> Thus lerede me ones a lemman – Loue was hir name'
> (13.137–9)[39]

to the end:

> 'Lerne to loue', quod Kynde, 'and leef alle oþere'
> (20.208)

But Langland's London emphases encompass not only the sanctified lay teacher but other themes as well. One might see the poem as particularly engaged in basic emphases of the London Apocalypse commentary. The recurring association of God and 'truþe' immediately recalls the definition of oppositional Antichrist as 'losengery' in that text and else-where (and automatically generates such chance personifications as Cov-eitise's lovely 'grace of Gyle', 5.205). Equally fundamental to the poem is the commitment to God's law and to laymen teaching it gratis, when and where they can (cf. pp. 184–91, and 5.556–9). Initially in the poem, accompanying this emphasis is a work ethic at least reminiscent of the Pepys *Riwle*; as I will argue, it comes to be replaced by the Apocalypse's insistence on the persecuted yet patient Christian teacher, who must contend with the world and see things through to the end.

Yet dialogic treatment characterises Piers's commitment to Truth every bit as much it does the first vision. There, the perception of what constitutes a justice or mercy to which one might commit oneself turns out to be constituted by political affiliation, lineage and household, special pleading for one's favourites. These expected patterns of courtly disruption will predictably eddy out to encompass a kingdom. Yet at bottom, discursive con-/profusion in the poem always addresses dearth, the finite quantum of power or food available to all. Justice problems recur in the second vision within a differently poised conception of 'commune'.

From the 22nd line of *Piers Plowman*, Langland universalises and morally marks 'winning' and 'wasting'. The terms refer differently than in his predecessor text – not to aristocrats, but most particularly to labourers, peasants. In this reformulation, 'winning' is privileged as work, honest labour, 'wasting' denigrated as idleness, consuming what you have not produced. Such peasant problems address dearth directly, in contrast to the rarefied atmosphere of aristocratic exchange. The second vision returns to the country, its turning away from the court basically a pastoral move. Implicitly, the argument follows out Con-science's metaphor: a hope that the village commune, the round of or-ganised dayworks, might be a focus of romanticisable cooperative social ideal (cf. Justice 141–92).

Piers leads this enterprise, already incipiently the 'procuratour and reue', *The Mirror's* good steward (see pp. 184–5, 187–8) the end of the poem imagines (19.258). A plowman is not a poor man but a village aristocrat, owner of the great machine of agriculture and requiring or-ganised cooperative labour to fulfil his function (Homans 45–50, 245–8; Hilton 21–7; Hanawalt 1986, 114). Thus, at the opening of passus 6, the 'commune' is refounded under directives inverting those of the Prologue. Instruction emanates from the leader of the work-force itself, and the knight is dragooned into a social order he did not create, in which even his sillinesses, blood sport for example (6.29–32), may be redefined as beneficial public contributions.

Yet whatever the high hopes and enthusiasms Piers can engender at the start, the results of this agrarian compact turn out to be depressingly familiar. The narrative exposes Conscience's naïveté in believing 'Lawe a laborer', Piers as governor of the village troop, will provide a universal panacea. Even in the best intentioned of worlds, what will ensue is not pretty – in fact a repetition of what happens at Court, although with a considerably more conscientious judge than Edward III.[40]

The crunch comes here when Piers finds his workforce includes those variously recalcitrant. As Aers points out, they are simply indulging in a common feature of late medieval peasant economy; rather than work to capitalise or to invest, peasants frequently sought to imitate their 'wasting' aristocratic betters and work only enough to ensure more productive and self-fulfilling leisure. But Piers, following the Prologue's various formulations, sees things through the poem's moralised take on peasants and labour, 'Ye ben wastours, I woot wel' (6.130). He is caught up in justice operations, the often-discussed fallout of the labour problems of 1349 *et seq.*, in which discernible productivity, acts with results, measure social viability/success.[41]

Faced with this perceived threat, Piers's solution is to call for the police, the knight (as typically, dispenser of the King's justice in the locale), who proves ineffectual. Not only is this individual hamstrung by his 'curteis kny3tly kynde' (6.164), but he equally knows one can't damage one's own capital, the work-force that produces the crop, whatever it's up to, and get it to work for you. This ineffectuality reflects the failure of The Statute of Labourers' projected wage controls and other rebarbative efforts to control labour in the wake of 1348 depopulation.

Thus, Piers is forced to seek other modes of social control. When he goes 'houp[ing] after Hunger' (6.172), he is essentially refusing food handouts, a customary part of day-wages, and starving his work-force into submission. Such punitiveness encourages actual production, indeed almost obsessively industrious cooperation. This situation obtains until Piers starts encouraging Hunger to go home and worries over how work will go on without his enforcement. At this point, he engages overtly in the problem that has been implicit from the first 'whoop'; having summoned Hunger up, he has created his own interlocutor, and as soon as he addresses him, they begin to offer differing interpretations of the situation, discourses in overt, although not always consistent, conflict.

To put matters rather crassly, Piers begins to see, as he has earlier when he coerced Hunger to stop tormenting Wastour and the Bretoner (6.179), his own brutality:

> And it are my blody breþeren for God bouȝte vs alle;
> Truþe tauȝte me ones to louen hem ech one,
> And helpen hem of alle þyng ay as hem nedeþ.
> Now wolde I wite, if þow wistest, what were þe beste,
> And how I myȝte amaistren hem and make hem to werche.
> (6.207–11)

Christian charitable impulses, couched in the language of London devotional literature – that all one's goods, temporal and spiritual, should help others in need – are getting violated. But simultaneously, Piers is flummoxed, because in addition to bloody brethren, these are his workmen. His responsibility as Truth's reeve is thus not to be brotherly, but masterly, to coerce their labour, to instigate their action and to get a visible product from it, a grain surplus. Of course, the indirect questions he is asking themselves remain problematic: what status does Hunger have, other than that Piers has accorded him, that would lead to taking his advice about anything?

Piers wishes he could recapture the idealism with which this whole show started, return to everyone's initial willingness to contract for a post. Instead, his having called Hunger, more clearly than the knight's threat, has echoed the moment in the first vision when the wrathful king insists that he will punish malefactors. Like the king's, Piers's words create Dread (cf. 2.208). And Langland describes the ultimate effects of loosing Dread in echoing language – 'Faytours for fere flowen into bernes' (183; cf. 2.236 'flowen into hernes').[42]

At this point, not only Piers but the poet was perturbed. The subsequent passage shows intensive revision in both later versions, as if

Langland was never quite satisfied with his formulation. The C revision should restrain discussions of that version as either simplifying or socially reactionary, since it includes a more extensive and emphatic insistence on Christian charity (including attention to building 'fiale/filiale' love in the workforce, C 8.215). This view creates a hunger-discourse additional to those I will discuss (spiritual hunger, treated ably by Trower).[43]

But in addition to Piers's second thoughts, another shift occurs here as well. Thus far in the narrative, Hunger has been comprehensible simply as dearth, starvation, the dire – and silent – tool of constraint. But at this point there occurs that 'wobble' in perspective on which Trower (241–2) and Aers (1988, 45) comment: Hunger starts offering instructions, not about starving, but feeding people. These instructions introduce further discursive complications about groups specifically deserving mercy, ones that echo Piers's earlier off-the-cuff pronouncements of 6.136–8 and 145–51. He has presumably internalised such charitable exclusions from his starvation regimen from the language of parish guild regulations (or, in the case of 'postles', the Pepys *Riwle* on itinerant priests; see p. 210).

Hunger's 'wobble' simply reflects the same allegorical instability always associated with Meed (reward or bribery?). Allegory always promises to clarify moral issues, but in fact always ambiguates and distances them by intruding a trope upon literal description (cf. Spenser's 'dark conceit'). To this difficulty, Langland's personification allegory adds a further problem, the very referential instability of language itself, the entitling name that should explain all as polyvalent disruptor of signification. Langland might well suspect the value of his poetic contribution precisely because the poem's language can never achieve that clarity that is an assumed property of the clerical language Piers's 'kynde knowyng' is supposed to subsume.

The character Hunger includes that ambivalence inherent in the varying senses of Latin *fames*. This word means both the external state 'famine' and the subjective perception (reminiscent of the king's 'wille') 'a desire for food'. Like the Latin word, the character joins both the external impersonal fact, starvation, with an inner human effect; compare for example, 6.183–5, where the faitours' energetic activity simultaneously suppresses desire and drives off dearth by earning the pittance

Piers now will give (cf. 186, 193). When Hunger comes to speak, he will necessarily express a subjectivity, cease to be an external physical process. Consequently, his speeches voice the subjective sense of *fames*, provide the opinions of a disgruntled poverty, far more grudging, in its desire to be fed before anyone else is, than is Piers. But the bottom line is pretty clear, and the bifurcation in points of view, between Christian charity and imperative to perform as labourer, simply widens.

Piers, apparently shocked to hear Hunger recommending feeding workmen – and indeed feeding some people for minimal or no work (contrast the crabbiness of the Pepys *Riwle* and London guild regulations, discussed pp. 210–12) – replies:

> I wolde noȝt greue God....
> Miȝte I synnelees do as þow seist?.
> (6.229–30)

The question, in logical terms, is ambiguous, but following on his preceding one, Piers must be asking whether God tolerates such a display of mercy to those who 'do evil', who don't work. His concern reflects London devotional worries that some charity could countenance sin and might thus *be* itself sinful (cf. pp. 211–12). Hunger's answer, scattily ascribed to the good offices of Kynde Wit (247), speaks to the opposite implication – a series of biblical citations, clerical textuality, the concording of similar written loci, demonstrating the moral imperative to starve folks.

Moreover, he goes on to answer Piers's requests for medical advice in a similarly grudging fashion. (As a natural thing or thing in nature, he can pose as expert in practical science.) Piers's workmen in fact have aching stomachs because empty (cf. 6.178), but Hunger asserts that this is so because they are fuller than his own – 'Ye han manged ouer muche' (258). While his homeopathic advice might seem to confirm Holychurch's 'Mesure is medicine' (1.35, cf. 25–6), Hunger remains also thoroughly and comically, if macabrely, self-interested. In a context where Piers could be construed a sumptuous waster, and thus he and others should eat less (for their health, understand), there will be more surplus food about for Hunger himself to eat.

The discussion then comes to rest in an aporia, Christian mercifulness against a self-interested harshness (echoing the king's of passus 4).

Additionally, the latter view threatens to justify itself by appropriating the discourse alleged to underwrite idealising Christian discussions. As Hunger's appeal to Kynde Wit implies, at stake are two versions of Nature. On the one hand, Piers appeals to 'blood', 'kynde' sympathy indeed, a metaphor for his natural love drawn towards other members of his incorporate community (and foreshadowing its incarnational embodiment in passus 18–19). On the other, Hunger cynically uses learned biblicism to support an almost Malthusian scientism in which dearth and want create boundless desire and require boundless repression (at least of others).

The second vision, at the moment Hunger needs to be driven off, has returned to an inverted version of Meed's banishment. Does one want tyrannical judicial harshness or possibly perturbing and indiscriminate operations of mercy? Yet the situation here is, ironically, a great deal more obfuscatorily inexorable, precisely in its echoic inversions.

For at this point one needs to recognise that Piers is getting Meed's lines. He is engaged in special pleading for members of his troop, based upon his recognition of obligations to a 'fellowship'. And to sustain this view, he must insist, as a serious reader of London texts would, upon his inner understanding of divine law, in the face of overwhelming textual citation (accurate citation, whatever Hunger's motivation).[44] Thus, to persist in unlearned 'kynde knowyng', he implicitly rejects his foundational text, Bible. Moreover, he must see Hunger, in his citations, as motivated to make the text say precisely what it shouldn't, but does. In his turn, Hunger provides a foretaste of the priest's 'I kan no pardon fynde' (7.115), a querulousness about a possibly inscrutable, yet nonetheless real, divine mercifulness (God does presumably 'pardon' on some basis).

But, in the context of the half acre, fundamental to both interlocutors' views is a troubling recognition. The act of agricultural labour will underwrite either option, punitive starvation or merciful provision, a perception signalled in the reinvocation of The Statute and the prophecy of dearth at the passus's end. But the situation only, once again, echoes the first vision. It reprises the generic distortions I have already outlined in the confrontation of Meed and Conscience, in which victory by argument has been replaced by victory, whoever should win, predicated on disruptive act.

I emphasise 'the act of agricultural labour' here, as I have done throughout, only partly to identify the historical material conditions that conflicting discourses attempt to situate to their social advantage. I am equally interested in seeing labour-issues as the continuing terms addressed in Piers's pardon, 'qui bona egerunt' (7.113), and in the realised actional gloss that here replaces the written text, Piers's speech after he has torn the document:

> 'I shal cessen of my sowyng', quod Piers, 'and swynke noȝt so harde,
> Ne aboute my bilyue so bisy be na moore;
> Of preieres and of penaunce my plouȝ shal ben herafter,
> And wepen whan I sholde werche þouȝ whete breed me faille.
> The prophete his payn eet in penaunce and in sorwe
> By þat þe sauter vs seith, and so dide othere manye.
> That loueþ God lelly his liflode is ful esy:
> *Fuerunt michi lacrime mee panes die ac nocte*'.
> (7.122–8a)[45]

Given the difficulties posed in passus 6, pardon-tearing might seem a classic example of explaining an *ignotum per ignocius* ('Canon Yeoman's Tale' G 1457). Yet the terms Piers here offers to justify his action should be familiar, for, as bishop Brinton saw, the pardon promises judgement of an action that will lead to an appropriate reward (cf. p. 251). But that is precisely the problem that has emerged in ploughing the half acre: just how does one identify good/bad action? how does one align that judgement with an appropriate reward? how does one retain confidence in the ability to judge acts in a situation of conflicting standards? In passus 6, Piers discovers the fruits of crisis and social faction in a situation of dearth – discursive overload. There exist too many possible standards, and their very profusion renders every individual one overtly faulted. At the simplest, justice appears inhumane and possibly self-interested, love or mercy too impossibly indulgent. Mensurability is baffled, and any act can look somehow compromised.

Tearing the pardon, replacing text with living gloss, tries to slice this Gordian knot. At the centre of everything in passus 6 and in the pardon stands 'labour', an act that merits reward. 'Kynde knowyng' leads Piers to tear the pardon, to destroy exactly that problematic equation (which can apparently produce no model exemplary behaviour) in favour of different terms. In his explanation, labour subsists, but in reduced and non-compulsive form; into the space opened by its absence, Piers inserts penitentialism, pain/tears and prayer, in exchange for the product labour has always sought (payn 'bread'). In the absence of any clear standard to judge acts, in a situation where everything seems up for questioning or negotiation, the overwhelming probability that one must face is that one's acts, whatever one's intention, are *mala*.

The sensible 'kyndely' conclusion is atonement in advance, perhaps unlikely ever to be enough. Piers underwrites this decision by an appeal to 'leel loue' for God, an answering echo of a faith in His freely given support, only believed because unsupported by circumambient conditions, the *in medio vmbre* of dea(r)th (121). Later, in the poem's greatest moment of discursive conflict, Wille stumbles, in digression, upon the name for the state Piers here enunciates, 'patient poverty' (cf. 11. 184–286a, 318–19).

Piers's explanation actuates 'leel loue', the 'kynde' feelings for his brethren that had originally invoked Hunger as speaker. But, in this new formulation, if the reeve is not working compulsively, then neither is anyone else, and the need for legal constraint, so central to passus 6, evaporates. Simultaneously, if the reeve is eating penitential tears (one of the four canonical prescriptions for 'satisfaction' is *ieiunium*, fasting), and not bread, he will have reduced general demand for foodstuffs. In his sorrowful love, he will have allowed others the space to eat and increased the margin that separates society from famine. (Cf. Carlyle's prescription in *Sartor Resartus* to reduce one's denominator.) Non-solicitousness thus is double-edged, not only faith in God to provide in the shadow of death, but also a rejection of Hunger's 'lechecraft', his particular voraciousness, predicated on a consciousness that someone somewhere has more to eat than he. Tearing the pardon rejects the act-measuring that created the situation in which fieldwork ground to a halt in passus 6.

If, as C 5 implies, plowing, looking for a treasure in the field, tropes continuation of poetic endeavour, a few further general observations follow. Piers's faithful and penitential subsistence, 'patient poverty', involves surrendering some economic supplement that might conceivably be his by right but that now can be seen as unnecessary, sumptuous. As my argument would indicate, tearing the pardon not only rejects measurement of finite act, plowing (well), in favour of perpetual state, lived penance, it implicitly rejects the poem's great temptation, to find a verbal supplement extrinsic to and explanatory of the only needful, 'kynde knowyng'.

One thing to be surrendered here, in the sundered pardon text, is learning. The priest's exegetical, documentary skill, like Hunger's capable of making texts mean as they palpably shouldn't, is left no material on which to work. Thus, the priest and Piers confront one another, and the scene proves intellectually fraught. As London devotional writers had argued, 'kynde loue' will always, in the company of sacrament, be enough. The scene provides a litmus for all the other confrontations of passus 8–15: under the rubric of 'patient poverty', subliterate genres, riddles for example (see Galloway), prove more productive than the high university learning of William Jordan OP (the model for the banquet scene's voracious friar, cf. 13.84) and Clergy.

Wille retrospectively defines Piers's state as 'patient poverty'. I initially consider the enabling adjective here, for it is not poverty *per se* that is blessed, but patient poverty, a sanctifying sorrow for one's debilitating sinfulness. Just as at the end of the first vision, where the king has internalised Meed, here Piers internalises what might appear to be the state opposed to his overtly stated position, that restraint sought in the field as coercive justice. One should see this action as a reflection of earlier London devotion, particularly the Pepys *Riwle*. That text has been rewritten to emphasise self-custody, the control of the senses that, unrestrained, will allow desire, the world, to corrupt the spirit. In the *Riwle*, this perception appears coupled with a firm sense of using the world in moderation and through the distribution of one's surplus, both material and spiritual, to others. Moreover, earlier London texts show a persistent interest in sacramental penitence, often expressed as an anxiety, analogous to Piers's bout with the priest, over its efficacy in the face of clerical abuses.

Further, identifying Piers's newfound state with patience associates it with, not an action, but an infinitely extensible state (cf. pp. 164–6). Paradoxically, this is the acceptance of finitude, of never being complete. Cicero defined this virtue in a form standard and ceaselessly invoked in the Middle Ages: 'Patience is the willed and continuous endurance of laborious and difficult things for the sake of virtue or benefit'.[46] But in this formulation, *patientia* (derived from *patiens*, the present participle of the verb *pati*, the inactive act 'to suffer') forms a temporally extended repetition of nothing except itself, 'diuturna *perpessio*' (for *per-passio*, derived from *passus*, the past participle of the same verb). Like 'kynde knowyng' in Wille and Holychurch's non-communication, patience is a continuous tautology, a state perpetuated all over again – and all over again. Undertaken for faith and love (Cicero's 'honestatis causa') and, more broadly in medieval accounts, with 'exspectatio' (Hope), patience can be seen to actuate all virtues; in a passage to which I have already referred (p. 215 n. 21), Gregory calls it 'the root and guardian of the virtues' ('radix et custos virtutum'). But the virtue actuates others, not as attainment, but as insistence that one never arrives at a definitive stasis, is always simply in development. Thus, in a piece of typically clergial Latin punning on similar verbal roots, the incremental textual division *passus* blurs into the extended and undivided *per-pass-io*.

V

So Piers vanishes, with the contentious priest, and will appear only twice more in the poem. At another moment of 'tene', he deals with a thieving wastour in passus 16, and in passus 19, he is central to a communal agrarian refoundation echoic of and spiritualising the old. The first replays the dreamer's earlier intersomnial excursion of passus 11 (his 'lond of longynge and loue' now a purified land of love alone) and dynamises a variety of old issues, as the plank 'spiritus sanctus' generates gospel narrative. Like the passus 5 pilgrimage to Truth, one returns to 'herte þe herber', where the tree Patience as root ('radix' – Piers is presumably 'custos') produces the fruit of the virtue Charity (16.4–17). Piers's second return, among other things, effects a full rapprochement with learning by rendering Clergy, textual culture, the bovine instruments that implement Piers's 'kynde wille' (19.262–73a), his vision of Christian cultivation.

But in spite of his general absence, the energy Piers conveys never vanishes from the poem. After all, at the opening of passus 6, it could engage a romance hero *manqué*, make him eager to grab up plough handles, not a destrier's reins (6.21–5). The remainder of the poem, quite against expectations perhaps, reaffirms and narrowly redefines the moment of pardon through a sequence of actions reminiscent of

Piers's appearance. The poem, its dreamer 'romynge in remembraunce', constructs itself as 'Memory' – both of a past lost to crisis and of the pastness created through its own repeated visioning. Like Thedmar's historicism, in its 'perpession' *Dialogus Petri Ploughman* 'ineches' the implications of what has been seen.

Throughout the 'Visio', Wille is basically an unengaged tourist (salient exceptions include 3.64–100, 5.61, 7.110); from the time he witnesses the pardon-tearing, he shifts to a yet more dialogic métier of 'inquisition' (see Joseph Wittig for the traditional background; Kirk 1972, 87–100, for the bible-theology). At least initially, the series of 'dialogi' appears but a large replay of 'the pilgrimage to Truth', just one more inconsequential 'road-trip', necessary, if for nothing else, to demonstrate its inconsequentiality. But in retrospect, it becomes properly and implicitly more active and engaged than it appears on its face:

> Ridyng ful rapely ...
> To a iustes in Ierusalem he iaced awey faste.
> (17.52–4)
>
> *
>
> I soiourned no3t but shoop me to renne
> And suwed þat Samaritan þat was so ful of pite.
> (17.86–7)

The Samaritan rides to catch Jesus, and stimulates thereby the active engagement of the Wille. But at earlier moments, Wille, unconsciously and often unpointedly (e.g. 'yarn into elde' 11.60), chases after Piers. This pursuit will lead to the informatively focussed moment at the climax of the poem (18.10–26) when all three objects of desire, who are equally the poem's most desire-filled subjects, Jesus/Piers/Samaritan, become associated in Crucifixion/Incarnation: Love incarnate and incarnadine, *in* the blood, and *for* the blood, longing for sustenance in dearth, to 'drynke ri3t ripe must' (18.370). This is sumptuousness itself, the replacement of peasant beverage 'atten ale' with a true luxury product. In this formulation, Wille becomes an engaged (?London) spectator of romance tournament, a role that carries over into passus 19–20.

But at earlier moments, 'inquisition' only generates Wille's discursive frustration, analogous to Piers's tearing. Wille keeps looking for a supplement to himself, and he keeps running up against the apparently unprovable negative that Piers has already discovered and that Anima will finally reiterate. In looking for an external answer to his early question, 'How [may I] saue my soule?' (1.84), with its implication that Christian self and soul are distinct, Wille discovers what he has been told all along: Soul itself provides sufficient answers. Anima, the integrated union of all the loose bits floating through passus 8–12 (and more), demonstrates the unanalysable integrity of the inner life (cf. 15.23–50) and its centre in Love (15.148–257, where the end has greater climactic force at C 16.374a).

In this process, the single constructive 'inquisicio' has been adumbrated by Piers at the pardon-tearing. This is the internal search of Conscience, the perpetual business of eating one's tears, in hope of instigating grace:

> [Scripture] sette a sour loof toforn vs and seide, '*Agite penitenciam*',
> And siþþe he drou3 vs drynke, *Diu perseuerans*,
> 'As longe', quod he, 'as lif and lycame may dure'.
> (13.49–51)

Through this seemingly inconsequent chase, Piers's absence is filled in by scenic echoes of the pardon-tearing. Through a sequence of circling approximations, the poem worries out the implications of his act. Strikingly, these echoes are associated with the poem's three or four great moments of collapse, of breach, in which apparent failure stands as generative intuition. Ultimately, all these echo the poem's great scene, where romance discourse evokes only the anti-romance prologue – chivalric victory by loss, death, and the discovery of the loving affinity of the blood (cf. the end of n. 35).

The first of these echoic moments appears in the dreamer's collapse at the juncture of passus 10 and 11:

> Tho wepte I for wo and wraþe of [Scripture's] speche.
> (11.4)

At this point, the C version (whose revisions are generally in the direction of allegorical precision and thus proves much the most intellectually demanding form of the poem) returns to the language of the first vision to offer a suggestive, if somewhat ineffectual, gloss:

> 'Allas, eye!' quod Elde and Holynesse bothe,
> 'That Wit shal turne to wrechednesse for Wil hath al his wille!'
> (C 12.1–2)[47]

While Wille is surely being will(ful) – indeed, he can't be anything else – the characterisation is not quite accurate. Up to his collapse, Wille thinks he is being witty, but as representative of the flaky logic-chopping wise guy Wit. Wille's collapse here follows from 9.121–57, where Wit uncomfortably raises a view of sin as predestinarian genetics, logical enough but removed from any gracious Christian premise. At the end of passus 10, in accord with this suggestion, Wille tumbles into a similarly depressing view, in which the internalised implications of Wit's 'lessons' are so terrifying as to lead him to cease emulating Wit altogether.[48]

This moment, rage before the inconsequences raised by learning, is further linked to Piers's tears by the fact that the dreamer in a dim way remembers him here:

> Ne none soner saued, ne sadder of bileue
> Than plowmen and pastours and pouere commune laborers,
> Souters and shepherdes; swiche lewed iuttes
> Percen wiþ a Paternoster þe pal[y]s of heuene
> And passen Purgatorie penauncelees at hir [partyng hennes]
> Into þe parfit blisse of Paradis for hir pure bileue.
> (10.465–70)[49]

The passage poises holy ignorance, a 'pure bileue' that hasn't tried to supplement itself with Wit's views, against a speaker who cannot believe he could be stupid. Yet Wille cannot see that the learned supplement to his 'kynde knowyng' he has been seeking will get him anywhere (cf. pp. 198–9). Wille recalls, but continues to misinterpret (as 7.173–8 does), what he saw Piers doing when he tore the pardon. The collapse that follows and precipitates Wille into the Land of Longing is essentially predicated upon despair, the acute sense that no conscious act could be sufficient to overcome the awareness of one's sinfulness:

Manye tales ye tellen þat Theologie lerneþ
And þat I man maad was, and my name y-entred
In þe legende of lif longe er I were,
Or ellis vnwriten for wikkednesse . . .
(10.378–81)⁵⁰

While the dreamer shares with Piers a horrifying sense of the potential ubiquitousness of sin, he lacks the faith Piers invokes as what allows him to address it. Patience fails, in Wille's paralysis before this enormity and in his sense that God is indifferent and uninterested in, if not downright hostile to, his plight.

The alternative to this paralysis turns out to be a protracted bout of forgetting (and return to a deeper past, memories of youth), the inner dream. Central to this indulgence is the character Rechelesnesse. In B, he merely 'st[ands] forþ in raggede cloþes' to encourage Wille to ignore repentance until he's old (11.34–6), but the more careful C version expands his role as the dreamer's *alter ego* enormously. Yet even in B, Rechelesnesse's poor appearance and his counsel echo Piers's determination to reduce his labour; he literalises Jesus's command, 'ne soliciti sitis' (7.131).

Cicero's definition, '*honestatis causa . . . voluntaria* perpessio', indicates what might be wrong with Rechelesnesse. True patience, according to the definition, requires two things, a will to endure and a virtuous cause to endure in. The character's name translates Latin 'negligentia', the term for a patience truly willed, but willed in a bad cause, traditionally defined as for an object lesser than God. Rechelesnesse expects a value in mere poor persistence, no matter what its goal. While this counsel approximates Piers's sorrow over sin and sees with him a long-term need to endure, it turns aside from the task, as the poem will persistently do until Wille's last trip at 20.213. As Ymaginatif sees caustically (and as C re-enforces monumentally), the poem isn't his, but has all along been the work of Rechelesnesse, of refusing the good cause of penance.

The point to this presentation, despair poised against heedlessness, is perhaps signalled by the appearance of 'poete Plato' (11.37). At this particularly erratic moment, Langland frames the narrative within a truly witty pre-Christian analysis, but one developing Wit's flirtation with predestination. The relevant text, however, isn't Plato, but Aristotle's analysis of virtue as a mean between excess and lack. To adopt the categories of *Nichomachæan Ethics* 1107b and 1115a-16a, Wille avoids virtue by opting erratically for one or another opposed extreme; he is capable of expressing only heedlessness or despair, either unduly audacious/arrogant or unduly pusillanimous attitudes towards the salvation he claims to seek. These bracket a mean that here can only be implicit (or allusive, the plowman reference of 10.466); one signal of a possible moderation between such flopping into extremes appears in the dreamer's waking from the inner dream to 'shame' (11.405, 425–38), guilty consciousness of a fault all his own. This reversion to a sense of guilt-inducing experience, the product of remembering youth, is equally associated with the cessation/forgetting of academic procedures.

Such clarification continues in Piers's second figural reappearance, in Hawkin's collapse into tears (cf. Maguire's discussion):

> 'Allas', quod Haukyn þe actif man þo, 'þat after my cristendom
> I ne hadde be deed and doluen for Dowelis sake!
> So hard it is', quod Haukyn, 'to lyue and to do synne.
> Synne seweþ vs euere', quod he and sory gan wexe,
> And wepte water wiþ hise eighen and weyled þe tyme
> That euere he dide dede þat dere God displesed;
> Swouned and sobbed and siked ful ofte ...
> (14.323–9)

This character takes one to the edge of the highflying castle world of romance. As 'minstrel', Hawkin is a necessary (but generally unfulfilled) accompaniment to great lords' feasts. He also sees himself as one of Piers's boys (13.237), since his wafers rely upon the grain-trade the central figure organises.[51] Equally, when Piers's name emerges in his speech, it accompanies a sequence of allusions to the punitive dearth of passus 6 and the hope for efficacious pardon (13.243–59). But Hawkin's social commendations clearly are faulted; as 'Actif þat ydelnesse hatie' (13.238), he resembles a Piers who didn't tear a pardon, who remained consumed by work-compulsion. His discovery concerns his limits (and through them, the dreamer's) as visionary, what he hasn't seen – the sin that has stalked him while he was too busy to look, the stains on his cloak that he's taken as just the normal working man's bake-shop soil.

Hawkin's breakdown recapitulates and develops a good many earlier moments in the poem. While he begins with an utterance of despair ('deed and doluen') analogous to the one that plunged Wille into the Land of Longing, he quickly moves past it, to an unremitting preverbal sorrow, Piers's 'payn', tears and sighs. But this gestural sorrow is here attached to another of the poem's emblems of memory, Hawkin's coat. He looks past sin to recall the intact garment he knew 'as a child þat in chirche wepeþ' (1.180). To undertake a recuperative journey towards that moment, he requires a memory that is penitential, not just 'recheles'. The allegory at this point insists, as Ymaginatif has stated it would (cf. 12.70–112), upon a Clergy (at this point abandoned in the dining hall) that can administer institutionalised sacraments. Hawkin's failure is measured by his baptismal garment, and his outcry, following elaborate contrition, the implicit confession of reading his coat, and his rejection of possession (14.330–1), portends a life devoted to satisfaction, addressing God in shame and desiring mercy.

Piers's (semi)final reprise – the ultimate one is the poem's end, the need to persist in it all over again – occurs in passus 17. The man fallen among thieves, the victim rescued by the Samaritan, might recall Ymaginatif's 'dronken daffe' (11.427, echoing 1.140). But rather than the plucky self-help the man in the ditch can give himself, the man fallen is so damaged by sin, 'semyvif' (17.58), that he cannot even cry for aid. He requires sustenance provided from somewhere, a freely given restorative grace, 'þe blood of a barn born of a mayde' (17.96). In all three of Piers's figural reappearances, one sees a pattern of increasing withdrawal from language, of silent subsistence in a state, an increasingly gestural recognition of human dependency.

To this point, I have examined reminiscences of Piers the Plowman in terms of that patience associated with infinite repentance. But, although I have been emphasising the virtue, it most often appears in my account as adjective 'patient', modifying the noun 'poverty'. As a final move, I briefly examine that governing noun. Poverty in the late Middle Ages is a contentious status, and not just one engaged in negotiating between holy suffering and imitative waster Rechelesnesse. Most oppressively in *Piers Plowman*, like the discourse of Law, the term is caught up in a factionalised appeal to a special status.

Thus, when penitential/patient poverty becomes central to the poem's 'inquisiciones', problems get redoubled within a new confrontation. For non-solicitousness or patient poverty is imbricated in a highly contested and pre-existing social discourse that threatens the poem's development. This concerns the history of Franciscan mendicancy and the possible mendicant claim to sanctified apostolic status (see Clopper 1997).[52]

Hence, paralleling efforts at gauging Piers's pardon-tearing, the second part of poem equally, if sometimes quietly, engages in a form of allegorical repetition. Through the 'inquisiciones', Langland indulges in versions of that metaphoric narrative of redefinition Burrow (1957) associates with the second vision. There, the analysis of Piers the pilgrim, in opposition to the tourist pilgrim (5.515–36), tries to measure the usefulness of an old professionalised status in a new contextualisation. Perhaps, Langland implies, one might move past crisis by recasting a threatened and remembered ideal as properly a metaphor literalised and co-opted by modern abuse. Through the 'inquisiciones', Langland measures Piers's penitential poverty against Franciscan (and other mendicant) professional commitment to a poverty equally presenting itself as penitential – although here combining living with providing hands-on purveying of the sacrament.

Fowler sees this major shift in interest (usually, satiric target) as a sign of a second poet. His perception that the poem has shifted gears is surely correct, as is his desire to associate the change with the poem's continuation past the pardon. But, although disruptive, this development testifies to the poem's organised deployment of its discourses, not to a new poet. Langland addresses mendicancy as the socially dispersed language most closely resembling that licensing the London lay teacher committed to poverty. The issue becomes more pressing because of the mendicants' possibly corrupted version of the most necessary sacramental act, penance.

The note is struck at the very head of Wille's search for Dowel, when in a waking interlude, he meets the Franciscans who tell him:

> 'Marie', quod þe maistres, 'amonges vs [Dowel] dwelleþ,
> And euere haþ as I hope, and euere shal herafter'.
> (8.18–19)

The masters allege a typically Franciscan claim, to a perfect life of non-possession. But it immediately sets the dreamer off, suspicious that it must be fake (the generative moment of the first *Piers* imitation, the

Lollard *Piers the Plowman's Creed*). Having been so ill-disposed to their pride from the start, Wille fails to heed their reasonably persuasive and perfectly orthodox teaching.

This is another moment in which Langland bares the device. One sees here the personalisation of instruction, its imbrication in a voice or a status (just as in the priest's snotty response to Piers). If the friars are proud, their problem as instructors is redoubled in the scene; their teaching techniques form part of a too recognisable discourse, in which their specific rhetoric is customarily taken as pernicious. Teaching by 'forbisne', a rhetoric of example that twins/echoes the friar as self-styled exemplary social figure, allows this instruction to be read differently than intended. In this formulation, friars may be seen as impeding instruction through anecdotal frivolity, offering vain inset romances and not sober gospel chastisement. In the face of engaged lay desire, they provide only pabulum, rather than instruction, indirection that serves mainly to highlight their own faults.

As I have argued, one generative force behind the poem is that suspicion of clerical speciality inherited from Pepys 2498 (cf. the late *Mirror* sermon discussed pp. 198–9). Clergy prides itself as delivering a unique instructional system; but equally, ordination does not necessarily convey a living understanding of 'God's law'. Wandering friars, social images of sanctified poverty and learning, may misrepresent both. The poem delights in suggesting the potentially bogus about them, the analogous emptiness of their pretensions to non-possession and to efficacy as instructors, particularly confessors (e.g., the invective against false hermits in C passus 9 or the appearance of William Jordan OP in passus 13). Such anti-mendicant complaint was a local and public development 'siþ þe pestilence tyme', preached 1356–7 in London and in English by bishop Richard FitzRalph of Armagh (see Walsh). The bishop on that occasion took on squarely mendicant claims to apostolic poverty.

But in passus 20, fraternal presence ceases to be a joking matter. The poem's final dream follows from the inversion of Piers's second social contract in the later stages of passus 19; it provides a reprise, savage and spiritualised, of the issues of passus 6. The central figure Conscience, Unity's castellan ('constable' 20.214), is, after all, from his first appearance simply a king's knight fresh from the French wars (cf. p. 265, as well as his too proximate resemblance to Wit's mainly sensory Dowel, 9.1–24). Thus, Conscience simply re-enacts the too courteous knightly kind that has already failed in passus 6 to deal with Waster (e.g., 20.106–9, 242–72, etc.). The policing elements Conscience thinks might work, Hunger redivivus, become more dire and extreme, Elde, Kynde, and Deeþ, signs of The End that demand, as the parable of the Unjust Steward teaches, a final account 'redde quod debes' (cf. Luke 16:2).

The direness of the occasion is, of course, signalled by the imbrication of the entire passus in language of that most generative London devotional text, the Apocalypse. One reflection of this move is compositional; while Langland's narrative is firmly and often allusively apocalyptic (e.g. in the context, 211–12 might allude to the woman in the desert, cf. chapter 4, n. 34), actual biblicism in fact shuts down. Particularly when compared with the several preceding passus, Latinate biblical citation, Langland's most prominent marking of clerical discourse, virtually ceases (256a, 279a only). The world has been abandoned to its *losengeries*, its non-sanctifying languages.

Most particularly, Langland offers one last, here scathing, look at a narrow stream of romance. Narratively pre-eminent, and re-enforcing the centrality of knightly Conscience, is the return to antique *Psychomachia*, battle-poetry, but often literalised (or perceived literally) in its integumen of 'Hende Speche', not its sentence. One might well be back in the world of aristocratic consumption of the Apocalypse (cf. pp. 166–72). By constant indirection, over and above Conscience's pleas for Clergy's aid (228–9, 375), the reader is presented with the value of clerical explanation as traditionally understood. (One could do worse than read the vision against some of its modern avatars, *Dunciad* 4 or *The Waste Land*, for example.)

But Langland's technique only fulfils the promise of the Apocalypse itself. The here absent Bible is the 'liber involutus' of Apoc. 6:14, precisely the absence of a zealous voice, the biographically imagined Revelator – or a figure like Piers (cf. p. 164). Pre-eminent among Antichrist's horde that immediately appears (52–64) are the friars. In the absence of both Piers and Grace, they threaten to subsume altogether the role of publicly available Clergy. But of course, they turn out to be precisely those ineffectual self-pluming fellows the dreamer has already met in passus 8. In Langland's most prominent recycling of anti-mendicant discourse, friars appear as corrupt penitencers, not the competent instructors, the chastisers, London devotional writing always demands.

The language returns, as Szittya cogently argues (3–10), to the font of anti-mendicancy, William of St Amour's *Tractatus de periculis novissimorum temporum*. Almost uniquely, friars come to stand in the poem for the hypocrites, heretics, and losengeors dear to Apocalypse commentary. Their one brush with Latinate Bible, the identification of the corrupt confessor as 'sire *Penetrans-domos*' (340) alludes directly to William's opening salvo against the orders. Moreover, it precisely indicates the problem of mendicants, especially as it appeared to FitzRalph, protector of the parish clergy. The jibe identifies the friar with the 'fur et latro' who is the antitype of the 'pastor bonus . . . qui intrat per ostium' (John 10:1–2). In such an account, friars have failed in their efforts to supplement, much less improve, parochial pastoral efforts.

The narrative outlines progressively the nature of this failure. Unity, stronghold of the Church Militant, should prefigure the 'tour on a toft', the Church Triumphant towards which its beleaguered remnant should pass. To accomplish this task, it must stand firmly, with a moat to keep besiegers off. In turn, this defensive function requires a filled moat, awash with devout penitential tears; it will thus answer 'the moot . . . of Mercy' (5.586) surrounding Truþe's place and thereby solicit from him His Grace. This narrative outline accords with Piers's discovery of patient poverty in the Pardon-tearing, and Piers's tutor, Kynde Wit, has reappeared to enjoin the plan on Conscience and his Londonish *ydiote* (19.360–80).

But just as Antichrist 'Torned al þe crop of Truþe tit vpsodoun' (20.53–4 paraphrased), the resulting narrative is savage parody. For example, as Unity comes under attack from the Seven Deadly Sins (214–27), its relation to the 'tour' comes to appear inverse, not complementary. In the 'tour', virtues precisely remedial to these assailants hold the posterns (5.618–24) – but as welcomers, to allow penitent entry. As zeal flags in Unity, the moat appears to dry up, promoting easy entry of sin instead. Downfall threatens the allegorical house – which is, of course, exactly the metaphorical anchorhold of the Pepys *Riwle*, the soul preserving itself against worldly incursion.

In this context, the fraternal imitation of instructional curacy proves only imitative – and thus appropriative. As Piers knows, following good

London precedent, only penitential chastisement seems to offer hope of salvation. But the grasping friars of passus 20 cannot provide such instruction; suave masters of 'Hende Speche' (and thus a good deal too attractive to the courtly Conscience), they enter Unity simply for 'a pryuee paiement . . . a litel siluer' (364, 367), not care over the penitent's soul or improvement. The poem concludes precisely by inverting one of its most powerful moments, in a parody of the man fallen among thieves, 'semyvif' yet cared for: Contrition 'lyþ adreynt and dremeþ . . . and so do manye oþere' (377). Friars consume the world in 'rechelees' torpor, clerically re-enforced *losengerie*, the absence of instruction and resistance to chastisement. Langland deliberately brings the poem to inertial stasis, a narration of the crisis that has inspired it, by making the 'drenching dreem', the very form of entire production, the primary referent of its narrative.

Yet simultaneously (as Clopper indicates), Langland does not come round to a full-scale rejection of the mendicants. In their Clergy, redeemed through Ymaginatif's measured explanation, and especially in their avowed interest in administering the sacrament of penance, mendicants are just too socially useful to ignore. While they lack Piers's zealous tears, they are potentially valuable allies and sacramental technicians, as Conscience hopes in his final wish that

> freres hadde a fyndyng þat for Nede flateren
> And countrepledeþ me, Conscience . . .
> (383–4)

They must become more like the dreamer, an uninspired lay model, in refusing his final temptation, to Need's license to pillage (20.1–50, 232–41). But equally, friars require a reform into another status in the poem again lay-enunciated, Piers's definition of non-solicitousness. Were friars given (and satisfied with) actual subsistence, they would not ceaselessly try to pillage it at the confessional. Socially useful as learned and public purveyors of penance, reformed orders would ensure that satisfaction payments, 'redde quod debes', remained spiritual goods ending up in Piers's tithe barn (and eventually souls in the 'tour'), not cash in their pockets, to the detriment of their patients, not to mention their own status and effectiveness. In arriving at this conclusion, the poem once again resituates its circumambient social models; a newly defined view of poverty, discovered in labour, displaces and remodels the now prevalent social form, apparently capable of producing only catastrophe.

But in choosing to follow Langland and let Conscience be my final poetic speaker, I am going, like the poem, full circle (and maybe, on to a D, E, or F Version). The end, including the cry to a corrective Clergy for help (375), resembles, a good deal too closely, Conscience's first ineffectual intrusion into the poem. On that occasion, I have argued, one may respect his motivation yet query the messianism that overleaps history, the material conditions of the present. Here at the end, one might wonder exactly how Clergy intends to combat Need with restraint, intends to make friars satisfied with subsistence, and recircling through the poem doesn't give one any sense of an answer. In the last analysis, Langland's desire to return to a purified older world remains just that, his continued 'perpession' in his poem as desire/Wille (but at least Wille, not that vapid resignation Chaucer learned from Boethius). While *Dialogus Petri Ploughman* addresses and analyses crisis with great fervour and intelligence, the power to enact its hopes finally lies with the enemy, the 'new men' whose interests and behaviours have inspired it in the first place.

NOTES

1. See Pearsall 1997 and Middleton's gloss at 1997, 234, 248.
2. On the A Version and some London lucubrations that can serve as prequel to this discussion, see 1996, 229–38.
3. On M's genetic relations (for much of the text, it is an independent derivative from Langland's papers, possibly directly so), see *B Version* 42–4, 50–1, 62; for Doyle's assessment of the hand, *B Version* 11 n. 73; 1986, 39–40.
4. At its end, R has both a guide and a rubric 'passus ij^{us}. de dobest'. The guide, in this case ignored, also appears in L.
5. Viz. Cambridge, University Library, MSS Dd.i.17 (less proximately related to Y than the remainder), Gg. iv. 31 (like S, s. xvi), Ll. iv. 14; and Oxford, Oriel College, MS 79 (CGC^{2}O).
6. 5.510–end, the pardon-tearing in 7, 8.1–75, 11.1–153, 13.1–216, and 20.199–end. Resemblances become attenuated as the poem proceeds, especially at the end as the scribes rush to complete their work.
7. The five copies WMLYR offer reasonably coherent evidence for probable authorial divisions of the text. (R frequently has only passus numbering, affixed mechanically and erroneously; L's evidence comes from its guides, presumably derived from the Langlandian papers that formed its exemplar, and not what the scribe eventually filled in red.) The evidence verifies those divisions conventional in discussions. Because it has been a matter of controversy (Robert Adams 1985, 1994; Clopper 1988, 1995), any

demonstration must occur elsewhere; but cf. 1996, 318 n. 41 and Vance Smith 2001, 44–5, 221 n. 13.

8. As well as, probably contemporary with Langland's C Version, the expatriate (and patronised) Oxford cleric John Trevisa's preface to his *Polychronicon*, a defence of translation, cultural appropriation into the vernacular of a sort prefigured by Pepys texts and, from that source, available to shape *Piers*.

9. 'Visio' as the title for the poem as a whole appears in the B tradition only affixed to Hm.

10. The Russell–Kane dissatisfaction with the form C revision, in their account, took, and their hypothesis of an editor represent one kind of response to this behaviour.

11. The reference to cardinals and papal elections (Pro.107–11) strikes me as potentially general, not necessarily to the Great Schism; those to warring popes (13.173–6; 19.417–23, 428–9, 442–6a) might reflect activities of Gregory XI in the early 1370s. Holmes 1975, 7–20, argues that these underlie complaints eventually productive of the 1376 Good Parliament – and of Langland's poem.

12. The block quotation above: '[Deus] benedictionem eande[m] usque ad interiora cordis tui penetrare faciat; quatenus hoc visibili et tractabili dono invisibilia percipere, et, temporali regno justis moderaminibus executo, æternaliter cum eo regnare, merearis' (Walsingham I, 334).

13. 'Dum rex a regere dicatur, utpote qui populum legibus gubernare et gladio debeat ab inimicis defendere, dum bene regit conuenienter rex appellatur; dum populum spoliat, tyrannus magis esse iudicatur' (75).

14. Cf. adjacent to Walsingham's account of Richard's coronation, Gaunt's difficulties with the City of London and efforts to propitiate him (325–6, 330–1). On the issue of the surrounding court factionalism, in addition to Holmes, see Given-Wilson 110–60, Ormrod 1987, and Michael Bennett 582–94, more consonant with the contemporary record than Goodman's recent biography of Gaunt, 48–86.

15. The anecdote at 317, 318/1–2 cited in the Latin. I am indebted to Andy Galloway for pointing this echo out to me, over a decade ago.

16. Cf. J. A. W. Bennett's note to 7.113 at 222–3, in which many of the cited analogues are simply, like Brinton, quoting Langland.

17. The author is enjoining his female reader to think on the crucifixion as an aid in temptation, and cites Latin bits from an antiphon in support: ' "Be strong in battle, etc." A stod and þoute in þe bellu[n]ge, and thus he promises you great praise when he says, "And you will receive the eternal kingdom". Do wel and aue wel, and, as St John says, "To him, that overcometh, I will give to eat of the tree of life, etc.". As helpe þe God, the person who understands this promise well will not go to be vanquished by death in battle' (' "Estote fortes in bello etc." A stod and þoute in þe belluge, e si vus promete grant luer quant ad dit, "Et accipietis regnum eternum" [cf. 1 Macc. 2:51]. Do wel and aue wel, e par Seyn Ion, "Vincenti dabo edere de lingno vite" [Apoc. 2:7, followed by vv. 17, 21, 28]. As helpe þe God, pur murir ne se lerreit veincre en bataile ke been enpreist cete promesse' (Hill 1978, 499, par. 22; cf. the summary of the piece 492–3 and discussion 496).

18. See the protracted discussion of magnatial lechery and adultery and an assessment of its disruptive power in the commune at 318–19; and ' "One worketh". Nor is it fitting or safe for all the keys to hang on a single woman's belt' (*'Operatur vnus* [1 Cor. 12:11, cited ironically]. Nec est decens vel tutum quod ad vnius vxoris cingulum pendere debeant omnes claues', 321). Cf. in this regard (and consonant with my discussion

of the Chandos Herald), the lament for the (overstated) loss of basic Anglo-Norman literacy at 15.372–6.

19. My general approach shares with Aers 1980, 1–80 (and cf. Lawton 1987), the view that, for Langland, forms of life have either been so emptied out and devalued or become so fraught with insolubilia that they require being ignored or resituated.

20. And not Bowers's speculations about the potential Wycliffism of the piece. As Hudson 1988, 398–408; Gradon, Lawton, von Nolcken, Scase 1989, 125–60; and Middleton 1997, 280–8, have shown, specifically Lollard opinions are unrecoverable from the text and remain about as evancescent as the Wycliffism Colledge wished to ascribe the Pepys *Riwle* (see p. 204).

21. Perhaps the foundational moralising discussion is Yunck's, a great deal more informative about a satirical tradition than it is about *Piers Plowman*; cf. Tavormina 1–47, although including interesting materials on the marital metaphors of this action. Contrast Mitchell's discussion. Similarly, Johnston (324–5, 344–5) and Musson–Ormrod (171–5) implicitly view Conscience as an idealised speaker, but then attack Langland's political naïveté; contrast the wiser Jenkins/Martin.

22. This form of reference indicates my preference for the archetypal reading of B, generally what the manuscripts provide, rather than Kane and Donaldson's reconstructed text.

23. In much the same vein, the agrieved Waster specifically complains against justices, and esp. Sir William Shareshull, 'þat saide I prikkede with powere his pese to distourbe' (314–19). See Turville-Petre's note to lines 126–33 (47–8).

24. Meed's status, as Tavormina sees, is that of magnatial heiress, hence Theology's 'She my3te kisse þe kyng for cosyn' (2.133). The king's interest in her marriage follows from the 'Prerogativa regis', probably 17 Edward II (1324), *Statutes* I, 226: as well as widows and royal wards, women holding of the king in chief require his license to wed. The statement of relationship foreshadows certain difficulties in regal action here, to be addressed below.

25. A signal of his difficulties marks the king's suspicious interruption of his grand grammatical effort in C 3, 'What is ... adiectyf an sustantyf, for Englisch was it neuere?' (342–3).

26. 20 Edward III, cc. 4–6, *Statutes* I, 304–5: 'We have commanded and utterly defended That none of our House ... nor Prelates, Earls, Barons, nor other great nor small of the Land, of what Estate or Condition they be, shall not take in hand Quarrels other than their own, nor the same maintain by them nor by other, privily nor apertly, for Gift [the most normative Mede-word for her action], Promise, Amity, Favour [cf. Wit's evocation of 'boote', 4.92–3], Doubt, nor Fear [cf. 'Drede at þe dore stood and þe doom herde, 2.208], nor for none other Cause, in Disturbance of Law and Hindrance of Right ... but that every Man may be free to sue for and defend his Right in our Courts and elsewhere, according to the Law ... ' (c. 4).

27. The question of church patronage that inspires the dreamer's outrage in 3.48–75 is similar; cf. Rosenthal's extensive documentation of the magnatial 'purchase of paradise'.

28. A view inherited in Brinton's comparisons of English conditions to beneficent French lordship, in his case implicitly glorifying not just Louis IX (whom he uses in an exemplum), but beyond him, the wise Charles V.

29. ' "Ego Dominus diligens justiciam et odio habens rapinam". Et si in hoc audieris populum et hoc illi concesseris, habebis *pacem* in terra ista cum subditis tuis. Unde ait Cassiodorus in quadam epistola, "In hoc gracia regis extollitur et servatur, si in *equitate pacis* populum dirigat et in justicie vigore conservet, et decet regem custodire

concordiam quoniam ad laudem gentis trahitur, si ab omnibus *pax* ametur. Quid enim est quod regem vel principem melius decet vel ipsum predicet, quam *quietus* populus, *concors* servatus, et tota respublica morum honestate vestita?" Si autem populum tuum in hoc non audieris, veniet super te tribulacio magna' (122, my emphasis). Cf. the later version 167–8; the earlier version contains a number of further touches resonant with *Piers*.

30. The 'escheat' reference probably attacks another widespread magnatial practice, business as usual: magnates ensured the perpetuity of their households by transferring the properties, in return for a life interest, to 'feofees'. These persons, usually the lord's closest associates, whom s/he could trust to transfer the assets to the agreed heir, formed a continuing corporation, and could not, consequently, be subjected to death duties.

31. And as once I pointed out (2002, 82–3, 91), is superseded as a character in the poem at the end of passus II. Cf. Simpson 1986; Simpson 1990 is the best general introduction, largely replacing Salter 1969.

32. Cf. Milemete's discussion of Justice, 'Through royal justice, those doing injury are punished, rebels oppressed, the oppressed poor aided' ('Per regeam iusticiam iniuriantes puniuntur, rebelles opprimuntur, *pauperes oppressi iuuantur*', fol. 52ᵛ, my emphasis), similarly fols. 15ᵛ–16 with explicit reference to aiding the oppressed.

33. For extensive discussion of arbitration, see Clanchy 1983, Powell, Hanawalt 1998, 29–31, 35–52; all revising Josephine Bennett; for examples from guild materials, see Barron–Wright 125, 130, 133, 135, 141. The emphasis on lechery, like her eventual condemnation as whore, here simply tropes on Meed as woman constantly open to any appeal for influence, and touches of the anti-feminist portrayal persist in the poem, e.g. 6.324–30.

34. Burdach aptly cites (194) Ps. 33:15: 'Turn away from evil and do good: seek after peace and pursue it' ('Diverte a malo, et fac bonum: inquire pacem et persequere eam').

35. The C passage includes further examples of projecting the poem as continuation, e.g. 84–8 (here a rather garbled account that Wille will learn to see straight), forecasting C 15.232–54 (in B, 14.46–54); these lines in the autobiography are brilliantly analysed Burrow 1993, 104. Any study of this portion of the poem must immediately acknowledge its debts to one of the most penetrating, and most unassuming, articles ever, Burrow 1965.

    Since my interests are other, I take the basics as *dejà lu*: Piers's genealogy is predicated on marrying the election of Peter as earthly heir of Jesus and keeper of grace on earth (Matt. 16:18–19) with the fallen universality of Adam the digger (Gen. 3:17–19) and agrarian parables of the Kingdom (Matt. 13, 20). See, most extensively, Burdach's distinguished treatment, as well as Coghill 1933 and Troyer, and the fine analysis Aers 1975, 77–109; on artistic parallels and shifts in the portrayal of labour, Camille 1987, more distantly Alexander, and Kirk 1988. This conception governs the entire portrayal, from Piers's oath of greeting/meeting (5.537, implying the appearance of Grace as 'gateward' to Truþe's castle 5.595) to his disappearance from the poem, '[Grace] hymself wente | As wide as þe world is wiþ Piers to tille truþe' (19.332–3).

    In addition, Milemete's treatise for young Edward III offers a further contemporary perception. If, as Milemete argues, warfare is a king's truest test, his advice would identify Piers Plowmen with romance preoccupations, as the basis of English military glory of mid-century: 'Country people are better with arms than city ones', 'An army's strength should be drawn from the fields', with lengthy praise of peasant stock ('Plebs rustica melior est ad arma quam urbana', 'ex agris suplendum uidetur robur exercitus', fol. 63). Cf. Spenser's association (ultimately from the *Legenda aurea*) of knightly George with penitential plowman, *Faerie Queene* 1.10.66; or disenfranchised Auchinleck heroes like Beves engaged in rural pursuits.

36. The salvific usefulness of learning is the major point of Ymaginatif's intervention in passus 12 and inherent in Clergy's farewell to Conscience at 13.198–204, a promise actuated at the end of the poem (20.375); see Martin 127.

37. For example, as my subsequent discussion will indicate, to imagine 'doing wel' as an imperative to act/'werche'; or such a locution as 'wher Dowel was at inne' (8.4); or the early (passus 8–9) appearance in the 'inquisiciones' of Wit, i.e. (quinque) sensus.

38. Cf. Donne, in a sermon at St Dunstan's, 1 January 1624/5, discussing sin: 'In young men, vanity begets excesse; excesse, licentiousnesse; licentiousnesse, envy, hatred, quarrels, murders; so here is generation upon generation, here are risen *Grandfather and Great-grandfather-sinnes* quickly. . . . And then they grow suddainly to be habits, and they *come to prescribe in us: Prescription is, when there is no memory to the contrary; and we cannot remember when that sinfull custome begun in us*; yea, our sinnes come to be reverenced in us, and by us; our sinnes contract a majestie and a state, and they grow sacred to us; we dare not trouble a sinne, we dare not displace it, nor displease it' (*The Sermons*, ed. George R. Potter and Evelyn Simpson, 10 vols. [Berkeley CA, 1953–62], 6:196, my emphasis), a citation I owe to Emma Rhatigan, a graduate at Magdalen College, Oxford.

39. The definition provided by Ymaginatif – whatever his mordancy about the prospect (12.16–19), the figure alleged to represent the poem's generating force – is the structural fulcrum, Faith–Hope–Charity (12.29–31; Ymaginatif only explicitly discusses the first of the three). But, in some sense, he generates, not only Patience's statement, but the remainder of the other variously overlapping structures of the 'inquisiciones':

Father (9.26)–Son (16.90)–Paraclete (19.201) (again, like Ymaginatif's definition, not at all separable, as the Samaritan instructs Wille at length 17.134–298, and as the general reference to Do-, 'Told hym of a trinite' [13.102] implies; cf. also Middleton 1972, equally relevant to Patience's definition, the contextual implication that remembering the forgotten consumes everything);

Creation–Gospel–Church Militant;

the belatedly developed romance knight–king–conquerour (cf. retrospectively, e.g., the *Ancrene Riwle* allusion at 9.11);

and, not least, the Ages of Man from at least Wille's schooling at six ('com[yng] to Clergie', 10.226) through Medill Elde (11.47, cf. Burrow 1981) to deathbed confession (20.212–13).

40. In discussing passus 6, like everyone else, I acknowledge the great stimulus of Aers 1988, 20–72, as well as 1980, 19–23, although I think we ultimately disagree about Langland's degree of self-awareness here. Aers's arguments are foreshadowed in Shepherd, and Trower provocatively analyses Hunger. On the topic of poverty, the essays of Mollat's seminar in 1974 are often more probing and suggestive than the general history of 1986.

41. There is, of course, an extensive literature on local, London enforcement of the Statute, most of it in the Letterbooks and Plea and Memoranda Rolls; see Riley 253–8 (and cf. 250–1, 256, 271, 293, 331, 347–8, 390). Particularly provocative, in the light of the poem, are the splendid 1359 attack on sturdy beggars (304–5) and the 1380 case of two men who faked being deaf mutes in hope of charitable support (445–6). One can get some sense of the wasters' alleged heaven, the tavern, from the inventory of two owned by Richard Lyons (like Betty Brewster, he kept spices in his house); see Myers 325–6.

42. Cf. the plausible, although I think ultimately misleading, gloss provided by Wit at A 10.76–84.

43. Although, as I have argued elsewhere (1996, 239), excision of the pardon-tearing from C may be a concession to events of 1381, that deletion is, in any event, balanced by compensatory additions elsewhere in passus 9 to the same purpose as the materials excised.

44. Cf. 6.237–46 with pp. 192–3 above.

45. Woolf seriously upped the explanatory ante necessary to any discussion; cf. Denise Baker and the earlier *lectio accepta*, Frank 1951.

46. In full, 'honestatis aut utilitatis causa rerum arduarum ac difficilium voluntaria et diuturna perpessio' (*De inventione* 2.54.163). For standard pastoral views of the virtue, see Hanna 1978 (for 'negligentia', to which I turn below, esp. 82 n. 14).

47. Reiterating C 11.185–92 = 11.27–32.

48. This passage should, retrospectively, lead one to reconsider Holychurch's view (2.20–35) that Meed is damned by her genetic background. Contrast Gratian, *Decretum* D.56.

49. I adjust Kane-Donaldson to indicate that Langland means palys = 'palisade, fence' and to correct a possibly unmetrical line.

50. Cf. the more allegorically careful C 11.205–6, an insertion, before the last line of the B passage of a bit of Lollard cant, thereby increasing the discursive tension:

> Predestinaet thei prechen, prechours þat this sheweth,
> Or *prescit* inparfit, pult out of grace.

See Hudson 1988, 314–5, 323–5, 328–9.

51. Hawkin, as waferer, does belong in the general class 'minstrels', i.e. festival entertainers. Rather ironically, the Good Parliament villain Richard Lyons functioned prominently in this status; he owned the manor of Overhall in Liston (Essex) which 'carried the right for its lord to make wafers for the king for his coronation feast and serve them to him on that very symbolic occasion. Lyons . . . exercise[d] his right at the coronation of Richard II' (Myers 302). For the Stratford bakers on whom Hawkin relies (13.265–70), see McDonnell 77–83, 90, 137–9.

52. One cannot, as Clopper copiously demonstrates, overestimate Langland's knowledge of the relevant materials. For example, 6.188 probably alludes to the Spiritual Franciscan remnant eventually deemed heretical in the 1320s; among other behaviours, they were accused of expressing their voluntary want by wearing tunics cut so short they exposed their arses. One might see such interest as far from unique in London; in addition to other examples I have cited, the prose Psalter MS, Additional 17376, in the blank lower half of fol. 149ᵛ, has an added series of notes on early Franciscan history (s. xv), ed. *Earliest English* vi.

The end of early London literature

I conclude at the temporal confluence of three widely acknowledged revolutions. Primary is, of course, the appearance of the canonical 'English national tradition', new 'Chaucerian' literature, *The Parliament of Fowls* in 1381, *Troilus* in 1386. These productions are contemporary with Samuels's postulated demise of an older variety of written London English (Type II) and the appearance of a new sort (his Type III, Chaucerian English), first recorded in the writings of Thomas Usk *c.* 1384–88 and in the London guild returns of 1389. Finally, the very writing system changed at this moment: just after 1375, a new variety of book-hand, 'Secretary', appears in English literary manuscripts.

Until this moment 'London literature' exhibited two distinct foci. One, Auchinleck romance, as I have argued above, Chaucer made every effort to laugh out of the canon in 'Thopas'. And while romance certainly has a London afterlife, e.g. Henry Lovelich's Arthuriana of *c.* 1420, Chaucerianism certainly came to dominate sophisticated local culture in its stead. But what of Langland's partial inspiration, the extensive body of bible-based prose texts communicated in Pepys 2498 and later books?

Here I consider the fate of the textual community created by these latter texts. What happened, at the very end of the fourteenth century and in the early years of the fifteenth, to mid-century London biblical translation? Where did it go? And what happened to the literary community, the readers, that had supported it? The most useful information may be derived from later copies of the London texts.

Four of the six copies of the Englished version of Gretham's *Miroir* were produced by Type II London scribes and constitute one focus of this local literary community. One can get some explicit clues to its fate by looking at the fifth, probably London manuscript of Gretham in English, Bodleian Library, MS Holkham misc. 40. The sermon collection here forms an 'expanded version', typical of the two later copies. The Holkham manuscript includes fourteen more sermons than does Pepys; the first of these occurs in some early *Mirror* MSS and is found in the Arundel scribe's Trinity 69 as an independent tract on charity.

Four scribes collaborated on the *Mirror* in Holkham 40, probably sometime in the first twenty years of the fifteenth century. But the fourth ('D') wrote more than 70 per cent of the text, in what appears Chaucerian Type III London, but with some Type II relicts, e.g. occasional 'hij' THEY and '-and(e)' PRES.P., probably inherited from his exemplar. The manuscript provides no information about its medieval provenance, but in 1552 belonged to an Essex rector.

The extra sermons are not the only expansion in Holkham 40, however. The producers of the manuscript display canonising procedures like those I have already described in Pepys 2498 – in the case of Holkham, an effort at providing a full English New Testament. In Pepys, the compilers emphasised narrative completeness – the gospel pericopes provided by the *Mirror* were supplemented by a unique diatesseron. In contrast, the Holkham team sought textual inclusiveness: after completing the *Mirror*, scribe 'D' provided, at fols. 133–62va, the general and Pauline epistles (ignored in the collection procedures underlying Pepys). These the scribe (or his director) acquired from that congeries of originally separate texts known as 'The Paues Version' (IPMEP 263). This biblical translation in its fullest form, exemplified by Cambridge, Selwyn College, MS 108.L.19, joins chunks from at least three different, and each partial, New Testament translations, one of them Wycliffite (but not The Wycliffite).

But the Holkham team's efforts at inclusiveness were not yet completed. After the procedures I have described, a fifth scribe ('E') worked on the manuscript and wrote into it a huge 'appendix', fols. 162va–257rb: his contribution is a full text of the gospels, in the Wycliffite early version. The Holkham manuscript enacts a subsumption of the Type II London canon into that of organised Wycliffism.

One can multiply book biographies like this in some profusion. They are endemic in a small but persistent class of volumes which present parts of Wycliffite scripture. These books generally differ from Pepys

2498 in two ways, partly related, comprehensiveness and size. First, a majority of the manuscripts includes only a single text (several of the exceptions, late Apocalypse manuscripts, represent a very different tradition of book-production and form Lollard anthologies of one stripe or another). Second, a very large number of the codices, especially of the Apocalypse, remind one of early copies of *Ancrene Riwle*; the volumes are portable, in a number of cases pocket-sized, and minimally decorated.[1]

As one further example of the handling of an early London text in a fifteenth-century book, consider the second manuscript (fols. 17–127) of what is now bound as Cambridge, St John's College, MS 193 (G.25). This originally separate volume begins in a predictably scriptural fashion – its first text is the Pepys prose Apocalypse, one of the nine later copies not written in Type II London English; it is succeeded, in a fashion which should now be familiar, by gospel – in this instance a Passion narrative, extracted from *Oon of Foure*, the unedited and possibly Lollard translation of Clement of Lanthony's diatesseron.

The St John's Apocalypse resembles other post-Type II copies in having been redacted. The recensions, of which two are typically recognised, share one feature: the biblical text, which originally had been translated from the Anglo-Norman source, has been replaced by that of the later Wycliffite translation. Unlike Holkham, Lollardised by accretion, here the earlier text has actually been infiltrated. But the revisions of the prose commentary (which distinguish the two recensions) do not reflect Wycliffism, or at least no strong or discernible variety of it (cf. Hudson 1988, 267).

Or so one would say of the Apocalypse in the St John's MS, viewed as an isolated text. But although two-thirds of the manuscript appears comparable to earlier books in being squarely biblical, the remainder is not. The manuscript again shows progressive expansion of contents; its concluding three texts were added, the last two as a separate booklet each. But all these added materials are emphatically Lollard, and of a particularly strident variety.

The first booklet of the manuscript, which contains the biblical texts, ends (fols. 85–93) with an unpublished tract 'how [in] þe sacrament of þe auter crist is [to] be resceyued worþili and deuotly'. This text addresses what is always taken as the defining heretical tenet of the movement and is neither overtly Lollard nor overtly orthodox, but accommodating of any view. The work may be construed as a bit of filler, since it occupies the blank end of the quire concluding the *Oon of Foure* excerpt. But it was important filler, since the scribe did not scruple to add an additional full quire to accommodate the end of the text, and this he only half-filled (the leaves at the end are blank, but bounded and ruled for writing).

Subsequent decisions about the production indicate that this is far from a random choice of text. The final two booklets (one for each item) present those most virulent appendages to the Lollard sermon cycle, the anti-fraternal 'Væ octuplex' and the anti-papal 'Of ministers in the church'.[2] As nearly unique loose copies of these works, their inclusion bespeaks deliberate religious provocateurism. In the St John's MS, the London prose Apocalypse has been recuperated for Lollard use, amid other biblical texts, themselves perhaps Lollard, and in the company of aggressive Lollard appropriations of scripture for the purposes of ecclesiology.[3]

Yet a further example of this behaviour concerns, once again, *The Mirror*. The second prologue to the text, continuous with preceding materials in Duncan's edition (at 7/15), includes a lengthy Apocalypse-inspired anti-clerical passage describing priests who abuse or avoid their teaching function. Much of this material expands decidedly shorter and more tepid discussion in the Anglo-Norman original. Portions of this second prologue, heavily cut and with provocative additions, form the eleventh tract in Cambridge University Library, MS Ii.vi.26 (fols. 51^v-58^v). The remainder of the manuscript is given over to shortish Wycliffite tracts advocating biblical translation (see Hunt 1, 83; 2, 330–6). Here those perhaps 'proto-Lollard' democratising themes of Pepys 2498 texts have been absorbed into the 'heretical' programme.

One may advance this account well into the fifteenth century by examining yet a further book. Manchester, John Rylands University Library, MS Eng. 77, a Wycliffite New Testament, contains the note 'This booke . . . was overseyn And redd by doctor Thomas Ebbrall and Doctor Yve or þat my moder bought it', a unique instance of an examined copy of Lollard scripture.[4] The names in the note place the event sometime in the 1460s and in London: Thomas Eborall and William Ive had Oxford degrees, Doctors of Theology both, and were in succession masters of Whittington College, London (1444–64 and 1464–70, respectively). Neither could be construed tepidly orthodox: both were among those who confuted Reginald Pecock. Moreover, Ive appears an outspoken vehicle of strict doctrine, committed to pulpit chastisement of royalty (even rejecting limitations on such 'assailing' proposed by the Dean of St Paul's) and to confuting the heresy of Christ's absolute poverty, which was bruited by contemporary London Carmelites (see BRUO 622–23, 1008; Scase 1992, esp. 273 n. 38).

Yet simultaneously, Mother (and her son), who were careful not to write an explicit note of ownership in the book, may have selected their examiners with a certain wary foreknowledge. Ive, who bequeathed books to various Oxford colleges, owned Magdalen College, MS Lat. 98, which includes Wycliffe on the decalogue.[5] Eborall, more provocatively still, was willed in 1465 two volumes of Latin and English New Testament (gospels and epistles); in addition, he owned Lambeth Palace Library, MS 541 (*The Pore Caitif*), as well as a more predictably clerical volume in Latin (British Library, MS Royal 5 C.iii). At this latish date, lines between orthodoxy and other endeavours would seem considerably blurred.

One might consider Mother a bit as well. She looks like the sort of person who, had she lived a century earlier, would have been reading at the archetypes behind Pepys 2498. She was quite clearly wealthy and pious. She was literate, wanted access to Scripture in English, and yet knew archbishop Thomas Arundel's 1409 Constitutions (which banned the Lollard Bible) well enough to be at least fastidious about the source of her textual access. Moreover, she was prepared to pay handsomely for her reading: her book although compact (190 mm × 130 mm) was thick, 266 folios worth, as well as expensive, priced in the note at £3 1*m*. Further, she had been able to find this large bible for open sale (although again, the note carefully does not say where), and, if the note is not just conspiratorial smokescreen (which seems unlikely – why name your examiners, if you've invented them?), in circumstances which allowed inspection by persons alleged impeccably orthodox.

In this account, Mother, Eborall, and Ive testify to a situation thoroughly removed from the crusades of extirpation by which Lollardy is often known. One witnesses here a transaction involving all the trappings at least of orthodoxy, with Lollard scripture at its centre. Although the text may be potentially dangerous, that possibility can be defused and the John Rylands volume declared safe pious reading matter. Rather than heresy, it has become the only game in town. This seems to me the most plausible reading of English biblical dissemination during the fifteenth century: the Lollard Bible was a huge success. For a time, it progressively infiltrated earlier, orthodox biblical versions, perhaps as a form of camouflaged circulation, for Arundel's constitutions only ban translations made since Wycliffe's time. But ultimately the banned text became a full substitute and drove out, destroyed the circulation of, competing biblical versions.

As this account also indicates, propagation of the heretical text was partly, if not prominently, London-based. Lollardy was already a public *cause célèbre* in 1386, when the activities of local sectarians produced the first search for written heretical texts (see Richardson). William Taylor's two surviving sermons were delivered in the London area in 1406, one at St Paul's Cross (see *Two Wycliffite*). Fairly thick evidence appears in the second decade of the fifteenth century, with John Claydon, who owned a copy of one of Taylor's sermons, and the discovery of a Lollard scribal community in Clerkenwell (see p. 188, Jurkowsky). Ian Doyle considers one of the five scribes responsible for Dublin, Trinity College, MS 75, Lollard scripture with an apparent 'John Purvey' rebus, likely to be John Seward, grammarmaster of Cornhill 1404 × 1436 and also the copyist of Corporation MS 4158 (see chapter 4, n. 64). Nicholas Belward, one of the Norfolk flock proselytised by William White, had bought the Wycliffite New Testament from which he taught others in London before 1429 (Deanesly 1920a, 358, cf. 355–7). Not only Mother as reader but book-producers as well appear to have converted from Pepys 2498 texts to the 'heretical' biblical version.

Whatever its ultimate source and mechanics of generation, Lollard scripture worked. While a tool that might foster heresy, the very fidelity to the Latin text and the absence of sectarian additions, both integral to sustaining literal Lollard biblical reading, also made the book useful to a general interested audience. Moreover, Lollard scripture had enormous advantages over any competitor: it was textually complete and an accurate rendition of its source,[6] relatively compact, and (in the Later Version) readily legible. The translation, in fact, turned out to be so good an idea that, whatever official pronouncements said, it could be re-appropriated to orthodoxy and used, without particular anxiety, as a convenient consultation text.

In this view, the Cultural Revolution of the 1380s, as I defined it at the opening, may be too narrowly conceived. Is there not a fourth revolution one might add to those I have mentioned: the appearance of 'public Wycliffism', certainly marked, but by no means contained, in the Blackfriars condemnations of May 1382?

This condemnation, like Arundel's later one, was surely abortive and failed to stem the composition and the later encroachment into non-heterodox circles of Lollard vernacular scripture. Such a view – which denatures the provocateurism of the Wycliffite biblical book – would suggest that the persistent interest in Wycliffism as oppositional and revolutionary may occlude much of the historical dynamic at work. Further, efforts to set Lollardy to one side of Middle English literary endeavours, as a religious extremism, may misrepresent as well. The *grande récit* of Middle English privileges as 'canon', of course, the development of 'the Chaucerian tradition'. And at its generative moment, for example with Hoccleve's stridency in the 'teens, this narrative requires the marginalisation of Wycliffism. From this perspective, the Lancastrians fostered one literary endeavour, courtly poetry, and tried to root out the other, Bible in English.

My account would suggest that both 'canonisation' and the parameters of London writing were considerably more fractured and less programmed than this retrospective teleology might imply. For example, the current view of Lancastrian suppressive behaviour (Hoccleve yes, Lollards no) must ignore some thought-provoking information:

First of all, Henry IV's father, John of Gaunt, was until mid-1382 one of Wycliffe's (and other named vernacular dissenters') protectors, certainly the most influential one and perhaps the only one powerful enough to ensure Wycliffe's personal safety.

Second, Henry's uncle and fellow Appellant, Thomas of Woodstock, owned at least four Lollard books (two of which survive) and organised at least one Lollard-friar debate on theological issues. Henry IV's son Thomas owned another surviving Lollard Bible, and although it does not survive, Henry himself appears to have had one, too.[7]

Third, chroniclers generally describe Henry himself as strenuously anti-clerical (most notably with regard to the 'illiterate parliament' of 1404), in contrast to either his predecessor or successor. One might notice, shortly after his usurpation, his order to reinstate in the University of Oxford Lollard troublemakers expelled by Richard II (Hudson 1988, 89).

Fourth, one 'commoner' member of his council, until removed in the putsch of 1410, Sir John Cheyne of Beckford (Gloucs.), was one of McFarlane's 'Lollard knights' and probably complicit in a Lollard library and book-production centre in nearby Kemerton (Gloucs.).[8]

Finally, on our way towards Mother, Eborall, and Ive, one could note just two figures of unimpeachable orthodox piety who transmitted Lollard scripture: John Lacy, Dominican recluse of Newcastle, book-active *c.* 1420–34, who probably ensured that Bodleian Library, MS Rawlinson C.258 was passed on, as was his home-made, but most professional, Book of Hours (now Oxford, St John's College, MS 94), to a local parish church; or King Henry VI, who donated his personal copy, now MS Bodley 277, to the London Carthusians (see Ker, MMBL 134, 222, and 284; 122 and 277, respectively).

One might consider that the development of a national literary canon in the early fifteenth century shows inconsistencies and divergent motivations. In my account, for example, the literary revolution of Type III London English could be construed as an irrelevance. Chaucerianism might well be disaggregated from other literary efforts, an indulgence in the literarily innocuous, the courtly game. Chaucer's career begins, after all, with the dream visions, all strongly imbricated in coterie *roman à clef* (as well as the decorous indirections, the refusals to counsel, with which John of Gaunt is addressed in *The Book of the Duchess*). The later works might be construed as showing similar social disengagement: the narrowing of the traditional public sphere of Troy narrative, alternately to amatory complaint or to Boethian non-engagement in *Troilus*, or the depoliticised narrativity of *The Canterbury Tales*.

One might contrast the more politically querulous inflections of Langlandian poetic. What advice might one offer Conscience (and other king's knights) at the poem's end? How is one to recapture the world of B passus 19, a reformed commonweal, directed by a kind-witted representative of the commune and susceptible to organised (and idealised) allegorical presentation? As one later Langlandian poet sees, modern courtliness is the literary mechanism for silencing older discourses of counsel, now deemed subversive, the 'sothsegger' with his composite medley of engaged (not just narrative) voices, literally a 'satyra', a grab-bag.[9]

In a further Langlandian contrast to the Chaucerian mode, biblicism, whether by allusion, paraphrase, or citation, has always been central to English literary production. Since the tenth century, this focus has been most powerfully expressed through a vernacular bible. And the Wycliffite effort proved an enormously successful consolidation of this interest – to the extent that it progressively supplanted, and then thoroughly extinguished, pre-existing indigenous efforts. Rather than an oppositional force, one might find in the Lollard translators and their efforts at propagating Scripture an example of the movement towards a continuing centre of a national literary tradition.

NOTES

1. For descriptions of Apocalypse manuscripts, see *Apoc* vii–xvi; Doyle discusses the manuscripts and their provenances at 1953, I, 120–5. The copies with Lollard associations include British Library, MSS Harley 1203, Harley 3913, and Royal 17 A.xxvi; Cambridge, St John's College, MS 193 (G.25); Bodleian Library, MSS Laud misc. 33 and 235; and Columbia University Library, MS Plimpton Add. 3. Pocket-sized, i.e. 5″–6″ high, are British Library, MSS Harley 3913, Royal; Cambridge, Gonville and Caius College, MS 231/117; Bodleian Library, MSS Laud 33 and Rawlinson C.750; somewhat larger, but not more than 8″ high, are St John's and Manchester, John Rylands University Library, MS Eng. 92.
2. IPMEP 127 and 738, now ed. Pamela Gradon, *English Wycliffite Sermons II*, 328–78; see also the discussion of the manuscript transmission, Anne Hudson, *English Wycliffite Sermons I*, 49–50.
3. Similarly, the Apocalypse copy closest to the St John's MS, Harley 3913 (see *Apoc* xxi), prefaces the text with three prologues, rather than the customary one. The first two unique passages have been derived from portions of the Lollard Psalter commentary (an identification for which I am grateful to Anne Hudson) and the whole bound with a Lollard theological notebook, mostly in Latin (see Hudson 1988, 204).
4. See Ker, MMBL 3, 404; Ker reports the note as having been added on a flyleaf somewhat later, 's. xv/xvi'.
5. Although what one may read as Ive's guilt of ownership is enshrined in the binding of the book. At some point in the mid-fifteenth century, the two texts in the volume were reversed, rendering the Wycliffe not so incriminatingly visible at its opening.
6. Indeed, more accurate than the clerical Latin, according to the author of the prologue to the historical books; see *Selections* 67/26–31, 69/72–8.
7. For Woodstock's books and the debate, see Hudson 1988, 12 and n. 29; A. I. Doyle notes his Bibles and John's at 1983, 168–9. For Henry's own Bible, see Summerson 112.
8. For Cheyne, see Roskell; and McFarlane's famous discussion, 162–76, etc.; on Kemerton as a copying centre, see Hudson 1988, 90–1.
9. Cf. *The Piers Plowman Tradition* 186–88, 194–202 (*Mum* 1343–1412, 1565–1752); see also Grady.

Bibliography

BOOKS ABOUT BOOKS: MANUSCRIPT REFERENCES

Baker, John H., and J. S. Ringrose 1996. *A Catalogue of English Legal Manuscripts in Cambridge University Library.* Woodbridge: Boydell.

Bloomfield, Morton W., *et al.* 1979. *Incipits of Latin Works on the Virtues and Vices, 1100–1500 A.D.* Cambridge MA: Medieval Academy of America.

Colker, Marvin L. 1991. *Trinity College Library Dublin Descriptive Catalogue of the Medieval and Renaissance Latin Manuscripts,* 2 vols. Aldershot: Scolar Press.

Corpus of British Medieval Library Catalogues . . . , gen. ed. Richard Sharpe 1990– . currently 10 vols. London: British Library.

Crick, Julia C. 1989. *The Historia regum . . . 3 A Summary Catalogue of the Manuscripts.* Cambridge: Brewer.

Dean, Ruth 1999. *Anglo-Norman Literature: A Guide to Texts and Manuscripts,* ANTS occasional publications 3. London: ANTS.

Dutschke, C. W. 1989. *Guide to Medieval and Renaissance Manuscripts in the Huntington Library,* 2 vols. San Marino CA: Huntington Library.

[Hardwick, Charles, and Henry R. Luard (eds.)] 1856–67. *A Catalogue of the Manuscripts Preserved in the Library of the University of Cambridge,* 6 vols. Cambridge: Cambridge University Press.

James, Montague R. 1900–4. *The Western Manuscripts in the Library of Trinity College, Cambridge: A Descriptive Catalogue,* 4 vols. Cambridge: Cambridge University Press.

1903. *The Ancient Libraries of Canterbury and Dover.* Cambridge: Cambridge University Press.

1905. *A Descriptive Catalogue of the Manuscripts in the Library of Pembroke College, Cambridge.* Cambridge: Cambridge University Press.

1909–12. *A Descriptive Catalogue of the Manuscripts in the Library of Corpus Christi College Cambridge,* 2 vols. Cambridge: Cambridge University Press.

1913. *A Descriptive Catalogue of the Manuscripts in the Library of St John's College Cambridge.* Cambridge: Cambridge University Press.

1921. *A Descriptive Catalogue of the Latin Manuscripts in the John Rylands Library at Manchester,* 2 vols. Manchester: Manchester University Press.

Bibliography

Jolliffe, P. S. 1974. *A Check-list of Middle English Prose Writings of Spiritual Guidance.* Toronto: Pontifical Institute.

Lewis, Robert E., and Angus McIntosh 1982. *A Descriptive Guide to the Manuscripts of the* Prick of Conscience, Medium Ævum Monographs ns 12. Oxford: Society for the Study of Mediaeval Languages and Literature.

McKitterick, Rosamond, and Richard Beadle 1992. *Catalogue of the Pepys Library at Magdalene College Cambridge, Vol. V: Manuscripts Part i Medieval.* Cambridge: Brewer.

Robinson, J. Armitage, and Montague R. James 1909. *The Manuscripts of Westminster Abbey.* Cambridge: Cambridge University Press.

Robinson, P. R. 1988. *Catalogue of Dated and Datable Manuscripts c. 737–1600 in Cambridge Libraries,* 2 vols. Cambridge: Brewer.

2003. *Catalogue of Dated and Datable Manuscripts c. 888–1600 in London Libraries,* 2 vols. London: British Library.

Rye, Reginald A. 1921. *Catalogue of the Manuscripts and Autograph Letters in the University Library.* London: University of London Press.

Watson, Andrew G. 1969. *The Manuscripts of Henry Savile of Banke.* London: The Bibliographical Society.

1979. *Catalogue of Dated and Datable Manuscripts c. 700–1600 in the Department of Manuscripts, the British Library,* 2 vols. London: British Library.

1984. *Catalogue of Dated and Datable Manuscripts c. 435–1600 in Oxford Libraries,* 2 vols. Oxford: Clarendon Press.

Young, John, and P. Henderson Aitken 1908. *A Catalogue of the Manuscripts in the Library of the Hunterian Museum in the University of Glasgow.* Glasgow: Maclehose.

PRIMARY SOURCES AND TEXTS

Adami Murimuthensis Chronica sui temporis, ed. Thomas Hog (London: [English Historical Society], 1846).

Aelred of Rievaulx. 'De genealogia regum Anglorum'. *Patrologia Latina* 195:711–38. 'Vita S. Edwardi regis'. *Patrologia Latina* 195:737–90.

Amis and Amiloun, ed. MacEdward Leach, EETS 203 (1937).

Anglo-Norman Political Songs, ed. Isabel S. T. Aspin, ANTS 11 (1953).

Anglo-Scottish Relations 1174–1328: Some Selected Documents, ed. E. L. G. Stones. Oxford: Clarendon Press, 1970.

Annales Londonienses and

Annales Paulini, Chronicles of the Reigns of Edward I. and Edward II., Vol. I, ed. William Stubbs, Rolls Series 76/1 (1882), 63–251, 255–370, respectively.

The Anonimalle Chronicle 1333 to 1381, ed. V. H. Galbraith. Manchester: Manchester University Press, 1927.

An Anonymous Short English Metrical Chronicle, ed. Evald Zettl, EETS 196 (1935).

Of Arthour and of Merlin, ed. O. D. Macrae-Gibson, EETS 268, 279 (1973–9).

Bibliography

The Auchinleck Manuscript: National Library of Scotland Advocates' Manuscript 19.2.1., ed. Derek Pearsall and I. C. Cunningham. London: Scolar Press, 1979.

Barber, Richard 1979, 1986. *Life and Campaigns of the Black Prince*. Woodbridge: Boydell.

Biblia latina cum glossa ordinaria, 4 vols. 1480/1; rep. Turnhout: Brepols, 1992.

Blumreich Moore, Kathleen M. 1992. 'The Middle English "Mirror": An Edition Based on Bodleian Library, MS. Holkham Misc.40 . . .' (unpub. Michigan State University Ph.D. diss.; see *Dissertation Abstracts International* 53 (1992):3598A).

The Book of Vices and Virtues, ed. W. Nelson Francis, EETS 217 (1942).

Bower, Walter 1993. *Scotichronicon 1*, ed. D. E. R. Watt *et al*. Aberdeen: Aberdeen University Press.

Brinton, Thomas 1954. *The Sermons of Thomas Brinton, Bishop of Rochester (1373–1389)*, ed. Mary A. Devlin, 2 vols. Camden Society 3rd ser. 85–6 (1954).

Brown, Carleton (ed.) 1924. *Religious Lyrics of the XIVth Century*. Oxford: Clarendon Press.

1932. *English Lyrics of the XIIIth Century*. Oxford: Clarendon Press.

The Brut or The Chronicles of England, ed. Friedrich D. W. Brie, EETS 131, 136 (1906–8).

Calendar of Select Pleas and Memoranda of the City of London, ed. A. H. Thomas, 4 vols. Cambridge: Cambridge University Press, 1926–32.

Cambridge University Library MS Ff.2.38, ed. Frances McSparran and P. R. Robinson. London: Scolar Press, 1979.

Chambers, R. W. and Marjorie Daunt (eds.) 1931. *A Book of London English, 1384–1425*. Oxford: Clarendon Press.

The Chastising of God's Children, ed. Joyce Bazire and Eric Colledge. Oxford: Blackwell, 1957.

Chaucer, Geoffrey 1987. *The Riverside Chaucer Third Edition*, ed. Larry D. Benson *et al*. Boston: Houghton Mifflin.

Chrétien de Troyes 1994. *Le Chevalier au lion*, ed. David F. Hult. Paris: Le livre de poche.

A Chronicle of London from 1089 to 1483 . . . , ed. Nicholas H. Nicholas and E. Tyrell (London, 1827).

Clanvowe, Sir John 1965, 1975. *The Works*, ed. V. J. Scattergood. Cambridge: Brewer.

Croniques de London depuis l'an 44 Hen. III. jusqu'à l'an 17 Edw. III., ed. George J. Aungier, Camden Society os 28 (1844).

Cursor Mundi, ed. Richard Morris, 7 vols., EETS os 57, 59, 62, 66, 68, 99, 101 (1874–93).

Davy, Adam 1873. *Adam Davy's 5 Dreams about Edward II.* . . . , ed. F. J. Furnivall, EETS os 69.

Donne, John 2002. *Selected Letters*, ed. P. M. Oliver. Manchester: Carcanet.

Dumville, David N. 1990. 'A Paraphrase of the *Historia Brittonum*: Two Fragments', in *Histories and Pseudo-Histories of the Insular Middle Ages*. Aldershot: Variorum. section XIII.

The Earliest Complete English Prose Psalter, ed. Karl D. Bülbring, EETS os 97 (1891).

The English Text of the Ancrene Riwle: Ancrene Wisse, ed. J. R. R. Tolkien, EETS 249 (1962).

Bibliography

British Museum MS. Cotton Nero A.xiv, ed. Mabel Day and J. A. Herbert, EETS 225 (1952).

Gonville and Caius MS. 234/120, ed. R. M. Wilson, EETS 229 (1954).

Magdalene College Cambridge MS. Pepys 2498, ed. A. Zettersten, EETS 274 (1976).

English Wycliffite Sermons, ed. Anne Hudson and Pamela Gradon, 5 vols. Oxford: Clarendon Press, 1983–96.

The Eyre of London 14 Edward II A.D. 1321, ed. Helen M. Cam, Selden Society 85–6 (1968–9).

FitzStephen, William. 'Descriptio nobilissimæ civitatis Londoniæ', the prologue to *Vita et passionis Sancti Thomæ archiepiscopi et martyris. Patrologia Latina* 190: 103–10.

Flores historiarum, vol. III A.D. 1265 to A.D. 1326 (partially Robert of Reading), ed. Henry R. Luard, Rolls Series 95/3 (1890).

Floris and Blauncheflur: A Middle English Romance . . ., ed. Franciscus C. de Vries. Groningen: Drukkerij V. R. B., 1966.

Fragments of an Early Fourteenth-Century Guy of Warwick, ed. Maldwyn Mills and Daniel Huws, Medium Ævum Monographs ns 4. Oxford: Blackwell, 1974.

Die Gesetze der Angelsächsen, ed. F. Liebermann, 3 vols. Halle a. S.: Niemeyer, 1898–1916.

The Great Chronicle of London, ed. A. H. Thomas and I. D. Thornley. London: G. W. Jones, 1938.

Havelok, ed. G. V. Smithers. Oxford: Clarendon Press, 1987.

Hengham, Ralph, *Radulphi de Hengham Summæ*, ed. William H. Dunham. Cambridge: Cambridge University Press, 1932.

Henry of Huntingdon. *Historia Anglorum: The History of the English People*, ed. Diana Greenway. Oxford: Clarendon Press, 1996.

Horn Childe and Maiden Rimnild, ed. Maldwyn Mills, Middle English Texts 20. Heidelberg: Winter, 1988.

Hunt, Simon 1994. 'An Edition of Tracts in Favour of Scriptural Translation and of Some Texts Connected with Lollard Vernacular Biblical Scholarship', 2 vols. unpub. Oxford University D.Phil. dissertation, Bodleian Library, MS D.Phil. c.11472–3.

Illingworth, William 1812. 'Copy of a Libel against Archbishop Neville, temp. Richard II . . .', *Archaeologia* 16:80–3.

Islip, Simon, see William of Paull.

John of Reading 1914. *Chronica Johannis de Reading et Anonymi Cantuariensis 1346–67*, ed. James Tait. Manchester: Manchester University Press, 1914.

Kempe, Margery. *The Book of Margery Kempe*, ed. Sanford B. Meech and Hope E. Allen, EETS 212 (1940).

Kyng Alisaunder, ed. G. V. Smithers, EETS 227, 237 (1952–7).

The Lambeth Apocalypse: Manuscript 209 in Lambeth Palace Library, ed. Nigel Morgan with Michelle Brown. London: Harvey Miller, 1990.

Langland, William 1960–97. *Piers Plowman*, ed. George Kane *et al.*, 3 vols.: *The A Version*, *The B Version*, with E. Talbot Donaldson, *The C Version*, with George Russell. London: Athlone Press, 1960, 1975, 1997.

317

Bibliography

2002. *The Piers Plowman Electronic Archive, Vol. 2: Cambridge, Trinity College, MS B.15.17*, ed. Thorlac Turville-Petre and Hoyt N. Duggan, The Society for Early English and Norse Electronic Texts. Ann Arbor MI: University of Michigan Press.

forthcoming. —, *Vol. 4: Oxford, Bodleian Library, MS Laud misc. 581*, ed. Hoyt N. Duggan and Ralph Hanna.

Latini, Brunetto 1948. *Li livres dou trésor*, ed. Francis J. Carmody. Berkeley CA: University of California Press.

Leges Henrici Primi, ed. L. J. Downer. Oxford: Clarendon Press, 1972.

Lybeaus Desconus, ed. M. Mills, EETS 261 (1969).

Life of the Black Prince, ed. Mildred K. Pope and Eleanor C. Lodge. Oxford: Clarendon Press, 1910.

'A Lollard Tract: On Translating the Bible into English' 1938, ed. Curt F. Bühler, *Medium Ævum* 7:167–83.

The London Chronicles of the Fifteenth Century: A Revolution in English Writing, with an Annotated Edition of Bradford, West Yorkshire Archives MS 32D86/42, ed. Mary-Rose McLaren. Cambridge: Brewer, 2002.

The London Eyre of 1244, ed. Helena M. Chew and Martin Weinbaum, London Record Society Publications 6 (1970).

The London Eyre of 1276, ed. Martin Weinbaum, London Record Society Publications 12 (1976).

Love, Nicholas 1992. *Nicholas Love's Mirror of the Blessed Life of Jesus Christ*, ed. Michael G. Sargent. New York: Garland.

Mannyng, Robert. *Robert of Brunne's 'Handlyng Synne' A.D. 1303*, ed. Frederick J. Furnivall, EETS os 119, 123 (1901–3).

Map, Walter 1983. *De Nugis Curialium: Courtiers' Trifles*, ed. M. R. James, rev. C. N. L. Brooke and R. A. B. Mynors. Oxford: Clarendon Press.

Matthew Paris. *La Estoire de Seint Aedward le rei, attributed to Matthew Paris*, ed. Kathryn Y. Wallace, ANTS 41 (1983).

Medieval English Songs, ed. E. J. Dobson and F. Ll. Harrison. London: Faber, 1979.

Meyer, Paul 1886. 'Les Manuscrits français de Cambridge. II – Bibliothèque de l'université', *Romania* 15:236–357.

The Middle English Genesis and Exodus, ed. Olof Arngart, Lund Studies in English 36. Lund: Gleerup, 1968.

The Middle English Translations of Robert Grosseteste's Château d'Amour, ed. Kari Sajavaara. Helsinki: Société néophilologique, 1967.

The Mirror of Justices, ed. William J. Whittaker (introd. F. W. Maitland), Selden Society 7 (1895).

'Die mittelenglische Übersetzung der Apokalypse mit Kommentar (Version B): Edition, Untersuchungen und Glossar', ed. Walter Sauer. Ruprecht-Karl-Universität zu Heidelberg Ph.D. diss., 1971.

'The monk of Malmesbury', see Walwayn.

Munimenta Gildhallæ Londoniensis ... Vol. II ... Liber Custumarum ..., ed. Henry T. Riley, Rolls series 12/2, 2 vols. (1860).

Bibliography

The Owl and the Nightingale: Text and Translation, ed. Neil Cartlidge. Exeter: Exeter University Press, 2001.

Parish Fraternity Register: Fraternity of The Holy Trinity and SS Fabian and Sebastian in the Parish of St Botolph without Aldersgate, ed. Patricia Basing, London Record Society Publications 18 (1982).

The Pepysian Gospel Harmony, ed. Margery Goates, EETS 157 (1922).

The Pierpont Morgan Library MS M.817 A Facsimile, ed. Jeanne Krochalis, The Facsimile Series of the Works of Geoffrey Chaucer 4. Norman OK: Pilgrim, 1986.

Piers Plowman: The Huntington Library Manuscript (HM 143) Reproduced in Photostat, ed. R. W. Chambers *et al.* San Marino CA: Huntington Library, 1936.

The Piers Plowman Tradition, ed. Helen Barr. London: Dent, 1993.

Prester John 1879: 'Der Priester Johannes', ed. Friedrich Zarncke, *Abhandlungen der philologisch-historischen Classe der königlichen Sächsischen Gesellschaft der Wissenschaften* 7:909–24.

'The Proclamation of Henry III [1258]', *Early Middle English Texts*, ed. Bruce Dickins and R. M. Wilson, 6th impression. London: Bowes & Bowes, 1965. Pp. 7–9.

The Recluse: A Fourteenth-Century English Version of the Ancren Riwle, ed. Joel Påhlsson. Lund: H. Ohlson, 1918.

Reliquiæ Antiquæ: Scraps from Ancient Manuscripts . . ., ed. Thomas Wright and James O. Halliwell, 2 vols. London: J. R. Smith, 1845.

Riley, Henry T. 1868. *Memorials of London and London Life in the XIIIth, XIVth, and XVth Centuries*. London: Longmans.

Robbins, Rossell H. (ed.) 1955. *Secular Lyrics of the XIVth and XVth Centuries*, 2nd edn. Oxford: Clarendon Press.

Robert of Gretham 1974. *Miroir, ou Les Evangiles des Domnees*, ed. Saverio Panunzio, 2nd edn. Bari: Adriatica.

Roger of Howden. *Chronica*, ed. William Stubbs, 2 vols., Rolls Series 51 (1868–71).

Rymer, Thomas 1745, rep. [1967]. *Foedera, conventiones, literæ, et cujuscunque generis acta publica, inter reges Angliæ . . .*, 3rd edn, 10 vols. [Farnborough: Gregg].

St Patrick's Purgatory, ed. Robert Easting, EETS 298 (1991).

Secretum Secretorum: Nine English Versions, ed. M. A. Manzalaoui, EETS 276 (1977).

Selections from English Wycliffite Writings, ed. Anne Hudson. Cambridge: Cambridge University Press, 1978.

The Seven Sages of Rome (Southern Version), ed. Karl Brunner, EETS 191 (1933).

The Simonie: A Parallel-Text Edition, ed. Dan Embree and Elizabeth Urquhart, Middle English Texts 24. Heidelberg: Winter, 1991.

Sir Tristrem, ed. George P. McNeill, Scottish Text Society 8. Edinburgh: Blackwood, 1886.

'The Song of the Husbandman'/'The Evils of Taxation', ed. Turville-Petre (see *Winner*), pp. 17–20.

The South English Legendary, ed. Charlotte D'Evelyn and Anna J. Mill, 3 vols., EETS 235–6, 244 (1956–9).

Speculum Vitae: see British Library, MS Additional 33995.

Spenser, Edmund 1977. *The Faerie Qveene*, ed. A. C. Hamilton, Annotated English Poets Series. London: Longman.

Statutes of the Realm, 9 vols. London: Eyre and Strahan, 1810–22.

Stow, John 1908. *A Survey of London*, ed. Charles L. Kingsford, 2 vols. Oxford: Clarendon Press.

Thedmar, Arnald. *De Antiquis legibus liber: Cronica maiorum et vicecomitum Londoniarum*, ed. Thomas Stapleton, Camden Society os 34 (1846).

Thomas Hoccleve: A Facsimile of the Autograph Verse Manuscripts..., ed. J. A. Burrow and A. I. Doyle, EETS ss 19 (2002).

Titus and Vespasian or the Destruction of Jerusalem in Rhymed Couplets, ed. J. A. Herbert, Roxburghe Club. London: Roxburghe Club, 1905.

Trevisa, John, 'Trevisa's Original Prefaces on Translation: A Critical Edition', ed. Ronald Waldron, in Kennedy *et al.* (eds.), pp. 285–99.

The Trinity College Apocalypse, ed. Peter H. Brieger. London: Eugrammia Press, 1967.

Two Wycliffite Texts, ed. Anne Hudson, EETS 301 (1993).

La Vie du Prince Noir by Chandos Herald, ed. Diana B. Tyson.Tübingen: Niemeyer, 1975.

Vita, see *Life*

Walsingham, Thomas. *Historia Anglicana*, ed. Henry T. Riley, 2 vols., Rolls Series 28/1 (1863–4).

[Walwayn, John], *Vita Edwardi Secundi/The Life of Edward II, by the so-called Monk of Malmesbury*, ed. N. Denholm-Young. London: Nelson, 1957.

William of Pauli 1891. *De speculo regis Edwardi III, seu tractatu quem de mala regni administratione conscripsit Simon Islip ...*, ed. Joseph Moisant. Paris: Picard.

William of Shoreham, *The Poems*, ed. M. Konrath, EETS es 86 (1902).

Winner and Waster, ed. Thorlac Turville-Petre, *Alliterative Poetry of the Later Middle Ages: An Anthology*. London: Routledge, 1989. Pp. 38–66.

'Wit and Will': *The Conflict of Wit and Will: Fragments of a Middle English Alliterative Poem*, ed. Bruce Dickins. Kendal: Wilson, 1937.

Woodbine, George E. (ed.) 1910. *Four Thirteenth Century Law Tracts*. New Haven: Yale University Press.

Worcester, William 1860. *The Boke of Noblesse*, ed. John G. Nichols, Roxburghe Club 77*. London: Nichols.

Wycliffe, John 1886. *Tractatus de Ecclesia*, ed. Iohann Loserth, Wyclif Society [8]. London: Trübner.

Yorkshire Writers, ed. C. Horstman, 2 vols. London: Sonnenschein, 1895–6.

SECONDARY SOURCES

Adams, Robert 1978. 'The Nature of Need in "Piers Plowman" XX', *Traditio* 34:273–301.
    1985. 'The Reliability of the Rubrics in the B-text of *Piers Plowman*', *Medium Ævum* 54:208–31.
    1994. 'Langland's *Ordinatio*: The *Visio* and the *Vita* Once More', *Yearbook of Langland Studies* 8:51–84.

Bibliography

Adams, Robert P. 1959–60. 'Bold Bawdry and Open Manslaughter: The English New Humanist Attack on Medieval Romance', *Huntington Library Quarterly* 23:33–48.

Aers, David 1975. *Piers Plowman and Christian Allegory*. London: Arnold.

1980. *Chaucer, Langland and the Creative Imagination*. London: Routledge.

1986. 'Reflections on the "Allegory of the Theologians", Ideology and *Piers Plowman*', in *Medieval Literature: Criticism, Ideology and History*, ed. Aers. Brighton: Harvester. Pp. 58–73.

1988. *Community, Gender, and Individual Identity: English Writing 1360–1430*. London: Routledge.

Aitken, Marion Y. H. 1922. *Etude sur Le Miroir ou Les Evangiles des domnees de Robert de Gretham*. Paris: Champion.

Alexander, Jonathan 1990. '*Labeur* and *Paresse*: Ideological Representations of Medieval Peasant Labor', *Art Bulletin* 72:436–52.

Alford, John 1988a. *Piers Plowman: A Glossary of Legal Diction*. Cambridge: Brewer.

1988b. 'The Idea of Reason in *Piers Plowman*', in Kennedy *et al.* (eds.), pp. 199–215.

Aston, Margaret 1984. ' "Caim's Castles": Poverty, Politics, and Disendowment', in Dobson (ed.), pp. 45–81.

Auerbach, Eric 1965. *Literary Language and Its Public in Late Latin Antiquity and in the Middle Ages*, Bollingen Series 74. Princeton: Princeton University Press.

Avery, Margaret E. 1969. 'The History of the Equitable Jurisdiction of Chancery before 1460', *Bulletin of the Institute of Historical Research* 42:129–44.

Baker, Denise N. 1980. 'From Plowing to Penitence: *Piers Plowman* and Fourteenth-Century Theology', *Speculum* 55:715–25.

Baker, John H. 1990. *An Introduction to English Legal History*, 3rd edn. London: Butterworths.

Barber, Richard 1978. *Edward, Prince of Wales and Aquitaine: A Biography of the Black Prince*. London: Allen Lane.

Barnes, Geraldine 1984. 'Cunning and Ingenuity in the Middle English *Floris and Blauncheflur*', *Medium Ævum* 53:10–25.

1993. *Counsel and Strategy in Middle English Romance*. Woodbridge: Brewer.

Barron, Caroline M. 1985. 'The Parish Fraternities of Medieval London', in *The Church in Pre-Reformation Society: Essays in Honour of F. R. H. DuBoulay*, ed. Barron and Christopher Harper-Bill. Woodbridge: Boydell. Pp. 13–37.

1989. 'The Later Middle Ages: 1270–1520', in Lobel (ed.), pp. 42–56.

1995a. 'Centres of Conspicuous Consumption: The Aristocratic Townhouse in London 1200–1550', *London Journal* 20, i:1–16.

1995b. 'London in the Later Middle Ages 1300–1500', *London Journal* 20, ii:22–33.

2000. 'London 1300–1540', in *The Cambridge Urban History of Britain Volume I 600–1540*, ed. D. M. Palliser. Cambridge: Cambridge University Press. Pp. 395–440.

2003. 'London and St Paul's Cathedral in the Later Middle Ages', in *The Medieval English Cathedral: Papers in Honour of Pamela Tudor-Craig*, ed. Janet Backhouse, Harlaxton Medieval Studies 10. Donington: Shaun Tyas. Pp. 126–49.

Bibliography

Barron, Caroline M. and Laura Wright 1995. 'The London Middle English Guild Certificates of 1388–9', *Nottingham Medieval Studies* 39:108–45.

Bateson, Mary 1902. 'A London Municipal Collection of the Reign of King John', *English Historical Review* 17:480–511, 707–30.

Beadle, Richard 1991. 'Prolegomena to a Literary Geography of Later Medieval Norfolk', in Riddy (ed.), pp. 89–108.

1994. 'Middle English Texts and their Transmission, 1350–1500: Some Geographical Criteria', in *Speaking in Our Tongues*, ed. Margaret Laing and Keith Williamson. Cambridge: Brewer. Pp. 69–91.

Beadle, Richard, and A. J. Piper (eds.) 1995. *New Science out of Old Books: Studies in Manuscripts and Early Printed Books in Honour of A. I. Doyle*. Aldershot: Scolar Press.

Beckerman, John S. 1999. 'Law Writing and Law Teaching: Treatise Evidence of the Formal Teaching of English Law in the Late Thirteenth Century', in Bush–Wijffels (eds.), pp. 33–50.

Beer, Jeanette (ed.) 1989. *Medieval Translators and Their Craft*. Kalamazoo MI: Medieval Institute.

Bennett, Adelaide 1986. 'Anthony Bek's Copy of *Statuta Anglie*', in Ormrod (ed.), pp. 1–27.

Bennett, J. A. W. 1943. 'The Date of the B-Text of *Piers Plowman*', *Medium Ævum* 12:55–64.

1969. 'Chaucer's Contemporary', in S. S. Hussey (ed.), pp. 310–24.

Bennett, Josephine W. 1958. 'The Mediaeval Loveday', *Speculum* 33:351–70.

Bennett, Michael 1998. 'Edward III's Entail and the Succession to the Crown, 1376–1471', *English Historical Review* 113:580–609.

Benson, Larry D. 1976. *Malory's* Morte Darthur. Cambridge MA: Harvard University Press.

Berger, Samuel 1884, rep. 1967. *La Bible française au moyen âge*. Geneva: Slatkine.

Bezzola, Reto R. 1958–63. *Les Origines et la formation de la littérature courtoise en Occident (500–1200)*, 3 vols. in 5, Bibliothèque de l'Ecole des hautes études, Science historiques et philologiques 286, 313, 319–20. Paris: Champion.

Binski, Paul 1986. *The Painted Chamber at Westminster*, Society of Antiquaries Occasional Papers ns 9. London: Society of Antiquaries.

1990a. 'The Cosmati at Westminster and the English Court Style', *Art Bulletin* 72:6–34.

1990b. 'Reflections on *La estoire de Saint Ædward le Rei*: Hagiography and Kingship', *Journal of Medieval History* 16:333–50.

1995. *Westminster Abbey and the Plantagenets: Kingship and the Representation of Power*. New Haven: Yale University Press.

Bird, Ruth 1949. *The Turbulent London of Richard II*. London: Longman.

Bliss, A. J. 1951. 'Notes on the Auchinleck Manuscript', *Speculum* 26:652–8.

Boffey, Julia, and Pamela King (eds.) 1995. *London and Europe in the Later Middle Ages*. London: Centre for Medieval and Renaissance Studies.

Bibliography

Boffey, Julia, and Carol Meale 1991. 'Selecting the Text: Rawlinson C.86 and Some Other Books for London Readers', in Riddy (ed.), pp. 143–69.

Bovey, Alixe forthcoming. *The Smithfield Decretals: Image, Text and Audience in Fourteenth-Century England*. London: British Library.

Bowers, John M. 1992. 'Piers Plowman and the Police: Notes Toward a History of the Wycliffite Langland', *Yearbook of Langland Studies* 6:1–50.

Boyle, Leonard E. 1955. 'The *Oculus sacerdotis* and Some Other Works of William of Pagula', *Transactions of the Royal Historical Society* 5th ser. 5:81–110.

———. 1970. 'William of Pagula and the *Speculum Regis Edwardi III*', *Mediaeval Studies* 32:329–36.

Brand, Paul A. 1974. 'The Contribution of the Period of Baronial Reform (1258–67) to the Development of the Common Law in England'. Unpub. Oxford D.Phil. thesis, Bodleian Law Library, MS D.Phil. c.1319.

———. 1992. *The Making of the Common Law*. London: Hambledon.

———. 1995. 'Westminster Hall and Europe: European Aspects of the Common Law', in Boffey–King (eds.), pp. 55–83.

——— (ed.) 1996. *The Earliest English Law Reports, Vol. I*, Selden Society 111.

———. 1999. 'Legal Education in England before the Inns of Court', in Bush–Wijffels (eds.), pp. 51–84.

———. 2000. 'The Languages of the Law in Later Medieval England', in Trotter (ed.), pp. 63–76.

Brandt, William J. 1966. *The Shape of Medieval History: Studies in Modes of Perception*. New Haven: Yale University Press.

Brantley, Jessica 2002. 'Images of the Vernacular in the Taymouth Hours', *English Manuscript Studies* 10:83–113.

Breder, Günter 1960. *Die lateinische Vorlage des altfranzösischen Apokalypsenkommentars des 13. Jahrhunderts (Paris, B.N., ms. fr. 403)*, Forschungen zur romanischen Philologie. Münster i. W.: Aschendorff.

Breslow, Boyd 1977. 'The Social Status and Economic Interests of Richer de Refham, Lord Mayor of London', *Journal of Medieval History* 3:135–45.

Brooke, Christopher 1989. 'The Central Middle Ages: 800–1270', in Lobel (ed.), pp. 30–41.

Broun, Dauvit 1999. *The Irish Identity of the Kingdom of the Scots in the Twelfth and Thirteenth Centuries*, Studies in Celtic History 18. Woodbridge: Boydell.

Brownrigg, Linda 1989. 'The Taymouth Hours and the Romance of *Beves of Hampton*', *English Manuscript Studies* 1:222–41.

Burdach, Konrad 1926–32. 'Beziehungen zum englischen Typus "Peter der Pfluger"', in *Der Dichter des Ackermann aus Böhmen und seine Zeit (Vom Mittelalter zur Reformation* 3.2). Berlin: Weidmann. Pp. 140–371.

Burrow, J. A. 1957. 'The Audience of *Piers Plowman*', *Anglia* 75:373–84.

———. 1965. 'The Action of Langland's Second Vision', *Essays in Criticism* 15:247–68.

———. 1971. *Ricardian Poetry: Chaucer, Gower, Langland, and the 'Gawain' Poet*. London: Routledge.

1981. 'Langland *Nel Mezzo del Cammin*', in *Medieval Studies for J. A. W. Bennett, Ætatis suae LXX*, ed. P. L. Heyworth. Oxford: Clarendon. Pp. 21–41.

1993. *Langland's Fictions*. Oxford: Clarendon Press.

Bush, Jonathan A., and Alain Wijffels (eds.) 1999. *Learning the Law: Teaching and the Transmission of Law in England 1150–1900*. London: Hambledon.

Butterfield, Ardis 1997. 'French Culture and the Ricardian Court', in *Essays on Ricardian Literature in Honour of J. A. Burrow*, ed. A. J. Minnis *et al.* Oxford: Clarendon Press. Pp. 82–120.

Camille, Michael 1987. 'Labouring for the Lord: The Ploughman and Social Order in the Luttrell Psalter', *Art History* 10:423–54.

1993. 'At the Edge of the Law: An Illustrated Register of Writs in the Pierpont Morgan Library', in Rogers (ed.), pp. 1–14.

1998. *Mirror in Parchment: The Luttrell Psalter and the Making of Medieval England*. London: Reaktion.

Cannon, Debbie 2003. 'London Pride: Citizenship in the Fourteenth-Century Custumals of the City of London', in *Learning and Literacy in Medieval England and Abroad*, ed. Sarah Rees Jones, Utrecht Studies in Medieval Literacy 3. Turnhout: Brepols. Pp. 179–98.

Carlin, Martha 1996. *Medieval Southwark*. London: Hambledon.

Catto, Jeremy 1981. 'Andrew Horn: Law and History in Fourteenth-Century England', in *The Writing of History in the Middle Ages: Essays Presented to Richard William Southern*, ed. R. H. C. Davis and J. M. Wallace-Hadrill. Oxford: Oxford University Press. Pp. 367–91.

Cavanaugh, Susan H. 1988. 'Royal Books: King John to Richard II', *The Library* 6th ser. 10:304–16.

Chaplais, Pierre 1971. *English Royal Documents: King John-Henry VI 1199–1461*. Oxford: Clarendon Press.

Chapters of the Augustinian Canons 1922, ed. H. E. Salter, Oxford Historical Society 74.

Charland, Th. M. 1936. *Artes Praedicandi: contribution à l'histoire de la rhétorique au moyen âge*. Paris: Vrin.

Childs, W. R. 1991. "Welcome my brother": Edward II, John of Powderham and the Chronicles, 1318', in *Church and Chronicle in the Middle Ages: Essays Presented to John Taylor*, ed. Ian Wood and G. A. Loud. London: Hambledon. Pp. 149–63.

Christianson, C. Paul 1990. *A Directory of London Stationers and Book Artisans 1300–1500*. New York: Bibliographical Society of America.

Clanchy, M. T. 1979, 1993. *From Memory to Written Record*. London: Arnold; Oxford: Blackwell.

1983. 'Law and Love in the Middle Ages', in *Disputes and Settlements: Law and Human Relations in the West*, ed. John Bossy. Cambridge: Cambridge University Press. Pp. 47–67.

Clark, John 1981. 'Trinovantum – The Evolution of a Legend', *Journal of Medieval History* 7:135–51.

Clarke, M. V., ed. L. S. Sutherland and M. McKisack 1937. *Fourteenth Century Studies*. Oxford: Clarendon.

Bibliography

Clopper, Lawrence M. 1988. 'Langland's Markings for the Structure of *Piers Plowman*', *Modern Philology* 85:245–55.

———. 1995. 'A Response to Robert Adams, "Langland's Ordinatio"', *Yearbook of Langland Studies* 9:141–6.

———. 1997. *"Songes of Rechelesnesse": Langland and the Franciscans*, Studies in Medieval and Early Modern Civilization. Ann Arbor MI: University of Michigan Press.

———. 2000a. 'The Engaged Spectator: Langland and Chaucer on Civic Spectacle and the *Theatrum*', *Studies in the Age of Chaucer* 22:123–47.

———. 2000b. 'London and the Problem of the Clerkenwell Plays', *Comparative Drama* 34:291–303.

———. 2001. *Drama, Play, and Game: English Festive Culture in the Medieval and Early Modern Period*. Chicago: University of Chicago Press.

Coghill, Nevill K. 1933. 'The Character of Piers Plowman Considered from the B Text', *Medium Ævum* 2:108–35.

———. 1946. 'The Pardon of Piers Plowman', *Proceedings of the British Academy* 30:303–57.

Colledge, Eric 1939. '*The Recluse*: A Lollard Interpolated Version of the *Ancren Riwle*', *Review of English Studies* 15: 1–15, 129–45.

Connolly, Margaret 1998. *John Shirley: Book Production and the Noble Household in Fifteenth-Century England*. Aldershot: Ashgate.

Courtenay, William J. 1987. *Schools and Scholars in Fourteenth-Century England*. Princeton: Princeton University Press.

Cox, D. C. 1976. 'The French Chronicle of London', *Medium Ævum* 45:201–8.

Crowfoot, Elisabeth, *et al.* 1992. *Textiles and Clothing c. 1150–c. 1450*, Medieval Finds from Excavations in London 4. London: HMSO.

Cunningham, I. C. 1972. 'Notes on the Auchinleck MS', *Speculum* 47:96–8.

Cunningham, I. C., and J. E. C. Mordkoff 1982. 'New Light on the Signatures in the Auchinleck Manuscript (Edinburgh, National Library of Scotland Advocates' MS. 19.2.1)', *Scriptorium* 36:280–92.

Dalrymple, Roger 2000. *Language and Piety in Middle English Romance*. Cambridge: Brewer.

Damian-Grant, Peter 1997. '*Estoire* as Word and Genre: Meaning and Literary Usage in the Twelfth Century', *Medium Ævum* 66:189–206.

Davies, J. Conway 1953–4. 'Common Law Writs and Returns: Richard I to Richard II', *Bulletin of the Institute of Historical Research* 26:125–56, 27:1–34.

Davies, R. R. 2000. *The First English Empire: Power and Identities in the British Isles, 1093–1343*. Oxford: Oxford University Press.

Davis, Brian P. 1997. 'The Rationale for a Copy of a Text: Constructing the Exemplar for BL Additional MS. 10574', *Yearbook of Langland Studies* 11:141–55.

Davis, R. H. C. 1976. *The Normans and Their Myth*. London: Thames & Hudson.

D'Avray, D. L. 1994. *Death and the Prince: Memorial Preaching before 1350*. Oxford: Clarendon Press.

Deanesly, Margaret 1920a. *The Lollard Bible and Other Medieval Bible Versions*. Cambridge: Cambridge University Press.

1920b. 'Vernacular Books in England in the Fourteenth and Fifteenth Century', *Modern Language Review* 15:349–58.

Denholm-Young, Noël 1943. 'Who Wrote *Fleta?*', *English Historical Review* 58:1–12.

1944. 'Matthew Cheker', *English Historical Review* 59:252–7.

1956. 'Who Was the Author of *Vita Edwardi secundi?*', *English Historical Review* 72:202–11.

Dennison, Lynda 1986. 'An Illuminator of the Queen Mary Psalter Group: The Ancient 6 Master', *The Antiquaries Journal* 66:287–314.

1990. ' "Liber Horn", "Liber Custumarum" and Other Manuscripts of the Queen Mary Psalter Workshops', in Grant (ed.), pp. 118–34.

1999. 'Monastic or Secular? The Artist of the Ramsey Psalter, now at Holkham Hall, Norfolk', in *Monasteries and Society in Medieval Britain*, ed. Benjamin Thompson, Harlaxton Medieval Studies 6. Stamford: Paul Watkins. Pp. 223–61 and plates 13–39.

Viscount Dillon and W. H. St. John Hope 1897. 'Inventory of the Goods and Chattels Belonging to Thomas, Duke of Gloucester . . .', *Archaeological Journal* 54:275–308.

Dobson, Barrie (ed.) 1984. *The Church, Politics and Patronage in the Fifteenth Century*. Gloucester: Alan Sutton.

Donaldson, E. Talbot 1949. *Piers Plowman: The C-Text and Its Poet*. New Haven: Yale University Press.

Doyle, A. I. 1953. 'A Survey of the Origins and Circulation of Theological Writings in English . . .', 2 vols. unpub. Cambridge University Ph.D. diss.

1958. 'Books Connected with the Vere Family and Barking Abbey', *Transactions of the Essex Archaeological Society* 25:222–43.

1981. 'University College, Oxford, MS 97 and its relationship to the Simeon Manuscript (British Library Add. 22283)', in *So meny people longages and tonges: Philological Essays in Scots and Medieval English presented to Angus McIntosh*, ed. Michael Benskin and M. L. Samuels. Edinburgh: privately. Pp. 265–82.

1983. 'English Books In and Out of Court from Edward III to Henry VII', in Scattergood–Sherborne (eds.), pp. 164–81.

1986. 'Remarks on Surviving Manuscripts of *Piers Plowman*', in *Medieval English Religious and Ethical Literature: Essays in Honour of G. H. Russell*, ed. Gregory Kratzmann and James Simpson. Cambridge: Brewer. Pp. 35–48.

1997. '*Stephen Dodesham of Witham and Sheen*', in *Of the Making of Books: Medieval Manuscripts, their Scribes and Readers: Essays Presented to M. B. Parkes*, ed. P. R. Robinson and Rivkah Zim. Aldershot: Scolar Press. Pp. 94–115.

Doyle, A. I., and Malcolm Parkes 1978. 'The Production of Copies of the Canterbury Tales and the Confessio Amantis in the Early Fifteenth Century', in *Medieval Scribes, Manuscripts and Libraries: Essays Presented to N. R. Ker*, ed. Parkes and Andrew G. Watson. London: Scolar Press. Pp. 163–210.

Drennan, Jean F. 1980a. '*The Complaint of Our Lady* and *Gospel of Nicodemus* of MS Pepys 2498', *Manuscripta* 24:164–70.

1980b. 'The Middle English *Gospel of Nicodemus*, Huntington Library MS. HM 144', *Notes and Queries* 225:297–8.

Bibliography

Duncan, Thomas G. 1968. 'Notes on the Language of the Hunterian MS of the *Mirror*', *Neuphilologische Mitteilungen* 69:204–8.

1983. 'The Middle English *Mirror* and its Manuscripts', in *Middle English Studies Presented to Norman Davis*, ed. Douglas Gray and E. G. Stanley. Oxford: Clarendon Press. Pp. 115–26.

1998. 'The Middle English Translator of Robert of Gretham's Anglo-Norman *Miroir*', in *The Medieval Translator Traduire au Moyen Age 6*, ed. Roger Ellis *et al*. Turnhout: Brepols. Pp. 211–31.

Durling, Nancy V. 1989. 'Translation and Innovation in the *Roman de Brut*', in Beer (ed.), pp. 9–39.

Ekwall, Eilert 1956. *Studies on the Population of Medieval London*. Stockholm: Almkvist & Wiksell.

Everett, Walter 1975. 'The *Clensyng of Mannes Soule*: An Introductory Study', *Southern Quarterly* 13:265–79.

Fellows, Jennifer 1986. 'Sir Bevis of Hampton in Popular Tradition', *Proceedings of the Hampshire Field Club and Archaeological Society* 42:139–45.

1993. 'St George as Romance Hero', *Reading Medieval Studies* 19:27–54.

Ferris, Sumner 1980. 'Chronicle, Chivalric Biography, Family Tradition in Fourteenth-Century England', in *Chivalric Literature: Essays on Relations Between Literature and Life in the Later Middle Ages*, ed. Larry D. Benson and John Leyerle, Studies in Medieval Culture 14. Kalamazoo MI: Medieval Institute. Pp. 25–38.

Fewster, Carol 1987. *Traditionality and Genre in Middle English Romance*. Cambridge: Brewer.

Field, Rosalind 1991. 'Romance as History, History as Romance', in *Romance in Medieval England*, ed. Maldwyn Mills *et al*. Cambridge: Brewer. Pp. 163–74.

2000. '*Waldef* and the Matter of/with England', in Weiss *et al*. (eds.), pp. 35–49.

Finlayson, John 1980–1. 'Defining Middle English Romance', *Chaucer Review* 15:44–63, 168–81.

1990. '*Richard Coer de Lyon*: Romance, History or Something In Between', *Studies in Philology* 87:156–80.

Fowler, David C. 1961. *Piers the Plowman: Literary Relations of the A and B Texts*. Seattle: University of Washington Press.

Fowler, Joseph T. 1882–1908. *Memorials of the Church of SS Peter and Wilfrid, Ripon*, Surtees Society 74, 78, 81, 115.

Frank, Robert W. Jr 1951. 'The Pardon Scene in *Piers Plowman*', *Speculum* 26:317–31.

1990. 'The "Hungry Gap," Crop Failure, and Famine: The Fourteenth-Century Agricultural Crisis and *Piers Plowman*', *Yearbook of Langland Studies* 4:87–104.

Freyhan, David C. 1955. 'Joachimism and the English Apocalypse', *Journal of the Warburg and Courtauld Institutes* 18:211–44.

Fryde, E. B. 1988. *William de la Pole, Merchant and King's Banker (+ 1366)*. London: Hambledon.

Fryde, Natalie 1979. *The Tyranny and Fall of Edward II, 1321–1326*. Cambridge: Cambridge University Press.

Fyler, John M. 1979. *Chaucer and Ovid*. New Haven: Yale University Press.

Galbraith, V. H. (with an appendix by G. D. G. Hall) 1969. 'Statutes of Edward I: Huntington Library ms. H.M. 25782', in Sandquist–Powicke (eds.), pp. 176–91.

Galloway, Andrew 1995. 'The Rhetoric of Riddling in Late-Medieval England: The "Oxford" Riddles, the *Secretum Philosophorum*, and the Riddles in *Piers Plowman*', *Speculum* 70:69–105.

Garnett, George, and John Hudson (eds.) 1994. *Law and Government in Medieval England and Normandy: Essays in Honour of Sir James Holt.* Cambridge: Cambridge University Press.

Gauchier, Elisabeth 1993. 'Entre l'histoire et le roman: la biographie chevaleresque', *Revue des langues romanes* 97: 15–29.

Gee, Loveday L. 2002. *Women, Art and Patronage From Henry III to Edward III: 1216–1377.* Woodbridge: Boydell.

Genet, Jean-Philippe 1984. 'Ecclesiastics and Political Theory in Late Medieval England: The End of a Monopoly', in Dobson (ed.), pp. 23–44.

Gillespie, Vincent 1994. 'Thy Will Be Done: *Piers Plowman* and the *Paternoster*', in *Late-Medieval Religious Texts and Their Transmission: Essays in Honour of A. I. Doyle*, ed. A. J. Minnis, York Manuscripts Conferences Proceedings Series 3. Cambridge: Brewer. Pp. 95–119.

Given-Wilson, Chris 1986. *The Royal Household and the King's Affinity: Service, Politics and Finance in England 1360–1413.* New Haven: Yale University Press.

Goodman, Anthony 1992. *John of Gaunt: The Exercise of Princely Power in Fourteenth-Century Europe.* Harlow: Longman.

Görlach, Manfred 1974. *The Textual Tradition of the South English Legendary*, Leeds Texts and Monographs ns 6. Leeds: University of Leeds School of English.

Gradon, Pamela 1980. 'Langland and the Ideology of Dissent', *Proceedings of the British Academy* 66:179–205.

Grady, Frank 1996. 'Chaucer Reading Langland: *The House of Fame*', *Studies in the Age of Chaucer* 18:3–23.

Gransden, Antonia 1974a. 'The Continuations of the *Flores Historiarum* from 1265 to 1327', *Mediaeval Studies* 36:472–92.

1974b. *Historical Writing in England c. 550 to c. 1307.* London: Routledge.

Grant, Lindy (ed.) 1990. *Medieval Art, Architecture and Archaeology in London*, British Archaeological Association 10.

Grassi, J. L. 1970. 'Royal Clerks from the Archdiocese of York in the Fourteenth Century', *Northern History* 5:12–33.

Green, Richard F. 1999. *A Crisis of Truth: Literature and Law in Ricardian England.* Philadelphia: University of Pennsylvania Press.

Griffiths, Jeremy J. 1992. 'A Newly Identified Manuscript Inscribed by John Shirley', *Library* 6th ser. 14:83–93.

1997. 'The Production of Copies of Vernacular Texts in London in the Fifteenth Century', unpub. and unsubmitted Oxford D.Phil. diss.

Haas, Elsa de, and G. D. G. Hall 1970. *Early Registers of Writs*, Selden Society 87.

Hallam, Elizabeth M., and Michael Roper 1978. 'The Capital and the Records of the Nation: Seven Centuries of Housing the Public Records in London', *London Journal* 4:73–94.

Hamilton, Bernard 1985. 'Prester John and the Three Kings of Cologne', in *Studies in Medieval History presented to R. H. C. Davis*, ed. Henry Mayr-Harting and R. I. Moore. London: Hambledon. Pp. 177–91.

Hanawalt, Barbara A. 1984. 'Keepers of the Lights: Late Medieval English Parish Gilds', *Journal of Medieval and Renaissance Studies* 14:21–37.

———— 1986. *The Ties that Bound: Peasant Families in Medieval England*. New York: Oxford University Press.

———— 1998. *'Of Good and Ill Repute': Gender and Social Control in Medieval England*. New York: Oxford University Press.

Hanawalt, Barbara A., and Ben R. McRee 1992. 'The Guilds of *Homo Prudens* in Late Medieval England', *Continuity and Change* 7:163–79.

Hanna, Ralph 1978. 'Some Commonplaces of Late Medieval Patience Discussions: An Introduction', in *The Triumph of Patience: Medieval and Renaissance Studies*, ed. Gerald J. Schiffhorst. Orlando FL: University Presses of Florida. Pp. 65–87.

———— 1989. 'The Scribe of Huntington HM 114', *Studies in Bibliography* 42:120–33.

———— 1993. 'Studies in the Manuscripts of *Piers Plowman*', *Yearbook of Langland Studies* 7:1–25 + plate.

———— 1996. *Pursuing History: Middle English Manuscripts and Their Texts*, Figurae: Reading Medieval Culture. Stanford CA: Stanford University Press.

———— 1997. *The Index of Middle English Prose Handlist XII: Smaller Bodleian Collections . . .* Cambridge: Brewer.

———— 2000. 'Reconsidering the Auchinleck Manuscript', *New Directions in Later Medieval Manuscript Studies*, ed. Derek Pearsall. Woodbridge: York Medieval Press. Pp. 91–102.

———— 2002. 'Langland's Ymaginatif: Images and the Limits of Poetry', in *Images, Idolatry and Iconoclasm in Late Medieval England*, ed. Jeremy Dimmick *et al.* Oxford: Oxford University Press. Pp. 81–94.

———— 2003. 'English Biblical Texts Before Lollardy and Their Fate', in *Lollards and Their Influence in Later Medieval England*, ed. Fiona Somerset *et al.* Woodbridge: Boydell. Pp. 141–53.

Hanning, Robert W. 1977. *The Individual in Twelfth-Century Romance*. New Haven: Yale University Press.

Harding, Vanessa 1995. 'Medieval Documentary Sources for London and Paris: A Comparison', in Boffey–King (eds.), pp. 35–54.

Heal, Felicity 1996. 'Reciprocity and Exchange in the Late Medieval Household', in *Bodies and Disciplines: Intersections of Literature and History in Fifteenth-Century England*, ed. Barbara Hanawalt and David Wallace, Medieval Cultures 9. Minneapolis: University of Minnesota Press. Pp. 179–98.

Hebron, Malcolm 1997. *The Medieval Siege: Theme and Image in Middle English Romance*. Oxford: Clarendon Press.

Henderson, George 1967. 'Studies in English Manuscript Illumination. Part 2: The English Apocalypse: I', *Journal of the Warburg and Courtauld Institutes*, 30:104–37.

Hill, Betty 1975. '*Epitaphia Alexandri* in English Medieval Manuscripts', *Leeds Studies in English* ns 8:96–104.

1977. 'The Twelfth-Century *Conduct of Life*, Formerly the *Poema Morale* or *A Moral Ode*', *Leeds Studies in English* ns 9:97–144.

1978. 'British Library MS. Egerton 613', *Notes and Queries* 223:394–409, 492–501.

Hilton, R. H. 1975. *The English Peasantry in the Later Middle Ages*. Oxford: Clarendon Press.

Hollaender, A. E. J., and William Kellaway (eds.) 1969. *Studies in London History Presented to Philip Edmund Jones*. London: Hodder & Stoughton.

Holmes, George 1957. *The Estates of the Higher Nobility in Fourteenth-Century England*. Cambridge: Cambridge University Press.

1975. *The Good Parliament*. Oxford: Clarendon Press.

Holt, J. C. 1974. 'A Vernacular-French Text of Magna Carta, 1215', *English Historical Review* 89:346–64.

Homans, George C. 1941. *English Villagers of the Thirteenth Century*. Cambridge MA: Harvard University Press.

Hopkins, Andrea 1990. *The Sinful Knights: A Study of Middle English Penitential Romance*. Oxford: Clarendon Press.

Horobin, Simon 2003. *The Language of the Chaucer Tradition*, Chaucer Studies 32. Cambridge: Brewer.

Horwood, A. J. 1877. 'A Manuscript Volume Belonging to Sir George Webb Dasent, D.C.L.', *Historical Manuscripts Commission*, 6th Report, Appendix, 407–18.

Howe, Nicholas 1989, 2001. *Migration and Mythmaking in Anglo-Saxon England*. New Haven: Yale University Press; and Notre Dame IN: Notre Dame University Press.

Hudson, Anne 1988. *The Premature Reformation: Wycliffite Texts and Lollard History*. Oxford: Clarendon Press.

2003. 'The Development of Wyclif's *Summa Theologie*', in *John Wyclif Logica, Politica, Teologia*, ed. Mariateresa Fumagalli *et al.* Florence: SISMEL Edizioni del Galuzzo. Pp. 57–70.

Hughes, Jonathan 1988. *Pastors and Visionaries: Religion and Secular Life in Late Medieval Yorkshire*. Woodbridge: Boydell.

Hunt, R. W. 1966. 'A Dismembered Manuscript: Bodleian MS. Lat. th. e.32 and British Library Add. MS. 17376', *Bodleian Library Record* 7:271–5.

Hussey, Maurice 1958. 'The Petitions of the Paternoster in Mediaeval English Literature', *Medium Ævum* 27:8–16.

Hussey, S. S. 1965. 'Langland's Reading of Alliterative Poetry', *Modern Language Review* 60:163–70.

(ed.) 1969. *Piers Plowman: Critical Approaches*. London: Methuen.

Hutton, Ronald 1994. *The Rise and Fall of Merry England: The Ritual Year 1400–1700*. Oxford: Oxford University Press.

Bibliography

Jenkins (Martin), Priscilla 1969. 'Conscience: The Frustration of Allegory', in S. S. Hussey (ed.), pp. 125–42.

Johnston, Andrew J. 2002. *Clerks and Courtiers: Chaucer, Late Middle English Literature and the State Formation Process*, Anglistische Forschungen 302. Heidelberg: Winter.

Jones, William R. 1974. 'English Religious Brotherhoods and Medieval Lay Piety: The Inquiry of 1388–9', *The Historian* 36:646–59.

Jordan, William C. 1996. *The Great Famine: Northern Europe in the Early Fourteenth Century*. Princeton: Princeton University Press.

Jurkowsky, Maureen forthcoming. 'Some Lollard Book Producers and Their Associates', in Hudson Festschrift.

Justice, Steven 1994. *Writing and Rebellion: England in 1381*. Berkeley CA: University of California Press.

Justice, Steven and Kathryn Kerby-Fulton (eds.) 1997. *Written Work: Langland, Labor, and Authorship*. Philadelphia: University of Pennsylvania Press.

Kauffmann, C. M. 1975. *Romanesque Manuscripts 1066–1190*, A Survey of Manuscripts Illuminated in the British Isles 3. London: Harvey Miller.

Keene, Derek 1989. 'Medieval London and Its Region', *London Journal* 14:99–111.

1990. 'Shops and Shopping in Medieval London', in Grant (ed.), pp. 29–46.

1999. 'Wardrobes in the City: Houses of Consumption, Finance and Power', *Thirteenth-Century England* 7:103–15.

2000. 'Metropolitan Values: Migration, Mobility, and Cultural Norms, London 1100–1700', in *The Development of Standard English 1300–1800: Theories, Descriptions, Conflicts*, ed. Laura Wright. Cambridge: Cambridge University Press. Pp. 93–114.

Kennedy, Edward D. *et al.* (eds.) 1988. *Medieval English Studies Presented to George Kane*. Cambridge: Brewer.

Ker, N. R., ed. Andrew G. Watson 1985. *Books, Collectors and Libraries: Studies in the Medieval Heritage*. London: Hambledon.

Kermode, Jenny 1998. *Medieval Merchants: York, Beverley and Hull in the Later Middle Ages*, Cambridge Studies in Medieval Life and Thought, 4th ser. 38. Cambridge: Cambridge University Press.

King, Andrew 2000. The Faerie Queene *and Middle English Romance: The Matter of Just Memory*. Oxford: Clarendon Press.

Kipling, Gordon 1998. *Enter the King: Theatre, Liturgy, and Ritual in the Medieval Civic Triumph*. Oxford: Clarendon Press.

Kirk, Elizabeth D. 1972. *The Dream Thought of* Piers Plowman. New Haven: Yale University Press.

1988. 'Langland's Plowman and the Recreation of Fourteenth-Century Religious Metaphor', *Yearbook of Langland Studies* 2:1–21.

Kisby, Fiona 2002. 'Books in London Parish Churches before 1603: Some Preliminary Observations', in *The Church and Learning in Later Medieval Society: Essays in Honour of R. B. Dobson*, ed. Caroline M. Barron and Jenny Stratford, Harlaxton Medieval Studies 11. Donington: Shaun Tyas. Pp. 305–26.

Klein, Peter 1983. *Endzeiterwartung und Ritterideologie: Die englischen Bilderapoka-lypsen der Frühgotik und MS Douce 180*, Codices selecti 72*. Graz: Akademische Druck.

Knowles, David 1963. *The Monastic Order in England: A History of its Development...*, *940–1216*, 2nd edn. Cambridge: Cambridge University Press.

Labarge, Margaret W. 1980. *Gascony: England's First Colony 1204–1453*. London: Hamish Hamilton.

Laing, Margaret 1992. 'A Linguistic Atlas of Early Middle English: The Value of Texts Surviving in More than One Version', in *History of Englishes: New Methods and Interpretations in Historical Linguistics*, ed. Matti Rissanen *et al.* Berlin: Mouton de Gruyter. Pp. 566–81.

   1993. *Catalogue of Sources for a Linguistic Atlas of Early Medieval English*. Cambridge: Brewer.

Laing, Margaret, and Angus McIntosh 1995. 'Cambridge, Trinity College, MS 335: Its Texts and Their Transmission', in Beadle–Piper (eds.), pp. 14–52.

Laird, Charlton G. 1942. 'Five New Gretham Sermons and the Middle English *Mirrur*', *PMLA* 57:628–37.

Lancashire, Anne 2002. *London Civic Theatre: City Drama and Pageantry from Roman Times to 1558*. Cambridge: Cambridge University Press.

Lawton, David A. 1981. 'Lollardy and the "Piers Plowman" Tradition', *Modern Language Review* 76:780–93.

   1987. 'The Subject of *Piers Plowman*', *Yearbook of Langland Studies* 1:1–30.

Leclercq, Jean, tr. Catherine Misrahi 1962. *The Love of Learning and the Desire for God: A Study of Monastic Culture*. New York: Mentor paper.

Legge, M. Dominica 1950. *Anglo-Norman in the Cloisters: The Influence of the Orders upon Anglo-Norman Literature*. Edinburgh: Edinburgh University Press.

   1963. *Anglo-Norman Literature and its Background*. Oxford: Clarendon.

   1965. 'La Précocité de la littérature anglo-normand', *Cahiers de la civilisation médiévale* 8:327–49.

Lewis, Suzanne 1986. 'Giles of Bridport and the Abingdon Apocalypse', in *England in the Thirteenth Century: Proceedings of the 1984 Harlaxton Symposium*, ed. W. M. Ormrod, 2nd edn. Woodbridge: Boydell. Pp. 107–19.

   1995. *Reading Images: Narrative Discourse and Reception in the Thirteenth-Century Illuminated Apocalypse*. Cambridge: Cambridge University Press.

Liebermann, F. 1913. 'A Contemporary Manuscript of the "Leges Anglorum Londoniis collectæ"', *English Historical Review* 28:732–45.

Lindenbaum, Sheila 1994. 'Ceremony and Oligarchy: The London Midsummer Watch', in *City and Spectacle in Medieval Europe*, ed. Barbara A. Hanawalt and Kathryn L. Reyerson, Medieval Studies at Minnesota 6. Minneapolis: University of Minnesota Press. Pp. 171–88.

   1990. 'The Smithfield Tournament of 1390', *Journal of Medieval and Renaissance Studies* 20:1–20.

Lobel, Mary D. (ed.) 1989. *The British Atlas of Historic Towns Volume III The City of London from Prehistoric Times to c.1520*. Oxford: Oxford University Press.

Loomis, Laura H. 1941, rep. 1968. 'Sir Thopas', in *Sources and Analogues of Chaucer's Canterbury Tales*, ed. W. F. Bryan and Germaine Dempster. New York: Humanities Press. Pp. 486–559.

1962. *Adventures in the Middle Ages: A Memorial Collection of Essays and Studies*. New York: Burt Franklin.

Loomis, Roger S. 1953. 'Edward I, Arthurian Enthusiast', *Speculum* 28:114–27.

Lysons, Samuel 1814. 'Copy of a Roll of Purchases Made for the Tournament of Windsor Park, in the Sixth Year of King Edward the First, Preserved in the Record Office at the Tower', *Archaeologia* 17:297–310.

Maguire, Stella 1949. 'The Significance of Haukyn, *Activa Vita*, in *Piers Plowman*', *Review of English Studies* 25:97–109.

Maitland, Frederic W., ed. H. A. L. Fisher 1911. *The Collected Papers*, 3 vols. Cambridge: Cambridge University Press.

Manley, Lawrence 1995. *Literature and Culture in Early Modern London*. Cambridge: Cambridge University Press.

Marshall, Linda, and W. Rothwell 1970. 'The *Miroir* of Robert of Gretham', *Medium Ævum* 39: 313–21.

Martin, Priscilla 1979. *Piers Plowman: The Field and the Tower*. London: Macmillan. See also Jenkins.

Masters, Betty R. 1969. 'The Mayor's Household before 1600', in Hollaender–Kellaway (eds.), pp. 95–114.

Matheson, Lister M. 1998. *The Prose* Brut: *The Development of a Middle English Chronicle*. Tempe AZ: Medieval and Renaissance Texts and Studies.

McClure, Peter 1979. 'Patterns of Migration in the Late Middle Ages: The Evidence of English Place-Name Surnames', *Economic History Review* 2nd ser. 32:167–82.

McDonnell, K. G. T. 1978. *Medieval London Suburbs*. London: Phillimore.

McFarlane, K. B. 1972. *Lancastrian Kings and Lollard Knights*. Oxford: Clarendon Press.

McIntosh, Angus 1976. 'The Language of the Extant Versions of *Havelok the Dane*', *Medium Ævum* 45:36–49.

McRee, Ben R. 1987. 'Religious Gilds and the Regulation of Behaviour in Late Medieval Towns', in *People, Politics and Community in the Later Middle Ages*, ed. Joel Rosenthal and Colin Richmond. Gloucester: Alan Sutton. Pp. 108–22.

1993. 'Charity and Gild Solidarity in Late Medieval England', *Journal of British Studies* 32:195–225.

Meale, Carol M. 1992. 'Caxton, de Worde, and the Publication of Romance in Late Medieval England', *Library* 6th ser. 14:283–98.

Michael, Michael 1994. 'The Iconography of Kingship in the Walter of Milemete Treatise', *Journal of the Warburg and Courtauld Institutes* 57:35–47.

Middleton, Anne 1972. 'Two Infinites: Grammatical Metaphor in *Piers Plowman*', *ELH* 39:169–88.

1982a. 'Narration and the Invention of Experience: Episodic Form in *Piers Plowman*', in *The Wisdom of Poetry: Essays in Early English Literature in Honor of Morton W. Bloomfield*, ed. Larry D. Benson and Siegfried Wenzel. Kalamazoo MI: Medieval Institute. Pp. 91–122.

1982b. 'The Audience and Public of "Piers Plowman" ', *Middle English Alliterative Poetry and Its Literary Background: Seven Essays*, ed. David Lawton. Cambridge: Brewer. Pp. 101–23, 147–54.

1990. 'William Langland's "Kynde Name": Authorial Signature and Social Identity in Late Fourteenth-Century England', in *Literary Practice and Social Change in Britain, 1380–1530*, ed. Lee Patterson. Berkeley CA: University of California Press. Pp. 15–82.

1997. 'Acts of Vagrancy: The C Version "Autobiography" and the Statute of 1388', in Justice and Kerby-Fulton (eds.), pp. 208–317.

Mills, Maldwyn 1992. 'Structure and Meaning in *Guy of Warwick*', in *From Medieval to Medievalism*, ed. John Simons. Basingstoke: Macmillan. Pp. 54–68.

Mills, Maldwyn, *et al.* (eds.) 1991. *Romance in Medieval England*. Cambridge: Brewer.

Minnis, A. J. 1984. *Medieval Theory of Authorship*. London: Scolar Press.

Mitchell, A. G. 1956. 'Lady Meed and the Art of *Piers Plowman*'. London: H. K. Lewis.

Mollat, Michel (ed.) 1974. *Études sur l'histoire de la pauvrété*. Publications de la Sorbonne, serie 'Études' 8, 2 vols. Paris: Sorbonne.

Mollat, Michel, tr. Arthur Goldhammer 1986. *The Poor in the Middle Ages*. New Haven: Yale University Press.

Monroe, W. H. 1981. 'Two Medieval Genealogical Roll-Chronicles in the Bodleian Library', *Bodleian Library Record*, 10:215–21.

Mooney, Linne R., and Simon Horobin forthcoming. Study of Cambridge, Trinity College B.15.17 and Early London Scribe B, *Studies in the Age of Chaucer*.

Mooney, Linne R., and Lister M. Matheson 2003. 'The Beryn Scribe and his Texts: Evidence for Multiple-Copy Production of Manuscripts in Fifteenth-Century England', *Library* 7th ser. 4:347–70.

Mordkoff, Judith C. 1981. 'The Making of the Auchinleck Manuscript: The Scribes at Work'. Unpub. University of Connecticut Ph.D. diss.

Morgan, Nigel 1982–8. *Early Gothic Manuscripts [I] 1190–1250: [II] 1250–1280*, A Survey of Manuscripts Illuminated in the British Isles 4.1–2, 2 vols. London: Harvey Miller.

Muir, Lynette 1968. 'King Arthur's Northern Conquests in the *Leges Anglorum Londoniis Collectae*', *Medium Ævum* 37:253–62.

Murray, Alexander 1978. *Reason and Society in the Middle Ages* Oxford: Clarendon.

Muscatine, Charles 1963. 'Locus of Action in Medieval Narrative', *Romance Philology* 17:115–22.

1972. *Poetry and Crisis in the Age of Chaucer*, Ward-Phillips Lectures in English Language and Literature 4. Notre Dame IN: University of Notre Dame Press.

Musson, Anthony, and W. M. Ormrod 1999. *The Evolution of English Justice: Law, Politics, and Society in the Fourteenth Century*. Basingstoke: Macmillan.

Myers, A. R. 1969. 'The Wealth of Richard Lyons', in Sandquist–Powicke (eds.), pp. 301–29.

Nicholls, K. W. 2003. *Gaelic and Gaelicised Ireland in the Middle Ages*, 2nd edn. Dublin: Lilliput Press.

Nightingale, Pamela 1989. 'Capitalists, Crafts and Constitutional Change in Late Fourteenth-Century London', *Past and Present* 124:3–35.

1995. *A Medieval Mercantile Community: The Grocers' Company and the Politics and Trade of London 1000–1485.* New Haven: Yale University Press.

1996. 'The Growth of London in the Medieval English Economy', *Progress and Problems in Medieval England: Essays in Honour of Edward Miller*, ed. Richard Britnell and John Hatcher. Cambridge: Cambridge University Press. Pp. 89–106.

Noel, William, and Daniel Weiss (eds.) 2002. *The Book of Kings: Art, War, and the Morgan Library's Medieval Picture Bible.* Baltimore: Walters Art Museum.

Nowell, Charles E. 1953. 'The Historical Prester John', *Speculum* 28:435–45.

Oakden, J. P. 1930–5. *The Alliterative Poetry in Middle English*, 2 vols. Manchester: Manchester University Press.

O'Connor, Stephen 1993. *A Calendar of the Cartularies of John Pyel and Adam Franceys*, Camden Society 5 ser. 2.

1994a. 'Finance, Diplomacy and Politics: Royal Service By Two London Merchants in the Reign of Edward III', *Historical Research* 67:18–39.

1994b. 'Adam Fraunceys and John Pyel: Perception of Status Among Merchants in Fourteenth-Century London', in *Trade, Devotion and Governance: Papers in Later Medieval History*, ed. Dorothy J. Clayton *et al.* Stroud: Alan Sutton. Pp. 17–35.

Ogle, Octavius 1892. *Royal Letters Addressed to Oxford.* Oxford: Parker.

Ormrod, W. M. (ed.) 1986. *England in the Fourteenth Century* Woodbridge: Boydell.

1987. 'Edward III and His Family', *Journal of British Studies* 26:398–422.

1989. 'The Personal Religion of Edward III', *Speculum* 64:849–77.

1990. *The Reign of Edward III: Crown and Political Society in England 1327–1377.* New Haven: Yale University Press.

1997. 'York and the Crown under the First Three Edwards', in *The Government of Medieval York: Essays in Commemoration of the 1396 Royal Charter*, ed. Sarah Rees Jones, Borthwick Studies in History 3. York: University of York. Pp. 14–33.

2000. 'Competing Capitals? York and London in the Fourteenth Century', in *Courts and Regions in Medieval Europe*, ed. Sarah Rees Jones *et al.* Woodbridge: York Medieval Press. Pp. 75–98.

Pächt, Otto, and J. J. G. Alexander 1966–73. *Illuminated Manuscripts in the Bodleian Library, Oxford*, 3 vols. Oxford: Clarendon.

Palmer, John J. N. (ed.) 1981. *Froissart Historian.* Woodbridge: Boydell.

1982. 'Froissart et le heraut Chandos', *Le moyen âge* 88:271–92.

Parker, Patricia 1987. *Literary Fat Ladies: Rhetoric, Gender, Property.* London: Methuen.

Parkes, M. B. 1969, 1979. *English Cursive Bookhands 1250–1500.* Oxford: Clarendon Press, and London: Scolar Press.

1973. 'The Literacy of the Laity', in *Literature and Western Civilization: The Medieval World*, ed. David Daiches and Anthony Thorlby. London: Aldus. Pp. 555–77.

1995. 'Patterns of Scribal Activity and Revisions of the Text in Early Copies of Works by John Gower', in Beadle–Piper (eds.), pp. 81–121.

1997. 'Stephen Batman's Manuscripts', in *Medieval Heritage: Essays in Honour of Tadahiro Ikegami*, ed. Masahiko Kanno *et al.* Tokyo: Yukodo. Pp. 125–56.

forthcoming. 'Richard Frampton: A Commercial Scribe *c.* 1390-*c.* 1420', in Takamiya Festschrift.

Parsons, John C. 1994. *Eleanor of Castile: Queen and Society in Thirteenth-Century England.* Basingstoke: Macmillan.

Pearsall, Derek (ed.) 1983. *Manuscripts and Readers in Fifteenth-Century England: The Literary Implications of Manuscript Study.* Cambridge: Brewer.

1997. 'Langland's London', in Justice and Kerby-Fulton (eds.), pp. 185–207.

Perroy, Edouard 1951. 'Gras profits et rançons pendant la guerre de cent ans: l'affaire du Comte de Denia', in *Mélanges d'histoire du moyen âge dediés à la mémoire de Louis Halphen.* Paris: Presses universitaires. Pp. 573–80.

Philbin, Patrick F. 1999. 'The *Excepciones Contra Brevia*: A Late Thirteenth-Century Teaching Tool', in Bush–Wijffels (eds.), pp. 133–56.

Phillips, J. R. S. 1986. 'Edward II and the Prophets', in Ormrod (ed.), pp. 189–201.

Plucknett, T. F. T. 1949. *Legislation of Edward I.* Oxford: Clarendon Press.

1958. *Early English Legal Literature.* Cambridge: Cambridge University Press.

Pollard, Graham 1937. 'The Company of Stationers before 1557', *The Library* 4th ser. 18:1–38.

Post, Gaines, *et al.* 1955. 'The Medieval Heritage of a Humanistic Ideal: "Scientia donum dei est, unde vendi non potest" ', *Traditio*, 11:195–234.

Powell, Edward 1983. 'Arbitration and the Law in England in the Late Middle Ages', *Transactions of the Royal Historical Society* 5th ser. 33:49–67.

Prestwich, Michael 1980a. *The Three Edwards: War and State in England, 1272–1377.* London: Weidenfield.

1980b. *Documents Illustrating the Crisis of 1297–98 in England*, Camden Society 4 ser. 20.

1988. *Edward I, King of England, 1239–1307*, Yale English Monarchs. New Haven: Yale University Press.

Price, Paul 2000. 'Confessions of a Godless Killer: Guy of Warwick and Comprehensive Entertainment', in Weiss *et al.* (eds.), pp. 93–110.

Rance, Adrian B. 1986. 'The Bevis and Ascupart Panels, Bargate Museum, Southampton', *Proceedings of the Hampshire Field Club and Archaeological Society* 42:147–53.

Reeve, Matthew M. 2002. 'The Former Painted Cycle of the Life of Edward I at the Bishop's Palace, Lichfield', *Nottingham Medieval Studies* 46:70–83.

Reichl, Karl 1973. *Religiöse Dichtung im englischen Hochmittelalter: Untersuchung und Edition der Handschrift B.14.39 des Trinity College in Cambridge.* Munich: Fink.

Reynolds, Susan 1989. 'Magna Carta 1297 and the Legal Use of Literacy', *Historical Research* 62:233–44.

Richardson, H. G. 1936. 'Heresy and the Lay Power Under Richard II', *English Historical Review* 51:1–28.

Richardson, H. G., and George Sayles 1934. 'The Early Statutes', *Law Quarterly Review* 50:201–23, 540–71.

Rickert, Edith 1932. 'Chaucer at School', *Modern Philology* 29:257–74.

Bibliography

Riddy, Felicity 1991. 'Reading for England: Arthurian Literature and National Consciousness', *Bibliographical Bulletin of the International Arthurian Society* 43:314–32.

(ed.) 1991. *Regionalism in Late Medieval Manuscripts and Texts*. Cambridge: Brewer.

Robinson, P. R. 1972. 'Some Aspects of the Transmission of English Verse Texts in Late Mediaeval Manuscripts'. Unpub. Oxford University B.Litt. diss.; Bodleian Library, MS B.Litt. c.240.

1980. 'The "Booklet": A Self-contained Unit in Composite Manuscripts', *Codicologica* 3:46–69.

Robson, C. A. 1952. *Maurice of Sully and the Medieval Vernacular Homily*. Oxford: Blackwell.

Rogers, Nicholas (ed.) 1993. *England in the Fourteenth Century*. Stamford: Paul Watkins.

Röhrkasten, Jehns 1998. 'The Origins and Early Development of the London Mendicant Houses', in *The Church in the Medieval Town*, ed. T. R. Slater and Gervase Rosser. Aldershot: Ashgate. Pp. 76–99.

Rosenthal, Joel T. 1972. *The Purchase of Paradise: Gift Giving and the Aristocracy, 1307–1485*. London: Routledge.

Roskell, J. S. 1956. 'Sir John Cheyne of Beckford, Knight of the Shire . . .', *Transactions of the Bristol and Gloucestershire Archaeological Society* 75:43–72.

Rosser, Gervase 1989. *Medieval Westminster 1200–1540*. Oxford: Clarendon Press.

1994. 'Going to the Fraternity Feast: Commensality and Social Relations in Late Medieval England', *Journal of British Studies* 33:430–46.

Rothwell, William 1968. 'The Teaching of French in Medieval England', *Modern Language Review* 63:37–46.

1976. 'The Role of French in Thirteenth-Century England', *Bulletin of the John Rylands Library* 58:445–66.

1978. 'À quelle époque a-t-cessé de parler français en Angleterre', *Mélanges de philologie romane offerts à Charles Camproux*, 2 vols. Montpellier: CEO. 2, 1075–89.

1983. 'Language and Government in Medieval England', *Zeitschrift für französische Sprache und Literatur*, 93:258–70.

1993. 'The "faus franceis d'Angleterre": Later Anglo-Norman', in *Anglo-Norman Anniversary Essays*, ed. Ian Short, ANTS occasional publications 2. London: ANTS. Pp. 309–26.

1994. 'The Trilingual England of Geoffrey Chaucer', *Studies in the Age of Chaucer* 16:45–67.

Rouse, Richard H. and Mary A. Rouse 1987. 'The Franciscans and Books: Lollard Accusations and the Franciscan Response', *Studies in Church History* subsidia 5:369–84.

2000. *Illiterati et uxorati: Manuscripts and their Makers: Commercial Book Producers in Medieval Paris 1200–1500*, 2 vols. London: Harvey Miller.

Rubin, Miri 1987. *Charity and Community in Medieval Cambridge*, Cambridge Studies in Medieval Life and Thought, 4th ser. 4. Cambridge: Cambridge University Press.

1991. *Corpus Christi: The Eucharist in Late Medieval Culture*. Cambridge: Cambridge University Press.

Rumble, Alexander 1996. 'The Known Manuscripts of the Burghal Hidage', in *The Defense of Wessex: The Burghal Hidage and Anglo-Saxon Fortifications*, ed. David Hill and Rumble. Manchester: Manchester University Press. Pp. 36–58.

St-Jacques, Raymond C. 1989. 'The *Middle English Glossed Prose Psalter* and its French Source', in Beer (ed.), pp. 135–54.

Salter, Elizabeth 1969. *Piers Plowman: An Introduction*, 2nd edn. Cambridge MA: Harvard University Press.

1983. *Fourteenth-Century English Poetry: Contexts and Readings*. Oxford: Clarendon.

Salter, Elizabeth, ed. Derek Pearsall and Nicolette Zeeman 1988. *English and International: Studies in the Literature, Art, and Patronage of Medieval England.* Cambridge: Cambridge University Press.

Samuels, M. L. 1963. 'Some Applications of Middle English Dialectology', *English Studies* 44:81–94; reprinted 1989 with some revisions, *Middle English Dialectology: Essays on Some Principles and Problems*, ed. Margaret Laing. Aberdeen: Aberdeen University Press. Pp. 64–80.

1972. *Linguistic Evolution with Special Reference to English*, Cambridge Studies in Linguistics 5. Cambridge: Cambridge University Press.

1985–6. 'Langland's Dialect', *Medium Ævum* 54:232–47, with necessary corrections 55:40.

Sandler, Lucy F. 1986. *Gothic Manuscripts 1285–1385*, A Survey of Manuscripts Illuminated in the British Isles 5, 2 vols. London: Harvey Miller.

1999. *The Psalter of Robert de Lisle in the British Library*, 2nd edn. London: Harvey Miller.

Sandquist, T. A., and M. R. Powicke (eds.) 1969. *Essays in Medieval History presented to Bertie Wilkinson*. Toronto: University of Toronto Press.

Saul, Nigel 1997. *Richard II*, Yale English Monarchs. New Haven: Yale University Press.

Saunders, Corinne 2003. 'Desire, Will and Intention in *Sir Beves of Hamtoun*', *The Matter of Identity in Medieval Romance*, ed. Phillipa Hardman. Cambridge: Brewer. Pp. 29–42.

Scase, Wendy 1989. Piers Plowman *and the New Anticlericalism*, Cambridge Studies in Medieval Literature 4. Cambridge: Cambridge University Press.

1992. 'Reginald Pecock, John Carpenter and John Colop's "Common-Profit" Books: Aspects of Book Ownership and Circulation in Fifteenth-Century London', *Medium Ævum* 61: 261–74.

1998. ' "Strange and Wonderful Bills": Bill-Casting and Political Discourse in Late Medieval England', *New Medieval Literatures* 2:225–47.

Scattergood, V. J. 1968. 'Two Medieval Booklists', *The Library* 5th ser. 23:236–9.

1970. 'Adam Davy's *Dreams* and Edward II', *Archiv für das Studium der neueren Sprachen* 206:253–60.

1983. 'Literary Culture at the Court of Richard II', in Scattergood–Sherborne (eds.), pp. 29–43.

1995. 'Misrepresenting the City: Genre, Intertextuality and William FitzStephen's *Description of London* (c. 1173)', in Boffey–King (eds.), pp. 1–34.

Scattergood, V. J., and J. W. Sherborne (eds.) 1983. *English Court Culture in the Later Middle Ages*. London: Duckworth.

Schofield, John 1994a. *Medieval London Houses*. New Haven: Yale University Press.

1994b. 'Saxon and Medieval Parish Churches in the City of London: A Review', *Transactions of the London and Middlesex Archaeological Society* 45:23–145.

Scott, Kathleen L. 1996. *Later Gothic Manuscripts, 1390–1490*, 2 vols. London: Harvey Miller.

Seipp, David J. 1999. 'The Mirror of Justices', in Bush–Wijffels (eds.), pp. 85–112.

Sharpe, Reginald R. 1889–90. *Calendar of Wills Proved and Enrolled in the Court of Husting, London . . .*, 2 vols. London: John C. Francis.

Sharpe, Richard 1994. 'The Prefaces of *Quadripartitus*', in Garnett–Hudson (eds.), pp. 148–72.

Shepherd, Geoffrey 1983. 'Poverty in *Piers Plowman*', in *Social Relations and Ideas: Essays in Honour of R. H. Hilton*, ed. T. H. Aston *et al.*, Past and Present Publications. Cambridge: Cambridge University Press. Pp. 169–89.

Sherborne, J. W. 1983. 'Aspects of English Court Culture in the Later Fourteenth Century', in Scattergood–Sherborne (eds.), pp. 1–27.

Shonk, Timothy A. 1985. 'A Study of the Auchinleck Manuscript: Bookmen and Bookmaking in the Early Fourteenth Century', *Speculum* 60:71–91.

Short, Ian 1980. 'On Bilingualism in Anglo-Norman England', *Romance Philology* 13:467–79.

1991. 'Patrons and Polyglots: French Literature in Twelfth-Century England', *Anglo-Norman Studies* 14:229–49.

Simpson, James 1986. 'From Reason to Affective Knowledge: Modes of Thought and Poetic Form in *Piers Plowman*', *Medium Ævum* 55:1–23.

1990a. 'The Constraints of Satire in "Piers Plowman" and "Mum and the Sothsegger"', in *Langland, the Mystics and the Medieval Religious Tradition: Essays in Honour of S. S. Hussey*, ed. Helen Phillips. Cambridge: Brewer. Pp. 11–30.

1990b. *Piers Plowman: An Introduction to the B-Text*. London: Longman.

1993. '"After Craftes Conseil Clotheth Yow and Fede": Langland and London City Politics', in Rogers (ed.), pp. 109–27.

Sinclair, K. V. 1992. 'The Anglo-Norman Patrons of Robert the Chaplain and Robert of Greatham', *Forum for Modern Language Studies* 28:193–208.

Skeat, Walter W. 1880–1. 'On the Only English Proclamation of Henry III., 18 October, 1258', *Transactions of the Philological Society* n.v.n.:*171–*77.

1911. *English Dialects from the Eighth Century to the Present Day*. Cambridge: Cambridge University Press.

Skemer, Don C. 1995. 'From Archives to the Book Trade: Private Statute Rolls in England, 1285–1307', *Journal of the Society of Antiquaries* 16:193–206.

1997. 'Sir William Breton's Book: Production of *Statuta Angliae* in the Late Thirteenth Century', *English Manuscript Studies* 6:24–51.

1999. 'Reading the Law: Statute Books and the Private Transmission of Legal Knowledge in Late Medieval England', in Bush–Wijffels (eds.), pp. 113–31.

Smith, D. Vance 2001. *The Book of the Incipit: Beginnings in the Fourteenth Century*, Medieval Cultures 28. Minneapolis MN: University of Minnesota Press.

2003. *Arts of Possession: The Middle English Household Imaginary*, Medieval Cultures 33. Minneapolis MN: University of Minnesota Press.

Smith, Jeremy J. 1983. 'Linguistic Features of Some Fifteenth-Century Middle English Manuscripts', in Pearsall (ed.), pp. 104–12.

1988. 'The Trinity Gower D-Scribe and His Work on Two Early *Canterbury Tales* Manuscripts', in *The English of Chaucer and His Contemporaries*, ed. Smith. Aberdeen: Aberdeen University Press. Pp. 51–69.

1996. *An Historical Study of English: Function, Form and Change*. London: Routledge.

Smith, John T. 1807. *Antiquities of Westminster....* London: T. Bensley.

Smith, Kathryn A. 1997–8. 'The Destruction of Jerusalem Miniatures in the Neville of Hornby Hours and Their Visual, Literary and Devotional Contexts', *Jewish Art* 23–4:179–202.

1999. 'The Neville of Hornby Hours and the Design of Literate Devotion', *Art Bulletin* 81:72–92.

Southern, R. W. 2001. *Scholastic Humanism and the Unification of Europe Volume II The Heroic Age*. Oxford: Blackwell.

Spencer, Brian 1998. *Pilgrim Souvenirs and Secular Badges*, Medieval Finds from Excavations in London 7. London: HMSO.

Staniland, Kay 1978. 'Clothing and Textiles at the Court of Edward III, 1342–1352', in *Collectanea Londiniensia: Studies in London Archaeology and History Presented to Ralph Merrifield*, ed. Joanna Bird *et al.*, London and Middlesex Archaeological Society special paper 2. London: London and Middlesex Archaeological Society. Pp. 223–34.

1986. 'Court Style, Painters, and the Great Wardrobe', in Ormrod (ed.), pp. 236–46.

Stokes, Myra 1984. *Justice and Mercy in Piers Plowman: A Reading of the B Text Visio.* London: Croom Helm.

Stones, E. L. G. 1969. 'The Appeal to History in Anglo-Scottish Relations between 1291 and 1401', *Archives* 9:11–21, 80–3.

Summerson, Henry 1997. 'An English Bible and Other Books Belonging to Henry IV', *Bulletin of the Johns Rylands University Library* 79, i:109-15.

Sutton, Anne F. 1992. 'Merchants, Music and Social Harmony: the London Puy and its French and London Contexts, circa 1300', *London Journal* 17:1–17.

1995. 'The *Tumbling Bear* and its Patrons: A Venue for the London Puy and Mercery', in Boffey–King (eds.), pp. 85–110.

Szittya, Penn R. 1986. *The Antifraternal Tradition in Medieval Literature*. Princeton: Princeton University Press.

Tavormina, M. Teresa 1995. *Kindly Similitude: Marriage and Family in* Piers Plowman. Cambridge: Brewer.

Taylor, John 1987. *English Historical Literature in the Fourteenth Century*. Oxford: Clarendon.

Theilmann, John M. 1990. 'Political Canonisation and Political Symbolism in Medieval England', *Journal of British Studies* 29:241–66.

Thompson, John J. 1991. 'Collecting Middle English Romances and Some Related Book-production Activities in the Later Middle Ages', in Mills *et al.* (eds.), pp. 17–38.

2000. '"Frankis rimes here I redd, / Communlik in ilk[a] sted...": The French Bible Stories in Harley 2253', in *Studies in the Harley Manuscript...*, ed. Susanna Fein. Kalamazoo MI: Medieval Institute. Pp. 271–87.

Thomson, J. A. F. 1960. 'Clergy and Laity in London, 1376–1531'. Unpub. Oxford D.Phil. diss., Bodleian Library, MS D.Phil. d.2413.

Thomson, Rodney M. 1982. *Manuscripts from St Albans Abbey 1066–1235*, 2 vols. Woodbridge: Brewer.

Thrupp, Sylvia 1948. *The Merchant Class of Medieval London* Chicago: University of Chicago Press.

Treharne, R. F. 1932. *The Baronial Plan of Reform, 1258–1263*. Manchester: Manchester University Press.

Tristram, E. W., ed. Eileen Tristram (with catalogue in collaboration with Monica Bardswell) 1955. *English Wall Painting in the Fourteenth Century*. London: Routledge.

Trotter, D. A. (ed.) 2000. *Multilingualism in Later Medieval Britain*. Cambridge: Brewer.

Trower, Katherine B. 1973. 'The Figure of Hunger in *Piers Plowman*', *American Benedictine Review* 24:238–60.

Troyer, Howard W. 1932. 'Who is Piers Plowman?', *PMLA* 47:368–84.

Turner, Ralph V. 1990. 'Who Was the Author of *Glanvill*? Reflections on the Education of Henry II's Common Lawyers', *Law and History Review* 8:97–127.

Turville-Petre, Thorlac, 'Some Medieval English Manuscripts in the North-East Midlands', in Pearsall (ed.), pp. 125–41.

1988. 'Politics and Poetry in the Early Fourteenth Century: The Case of Robert Manning's *Chronicle*', *Review of English Studies* 39:1–28.

1996. *England the Nation: Language, Literature, and National Identity, 1290–1340*. Oxford: Clarendon Press.

Tyrwhitt, Thomas 1775, rep. 1868. *The Poetical Works of Geoffrey Chaucer*. London: Routledge.

Tyson, Diana B. 1977. 'The Epitaph of Edward the Black Prince', *Medium Ævum* 46:98–104.

Vale, Juliet 1982. *Edward III and Chivalry: Chivalric Society and its Context, 1270–1350*. Woodbridge: Boydell.

Vale, Malcolm 1996. *The Origins of the Hundred Years War: The Angevin Legacy, 1250–1340*. Oxford: Clarendon Press.

Veale, Elspeth M. 1969. 'Craftsmen and the Economy of London in the Fourteenth Century', in Hollaender–Kellaway (eds.), pp. 113–51.

1991. 'The "Great Twelve": Mistery and Fraternity in Thirteenth-Century London', *Historical Research* 64:237–63.

von Nolcken, Christina 1988. '*Piers Plowman*, the Wycliffites, and *Pierce the Plowman's Creed*', *Yearbook of Langland Studies* 2:71–102.

Wagner, Anthony R. 1939, 1956; rep. 2000. *Heralds and Heraldry in the Middle Ages: An Inquiry into the Growth of the Armorial Function of Heralds*. Oxford: Oxford University Press.

Walker, Simon 1995. 'Political Saints in Later Medieval England', in *The McFarlane Legacy: Studies in Late Medieval Politics and Society*, ed. R. H. Britnell and A. J. Pollard. Stroud: Alan Sutton. Pp. 77–106.

Wallace, David 1997. *Chaucerian Polity: Absolutist Lineages and Associational Forms in England and Italy*, Figurae: Reading Medieval Culture. Stanford CA: Stanford University Press.

Walsh, Katherine 1981. *A Fourteenth-Century Scholar and Primate: Richard FitzRalph in Oxford, Avignon, and Armagh*. Oxford: Clarendon Press.

Wathey, Andrew 1992. 'The Marriage of Edward III and the Transmission of French Motets to England', *Journal of the American Musicological Society* 45:1–29.

Waugh, Scott 1991. *England in the Reign of Edward III*. Cambridge: Cambridge University Press.

Weiss, Judith 1979. 'The Major Interpolations in *Sir Beues of Hamtoun*', *Medium Ævum* 48:71–6.

Weiss, Judith, *et al.* (eds.) 2000. *Medieval Insular Romance: Translation and Innovation*. Cambridge: Brewer.

Westlake, H. F. 1919. *The Parish Gilds of Mediæval England*. London: SPCK.

Whitwell, Robert J. 1905. 'The Libraries of a Civilian and Canonist and of a Common Lawyer, an. 1294', *Law Quarterly Review* 21:393–400.

Williams, Gwyn A. 1963. *Medieval London From Commune to Capital*. London: Athlone Press.

Withington, Robert 1917. 'The Early "Royal Entry"', *PMLA* 32:616–23.

Wittig, Joseph J. 1972. '*Piers Plowman* B, Passus IX-XII: Elements in the Design of the Inward Journey', *Traditio* 28:211–80.

Wittig, Susan 1978. *Stylistic and Narrative Structures in the Middle English Romances*. Austin TX: University of Texas Press.

Wogan-Browne, Jocelyn 2001. *Saints' Lives and Women's Literary Culture c. 1150–1300: Virginity and its Authorizations*. Oxford: Oxford University Press.

Wood, Robert A. 1984. 'A Fourteenth-Century London Owner of *Piers Plowman*', *Medium Ævum* 53:290–4.

Woodbine, George E. 1943. 'The Language of English Law', *Speculum* 18:395–436.

Woolf, Rosemary 1969. 'The Tearing of the Pardon', in S. S. Hussey (ed.), pp. 50–75.

Wormald, Francis 1966–8. 'Some Pictures of the Mass in an English XIVth Century Manuscript', *The Walpole Society* 41:39–45.

Wormald, Patrick 1994. '*Quadripartitus*', in Garnett–Hudson (eds.), pp. 111–47.

    1999. *The Making of English Law: King Alfred to the Twelfth Century*. Oxford: Blackwell.

Bibliography

Wright, Laura 1996. *Sources of London English: Medieval Thames Vocabulary*. Oxford: Clarendon Press, whatever the rebarbative quality of Michael Benskin's review, *Medium Ævum* 66 (1997), 133–5.

2000. 'Bills, Accounts, Inventories: Everyday Trilingual Activities in the Business World of Later Medieval England', in Trotter (ed.), pp. 149–56.

Wright, Rosemary M. 1991. 'Sound in Pictured Silence: The Significance of Writing in the Illumination of the Douce Apocalypse', *Word and Image* 7:239–74.

Yunck, John A. 1963. *The Lineage of Lady Meed: The Development of Medieval Venality Satire*, University of Notre Dame Publications in Mediaeval Studies 17. Notre Dame IN: University of Notre Dame Press.

Index of manuscripts cited

In both indexes, references in bold identify extended and detailed discussions.

General index

Medieval names are entered under their common forms, e.g. 'Chaucer, Geoffrey' but 'John of Reading'. Modern scholars only appear when integral to the argument (rather than in parenthetical or footnote references).
All references to *Piers Plowman* and to figures from the poem are grouped under 'Langland, William'.

Burrow, John 247, 294
Buxhill, Alan, constable of the Tower 1378 234
Byzantium 85, 92

Caernarfon and its castle 92
Calais, siege of (1337) 95
Cambridge 25
canons (generally of collegiate churches like
  St Paul's) 81–2, 124, 145 n. 30, 161, 187
Canterbury, archbishops' Chancery 226
  Prerogative Court of 226
  Cathedral 39 n. 4; tomb of the Black
    Prince 223, 225
  St Augustine's abbey (OSB) 82
Carlton Miniott (N. Yks.) 95
Carlyle, Thomas, *Sartor Resartus* 285
Carmelite friars 309
Carrow (OSB nuns, Norwich) 214 n. 16
'Carta mercatoria' and trade protectionism 58,
  60–1, 66, 146–7 n. 43
The Castle of Perseverance 38
castles in procession and illumination 38, 120,
  122, 249; the towers of *Piers Plowman*
  297–8
cathedral schools 161, 187
'central Midland standard' English 26–7
Chalket, Roger, London pepperer bankrupt
  in 1361 12
Chandos, Sir John (d. 1370) 222, 223, 229,
  231, 233, 237, 239, 240 n. 11, 242 n. 29
The Chandos Herald, *La Vie du Prince Noir*
  222–32, 257
chapel or chantry 125, 153, 199, 201, 212, 253;
  see also guild
Charlemagne 105, 151; see also Roland
Charles V, king of France (d. 1380) 301 n. 28
Chart iuxta Leeds (Kent) 39 n. 6
charters, see documents
The Charterhouse 39 n. 1, 41 n. 16, 312
Chartres Cathedral 144 n. 19
chastisement 172–5, 178, 184, 191–2, 194–5,
  197, 199–201, 205, 295, 297–8, 309; see
  also penance, work
The Chastising of God's Children 15
Chaucer, Geoffrey xiii–xiv, 1, 5, 10–11, 16, 41
  n. 20, 42 n. 28, 106, 108, 153–4, 232,
  238–9, 247–8, 305, 311, 312
  and Boethius 299, 312
  and Langland 253–7
  The Book of the Duchess 312
  The Canterbury Tales 312
  'The Canon Yeoman's Tale' 284
  'The General Prologue' 253–4
  manuscripts 79, 245

'Melibee' 9
'The Monk's Tale' 241 n. 17
The Parliament of Fowls 305
'Sir Thopas' xiv, 25, 107–8, 253, 257, 258,
  308
Troilus and Criseyde 238, 305, 312
'The Wife of Bath's Tale' 258
Cheapside 43 n. 36, 73, 262
Cheker, Matthew, author of *Fleta* (?) (d. after
  1312) 47, 53, 83–4, 87
Cheshire 229
Chester Inn, the Strand 145 n. 32
Cheyne, Sir John of Beckford (Gloucs.)
  (d. 1414) 312
Chrétien de Troyes, *Yvain, ou le chevalier au
  lion* 109–10, 115
Christmas 34–5, 140
chronicles 25, 90, 121, 227; see also
  'romance'-history, individual titles
  and legal writing 54, 55, 59–60, 62–72, 74
Cicero 88, 165–6, 286–7, 291
Cinque Portes 47
Clanvowe, Sir John, 'The Two Ways' 149, 152
Claydon, John, London Lollard (executed
  1415) 188, 310
'þe Cleansing of Man's Soul' 14–15
Clement of Lanthony, translated as *Oon of
  Foure* 161, 307–8
clerics 21–3, 81–2, 168–70; see also
  chastisement etc., Latinate culture
  in control of instruction and religious
    intermediaries 167–71, 183, 187–8, 295
  clerical administrative and state service
    126–8, 146 n. 35, 254–6; see Chancery
    s.v. government
  clerical mal-/non-feasance 22–3, 174–5,
    178–9, 183–4, 187–8, 190, 192–4,
    195–7, 205–6, 208–11; see false
    teaching
  suspicion of clerical speciality, esp. learning
    197–9, 207–8, 295; see also the
    character Ymaginatif
  subsumption of clerical roles by English
    readers 163–212 *passim*, 302 n. 36; see
    also Piers the Plowman
  financial support for clerics 191, 219 n. 55
Cleveland 130
Clifford, John, mason of Southwark (d. 1417)
  12
Clifford, Lewis, king's knight (d. 1404) 10–11
Clifford's Inn 126
Clopper, Lawrence M. 298
cloth trade guilds 73
Cobham (Surrey) 52

351

General index

'romance', general discussions and references 12, 84, 106–8, 116, 124, 164–6, 167, 169, 172, 175, 177, 214 n. 19, 257, 258–9, 287, 292, 296
and history 39 n. 5, 82–97, 105, 116–22, 148–9, 227; and sacred history 171–2, 255; see also chronicles, jurisdiction
'English romance' 96–7, 105–6, 111, 113, 114–15, 122, 129–32, 133–4, 136, 137, 140, 143 n. 10, 151
exile and return patterns 129, 133–4, 141, 147 n. 50, 150, 153, 164–6, 237, 276
fictive selfconsciousness 134–9, 149–50; see also guile, rhetoric
type-scene or -image 108–9, 116, 121, 138–9, 169
The Romance of the Rose 122
Rome 92
Roncevaux 228
'rorers' 43 n. 34
Russell, George 243

the Saddlers and associated crafts 73
St Albans (OSB, Herts.) 106, 167; see also Matthew Paris
St Etheldreda, Ely Place 145 n. 31
St Helen Bishopsgate, parish church 220 n. 64
St John Street, Clerkenwell 146 n. 33, 310
St Martin Outwich, parish church 220 n. 64
St Nicholas of Acon, parish church 35
St Patrick's Purgatory 144 n. 22
St Paul's 18, 32–3, 39 n. 4, 41 n. 18, 57, 61, 81–2, 87, 102 n. 59, 187–8, 310
Ste Chapelle, Paris 144 n. 19
Salman, John, Brugges merchant in action for debt 1382 41 n. 13
Samuels, M. L. 4–5, 7, 26–32 *passim*, 305
Sandele, John, bishop of Winchester (d. 1319) 12
satire 34
Saul 95
Scattergood, John 87
Scota, foundress of Scotland 91, 93–4
Scotland and The Great Cause 89–93, 121, 126–7, 143–4 n. 17
scribes: London Scribe B 244; London Scribe D 243–4
scriptorium, see book-production
the Scriveners 1–2, 34, 45, 126
seals of the City of London 87
secretary script 225–7, 238, 305
Secretum secretorum 116–17
Seneca 88

sermons 177, 181, 252, see chastisement, *Mirror*, preaching, work
Seven Deadly Sins 10, 37, 176–7, 297
The Seven Sages of Rome 9, 105, 132
Seward, John, grammarmaster of Cornhill (d. 1435) 310
Seymour, Edward, duke of Somerset, Lord Protector (executed 1549) 69
Shakel, John, captor of the count of Denia 233–4
Shane 107
Sharnebrok, John, London chandler in action for debt 1376 14–15
Shirley, John, London scribe (d. 1456) 229
Shonk, Timothy 75
shunning the sinful 192, 196, 211–12
The Simonie 22–4, 105, 263
the Skinners 36
Skip, John, rector of St Martin in the Vintry (c. 1300–18) 6, 14
Sleford, John de, Keeper of the Wardrobe in the Tower (fl. s. xiv ex.) 127
Smith, Jeremy 243
Smithers, G. V. 104, 120
Smithfield 37, 43 n. 36, 124, 229
Sopar Lane 43 n. 36
South English Legendary 7, 13–14, 19, 104, 106, 149–50, 164; other saints' lives 12, 13
Southampton 133
Southwark 12, 145 n. 31
Speculum Cristiani 219 n. 56
'Speculum Gy de Warwyke' 6, 9, 104
Speculum Vitæ 149, 218 n. 50, 219 n. 56
Spenser, Edmund, *The Faerie Queene* 108–11, 115, 129, 140, 258, 281, 302–3 n. 35
the Spurriers 42 n. 34
Stapeldon, Walter, bishop of Exeter (assassinated 1326) 62
The Statute of Gloucester (and its 'explanationes', 1278) 46, 59–60
The Statute of Labourers (1349) 279, 283, 303 n. 41
The Statute of Marlborough (1267) 46, 63
The Statute of Pleadings (1363) 46
The Statute of Westminster I (1275) 46, 52–3
Statutes and *Statuta Anglie* 45–6, 47–54, 69, 70, 82, 84, 100 n. 39, 101 n. 43, 119
The Steelyard, Hanseatic trading entrepot 63
Stepney 37, 43 n. 37, 59
stewards 112–13, 130–2, 187–8, 211–12, 218–9 n. 53, 278–80, 296
The Stone of Scone 92–4

357